ECONOMY AND SOCIETY

ECONOMY AND SOCIETY

Essays in Indian Economic and Social History

EDITED BY

K. N. CHAUDHURI

CLIVE J. DEWEY

DELHI

OXFORD UNIVERSITY PRESS

BOMBAY CALCUTTA MADRAS

1979

Oxford University Press
OXFORD LONDON GLASGOW
NEW YORK TORONTO MELBOURNE WELLINGTON
NAIROBI DAR ES SALAAM CAPE TOWN
KUALA LUMPUR SINGAPORE JAKARTA HONG KONG TOKYO
DELHI BOMBAY CALCUTTA MADRAS KARACHI

Printed in India by P. K. Ghosh
at Eastend Printers, 3 Dr Suresh Sarkar Road, Calcutta 700 014
and published by R. Dayal, Oxford University Press,
2/11 Ansari Road, Daryaganj, New Delhi 110 002

PREFACE

The papers included in this book were originally delivered at a conference held at St John's College, Cambridge, in July 1975. The conference was sponsored by the Economic and Social History Committee of the U.K. Social Science Research Council, and it was the first meeting specifically designed to bring together a number of economic historians working on the economic and social history of South Asia. While exciting developments had taken place in the historiography of the West since the early 1950s, the economic history of the Indian subcontinent remained a relatively neglected subject. But in the late 'sixties and early 'seventies a number of young research students began work—in India, America, Western Europe and Australia—under the guidance of a handful of established scholars. By 1975 they and their supervisors had produced a corpus of new ideas and findings on most aspects of India's economic and social history. The bulk of their work, however, was still unpublished; and the conclusions to be drawn from the new research remained buried in doctoral dissertations, seminar papers, and preliminary drafts scattered over four continents. Apart from the groups which existed for a time at centres like Cambridge, London, or Chicago, the new generation worked in virtual isolation. It was impossible to discover from casual academic contacts and discussions who else was working on one's speciality or what they had discovered. Only personal contact could do that, and preferably within the context of a general meeting of all those actively engaged in research.

It seemed that the time was ripe for the 'invisible college' of South Asian economic historians to materialize. When it did no one was more surprised than the participants at the extent and advancement of their discipline. Each participant was more or less aware of developments in his or her own particular sphere of interest, but not perhaps of the changes which had overtaken the subject as a whole. It was enormously encouraging to discover that, however solitary one had supposed one's own research to be, there was in fact someone else capable of discussing it critically, and an interested audience eager to follow the debate. Besides improving the collective morale of the historians present, the conference helped refine 'work in progress', and suggested directions in which future research might usefully be done. There was, as usual, much more discussion following the formal sessions, and welded together in this way over three days, the conference proved a severe test of concepts, methods, and conclusions. It acted, in a sense, as a censor of professional standards at a time at which a newly-expanding profession was struggling to create criteria of evaluation. Not all criticism, moreover, was negative. If the general drift of the discussion was towards qualification and refinement, the value of an idea in history, it has been said, lies in discovering the limits of its validity.

A total of twenty-two papers was presented at the conference, and discussed in eight sessions. Unfortunately, it has proved impossible to publish them all. To do so would have meant a book perhaps a quarter of a million words long, far too costly to be an economic proposition. Fortunately for the editors, the invidious task of selecting papers for inclusion was greatly simplified by the appearance of a number of papers elsewhere, and the inability of a number of paper-givers to revise their papers in time. Those that remain—thirteen out of the original twenty-two—are a reasonably representative selection of the work of younger historians engaged in research on Indian economic and social history. The editors are conscious of gaps they would have liked to have filled, and biases they would have wished to correct; and if no collection of thirteen papers can hope to reflect the full range of research now being done in the field, it is some consolation to know that the reason is the 'explosion of knowledge' which has taken place.

We are indebted to a number of individuals and institutions for making the conference a success. Our first thanks must go to the U.K. Social Science Research Council, to whose enlightened patronage Indian economic and social historians are everywhere indebted. Without the funds which the Council has provided, it is unlikely that the subject would ever have 'taken off' in the U.K. in the way that it has, and it is to be hoped that the Cambridge conference will increase the return on their already-generous investment. The accommodation provided by St John's College was superb, and we are grateful to the College staff who looked after us so well. We must thank the School of Oriental and African Studies, University of London, for administering the research grant. Our special thanks are due to the non-specialists who acted as commentators, bringing a breadth of knowledge and a wealth of insight into our deliberations, which they would not otherwise have had. Most of all, we are grateful to the participants, our colleagues, whose enthusiasm made the conference what it was, and whose helpfulness simplified the task of organizing it. It is to them that we would like to dedicate this volume.

K. N. CHAUDHURI
C. J. DEWEY

CONTENTS

Part III: INDUSTRY AND LABOUR

Part IV: TOWNS

Part I

AGRARIAN STRUCTURE AND AGRICULTURAL DEVELOPMENT

1

Social Power and Social Change in the United Provinces 1860-1920

P. J. MUSGRAVE
University of Leicester

It is a commonplace—and a truism—of historians and others that, in societies before the stage of mass literacy, it is the upper strata of society, and in particular those connected with institutionalized power and control which leave the traces we call sources and, even more pervasively and more insidiously, the unspoken assumptions and structures upon which any interpretation of the sources and the society which produced them are based. Even in English history, however, largely as the result of studies of local and regional societies, some of the unspoken but nonetheless profound assumptions are being revealed as the polemic of the political and social elite, rather than sound interpretative generalizations.[1] In particular, it is becoming increasingly possible to see rural society not simply in terms of the great barons and the great landlords—of the de Clares, the Cecils or the Cavendishes—but also in terms of the inhabitants of the villages, of the villeins, the copyholders and the cottars, and of the considerable tenants and small independent landholders. Looked at in this way, from the position of the people inside the system rather than from the position of the people on the top of the system, Professor Elton's 'historian's commonplace that in the Tudor age power and control percolated downward through the hierarchy of the landed classes',[2] ceases to be quite such a truism; it becomes rather a matter of contention, a restatement in historical terms of the overtly propagandist view of the homily 'Of Obedience'[3] and the proclamations against rebels; as a view of English society in the Tudor period, it assumes the same status as Shakespeare's view of the reign of Richard III.

The historian of India who seeks to carry out the same sort of re-analysis of rural society during the British period is faced in many ways with problems even more considerable than those facing the English historian. Like Tudor rule in England, the British Raj in India was, above all, a political exercise: at base—during the late nineteenth century admittedly very deep down—the aim of British rule was its own maintenance in peace and order. Underlying all the complexity, practical, theoretical and ideological, of the settlement systems, and of their later modifications, was the basic need to come to some compromise with the existing structures of rural society as the foundation for the continuance of British rule and the Pax Britannica. In addition, therefore, to all the problems of perceiving any rural society through the eyes of its political elite—in particular where that political elite was increasingly divorced from the rural society which it was supposed to dominate—are added the problems of seeing that society not as the imperial power had perforce to see it as a system of control—and hence potentially as a system of opposition—but as a system within which people lived and worked and organized their lives.

The United Provinces, and in particular the province of Oudh (Avadh), was the scene of the working out of a number of the social and political constructs erected by the British. From the earliest period of British rule in the provinces, the period of Jonathan Duncan's residency in Benares,[4] political problems, and the need for political stability, were the central issues in the development of the relationship between state and rural society, a relationship which rapidly developed and ossified into a system not merely of rural relations but one of landholding and—at least in theory and in the eyes of the British—of social and political relationships. In the period after 1858, the strand in rural policy which saw the countryside as being organized into large, vertical tenurial and political groups—'estates'—and which had been somewhat in retreat in the period before the Rising of 1857–8,[5] enjoyed a period of temporary and partial predominance. This series of political expedients was based on a set of assumptions, spoken and unspoken, about the organization of Indian society; the 'Oudh School' had, as did all the other 'schools' of political and economic policy, a construct picture of Indian society, in part based on the apparent needs of government, in part based on observation and on real or imagined parallels with other societies, and in particular with European and other Indian societies. In many ways, the assumptions which underlay the Oudh school differed in detail and in prescription rather than in type from those of the other schools, and hence it is perhaps permissible to use the Oudh school as an illustrative example of the sorts of problems which the assumed framework presents and of some of the ways in which that framework can usefully be altered.

This paper, then, seeks to isolate and illustrate some of the assumptions upon which the Oudh school was based, and then to consider them critically, not in the sense of subjecting individual assumptions to factual criticism, finally tallying the pros and cons and hence proving or disproving them, but rather by examining them from a different angle; from the position of the 'man in the village', from the point of view of the man in the system who had, as I have suggested elsewhere,[6] to operate the system, and for whom, it is my contention, the system provided advantages, political and social as well as economic, which made its continuance worthwhile. From this position it is possible to go further and rephrase some of the basic questions about, for instance, the 'collapse of landlord power' in the U.P. in the 1920s and 1930s and, hopefully, to suggest some more convincing answers to them than have hitherto been advanced. The first section of the paper, therefore, seeks to outline some of the assumptions upon which the Oudh school—and with certain necessary but not fundamental variations, most of the other schools—based their view of Indian rural society and hence their remedies for its developing and spreading ills. In the second section, a counter-argument is advanced which, albeit very much in outline, seeks to establish a rather different, and more inclusive structure of society and social relations. The final section proceeds from the second to pose, and to answer in a very tentative way, some of the questions about the development of society—and of politics—in the Indian countryside in the late nineteenth and early twentieth centuries, which both the 'Oudh construct of society' and also the construct advanced in the second section raise.

I

It is ever a danger of outsiders attempting to rule alien societies that the technical vocabulary of their own society springs unbidden to mind. Ever since the Spaniards created middle-American *hidalgos* from the *caciques* of Mexico in the sixteenth century, foreigners have attempted to describe unfamiliar societies by comparison with and in the terms of their own society, and equally universally, the metaphor has been converted from description to analysis. Arguably the late nineteenth century, influenced by the discovery of the common Indo-European past and by the new 'sciences' of evolutionary sociology and diffusionist archaeology,[7] was more likely than its predecessors to see in analogous organizations not merely interesting parallels but direct and important derivations and inter-relationships. Whether or nor this was the case—and it must be emphasized that every British administration from the time of Cornwallis onwards made the same kind of judgement—the late nineteenth century administrators transferred to north India the vocabulary and with it the concepts of English rural society, and above all of English medieval society. When the *talukdars* of Oudh became the Rajput Barons of Oudh[8] and when a settlement officer in one of the most highly developed districts of the province could state categorically,

> The cultivators, the *asamis*, are the villeins of the Middle Ages and the Lord of the Manor reckons them amongst his goods and chattels, his they truely are, the *adscripti glebae*.[9]

many issues were surely being decided not by ratiocination but by metaphor.

The 'Oudh Policy' presupposed a dominant 'landlord', usually of 'ancient and military race', granting his 'kinsmen', 'clan', or 'followers', lands for their maintenance, perhaps on payment of rent but in essence in return for military support. In return, the clansmen gave their leader their support in war and in peace, came to him as their arbitrator and protector and as a substitute for other jurisdiction.[10] The whole system implies a very strong control by the landlord, not merely in social but also in economic terms.

> There used to be fair and equitable rates fixed with the mutual consent of the landlord and his tenant, yielding a just proportion of profit to either party according to which generations of tenants continued cultivating fields without showing the least sign of recusancy and improved their lands with their energies and resources as if they were their only inestimable treasure in the world,

remarked Babu Ganga Pershad, the son of Misr Baijnath, a famous banker turned landlord of Bareilly, in opposing the 1873 Rent Act.

> The landlord on his part used to regard his such tenants as his useful children and to sympathise with them in all their times of need or emergencies. The contrivance of such harmony was highly gratifying to both, the tenant being affectionately obedient to his landlord. In such happy days, had government by way of testing the fidelity of such tenants condescended to apply to such landlords

for their help with men and money, I can confidently say that on the call of their landlords, their whole tenantry would gladly come forward to sacrifice their lives. . . . In former times the tenants of a landlord would be regarded as his feudal army.[11]

The landlord was truly lord of the land and all that therein is, a 'ruler of men not an owner of land'.[12]

Significantly, the original justification of the Oudh policy and its view of society rested very firmly on the studies of the Rajput clan systems of Oudh—such as Elliott's *Chronicles of Oonao*[13] or Benett's *Report on the Family History of the Rajput Clans of Roy Bareilly*[14]—and on the behaviour of the Rajput clans of South Oudh—and to a certain extent those of the east of the N.W.P.—during the Mutiny. But in the same ways as the proponents of the 'village zamindar' had seized on the descriptions of the village communities within the Delhi territory and applied them to a province-wide policy, so the Rajput landlords of Oudh were used as an exemplar for the landed relations of the whole United Provinces. While some distinction was made in favour of the 'martial races' and the 'ancient masters of the people', when the time came in the 1870s and 1880s to delegate power from an overburdened and inadequately financed government to a voluntary and honorary group of natives, that group was, perhaps inevitably, the landlords, and this delegation was justified on the grounds of their 'social position' as the 'natural leaders of society'.

Underlying this idea of the landlord as the natural leader of society, a society which operated on deference and following, throughout which power was operated and influence exercised ultimately as a delegation from the landlord, is one very basic but unformulated assumption. For such a system to operate successfully, the landlord must be able to exercise a monopoly or at least a near-monopoly of resource within rural society. Perhaps this can be seen most clearly in terms of the supply of land; the lord can only be seen as the all-provider if he is the sole source of land within the estate. If he is not the sole supplier of land, obviously his position is thereby the weaker in any attempt to control the actions of his so-called followers. Again, if he is to be truly dominant, in the way which the Oudh construct sees him as being, he and he alone must be the source of other forms of resource within the local situation—the sole outside source, that is, of credit and finance, the sole channel through which the follower can contact the outside powers which play on the village, above all government, its courts and its taxation machinery. For the Oudh system to work, the landlord must, very clearly, be the 'earthly providence' of his tenants and followers.[15]

Growing from both of these assumptions was the central tenet of the Oudh creed. Far from being purely the creations of external governmental action—as the *zamindars* of Bengal all too clearly were—or of usurpation during the military chaos of the eighteenth century or during the legislative chaos of the first years of British rule—as far too many of the landlords of the United Provinces were proved to be during the 1857–8 rising—the landlords, in particular the great Rajput landlords of Oudh, were the products of processes of social evolution, the natural outgrowths of the 'sentiments of the people'. A system of social control which made use of institutions and organizations which depended on the sentiments of the people, in which the position of the landlord grew not out of a particular relationship with government, or out of a purely economic relationship between landlord and tenant, obviously had many advantages for the ruling power; as the foundation for a system of indirect rule, or even more of partial indirect rule, it could have few equals. But it does have its drawbacks; above all, it can hardly be regarded as stable, particularly in a situation where the economic facts are changing, or where one of the parties, as it were, became, for some reason, able to exert undue pressure. It was perhaps an 'equilibrium system', which only worked when the forces within society were in their correct balance, the landlord being able to maintain his status through, for instance, protection, or through regulating the supply of land, and on the other hand, the tenants being able to bring a meaningful force to bear by the threat of sanctions, either military—that is by the withdrawal of 'feudal service'—or economic—by the withdrawal of labour and cultivation. Above all, it was paradoxical for a system which was based on the natural development of society, and the sentiments of the people, that it should have needed constant interference and regulation to keep its parts in proper balance.

Much of the agrarian policy of the late nineteenth century in the United Provinces can be seen as part of an attempt to maintain this balance. While in 1890 the Revenue Commissioner of Oudh could report that 'there survives a strong feeling of attachment and regard for the hereditary leaders which will continue as long as the landlords treat [the tenants] with moderation and the disappearance of which will be a calamity to the country',[16] his was a voice crying against the wind. 'The relations of landlord and tenant are not in a satisfactory state and are getting more and more strained',[17] roundly declared two of the most influential revenue officers in the United Provinces in their evidence to the 1880 Famine Commission. Even the Board of Revenue itself officially reported 'the growth of a sturdy conflict between the proprietor and the tenant'.[18]

This steady conflict was evidenced by growing disorder and non-cooperation in the countryside,[19] but also and perhaps primarily by the rapid increase in the volume of litigation.[20] The basic assumptions of the Oudh system implied a specific approach to the causes of the decline of this system. Landlords, so the theory ran, owed their position to a certain very definite social and political status; they were a function of the social system. If the landlords, dependent on the 'sentiments of the people', were a declining group, the reason must lie in some deep social change. If the 'natural leaders of society' were becoming a thing of the past, it must follow that society was succumbing to forces of change and disintegration. Hewitt and Butler believed—a view curiously similar to Marx's—that Indian rural society was in imminent danger of collapse under the pressures of economic change, and in particular under the pressures of British bureaucracy. Nor was this view limited to the extremists of the Oudh policy. T. A. Martin, failed civilian, indigo-planter and russophobe, who pestered governments in Allahabad, Calcutta and London for twenty years with memoranda offering irrefutable proof that tenancy legislation, the introduction of municipal self-government and the famines of the 1890s were an open invitation to the Russians to pour over the Khyber, complained of one of the more backward districts of the eastern United Provinces, Azamgarh, that:

> The *mahal* system has broken down the village system and done no good—enormous harm. I remember an old zamindar saying in '93 that the Sirkar had ruined the village by the *mahal* system, taken away his power and his young bloods would not obey him and would go to the riots and now [his son] may be hanged.[21]

Even cooler heads in the Secretariat in Allahabad could complain that in the early 1890s:

> Whether it be lambardar or landholder, the influences which have hitherto held and controlled the masses are gradually being weakened under the levelling influence of British rule.... In rural as well as in urban life changes are taking place of which the result is to bring obscure men to the surface and to relegate to comparative obscurity the classes on whom the public attention has been up

to recent times concentrated. The structure of the old society is becoming unstable throughout. These changes may be for good or evil: this is not the place to discuss that aspect of the matter; but there can be no doubt that, one by one, the forces which have hitherto held native society together are being loosened.[22]

Not merely was the superstructure of society tottering; even the lowest levels were shaken. From the length and breadth of the province, cries went up that the village system, the essential basis of society, was collapsing; landlords were complaining that their tenants were unruly and lacking in due deference, tenants in their turn were complaining of the exactions and oppressions of their landlords. The reasons advanced for this decline were, above all, social and political reasons, reasons which visualized change within the society as the result, at least in major part, of the interference of Government in rural relationships, in particular by freezing the patterns of social relationships by giving them the force of legal relationships. They were, however, reasons within the span of the basic assumptions of the Oudh system; changes in the general economic and political framework were tempting—in some cases forcing—the landlord to abandon his traditional role as the leader of society and become no more than a parasite. The disappearance of the military role of the landlord had 'de-militarized' his relations with his followers, while growing demand for land had increased the importance of his control over the basic resource of rural society; the landlord was at once strengthened and weakened. The balance was shifting but not in any clear direction, and consequently had to be constantly redressed first in one direction, and then in another. In many ways it is tempting to see the apparent vagaries of tenancy and landlord policy in the United Provinces as being the working out of this constant balancing act, rather than in terms of the victory of first one, and then another ideological slant.

The 'Oudh construct', then, was not simply a justification for a particular policy of the United Provinces government; it was rather one aspect of a general and pervasive view of the organization of Indian rural society. It was a view very like Professor Elton's view of Tudor England, a system of concentrated power being demitted downwards to relatively powerless followers, followers who were followers because it was in the nature of the system that they should be so, and also because they had no choice but to be followers.

II

The 'Oudh Policy' and the 'Oudh Construct', then, provided a very useful framework within which government could comprehend and administer rural society; a society whose organization was based on the 'sentiments of the people' could be safely administered in the semi-indirect way which many officials preferred, on ideological as well as financial grounds. If power was concentrated in the higher levels of society, imperial power simply had to impose itself as a further, higher level of power and operate the existing system, from time to time interfering in it to ensure its continued existence and balance, to prevent the imbalances in power in the system reaching the point where they became open abuses or where they threatened the existence of the system. It was, inevitably, an interpretation of society and of social change which concentrated on society as seen from the top, as a system of political control rather than as a system of social organization into which not merely the province-wide society of *zamindars* and *talukdars* but also the local society of tenants, rich and poor peasants and labourers—and others not directly connected with the land—has to be fitted. If the Oudh system worked, it worked not because of the nature and ancestry of the landlords, but because, in thousands of villages, and in thousands of local societies, men found the system of value to them in organizing their lives. If the Oudh system—or any other system—rested on 'the sentiments of the people', it was in this very concrete local context, rather than in the traditions of leadership, or the deference due to the great—important though these no doubt could be—that the basis of those sentiments lay.

Looked at in this way, from within the local context rather than from outside, the structure of almost any rural society would appear very different; nineteenth century north Indian society is no exception to this rule. Far from appearing a system of oppression, of power concentrated and delegated almost irresponsibly, the outside 'systems of social control' are to be seen as part of the overall political and resource framework of local society and local politics, as counters in a political game being played by local 'politicians', by, that is to say, the leaders—and others—in local society. Viewed from this angle, too, the 'decline of the power of the landlords' appears not so much as a symptom of a catastrophic and far-reaching revolution in rural society as the result of the continued and continuing working out of the in-built patterns of social and political change within the society.

In attempting to discuss the 'local political unit' and the 'local political context', the historian of the United Provinces is immediately faced with an almost insoluble problem of definition. By training and by the persuasive and pervasive influence of much anthropological work, we are almost driven to see 'the village' at the centre of this local unit, as virtually being this unit. Such a conclusion is natural but misleading. Even in areas of heavily nucleated settlement such as the Meerut division, as Professor Kessinger has pointed out for the Punjab,[23] the effective local political unit is wider than the village. 'Clan' groups and 'clan lands' spill from village to village, men held land in a number of villages, labourers moved from village to village in search of work. In the eastern parts of the United Provinces, even the apparent unity of the nucleated village does not exist.[24] Consequently, in the United Provinces at least, the local political unit has to be seen as something wider than the village. It is not the aim of this paper to attempt to define this unit; indeed, it seems very likely that there was no consistent, local unit in the province; it almost certainly differed from region to region, as indeed it varied in one area over time; it may even have varied in the same area at the same time, having different sizes and different composition for different functions. For the purposes of this paper, the local political unit must remain as nebulous as the village before it.

The local political unit was not a totally undifferentiated mass of peasants or peasant proprietors; the most significant factor in local society was not equality but stratification. Far from being sunk into some kind of common mediocrity or misery, it is becoming increasingly clear that the inhabitants of the countryside had their own complex system of economic and social ranking, a system which is only partially, often apparently accidentally, congruent with the imposed imperial system of village organization, or with the *varna* system of caste. Whatever its causes—and they are many and varied—stratification was a major factor in village life; not merely can this be seen in the social relationships which have been the concern of the anthropologists, but it is clear also in the economic and landholding structure of that village. It is an obvious point that not all villagers held land and that not all villagers who held land held the same amount of land. Not merely, however, was there a disparity in holdings; there was also a pattern in this disparity.[25] The pattern of disparity seems to have been common to the vast range of local contexts: a large number of very small holdings, a number of middle-sized holdings and a few large holdings; such a pattern almost exactly matches the idea of village and local stratification as it emerges from other sources. The local community is dominated economically and politically by a group of relatively well-to-do men, often including village officers and virtually always including the official village headman, the *chaudhuri, muqaddam* or *mukhya.* Their position was not simply dependent upon their caste or ritual status as members of a dominant group; it had firm economic foundations. As controllers of disproportionate shares of the land of the village (either as 'owners' or 'tenants'—the distinction is of relative unimportance within the local context) they were able to tie the other villagers to them either as seasonal labourers or as tenants or sub-tenants; a very high proportion of the occupancy tenure land of the provinces—the land held by the longer-standing tenants who were likely to be members of this dominant group—was sublet.[26] The wealth of the dominant group also made them potentially and actually an important source of credit in the local community. Beneath them were a mass of middle-ranking men, in some ways closely similar to the Wisers' 'followers',[27] some of the subordinate members of the ruling elite, others members of other groups—*kurmis, kacchis, muraos,* for instance—whose social and ritual position did not necessarily match their economic position. Finally at the bottom of the society were the great mass of landless and almost landless labourers, often compounding the sin of being poor with that of being untouchable.

The organization of the local community was not, however, as simple as this kind of horizontal description would suggest; the 'class' divisions in the village were cut across by the kind of vertical connections which are so clear in the wider and more open situation of the towns.[28] As with so many forms of social organization in India, these networks were in part based on traditional structures of relationship—on the *jajmani* relationships which play such a large part in the anthropological view of the Indian village, for instance—in part on family relationships, whether real or putative; but also upon some kind of social and political status and upon a generally recognized need not to be left alone, an individual in a world of connections and followings. The Deputy Commissioner of Rae Bareli observed in 1870: 'The population seems to be divided into four classes viz.:

Masters and Dependents
Borrowers and Lenders.

Not a man who has the slightest means of support but has one dependent at least; no vagrant without ostensible means of support but has one patron at least.'[29] It was advisable for a cultivator or a labourer to belong to the connection of one of the local leaders, since it was only in this way that he could guarantee that his case would not be forgotten in the division of spoils within the local political arena; but it was also useful for the local leader to have some kind of connection or faction, since not only was the backing of followers a helpful card to play in the politics of the locality, but in addition, the presence of large numbers of followers at those times of spectacle—funerals, marriages, *Dasehra*, *Holi* and so forth, when the standing of the leader could be enhanced by a display of his *izzat*, his wealth and importance—enabled him to increase further his standing in the village as a *burra admi*. Potentially and very frequently in fact, the local polity was a factional struggle in the same ways as the town; local connections were never stable and hence ever in competition. The work of a number of anthropologists, in particular Oscar Lewis,[30] and more recently M. N. Srinivas,[31] has highlighted the importance of faction, whether traditional or fluctuating. Nineteenth century United Provinces officers were making much the same sorts of comments about villages: the Deputy Commissioner of Partabgarh, for instance, commented in 1865:

> Often as I have toiled through the history of a village, I have seen evidence of such a state of struggle and tension between the parties, the equilibrium being disturbed now in favour of one, and now of another that I have been obliged to confess that in many instances, zamindari in India is an idea and not a tangible, proveable thing.[32]

The 'stable unchanging' village community of India was perpetually in a state of flux; it was only the outward structure which maintained some show of stability.

It is with this political universe, and in particular with the role within it of the local leaders, that the remainder of this paper is concerned, since it is at this level that it is most possible to get a view of the operation of the local political system, and of its relations with the wider world. In many ways, this relationship of the local leaders to the outside world was, and always had been, crucial to their position. The position of the local political leader was, in most cases, generated at least partly within the locality; it was based not simply on economic leadership. Amongst other factors which played a part in the creation and maintenance of leadership were kinship, ritual and caste status and 'respect'—personality. A leading position in the kinship structure of caste or clan within the local context could be a considerable advantage in the factional structure of the locality. Kinship or caste leadership did not, however, guarantee to a family or a person a leading position in the locality; kinship was, and is, almost as flexible as all the other changing components of the village community. In a situation in which a number of families, or a number of men, could claim to kinship leadership, what was likely to distinguish them in terms of local leadership was the ability of particular individuals to operate the connectional structure of the village. The same, to some extent, holds true of the even more nebulous 'respect'; one of the ways in which a man could gain respect was by operating the systems of external influences, by demonstrating that he could provide goods or services for his followers. Perhaps more important were the directly economic ways in which the local leader could control his followers: employment, the tenancy or subtenancy of land, credit, were all prizes with which the leader could reward the loyal and, by withholding or withdrawing them, punish the disloyal. In areas of precarious climate, the local leader, too, could use the economic power which allowed him to store and hoard foodgrains as a sanction over his followers in times of shortage.[33]

The position of the local leader did to some extent depend on his standing simply within the enclosed local society. Few, if any, local societies, however, were closed; all of them were influenced by outside forces, by just those forces of outside control with which the Oudh policy was concerned. From within the local community and its local politics, however, these forces appear rather differently, as resources available within the local political system, as counters available to local politicians within their political game. It is only necessary to list these outside influences to realize their importance. Up to this point this paper has been largely concerned with one of these, the great estates, which could, through their local bureaucracy, control, to some extent at least, the supply of land in the locality and the levels of rent for those lands; a local leader who had, and was known to have, influence with the landlord or his servants obviously had a major advantage in the struggle to gain and keep followers. The landlord, too, performed other functions and supplied other resources than land; he had, in many cases, a jurisdictional function, whether it be traditional or one delegated to him by the imperial power; he was, in some cases at least, an important source of credit.[34] An important distinction, too, can be made between the landlord and his bureaucracy; just as the lower levels of the official bureaucracy possessed an initiative and an influence of its own, so too did the unofficial bureaucracy of the estates. The estate and its bureaucracy were not, even in those villages wholly or partly included in great estates, the sole source of external resource and influence available within the local context.

The government itself and the official bureaucracy had important power and influence in the locality. It was the government or rather its officials who set the level of taxation on the village, and the records are full of complaints, in some cases justified, of officials—usually native—favouring particular lands and particular groups.[35] Again, officials also gave out the titles to land—or rather engagements to pay revenue—which could obviously have major importance in any factional struggle in the village.. The government appointed and dismissed the village officers—*muqaddams*, *patwaris* and *chaukidars* amongst others—thus giving individual villagers and individual connections the lucrative opportunities these offices presented. Increasingly, too, the government became a supplier of irrigation; the political opportunities which arose from this vital resource were immense. So serious did the problem of 'corruption' in the irrigation department become that, in the words of A. P. Webb:

> There is, in every village, a strong faction which fattens under the shadow of canal favour. These, chiefly lumbardars and their relations, in return for large supplies of water, promote canal oppression in all its forms.[36]

The local community was also linked to the outside world by ties of trade and credit. Foodstuffs, cloth, metals, and many other necessities had to be imported; some provision had to be made for marriages, festivals, funerals and agricultural disasters. The village too had to export, above all, cash crops—sugar, cotton, wheat, opium and many others. In all these cases the resource of the village was widened, and the function of the local leader as a link strengthened.

Far, then, from being tied into a system in which power and influence were monopolized by a single source, the landlord, the local political leaders were able to make use of a wider-ranging pattern of resources in their local political game. On the one hand, different leaders in the same locality might have access to sources of different types of resource, and consequently local politics came down to a playing off of, for instance, government against estate or *karinda* against *bania*. On the other hand, an individual leader might have access to a number of differing sorts of influences—this is perhaps the most typical situation—and could play one system off against the other as part of his own political game. Far from being an oppressed peasant the local leader was an independent and powerful political figure in a surprisingly open political system.

The history of the Kisan Sabha Movement of 1921–2 in Rae Bareli district holds a fascinating example of this; an example which is interesting for a number of reasons.[37] The village of Ramnagar—or rather the Murai group—had for a considerable period been in conflict with their landlord, the *talukdar* of Rasulpur. In the period before 1920 the conflict had been carried on in the usual ways—violence and refusal to pay rents on the part of the Murais, threats of eviction and writs on the part of the estate—culminating in *fasli* 1326 (= 1918/9) with a clear threat by the landlord to evict the Murais at the end of their leases. There was no reason why the pattern should not have been continued; however, the Ramnagar situation was complicated by the ability of the Murais and their connections to seek help elsewhere. The most 'traditional' of these outside connections was with government: one of the Ramnagar Murais had a brother-in-law who was the servant of the wife of a zamindar who was the sister of the tahsildar of Salone. This indirect connection was strong enough to get the Murais' complaint brought to the attention of the Sub-district officer. In fact, in the short run this approach failed (it was later renewed). One set of connections having failed, further ones were brought into use. The presence of a 'non-*talukdar*' candidate, B. Kismat Rai, in the Salone tahsil, may have drawn the attention of the Murais to the new form of influence being provided by the politicians, but it was to the leader of the 'provisional' Kisan Sabha, Ram Chandra, that the Murais turned. Their approach, however, does not suggest an 'upswing of political feeling', nor a radical change in the framework within which rural society operated; rather than approaching Ram Chandra direct, they got in touch with him through their connectional system—in fact through the tahsildar of Salone's family.[38]

For the system to be so open, however, at least two basic conditions had to be fulfilled, one in line with the assumptions of the Oudh policy, the other in direct contradiction to it. To take this latter first: the system can only work if, rather than being the 'sole earthly providence' of the inhabitants of the countryside, the landlord was merely one of a number of potential sources of influence and resource. As has already been pointed out, in fact a whole range of other types of resources was available, but almost as important as all these other systems is the fact that any single landlord very rarely monopolized even the supply of the 'landlord-resources' in a locality. I have pointed out earlier, with particular reference to eastern Oudh, that the complexities of settlement policy and of the history of transfer of land had left few villages, and fewer localities, in the sole control of single landlords.[39] This point can be extended to much of the rest of the province; even in those areas such as the Himalayan Tarai areas in Oudh where single landlords such as the Maharaja of Balrampur controlled large tracts of land, the apparent strength of the landlord was reduced by the shortage of labour rather than of land.[40] Even within the locality, however, the landlord's control of the land which was nominally his was limited in part by the legislation introduced to protect tenants and, above all, by the subletting of tenant land to smaller tenants, usually by the village leaders themselves; it was calculated that in 1919/20, some 17.4 per cent of the land held on protected occupancy tenures in the Agra Province (e.g. the U.P. without Oudh) was sublet.[41] Far from being the lord of the land, the sole supplier of the basic resource of rural society, the landlord was only one of a number of potential sources within the locality.

All this available resource, however, would not have made the society and polity so open had the local leader nothing to offer to the outsiders; it must be emphasized constantly that this society was not one in which power was concentrated at any single level; power was diffuse, some resting with the landlord as well as with the local leader. What the local leader could offer to the outsiders was his support; this support, however, was not the rather nebulous feudal support which the Oudh policy supposed. It was, rather, something much more concrete, and much more immediate; the great strength of the local leader lay in his ability to control and direct local coercive force. Not only the great estates, but also the government and creditors and traders, lacked, ultimately, any form of really effective force within the village; to make their position felt, to enforce any of their decisions, they required such local effective force.[42] While some of the external leaders made use of hired external force, or of the force of officialdom, the great mass of outsiders perforce relied on the coercive power held by the local leaders. The estates and also the government and the networks of credit were coalitions between the higher levels of society and local leaders, just as the local connections were coalitions between leaders and followers. Far from being a society with power concentrated at the top, north Indian rural society was a complex and changing political system, in which power was more equally divided between a number of levels, and in which all levels of society were able to take part in a complex system of politics and to make use of the patterns of resources available to them.

III

This open polity was no more static than the Oudh construct—indeed it is in its very nature that it should be unstable and ever-changing. The same historical problems that the Oudh construct sought to explain, the decline of the landlords, the apparent collapse of rural society, have to be explained within the terms of this local political network. Unlike the Oudh construct, however, this pattern does not require the assumption of a major social revolution, of a complete change in the patterns of social organization; rather than postulating a wholesale re-structuring of society, it is possible to explain the changes which are visible in society as being the result of a shifting pattern of resources, and in particular of external resources.

The later part of the nineteenth century saw a major expansion in the number and range of the external influences which made up the political galaxy of the local leader. Very crudely it is possible to say that, in particular during the eighteenth century, a large number of the potential external resources came to be concentrated in the hands of the 'landlord': the collapse of administration gave the landlord increased jurisdictional and fiscal freedom, the landlord, to some extent at least, became a leading creditor and, since the ability to cultivate land may have rested on the ability of the landlord to organize its military protection, the control of land may have been more completely in the hands of the military landlord. The nineteenth century saw, first of all, a re-exertion of the powers of government; the government again took over the great mass of jurisdiction, again took control of the assessment and collection of revenue. The revival of long-distance trade and the introduction of export cropping introduced new forms of influence and power to be placated and used. Not merely were these old forms of resource and power being revivified; a large number of new and potentially important powers were brought into the countryside. One of the most important of these was the expansion of government intervention. The most spectacular form of this was perhaps the development of a government-controlled system of canal irrigation centred in the Meerut, Agra and Rohilkhand divisions, which brought not merely a whole new resource on a spectacularly large scale into the locality but also a wider-ranging and powerful new bureaucracy into the structure. The government, too, began to interfere with the position of the village officials, to become a lender of money and to create, in the cooperative societies, new arenas for local political struggles with new resources. The expansion of the law courts and the massive litigation which went with it can perhaps best be seen not as a cause and a symptom of the collapse of the social structure, but rather the seizing by local—and external—leaders of a new form of political opportunity. At the same time, the tenancy legislation of the later part of the century undoubtedly reduced the importance of the resources which the landlord could offer. The balance of external resource was shifting and becoming more complex; into this picture, too, has to be added the expansion of trade and commerce which came with the growth of the railways in the later nineteenth century. Traders became important sources of resource for the village leader; an ability to get the best—or at least a better—price for the produce of his followers could be an important advantage for the local leader. External creditors, too, played an increasing part in the economic structure, both providing a new resource and seeking the support of the local leaders.

The political system within which the local leaders were operating thus became a much more open one; there were many more potential sources of resource and power to be tapped, many more external powers seeking village support which could be played off against each other in local political struggles. The apparent weakening of the social structure, which the Oudh construct saw in terms of the collapse of traditional ties and a wide-ranging social revolution, was to imply the widening of the political context within which society worked; as the range of choice available to the local leader became wider, so his dependence on any single source of power and influence was lessened; as the local leader could get similar resources, or different resources of similar weight and value, from other sources, so the importance to him of the single landlord declined. Rather than the structure of society being destroyed, a re-balancing within an elastic and resilient structure was taking place.

This analysis of society must, however, be carried a stage further to avoid creating a new Oudh construct, substituting the village leader—'the rich peasant'—for the landlord as the node of political, social and economic power. In the diffuse society which has been described above, there was no single, simple node of power. The local leader, as much as the landlord or the government official, operated in a world in which everyone around him had some freedom of action, some ability to choose between available resources and available connections; no more than the government or landlords did the local leaders lead connections of the inert. Followers too possessed freedom of action, a freedom which obviously varied with their economic status, and in particular with the value of any skills they possessed: the freedom of a *chamar* ploughman or a *kumhar* potter was, perhaps paradoxically, given their devalued caste status, much greater than that of a small tenant. The freedom of action of the local leader was always limited by the need to hold his connection together. In many ways, the local leader was presented in the nineteenth century with the same sorts of problems which the landlord or the government official had to face; a widening range of opportunities for his followers which inevitably meant a much greater mobility and fluidity of connections. The 'rich peasant' was no more the sole node of power, even in the small locality, than was the government officer or the nominal owner of the land. It is as dangerous, and as much a part of the same misconception of the nature of north Indian rural society which informed the 'Oudh Construct', to see the late nineteenth century as marking the 'Rise of the Rich Peasant', as it is to see the same period as the period of decline of the great landlord and the great estate. In the diffuse society of rural north India, what was occurring was not the rise and fall of classes or categories, nor yet the collapse of a society based on the 'sentiments of the people', but rather a re-balancing of a complex structure in which power, social, economic, and political, was diffused amongst a whole range of men, all of them dependent to a greater or lesser extent upon the support or acquiescence of other men. Though the landlords, the government or the traders did not possess a monopoly of power, neither were they without it; rural society, or rather the control of rural society, was, and remained, a coalition between the many levels of society, levels which governed and controlled, and were governed and controlled by consensus rather than by dominion.

Rather than being a period of the growing dominance of the rich peasant, or the money-lender or any other single level in the society, the nineteenth century can be seen as a period in which the changes which occur in the apparent structure of society are largely a result of the increasing openness of society, of the expansion of ranges of outside opportunities available to all levels of society. The diffuse society was becoming more diffuse; rather than becoming concentrated, power within society was being spread further and further through the society. The second half of the nineteenth century in the United Provinces is no more the age of the *kulak* than the early nineteenth century had been the age of the great landlord. North Indian society in the late nineteenth century must be seen as a complex and mutually qualifying series of centres of influences and potential leadership rather than as a society with clear-cut power relationships and distinctions, and change can, in consequence, be seen not as the simple decline of centres of power and the rise of new ones but rather as a continuous and continuing shift in the balance between a galaxy of centres in the society. If the Oudh policy failed it did so not because of the machinations of nationalist politicians or the clumsiness of the governors, but rather because it sought to treat as a social revolution of massive proportions what was no more than the normal ebb and flow of a highly sophisticated and highly adaptable society.

The issues raised in this paper are discussed at greater length in my doctoral dissertation (P. J. Musgrave: 'An Indian Rural Society; Aspects of the Structure of Rural Society in the United Provinces 1860–1920', unpublished Ph.D. dissertation, 1976, University Library, Cambridge).

NOTES

1 See, for instance, D. G. Hey, *An English Rural Community: Myddle Under the Tudors and Stuarts* (Leicester, 1974). R. M. Spufford, *Contrasting Communities, English Villages in the 16th and 17th Centuries* (London, New York, 1974).

2 G. R. Elton, *Review* of R. V. Smith, 'Land and Politics in the England of Henry VIII', *Historical Journal*, 14:1 (1971), 221.

3 G. R. Elton, *The Tudor Constitution* (Cambridge, 1962), pp. 13, 15.

4 Duncan was Resident in Benares from 1788 to 1795. See B. H. Baden-Powell, *Land Systems of British India*, 3 vols (Oxford, 1892), II, pp. 5–8.

5 For an outline of this, see T. R. Metcalf, *The Aftermath of Revolt* (Princeton, 1965), especially chapter V; E. T. Stokes, *The English Utilitarians and India* (Oxford, 1959); and D. Rothermund, 'Government, Landlord and Tenant in India, 1875–1900', *Indian Economic and Social History Review*, 6:4 (1969), 351–67.

6 P. J. Musgrave, 'Landlords and Lords of the Land: Estate Management and Social Control in Uttar Pradesh 1860–1920', *Modern Asian Studies*, 6:3 (1972), 273–5.

7 C. J. Dewey, 'Images of the Village Community: A Study in Anglo-Indian Ideology', *Modern Asian Studies*, 6:3 (1972), 291–328.

8 Darogah Haji Abbas Ali, *An Illustrated Historical Album of the Rajas and Talukdars of Oudh* (Allahabad, 1880), p. 1.

9 H. H. Butts, *Report of the Land-Revenue Settlement of the Lucknow District* (Lucknow, 1873), p. 76.

10 This view has been restated somewhat opaquely by T. R. Metcalf, 'From Raja to Landlord', in R. E. Frykenberg, ed., *Land Control and Social Structure in Indian History* (Madison, Milwaukee and London, 1969), pp. 123–41 and more clearly by Walter C. Neale in the same volume.

11 National Archives of India, New Delhi [hereafter NAI], Government of India Legislative Department Proceedings, January 1874, Appendix O, 64, p. 16.

12 T. R. Metcalf, 'From Raja to Landlord', in R. E. Frykenberg, ed., *Land Control and Social Structure*, p. 124.

13 C. A. Elliott, *Chronicles of Oonao, a District in Oudh* (Allahabad, 1862).

14 W. C. Benett, *A Report on the Family History of the Chief Clans of Roy Bareilly* (Lucknow, 1870).

15 H. C. Irwin, *The Garden of India or Chapters on Oudh History and Affairs* (London, 1880), p. 12.

16 *Report on the Administration of the North Western Provinces and Oudh*, 1889–90, p. 168.

17 C. A. Elliot and W. Buck, 'The Condition of the Agricultural Classes in the North Western Provinces', in *Evidence Presented to the Indian Famine Commission, 1879–80*, Parliamentary Papers, Session 1881, vol. lxxi, Part 1, p. 493 (169).

18 *Report on the Administration of the Revenue of the North Western Provinces and Oudh*, 1881/2, p. 39, quoting NWP Progs, Revenue Proceedings, [hereafter NWPR], November 1885, file 292, serial 15, p. 125.

19 There were, for instance, a number of rent strikes: in Allahabad in 1866 (NWPR, April 1866, p. 22); eastern Oudh in the late 1860s and early 1870s (Metcalf, 'Raja to Landlord', in Frykenberg, ed., *Land Control and Social Structure*, pp. 132–3); in the Bulandshahr *Lalkhani* estates in the late 1880s (NWP & OR, September 1888, p. 1); and in the Gursarai *ubari* in Jhansi in the 1890s (NWP & OR, December 1896, p. 106).

20 E. M. Whitcombe, *Agrarian Conditions in Northern India: The United Provinces under British Rule, 1860–1900* (Berkeley, Los Angeles and London, 1972), chapter V.

21 NAI, Government of India Revenue Proceedings, Land Revenue, August 1901, Prog 64B quoting Legislative Proceedings, July 1901–2 B, Appendix H, Opinion 30, p. 105.

22 Report on the Administration of the NWP & O, 1890–1, p. xxvii.

23 T. G. Kessinger, *Vilyatpur 1848–1968: Social and Economic Change in a North Indian Village* (Berkeley, Los Angeles and London, 1974), p. 5.

24 R. L. Singh and K. N. Singh, 'The Middle Ganga Plain', in R. L. Singh, ed., *India: A Regional Geography* (Varanasi, 1971), pp. 213–14.

25 Some impression of the distribution of holdings can be gained from the following table:

SIZE OF TENANT-HOLDINGS IN 10 TALUKDARI VILLAGES OF SANEHIGHAI TEHSIL, DISTRICT BARA BANKI, 1881

Numbers of Holdings by Area in Bighas

Village	Number of Holdings	0–4	5–10	More than 10
Muttranagar	155	88	34	34
Danapur	34	17	14	3
Pattipur	21	10	8	3
Jithani Kurmiyon	38	35	3	0
Jithani Rajputon	160	85	31	44
Sarai Barai	120	64	33	23
Sarai Ahmad	95	42	33	20
Fatehpur	69	31	24	15
Pakariagaon	50	30	13	7
Berhar	82	60	16	6

SOURCE: W. Erskine, *Collection of Papers Relating to the Condition of the Tenantry and the Working of the Present Rent Act in Oudh*, 2 vols (Allahabad, 1883), p. 220.

26 See below, p. 18.

27 William and Charlotte Wiser, *Behind Mud Walls 1930–1960* (Berkeley and Los Angeles, 1963).

28 C. A. Bayly, 'Patrons and Politicians in Northern India', in J. A. Gallagher, G. Johnson and A. Seal, eds., *Locality, Province and Nation* (Cambridge, 1973), pp. 29–68.

29 State Archives of Uttar Pradesh, Allahabad, Files of the Board of Revenue, Rae Bareli, file 24, p. 308.

30 Oscar Lewis, *Group Dynamics in a North Indian Village: A Study of Factions* (Delhi, 1954).

31 M. N. Srinivas, 'The Indian Village: Myth & Reality', in J. H. M. Beattie and R. G. Lienhardt, eds., *Studies in Social Anthropology: Essays in Memory of E. E. Evans-Pritchard* (Oxford, 1975), pp. 41–85.

32 NAI, Government of India Foreign (Revenue) Proceedings, February 1865, p. 187.

33 Both Michele McAlpin and David Washbrook (M. B. McAlpin, 'The Effects of Markets on Rural Income Distribution in Nineteenth Century India', *Explorations in Economic History*, 12:3 (1975), 289–302; D. A. Washbrook, *The Emergence of Provincial Politics: The Madras Presidency, 1870–1920*, Cambridge, 1976, pp. 74–8) have suggested the importance of storage in the Indian agricultural economy; both have been concerned more with the economic than with the social aspect of storage; the social power of the storer is probably closely proportional to the threat of violent subsistence crises; in an area like the Meerut Division where the expansion of irrigation reduced the threat of crop failure, the importance—social and economic—of storage declined, perhaps to be replaced by cartage, access to transport to the growing markets, increasingly controlled by the dominant groups in the local community.

34 P. J. Musgrave, 'Rural Credit and Rural Society in the United Provinces, 1860–1920', in Clive Dewey, and A. G. Hopkins, eds. *The Imperial Impact: Studies in the Economic History of Africa and India* (London, 1978), pp. 216–32.

35 E.g., State Archives of Uttar Pradesh, files of the Board of Revenue, Oudh General Series, file 2235.

36 A. P. Webb, 'Irrigation Topics', reprinted in NWP & O Progs RA, October 1879, No. 62, p. 139.

37 W. F. Crawley, 'Kisan Sabhas and Agrarian Revolt in the United Provinces, 1920–1', *Modern Asian Studies*, 5:2 (1971), 95–109.

38 Uttar Pradesh Secretariat Record Room, Lucknow, General Administration Department, file 50 of 1920.

39 P. J. Musgrave, 'Landlords and Lords of the Land', pp. 261–4.

40 See, for instance, NWP & OR, July 1888, pp. 8–16.

41 Uttar Pradesh Secretariat Record Room, Revenue Department file 166/1920.

42 Musgrave, 'Landlords and Lords of the Land', pp. 268–74.

2

Madras Headmen

CHRISTOPHER BAKER

Queens College, Cambridge

In much of rural British India, where the writ of the civil servant ended the regime of the village officer began. In 1807, Thomas Munro wrote of the village headmen: 'whoever rules the province, they rule the village'.[1] In the nineteenth and early twentieth centuries, they formed a crucial link between the new systems of administration spreading out from government headquarters and the internal processes of rural India. The achievement of administrative policies in the rural areas often hinged upon the government's relations with village officers, and the shape of village society was fundamentally influenced by the nature of the village officers' contact with the state. Thus a study of the village officer can illuminate both the character of the government control and the structure of rural society, and, more importantly, the interdependence of the two.

In many parts of British India, the relationship of the government and the village was complicated and obscured by the existence of *talukdars*, *zamindars* and similar agents interposed between the two. In the *ryotwari* areas of the Madras Presidency, that was not so. Indeed, the operation of the *ryotwari* administration came to depend crucially on the co-operation of the village officers.[2] This essay starts out by sketching the history of village office in Madras from the early years of British rule. This serves as background for a study of the subtle yet fundamental change in the position and role of village officers in the last quarter-century of imperial control.

The two principal village officers were the headman, known in various areas of the region as *maniakkarar*, *potail*, *peddakarar* or *pedda ryot*, and the accountant known generally as the *karnam*. There was usually one of each of these officers in every 'revenue village', an official term which did not define each separate settlement but generally included a number of adjacent hamlets. In 1927 there were

16,411 headmen and 14,868 *karnams*[3] and the 'revenue village' had on average nearly seven hundred acres of occupied holdings.[4] There was also a number of assistants (watchmen, irrigation overseers, crop inspectors, runners and general dogsbodies), known collectively as the village menials. Their names, numbers and functions differed greatly from tract to tract, but in 1927 they totalled 47,100.[5]

The relative power of the two principal officers, and the status (both economic and social) of the headman with regard to the other villagers, differed greatly from tract to tract and perhaps also from village to village. At the start of the nineteenth century, in many upland areas where governmental control was remote and where local defence against marauders was vital, the headman was generally a powerful figure.[6] Similarly in those areas where successive governments and successive invasions had done little to dislodge the local pre-eminence of the communities who had made the initial colonization, big landowners often controlled the village headship as part of a more general assertion of *mirasidari* rights.[7] Yet, in Tanjore, which had been the seat of power and the major source of governmental income for several generations of kings and princelings, the headmen had almost been crushed out of existence while the *karnams*, who controlled the local records necessary for any close administration, had risen into prominence.[8] Nor did the imposition of British administration bring about a much greater level of uniformity. Until late in the nineteenth century, the British schemes of rural administration in Madras provided only a loose framework in which a huge variety of local systems could persist side by side. This variety makes it difficult to generalize about the position of the village officers, but at a reasonable level of abstraction, and with considerable concession to local diversity, it remains possible.

I

Village officers were in no way creations of the British. Some kind of village leader with official duties appears to have existed in south India from the time of the first records of central administration of rural areas in the Sangam period.[9] In the twentieth century, nationalistic writers (and village officers themselves) were to portray the role of the officers in pre-British times as one of benign 'natural' leadership.[10] This was certainly a gross distortion, and indeed it is hard to see how the pristine innocence of the institution could have survived several centuries of use by a variety of political overlords. In most parts of south India, village officers had long since become intermediaries between government and the village, mediating the demands and desires of both parties, and levying some sort of fee on both parties for this service. A. Sarada Raju quotes Telugu poetry to illustrate the consequent distrust felt by the villagers, and quotes the *Fifth Report* (the pilot survey of the British administration) to illustrate the distrust which the British inherited from their predecessors.[11] Even so, the British soon seized on the institution of village office. In 1817 Munro, the architect of the Madras revenue system, wrote:

> Our Government rests entirely upon the single point of military power: there is no native one which rests so exclusively upon it. Where there is no village establishment we have no hold upon the people, no means of acting upon them, none of establishing confidence. Our situation, as foreigners, renders a regular village establishment more important to us than to a native government: our inexperience, and our ignorance of the circumstances of the people, make it more necessary for us to seek the aid of regular establishments to direct the internal affairs of the country, and our security requires that we should have a body of head men of villages interested in supporting our dominion.[12]

But the British did not adopt the system of village office without modification. In the disorders of the late eighteenth century many village officers had been able to extend their powers and to engross lands. In their early surveys, the British found several villages where the officers claimed to hold up to a third of the land as service *inam*.[13] Thus in the early nineteenth century the British felt that the village officers had to be wooed, but they also had to be cut down to size. The result of this rather contradictory policy was to humble the headman and strengthen the *karnam*. In many districts the settlement officers (who were allowed considerable liberty to make their own local policy) took away most or all of the large amounts of land claimed by headmen. Then during the period of village leases between 1803 and 1818, the headmen lost their duties as government revenue officers. Some headmen of course were transformed into lessees of their villages, but many others found that the lessees were not interested in their services and preferred to work directly with the *karnam*. When the lease system was abandoned and government declared itself in favour of the *ryotwari* principle, the local situation did not undergo any dramatic change. Until the government compiled a full survey in the second half of the nineteenth century, the *ryotwari* system was little more than a settlement between the Collector and the *karnams*. Local tenures remained largely unchanged and the Collectors relied upon the *karnams*' records for their knowledge of, and access to, these systems.[14] When, in the 1850s and 1860s, the government set about the land survey and the administrative reorganization necessary to implement a proper *ryotwari* system, it discovered that in Tanjore the important office of headman had become a 'sinecure', while elsewhere, 'in very many instances the emoluments of office have been frittered away, or the man is incompetent, and his powers and duties have in consequence been usurped by the curnum or taken by the taluk officials'.[15]

When Fort St George began to establish the new *ryotwari* system in the second half of the nineteenth century, it found it necessary to reorganize the village officers. As one senior official noted about the old system in which magisterial and revenue duties were held by separate officers: 'This divided power constantly breeds discord. . . . There is no fulcrum on which to rest the lever.'[16] The new revenue system was a strong lever for prising wealth out of the rural areas and it required a substantial fulcrum. Thus from about 1860, Fort St George set about strengthening the village headman. The Secretary of the Board of Revenue noted:

> To give this office a real and important position, it is requisite that the best and most influential men of a village community, having hereditary claims to the office, should be selected to fill it, and that all the emoluments and privileges of the office should be transferred solely to him.[17]

This became government policy. In about half of the Madras districts, the headman's post was decreed to be hereditary, while in the other districts succession to the post was administered as if the hereditary rule applied there as well. This principle served to keep the village headship in the hands of rich and respectable families, and of course to allow those families to consolidate their wealth and their prestige over the years. Government also began to destroy all rivals for the headman's power. Within the next twenty years, the headmen of most of the Madras villages had taken on the office of *munsiff* (village magistrate) and had become the official heads of the village police.[18] Thus in a large number of cases, the headman was accuser, chief witness and judge. The new revenue survey and the new, more formal and bureaucratic system of revenue assessment and collection, certainly limited the village officers' personal discretion and reduced their ability to appropriate to themselves a part of the revenue which the government believed was its due. In the 1870s and 1880s many village officers were found guilty of embezzlement;[19] clearly such men had not adjusted to the new conditions and were still trying to exact their customary percentage. But as a counterweight to these diminutions of power, the headmen found themselves made executors of a large number of rules and regulations. They could thus wield the power of government, and since the agency for checking their actions was light and flexible, they could often do this in a highly personal way.[20] Moreover, while the British administration gradually extended its scope in the later nineteenth century, there was no parallel expansion of government's agency in the village but rather a steady accretion of powers in the hands of the village officers, especially the headman. By the end of the century, the headman had new duties under the Arms Act, excise rules, irrigation laws, salt laws and the new institutions of local government.[21]

The position of the headman was further strengthened by the relative decline of the *karnam*. The revenue survey completed between 1864 and 1895 reduced the importance of his personal records and accounts. The more formal bureaucracy of the revenue system transformed him from an arbiter to a functionary. The government demanded that the *karnam* be an efficient part of a smoothly functioning machine and to that end it forced the *karnams* to sit for proficiency examinations, and placed them under fairly close supervision by the *tahsildars* and the deputy collectors. Whereas the *karnams* had once been left to write up the village accounts at their leisure, each year they were now hauled into the *taluk* headquarters and forced to write up the accounts under close supervision. 'Until he has bribed the Gumastah [clerk] who is supposed to examine his accounts,' noted a senior government officer, 'no karnam can hope to get back to his village with his accounts passed.'[22] The *karnams* still earned some power and prestige from their official duties, but they could no longer lord it over the headman and only rarely could they build up a faction in village politics to rival and check that of the headman.

Thus by the turn of the century, the powers of the village officers, and especially those of the headmen, were considerable. At the base of the sprawling superstructure of imperial government, the British had built a little monolith. His power came from the role as executor of government, his perquisites from the ability to wield this role to personal advantage, his prestige from the independence of action permitted by the remote, flexible supervision to which he was subjected.

Even after the new surveys, it still remained fairly simple for the village headman to make his own distribution of the revenue demand within the village. In the extreme case in certain villages of Chingleput, the village headman possessed the only *patta* (land deed) and he organized his own internal settlement within the village.[23] In many other villages the headman paid the government revenue demand from his own pocket and collected dues from the villagers with little reference to the official system and the official records.[24] With some ingenuity, village officers could still appropriate some proportion of government dues. In 1929 the Board of Revenue admitted, 'It is difficult to detect cases in which a village headman collects money and grants receipts and does not bring the amount to account. It is too much to expect the Revenue Inspector to be able to make a detailed examination of the receipts in the possession of ryots and a comparison of these with the credit in the various accounts to ensure that no loophole is left.'[25]

It was notorious that the lands of the headman and his cronies bore a light assessment, while others had to make up the deficit. The officers also had considerable control over any extension of cultivation. Until as late as 1919 the rules for assignment of new land (*darkhast*) ordained that the established landholders of a village would have first claim to the deeds (*patta*) for any land newly brought under the plough; and it was the village officers who recommended assignments. This in effect meant a labourer, even if he cleared a new bit of land for himself, was likely to find that the village officers or their friends acquired the *patta* for it and he had to remain as a labourer or tenant on the holding.[26] At sales of land for arrears of revenue, the village officers again enjoyed a privileged position. The village officers conducted the sales, and were also allowed to bid at them. It was folklore that such sales were rarely publicized and that the prices fetched were derisory; in other words, the headman could virtually assign the land to himself or his friends.[27]

Other profits came in cash. 'Some years back', wrote an Indian administrator in the early twentieth century, 'the village munsiffs were getting from each ryot during the kist [revenue payment] season an extra remuneration of annas four for each patta—what is known as *Cheetu Vari* in these parts—making it appear to the villagers that the amount is needed for jamabandi expenditure.' The *karnams* could charge fees for revealing excerpts from the records to other members of the village, and other fees for writing up all the accounts correctly at harvest-time.[28]

Thus both officers could charge the villagers for doing their job properly, and without prejudice to a particular individual. They could also charge for ignoring or perverting the laws. The same administrator talked of the 'illegal and extortionate demands made by the karnams in supporting claims in contesting encroachment, water-rate, patta transfer, sub-division cases, etc,' and noted that 'it is also a well-recognized fact that a very high percentage of the ryots in villages are offenders in trespassing on public ways or taking government water before time or in clandestine use of it, or numerous other ways. The karnam has always to be kept in good humour.'[29] The headman could arrange for a profitable future in the liquor trade; liquor could only be sold under government licence and again it was the headman who vetted an applicant.[30] He and the *karnam* could reduce a man's revenue-demand, by omitting to record the use of government water or the occupation of common lands. They could even free land from the encumbrances of mortgage or hypothecation. By a quirk of the revenue law, land sold for arrears of revenue was deemed free of encumbrances unless the parties involved put in a claim before the sale. If the headman covertly arranged for land to be sold for arrears and knocked down to its owner at a nominal price, the encumbrances disappeared.[31]

There were of course very substantial boundaries to the powers of the village officers. The most important were those operated by fellow villagers. Most *ryots* were reluctant to protest against the operations of the village officers and risk retribution in the future; the village officers commanded the ear of government, and the records which would be important in any court cases, and thus had natural advantages in any contest which followed from an appeal for help beyond the confines of the village. But there were of course often rich *ryots*, strong factions, or even sometimes combinations of poor *ryots*, who could oppose the village officers should the latter engage in a particularly flagrant exercise of power. The village officers, then, had to accommodate other powerful agencies in village society. Two examples will show the possibilities for retribution.

In one Trichinopoly village, a low-caste man secured the headman's post, to the annoyance of the majority of landowning Reddies, who quickly rendered the headman absolutely powerless. They refused to pay their revenue, which got the headman into trouble with his superiors for slackness, and (according to the headman) they bribed the *karnam* and the Revenue Inspector to make false reports about him. Within two years, he had been dismissed.[32] In a Madura village of Kallars, a caste notorious for their lawlessness, a *karnam* tried to exercise the letter of the law too exactly. As he told the government: 'They used to occupy Government lands and irrigate them unauthorisedly for which they are penalised heavily. They think that but for the karnam, their unauthorised occupation would go unnoticed and hence they would bear a grudge towards me. . . . They committed thefts in my house three times, set fire to my house once and beat me once while I was undefended. They are even threatening my life. . . . They beat the man who used to watch my house and did not allow him to do service under me. . . . I was returning from the field inspection . . . when I was beaten very severely and some of my accounts taken away.'[33] The message was that the *karnam* must share the benefits of the system.

The other limitation was government supervision, which operated largely through the institution of *jamabandi*, an annual visit by the Collector or one of his assistants, to check and close the village accounts and hear any petitions against the village officers' administration. This peculiar peregrination possibly holds more significance for the cultural anthropologist than for the student of economic or administrative history. In 1883, J. H. Garstin called it 'unnecessary and but little more than a farce'.[34] The *jamabandi* officer visited three or four villages in each *taluk*, and the village officers and interested *ryots* from other villages had to trek into these centres. Each village was allotted a certain few hours in which the *karnam* presented the accounts and any petitions were heard. A Collector, reminiscing about the 1880s, admitted that little serious business was done and talked of 'the old gathering and leisurely proceedings, the reception of the Collector or Jamabandi officer *en fête* with the temple music, umbrellas and all the rest of the paraphernalia, the erection and decoration of elaborate pandals'.[35] In the 1890s the government reorganized the institution and brought in a strict form of bureaucratic checks. After this reorganization, the village accounts became impossibly large and complex. The *karnams* kept two registers (of fields, and of *inams*), a diary of operations, twenty-four annual statements of account (including a record of cultivation by crop, records of irrigation, day-to-day records of revenue payments, lists of remittances to the treasury, statistics on rainfall, agricultural stock and crop yield, details of pattas, and a demand collection and balance statement). A (very incomplete) example in a government manual ran to 108 pages of printed foolscap.[36] These accounts could not be checked so easily at a *jamabandi* camp. Another Collector noted about *jamabandi*:

From the 'redress of grievances' angle it seemed to me to be admirable, but the rest of it struck me as having become so overloaded with detail as to be beyond the capacity of any single person to deal with efficiently. One's clerks went through all the accounts in advance and filled in the answers in enormous printed questionnaires. One just had to accept many of the answers on trust. I suppose it did keep the village officers on their toes and enable one, here and there, to detect a bad one. But equally it must have provided many opportunities for bribery.[37]

Indeed the system helped to create a formidable, almost impenetrable, layer between the Collector and the village. Another Collector left a fine picture of the actual operation of *jamabandi,* in which the placing of the characters symbolizes the relation of forces:

Every morning I took my seat on the verandah of the travellers' bungalow, with the tahsildar seated by me and the revenue inspector standing on one side of us and my head clerk on the other. In the front of us were two village officers, standing with arms folded and all the village accounts on the ground in front of them, while the village menials stood in a semi-circle behind them and still further away would be a crowd of petitioners and interested spectators.[38]

Evidently this Collector found the hurdles placed in his path simply too great and the burden of delivering economic justice to half a million *ryots* in a few days simply too much, for he devoted one of every two days of his *jamabandi* season to shooting the local snipe.[39]

Certainly in practice *jamabandi* did not provide the occasion for other villagers to challenge the administration of the village officers. In a petition entitled 'The Jamabandi Farce' one landowner wrote: 'The Revenue Inspector or the clerk glance through the petitions and hush up those that contain any allegation against the revenue or village officials. On the rest they put short notes and place them before the Jamabandi officer for normal disposal. It would be surprising to note that the disposals in most cases would be nothing but "petition dismissed".'[40] Most Collectors found that there were few petitioners. 'I have done the jamabandi of over 250 villages', wrote one, 'and not more than two or three dozen have appeared before me from the first to the last.' Others found petitioning *ryots* were even rarer than that, and in ten years they had seen only a handful.[41]

Indeed other reports alleged that *jamabandi* resulted not in a correction of accounts, or an occasion for a display of patriarchal justice, but in a dramatic redistribution of wealth among landowners, village officers and government officials. A Tanjore landowner wrote: 'Bribery and corruption are the chief outstanding features of this so-called Jamabandi or checking of accounts, in fact no checking of accounts is made excepting the festive celebration.' He followed this assertion with a detailed description of the payments made by each member of the revenue machinery to his immediate superior.[42] It was the occasion for the village officers to buy their immunity from higher authority and it was hardly surprising that village officers themselves complained that the *jamabandi* officer and his clerks 'sit in the place like a flight of locusts'.[43]

Most of the *karnams* did not or could not use their position to acquire lands. By the end of the nineteenth century, their official responsibilities occupied them full-time, and they evidently considered themselves as skilled professionals living off pay and perquisites, rather than as lords of the soil. Most *karnam* posts were hereditary, and were held by families from non-cultivating castes. Many were Brahmans and others came from specialist *karnam* communities, such as Karnikkarar. The headman, on the other hand, was nearly always drawn from the dominant landholding caste in the area. His official responsibilities occupied him for only four or five months of the year, and for the rest he could devote himself to his lands. It had been British policy from the beginning to choose (or confirm) the most authoritative men in the locality as headmen. This policy not only harnessed the authority of the village leader for the benefit of the tax-collection effort, but also provided an insurance against any assertion of independence by the village officers; if a headman refused to remit revenue collections, the government's only recourse was to proceed against the headman's property, and thus the government was anxious that the headman's property should be substantial. By the early twentieth century there was a rule of thumb among Collectors that the property of a headman should be worth as much as one revenue instalment of the whole village (there were three or four a year according to the district), or, preferably, worth as much as the entire annual demand of the village.[44] By the early twentieth century, the latter was generally in the region of Rs 5,000–15,000.

This meant that headmen had to be of considerable substance in the village. Choosing men of wealth in the first place, allowing them considerable opportunities to profit from the system, and making the post in most cases hereditary, did of course ensure that this was generally the case.[45] Many paid large sums in land revenue and boasted that they came 'of noble family'. Others were proud to add to their claims of wealth, their pretensions to belong to an extensive village elite; such men listed their kin relationships with local *zamindars*, other headmen, important men in the co-operative movement, luminaries from local politics, government servants and other prominent landowners.[46] In quite a number of cases, however, the headman was not himself wealthy. Indeed in many villages the men of undoubted influence were not anxious to undertake the burdens of office, and allowed it to fall to some lesser mortal whom they kept under close control. But whatever the local circumstances, the office was undeniably important, and its increased power in the late nineteenth century played a large part in the emergence of a distinctive rural elite. As David Washbrook has noted, over most of south India the expansion in the power of the village officers coincided with the expansion of wealth in the hands of major landowners: in the late nineteenth century 'the distance between the rich and the poor, between those with administrative power and those without it, was becoming greater'. The two developments, administrative and economic, corroborated one another and helped to create 'a small and resilient village elite'.[47] This fact underlay the development of rural politics until the 1920s. Thereafter the situation changed subtly but rapidly.

II

In 1947, a commentator wrote of the village officers: 'They are no longer the natural leaders and representatives of the village community, but are the salaried employees of the Government.'[48] Their formal powers were still considerable, and indeed with the advent of new taxes and the new food administration, they had in some ways increased. The same author noted that 'with the revenue powers vested in them . . . they are still the demigods of the village.'[49] But while they had retained their administrative powers, they had lost much of their status and prestige. This was of crucial importance.

Their decline was the result of a series of small reforms which qualified the independence of action of all village officers, but particularly the headmen, and made subtle changes in their relationships with other villagers and with the machinery of government; the headmen lost their unique importance to government, and their elbow-room, and as a consequence lost the power to command respect.

One of the most important changes came in the way village officers were paid. In 1906, the government took over the entire responsibility for paying village officers, thus relieving them of any dependence on *inam* lands or on fees collected from the other villagers.[50] This completed a process begun in 1865, and could not avoid giving the impression that the village officers had ceased to be local satraps and had become a lowly component of the government machine. As far as the *karnams* were concerned, this was the effect the government intended; but at the same time the government was anxious to preserve the illusion of the headman's independence and thus styled his pay as 'a mere honorarium'. However, when the government decided to raise the village officers' pay in 1919, and announced that while the *karnams* and menials would benefit, there was no need to raise the headman's pay since it was only an honorarium, the headmen were incensed. 'That a talaiyari [watchman] under him should draw more pay than a village munsiff', warned one politician, 'is a thing which touches his honour and sentiment.'[51] The government was forced to give way and the illusion of the headman's financial independence faded away.

Between 1915 and 1925, the government altered the relationship of the headman to his immediate superiors and inferiors. Firstly, they cut back on the number of village menials. While this seemed to the government to be a rational measure of retrenchment, to the headman it was a physical reduction of his private army, and thus a visible blow to his local prestige.[52] Secondly, the government gave new disciplinary powers to the *tahsildars*. The relationship between the headman and his immediate supervisor had always been finely balanced and many headmen were disturbed at this alteration. 'Does the resulting corruption', argued a local vernacular paper, 'need to be described? . . . How many tahsildars are not building palatial houses and acquiring lands? . . . Even now there are many Achari tahsildars who beat karnams, and many Nayudu tahsildars who abuse them. . . . Is there any doubt that in future tahsildars will expect all sorts of services from village officers . . . the poor village officers pay four out of eight rupees of their salary for the feast of the officer. Will the matter end there?'[53]

Thirdly, the government restricted the village officers' independence of action in matters of revenue. They deprived the headman of the power to issue demand notices for arrears and to conduct on their own authority sales of property for arrears.[54] They also tightened up the laws relating to village common land which meant that the headman could no longer make money on the side by selling off the fruit, timber and other material which grew there, but was instead himself now financially liable for any depredation of this communal property. Next, the headmen were obliged to produce a provisional demand statement before *jamabandi*, which enabled revenue officials to check their activities inside the village with more time than they had in a *jamabandi* camp,[55] and later forced to send in the record of day-to-day revenue payments at the end of the year rather than keeping it in the village. The village officers protested that 'that is the only account on which they can rely to meet vexatious charges of misappropriation' but the government evidently felt that the account was necessary to *prevent* misappropriation.[56] In 1920 the *karnams* were ordered to allow all *pattadars* to inspect the village records and in 1929, the government took further steps to facilitate access.[57] Finally, the assignment of new land, an important piece of patronage, tailed off, and changes in the *darkhast* rules made it far more difficult for the officers to divert what little there was to themselves and their friends.[58]

All these reforms contributed to the impression that the village officer was no longer lord in his own domain, but the minor functionary of a superior power. Much the same story was repeated in the case of the headman's political and judicial functions. In 1920 the government started a scheme of village *panchayats*, and intended at first to make the village headman the ex-officio chairman. But as part of the same scheme the government wanted to reorganize the areas and slightly reduce the numbers of the official 'villages', and take on powers to select headmen suitable for their new responsibilities in the *panchayats*. This meant not only that some headmen would lose their jobs, but that the idea of hereditary succession to village office would be abrogated. In this scheme, the village officers saw their final conversion into government servants, and they rebelled. Village officer associations mushroomed, and in the turbulent area of the Kistna–Godavari deltas, the village officers struck work and thereby created a Non-cooperation campaign of tax refusal. The government was obliged to abandon its scheme of re-organization and to allow hereditary right to remain, but it also decided that it could not permit the unreconstructed village headmen to command the *panchayats*. Ironically the headmen's intransigence shut them out of command of an institution which in the years to follow became a serious rival to their own power.[59]

Also in 1920, the government set up new village courts, staffed by locally elected magistrates. Soon these courts began to supplant those of the village headman in his role as *munsiff*. Indeed, in many districts, feuding between headmen and the elected leaders of these new courts became so violent that elections were fought wildly and court meetings often disrupted. Within a decade 2,030,401 suits, or 96 per cent of the total number of suits submitted to village courts, were submitted to the panchayat courts and only 4 per cent to the *munsiffs*.[60] Many headmen were completely deprived of their magisterial role. (Incidentally, under the same Act the headman lost the authority to put a low-caste villager in the stocks for six hours.)[61] Many headmen protested against the judicial changes; in 1924 one petition urged that 'in the absence of civil and criminal powers, the village munsiffs are practically unable to command any sort of influence in the village'.[62]

Finally, the village officers had shown their political muscle and thereby earned the enmity of the government. Before 1920, the government had been nervous about the power of the village officers. Indeed it had tried to pass a law abrogating hereditary right in a hurry in 1920 before the Montagu–Chelmsford reforms because, as the Chief Secretary noted, 'the village officers are likely to have so much power over the electorate under the Reforms that it would be easy for them to secure a mandate to elected members to oppose interference with hereditary right'.[63] The government had refused to be moved by the early signs of village officer disgruntlement because, as another leading civilian noted, 'once the village officer associations have "tasted blood" in that way they may be expected to give trouble'.[64] The signal victories of the village officers in this crisis strengthened government's resolve to cut them down to size.

By the 1920s, many substantial families found that village office had become more of a burden than an asset. The reasons were not only the decline in prestige and the subjection to minor government officers, but also changes in the economic options open to the village elite. In the early twentieth century, there were many new and spectacular opportunities for profit within reach of a substantial landlord who was prepared to venture beyond the village; extensive money-lending, investment in the purchase of good land wherever it might be, commission agency business in cash crops, building small processing factories and entering law or politics were the most common. Such activities drew many substantial landowners to reside in the towns and cities of the region. A village officer was strictly forbidden to reside outside his village, and had to humble himself before the *tahsildar* to get permission for even a short absence.[65] Of course many families were able to share the entrepreneurial and the official activities among different members, but often it was not so simple. In the 1920s, the government was for the first time faced with large numbers of resignations from village office.

During the 1920–1 crisis, over 200 village officers in the Andhra deltas alone resigned their office and there were occasional instances of resignations in other districts during the 1920s.[66] Fifty-two resigned or were dismissed during the first phase of Civil Disobedience in 1930. Twenty-five of these were subsequently reinstated, and another thirty-six resigned in the later part of the agitation.[67] In Salem the Collector complained that it was difficult to replace those who died or retired,[68] and in North Arcot it was reported that many *karnams* had decided to 'resign their posts and seek employment as vakils' clerks under mittadars. . . . Resignation by karnams are frequent and it is difficult to find respectable residents in the village [to replace them].'[69]

The next decade witnessed the great agricultural depression. Throughout southern India it was the families who had invested money in land, money-lending and crop dealing that bore the brunt, and many village officers fell into these categories.[70] Besides, there were many village officers who had deployed their official power to command credit and had got deeply into debt. While in the conditions of depression most creditors were not anxious to proceed against the lands and possessions of defaulting debtors and then see their liquid capital solidify and stagnate, there were political as well as economic considerations in the case of defaults by men who were headmen. In many cases rivals and enemies saw that if they started proceedings against a headman or *karnam*, they could either embarrass him or succeed in having the government remove him from office. Evidently, many village officers suffered in this way. An example was a Tanjore headman who was arrested on a debt decree in 1931 'out of spite', he claimed, 'at the instigation of some of his enemies'. He survived that affair but was then arrested on another decree in 1933 and subsequently dismissed from his post.[71] Another Tanjore headman was dismissed in 1938; his family had held the post for 75 years, his property was worth nearly Rs 16,000 and he had good connections in government service and the local elite; yet all his properties were mortgaged and 'interested individuals' managed to persuade the authorities that his liabilities far exceeded his assets.[72] Another dismissed in 1939 had inherited his debts, along with the village office, over a quarter of a century before and had survived without trouble until the depression, when he was brought to court by his enemies, judged insolvent and dismissed.[73]

On top of all this, the headmen were faced with the problem of collecting a revenue demand which, in real terms, almost doubled in the four years following 1929. Those village officers who still paid the revenue from their own pocket and then operated a private system inside the the village were especially vulnerable.[74] The result was a rash of defalcations by village headmen. There were numerous cases in which the headman tried to maintain his revenue collections (or at least the appearance) by collecting excess amounts from the less truculent, less powerful and less intelligent members of the village, or by manufacturing false records to show that he had tried using coercive processes or had even sold off lands for arrears.[75] If these measures failed, he might then be sacked for 'slackness in collection'.[76] Some avoided this indignity by committing suicide,[77] while many others collected all that they could and made off. In 1940, the government found that while in the late 1920s the yearly average of embezzlements by village officers had been only 11, throughout the 1930s the number was 152. They suspected that a large number of other cases had escaped detection.[78]

It was this same investigation that revealed to the government how poor many of its village headmen had become. The Collector of South Arcot, the district with most defalcations per year (29), reported:

The majority of the village headmen in this district are poor and depend mainly upon their pay. The worst of them misappropriate Government money.... The existence of a large number of small holdings in the district facilitates the manipulation of accounts to misappropriate Government money and this fact also renders detection difficult.... It is reported that many of the headmen do not keep the Government money separate from their private money and spend from the common fund. The illiteracy of the ryots renders misappropriation easier as most of them do not take care to verify whether the amounts entered in the Kachayats [receipts] given to ryots are brought to the village monetary accounts. Even where misappropriation is detected the more influential of the headmen square up the parties who are illiterate and make it difficult to prove the fact of misappropriation.[79]

Another inquiry found that a large number of village headmen in Ramnad were 'impoverished', most in South Arcot were 'very poor', and many in Madura were 'dependent on their meagre honorarium'.[80] It was hardly surprising that the government was now assailed every year with demands for a rise in village officers' pay. Because so many of the defalcating village headmen had little or no property which the government could seize and sell off to realize the stolen amounts, the government in 1936 amended the rules to allow Collectors to sack village officers who were insolvent.[81]

III

Thus by the second quarter of the twentieth century, the village establishment had become an awkward and embarrassing institution. On the one hand, many headmen no longer commanded the prestige and the material resources required for the job that the government wanted them to do. On the other hand it would be impossibly expensive to erect a different system of revenue collection. On the one hand, the village officers constantly complained about the decline in their powers, prestige and wealth and thus were a ready audience for nationalist and later socialist propagandists. On the other hand, they still possessed enough formal power to be able to coerce their neighbours and thus be a political threat to the government. Fort St George had created a Fifth Column.

There had been occasional conferences of disgruntled village officers since the early years of the century, and a number of meetings and new associations appeared during the agitation of 1920–1. These conferences continued sporadically throughout the 1920s, and matured into a Madras Presidency Village Officers Association at the start of the depression.[82]

Moreover, as the government had feared in 1920, the village officers gained disproportionate power in the new constitutional structure of local and provincial councils. Many of the candidates at the 1920 elections courted the support of individual village officers and then deployed this agent's powers to bring several local electors to heel. The village officers extracted their reward; in the first sitting of the new legislature, many of the members brought up the question of village officers' pay, jobs and hereditary rights; and within five years this legislature forced government to undo all the reforms of village office it had introduced in 1920. In 1926, the government cut village officers' pay, and at the elections at the end of the year many candidates were only too willing to promise to undo this measure, in order to gain the necessary help from the village officers on polling day. Again after this election village office was one of the first subjects raised in the legislature, and the pay cuts were restored in 1927.[83]

The government had hoped the reforms of 1920–1 and the *panchayat* scheme would set out a new role for the village officers, but by 1927 the scheme lay in ruins. From this time on, the government gave little constructive thought to the institution of village office. It tried instead to limit their powers as far as it was possible without impairing their usefulness. The result was a series of reforms which only added to the village officers' discontent, and a series of abortive schemes which illustrated Fort St George's uncomfortable predicament. In 1925 the government debated making village office honorary (i.e. unpaid) again. They believed this would not only halt the decline of the village officer from a local leader to a petty bureaucrat but it would also save important government cash. The Board of Revenue wrote an alarmist note: any reduction 'would mean widespread discontent and many headmen would doubtless resign'; and any attempt to tamper with the village establishment would mean 'villages already torn by faction would be in a state of civil war in a very short time'.[84] In 1932, during the financial turmoil of the depression, the government again sought to cut costs in the revenue system and quickly lighted on the village office establishment, which cost more than all the rest of the revenue machinery put together. Many district Collectors reported that a pay cut would probably cause agitation, and the Board concluded that 'at the present time of political unrest the cut is inexpedient'.[85] Another retrenchment proposal four years later met the same fate. In 1937, the government again thought about abolishing hereditary right as a prelude to remodelling the village establishments. Fifteen Collectors, and all the village officers consulted, objected strongly and the proposal was shelved.[86] In 1938 the government considered getting rid of more of the menials since they were probably more useful to the *karnam* and headman personally, than to the government. The Board and Collectors told the government that the menials were vital to the ever more difficult process of collecting the revenue, and that they were overworked already; any reduction in number (and consequent increase in duties for those remaining) would harm recruitment.[87] The outlines of the village establishment had become sacrosanct.

If it could not really change the village officers' role, the government at least wanted to contain their power. In 1915, the government laid down that it was 'undesirable' for village officers to join political organizations or parties, and in 1920 it banned *karnams* (but not headmen) from standing for election to legislatures or local boards.[88] In 1924, three North Arcot headmen took a prominent part in a Congress meeting, and the Secretariat cast around frantically for a rule which declared this illegal. It took them seven months to establish that there was no rule banning involvement unless the political organization concerned was blatantly subversive, and that the current Swarajist policy of the Congress could in no way be portrayed as subversive. Nor was it possible to invent a rule, for village officers were not public servants—they occupied a rather odd position somewhere between public service and private citizenship. The government had to be content with laying down that 'the case will be met if Collectors discreetly use their authority over village officers to discourage them from taking any active part in political movements of any description or in political elections.'[89]

It was an order that had little weight, and by the early 1930s village officers were showing considerable interest in local elections, and several had even participated in Civil Disobedience (and been punished). In 1932 the government 'advised' village officers to take no part in elections, and then in 1934 ordered that *karnams* must resign and headmen go on leave if they wished to stand at any election to a legislature or local board.[90] Several headmen did in fact go into local government in the next few years. The government soon discovered, however, that the decision to allow headmen to retain their post (yet go on leave) while occupying a place in local government, was being assiduously abused. Many of the acting headmen inserted while the incumbents went into local government were nothing less than agents for the incumbents. In 1939, the government ordered that any village officer must resign his post conclusively before entering local government.[91]

The Congress had for a long time been anxious to make political capital out of the government's embarrassment in its relations with the village officers. Individual Congressmen were involved in the earliest village officer associations, and Congressmen in the Andhra deltas helped organize the protests and resignations that resulted in the Non-cooperation no-tax campaign in 1921. Again in 1931, Congress leaders urged beleaguered village officers to throw in their lot with the Congress, and several lost their jobs for helping agitators.[92] Then as the Congress turned back to an electoral strategy in the mid-1930s, it courted the village officers' help. 'Village officers occupy today a position of advantage in the electorates that have been formed,' noted one Congress leader in 1935, 'and their influence rightly directed cannot fail to yield results.' He urged them to support the Congress and hinted strongly that the Congress in power would meet their demands over pay, hereditary rights, political participation and other privileges.[93]

Once in power after 1937, the Congress flamboyantly restored all the village officers who had been dismissed for aiding the Civil Disobedience campaign.[94] It was a clever way to demonstrate the ascendancy of the Congress to rural Madras, and to inform village officers where they should now bestow their allegiances. The Congress Chief Minister, C. Rajagopalachari, then turned to the question of the village officers' participation in politics and wrote:

> I am of opinion that the exception of karnams being made, as one accepted generally without demur, all other village officials including the headman or munsiff may be treated as 'free' citizens. If we keep out of elections and politics all responsible and decent citizens, the residue will not be a good one. . . . I am therefore for issuing a Government Order releasing the village munsiffs from all bans.[95]

But at this point the Congress leaders came up against much the same problem of 'who rules who' that had so vexed the British administrators. Those who aspired to command the loftier heights of the south Indian polity could not afford to let those on the baser levels abscond with much of their patrimony.

The Congress Ministry soon found that there were severe practical difficulties in the way of allowing the village officers into the political arena. Whether they were officially government servants or not, they certainly served the government, and in ways that had a direct bearing on electoral politics. As another Congress minister noted:

> The village munsiff signs literacy and residence applications of voters in the village. He is in charge of the preparation of the electoral rolls. If he were to

be a prospective candidate, it would be unfair to other candidates. As an agent of the government, the village munsiff has many powers. A politician village munsiff most often abuses his powers and victimises his opponents. It is an undesirable concentration of power, if the village officer is allowed to take charge of a Panchayat Court or Board. . . . I know many cases of village munsiff presidents being nothing short of Hitler.[96]

In the end, Rajagopalachari and his lieutenants agreed that village officers must be barred from any kind of political activity, since 'the village headmen should be representatives of the Government in every respect and not participate in things that are likely to create an anti-Government feeling'.[97] In the end, then, the Congress put the finishing touches to the transformation of village officers from leaders of rural society to petty bureaucrats.

IV

This essay has traced the transformation of the Madras village officers, and particularly the headmen, in the first half of the twentieth century. It has concentrated on the 'administrative' side of the story, but it has tried to point out that questions of administration and economics interlocked. The administrative arrangements for village government in the late nineteenth century succeeded because they matched and corroborated developments within the society and economy of the village. Fort St George deliberately tried to build up powerful village headmen, and the attempt largely succeeded because the development of the village economy was helping to carve out a strong village elite. Men could lend their personal power and prestige to the administration and be rewarded with a substantial rate of interest. But in the twentieth century, administrative policy and economic opportunities both altered, and now pulled not together, but apart. On the administrative side, the village officers were affected by a general change in which the machinery of government was pressed down more firmly on the society and the lower ranks of the bureaucracy were drawn under closer central control. The village officers in fact loitered around the ragged edge of this process. They found their powers and their perquisites steadily diminished as the government gained more knowledge about, and a stronger bureaucratic hold over, the Madras countryside. Yet except with the scheme of 1919–20, which was abortive, the government never applied serious thought to the role of the village officers in the new organization. Thus, while the scheme of village office was ideally suited to the conditions of remote government of the nineteenth century, and had at that time helped to make the administration of Madras the envy of officials in other parts of India, it could not respond to the demands of the twentieth. Village office became not an aid to good government, but a hindrance to schemes of reform and development. It remained the vital link between the administration and rural society, but it could not be employed for schemes of improvement because the government no longer had any confidence in it. It was hardly surprising that one of the first problems taken up by the post-Independence governments in south India was the reorganization of government agency in the village, and that that reorganization should seek not to resurrect the village officers but to establish a wholly new agency.

The decline of village office in the twentieth century was hastened because men of prestige within the village became more reluctant to take up the posts. Many distinguished families resigned from village office, while others who stayed on went into decline. The dissociation of village office and local ascendancy was part of a more general process in which economic and political power in south Indian rural society came to depend less on factors internal to the village itself, and more on access to economic and political opportunities in a wider world. By the 1920s the men emerging as rich and powerful in rural society were those who had foregone the advantages of constant residence and local monopoly, in order to take up new opportunities in export trading, industrial investment, the professions and extensive land speculation. These activities had ripped them out of the closely woven texture of village life, and while they were the undoubted luminaries of rural society, their power came from lording it over the villages, not from lordship within them. By the end of the 1930s, when the depression in agricultural profits had induced many to seek a more urban career, the process was more or less complete.

This development helped to belittle the prestige of the village officer. Meanwhile, the sum total of economic and administrative change caused a sea-change in the character of rural politics. The era of dominance by powerful rural bosses gave way to one in which rural agitations suggested the lack of strong leadership, or the confused emergence of a new and inexperienced stratum of leaders, and in which the rural areas proved something of a *tabula rasa* for politicians who often had started out as rural leaders but who now drew their strength from access to economic opportunities and party machineries rooted in the towns.

NOTES

Research on which this article is based was financed by the S.S.R.C.

1 Munro to Board of Revenue, 15 August 1807, quoted in A. Sarada Raju, *Economic Conditions in the Madras Presidency 1800–1850* (Madras, 1941), p. 16.

2 'The village system is the keystone of the arch.' J. H. Garstin, *Report on the Revision of Revenue Establishments in the Madras Presidency* (Madras, 1883), p. 4.

3 G.O. 1476, Revenue, 29 July 1927, Tamilnadu Archives [hereafter TNA]. In some small villages, the headman also took on the *karnam's* role, and in some large villages there were assistant headmen and *karnams*.

4 This figure is reached by a simple division of the area of *ryotwari* holdings given in the *Report on the Settlement of the Land Revenue in the Madras Presidency for fasli* 1335 (1925–6) (Madras, 1927), and is thus only a rough guide. The same method gives an average of about 360 landholders per village.

5 G.O. 1476, Revenue, 29 July 1927, TNA.

6 H. A. Brett, Collector of Salem, 16 October 1856, in *Correspondence relating to the Revision proposed in the Village Revenue Establishments of the Madras Presidency*, Part 1 (Madras, 1867) [hereafter *Village Revenue Establishments*].

7 Extract from proceedings of Board of Revenue dated 4 December 1820 in *Selections from Old Records of South Arcot, containing Mr Hyde's Report on the Introduction of a Ryotwari Settlement into the South Arcot Collectorate and the Correspondence relating thereto* (Cuddalore, 1904), p. 22.

8 R. Ragoonatha Row, Collector of Tanjore, January 1860, in *Village Revenue Establishments*, p. 56.

9 T. V. Mahalingam, *South Indian Polity*, second edition (Madras, 1967), pp. 344–5.

10 See, for instance, M. S. Sesha Ayyangar, *Madras Village Panchayats* (Madura, 1916); J. Matthai, *Village Government in British India* (London, 1915); K. Jayaraman, *A Study of Panchayats in Madras* (Bombay, 1947).

11 A. Sarada Raju, *Economic Conditions*, p. 17.

12 Munro to Government of Madras, 4 July 1817, quoted in T. H. Beaglehole, *Thomas Munro and the Development of Administrative Policy in Madras* (Cambridge, 1966), pp. 116–17.

13 *Selections from the Records of the Madras Government, New (Revenue) Series No. 1, A Collection of Papers relating to the Inam Settlement in the Madras Presidency* (Madras, 1948), *passim*, especially reports from Collectors.

14 'There are many [districts] even at the present day wherein the land revenue

demand is based merely on the unchecked statement of the Curnum, who thus has vast opportunity both of making exaction on the Ryots and in collusion with them of defrauding the Government.' Revenue Department No. 951 dated 14 August 1855, reproduced in *Selections from the Records of the Madras Government No. LIII. Papers relating to the General Revenue Survey of the Madras Presidency* (Madras, 1858) [hereafter *General Revenue Survey*].

15 *Village Revenue Establishments*, iii–iv, pp. 74–5.
16 C. S. Hearn, Deputy Inspector General of Police, in ibid., pp. 301–2.
17 Charles Pelley, introduction to ibid.
18 Ibid., *passim*.
19 J. H. Garstin, *Report . . .*, p. 4.
20 One of the aims of the revised *ryotwari* system was 'getting rid of the constant interference of the Talook offices in the concern of the individual ryots'. *General Revenue Survey*, p. 17.
21 See *The Village Officers' Manual* (Madras, 1913).
22 J. H. Garstin, *Report . . .*, p. 15.
23 Collector of Chingleput, 1 June 1938, in Board of Revenue proceedings in the department of Land Revenue and Settlement [hereafter LRS] 288, 28 January 1939, TNA.
24 G.O. 1589, Revenue, 27 June 1939, TNA.
25 LRS 3491, 15 November 1929, TNA.
26 G.O. 2435, Revenue, 26 June 1918, TNA; G.O. 859, Development, 27 May 1936, TNA; *The Village Officers' Manual*, p. 38.
27 'No due publicity is given of the sale. Some hangers-on of the village officer are collected together and a farce of a sale is gone through.' 'Land in government auction is chiefly bought in by the big landholder of the village, either the karnam or the Reddi [headman].' *Madras Provincial Banking Enquiry Committee* (Madras, 1930), volume II, pp. 94, 302; see also LRS 265, 24 January 1928, TNA; G.O. 2435, Revenue, 26 June 1918; note by Hopetoun Stokes dated 12 September 1933 in G.O. 859, Development, 27 May 1936, TNA.
28 Note by a Revenue Divisional Officer dated 30 May 1926 in G.O. 1006, 23 June 1926, TNA.
29 Ibid.
30 LRS 1254, 10 May 1927, TNA.
31 See an example in LRS 2421, 13 August 1930, TNA, and another where a village officer used this device to free land from hypothecation to government in G.O. 3068, Revenue, 20 November 1939, TNA.
32 Petition of O. M. Subramania Pillai dated 30 August 1938, in G.O. 1687, Revenue, 8 July 1939, TNA.
33 Petition of V. Kethiripal Pillai dated 24 August 1931, in LRS 3583, 12 November 1931, TNA.
34 J. H. Garstin, *Report . . .*, pp. 14–15.
35 L. M. Wynch, 10 May 1913, in G.O. 8, Revenue, 2 January 1914, TNA.
36 See *Revised Form of Village Accounts* (Madras, editions in 1910, 1930, etc.).
37 Papers of Sir Richard Tottenham, Cambridge South Asian Archive.

38 S. Wadsworth, 'Lo, the poor Indian', typescript memoir, p. 126, Cambridge South Asian Archive.

39 Ibid. His frustration was shared. Another Collector, J. C. Molony, wrote: '[The petitioner] seems to have a vision of a Jamabandi officer dispensing patriarchal justice to the ryots. Unfortunately this is exactly what does not happen. Between the two is built a mighty wall of constitutional forms, notices etc.' Letter dated 8 May 1913 in G.O. 8, Revenue, 2 January 1914, TNA.

40 Petition of M. S. V. Murti dated 5 April 1938, in LRS 2000, 20 July 1938, TNA.

41 See Collectors' letters in G.O. 8, Revenue, 2 January 1914, TNA.

42 'All the clerks without a single exception, including the Head Clerk, insist and compel the poor village officer . . . through their respective Revenue Inspectors to pay down Rs 10 for every village or vattam. Further the clerk who checks or is supposed to check the accounts of the village demands a payment of Rs. 5 per village, or else he refuses to touch the books. If the poor Karnams do not pay, the accounts are delayed. . . . The Revenue Divisional Officer, without any investigation, suspends or punishes the poor Karnam. The Crocodile Head Clerk demands Rs 50 per range in lump sum besides getting all his household requirements from the respective Revenue Inspectors of the Taluk. . . . Even the peons who put the seal on the papers claim a mamul of Rs 5 per range besides getting as much from the poor Karnam, the least being Re 1 per vattam. On the whole from top to bottom, corruption and bribery is rampant in the Revenue Department.' Petition of K. Krishnamurti dated 7 April 1938, in LRS 2000, 20 July 1938, TNA.

43 V. K. Ramanujachariar speaking in the Madras Legislative Council, quoted in G.O. 8, Revenue, 2 January 1914, TNA.

44 See, for example, LRS 1947, 10 June 1936, TNA.

45 LRS 1254, 10 May 1927, TNA; LRS 451, 8 February 1930, TNA; LRS 336, 30 January 1933, TNA; LRS 716, 3 March 1933, TNA; LRS 2837, 19 October 1933, TNA; LRS 1947, 10 January 1936, TNA; G.O. 64, Revenue, 10 January 1939, TNA; G.O. 1662, Revenue, 5 July 1939, TNA.

46 LRS 451, 8 February 1930, TNA; LRS 2187, 2 July 1936, TNA; G.O. 64, Revenue, 10 January 1939, TNA.

47 D. A. Washbrook, 'Country politics: Madras 1880–1930', *Modern Asian Studies*, 7: 3 (July 1973), quoted in pp. 498 and 530.

48 K. Jayaraman, *A Study of Panchayats in Madras*, p. 55.

49 Ibid., p. 56.

50 See the history of the village service cess in G.O. 664, Revenue, 5 May 1925, TNA; note by Revenue Department dated 23 April 1926 in G.O. 1006, Revenue, 23 June 1926, TNA.

51 G.O. 1958, Revenue, 14 August 1920, TNA; T. N. Ramakrishna Reddy to C. R. Reddy dated 5 August 1920, in C. R. Reddy papers file 52, Nehru Memorial Museum, New Delhi.

52 'The last and decisive factor in the revolt is the recent reduction in the village establishment by which they are deprived of assistant karnams, assistant headmen, vettis and mohads. Even the loyal headmen complaiu

bitterly of this.' Collector of Guntur dated 10 January 1922, quoted in M. Venkatarangaiya, *The Freedom Struggle in Andhra Pradesh* (Hyderabad, 1965), volume III, pp. 263–5.

53 *Sudarsini*, 1 January 1918, Madras Native Newspaper reports.

54 See petitions of village officer associations in G.O. 1958, Revenue, 14 August 1920, TNA.

55 G.O. 2742, Revenue, 23 November 1928, State Archives, Hyderabad.

56 Petition of Srivilliputtur Taluk Village Officers' Association dated 30 December 1940, in G.O. 157, Revenue, 27 January 1944, TNA.

57 LRS 64 (Press), 13 August 1929, TNA.

58 G.O. 859, Development, 27 May 1936, TNA; LRS 988, 31 March 1932, TNA.

59 G.O. 1958, Revenue, 14 August 1920, TNA; see also C. J. Baker, 'Non-co-operation in South India', in C. J. Baker and D. A. Washbrook, *South India: Political Institutions and Political Change 1880–1940* (Delhi, 1975).

60 These were the figures for 1929, see LRS 2123, 12 July 1930, TNA.

61 *Village Officers and Ryots Manual* (Madras, 1931), p. 38.

62 Petition dated 26 May 1924 in LRS 1994, 26 August 1924, TNA.

63 Note by C. G. Todhunter dated 10 December 1919, in G.O. 1958, Revenue, 14 August 1920, TNA.

64 Note by A. R. Knapp dated 15 December 1919, in ibid.

65 Not surprisingly, the question of leave of absence was one of the items most commonly and most urgently pressed in all village officer petitions in the early twentieth century.

66 See Baker, 'Non-co-operation in South India'.

67 G.O. 818, Public General, 31 May 1932, TNA; G.O. 587, Revenue Confidential, 3 March 1938, TNA.

68 Collector of Salem dated 24 February 1932 in LRS 988, 31 March 1932, TNA.

69 Board of Revenue note dated 13 July 1927, in G.O. 2647, Revenue, 17 December 1927, TNA.

70 See C. J. Baker, *The Politics of South India* (Cambridge, 1976), pp. 170–200.

71 An example is a village officer with some twenty acres who had 4.5 acres under a usufructuary mortgage for Rs 700, another 2.66 acres under usufructuary mortgage for Rs 400, 0.53 acres under a simple mortgage for Rs 100, 0.95 acres under another mortgage for Rs 200, 5 acres mortgaged to a brother in return for the latter taking over a debt of Rs 500, the remaining 7 acres encumbered with a debt of Rs 670, and a Rs 500 debt on top. He found nothing extraordinary in this and argued, 'my financial position is quite sound'; LRS 2837, 19 October 1933, TNA.

72 G.O. 64, Revenue, 10 January 1939, TNA.

73 G.O. 63, Revenue, 10 January 1939, TNA.

74 See the case of a Chidambaram headman in G.O. 2273, Revenue, 3 September 1938, TNA.

75 LRS 2331, 14 August 1932, TNA; LRS 716, 3 March 1933, TNA; LRS 1387, 16 May 1933, TNA; LRS 2837, 19 October 1933, TNA; LRS 1771, 8 May 1935, TNA; G.O. 2773, Revenue, 26 October 1938, TNA.

76 See, for example, G.O. 295, Revenue, 1 February 1938, TNA.

77 See, for example, G.O. 1131, Revenue, 20 May 1938, TNA.
78 LRS 1523, 7 June 1941, TNA.
79 Ibid.
80 LRS 2910, 18 October 1938, TNA; LRS 2549, 9 August 1937, TNA.
81 LRS 3009, 31 August 1936, TNA; the rule was enshrined in legislation in 1941, see LRS 6 (S) Press, 6 February 1942, TNA.
82 G.O. 1323, Revenue, 3 July 1929, TNA.
83 G.O. 1473, Revenue, 28 July 1927, TNA.
84 LRS 512, 16 March 1925, TNA.
85 LRS 988, 31 March 1932, TNA.
86 LRS 2910, 18 October 1938, TNA.
87 LRS 288, 28 January 1939, TNA.
88 G.O. 833, Revenue, 6 June 1925, TNA.
89 Ibid.
90 LRS 19 (Press), 7 February 1934, TNA.
91 G.O. 2214, Revenue, 28 August 1939, TNA.
92 G.O. 639, Public, 5 June 1931; G.O. 690, Public, 22 June 1931; G.O. 760, Public, 16 July 1931; G.O. 938, Public, 11 September 1931; G.O. 939, Public, 11 September 1931; G.O. 980, Public, 21 September 1931; G.O. 1075, Public, 20 October 1931; all in State Archives, Hyderabad.
93 *The Hindu*, 1 February 1935.
94 G.O. 587, Revenue Confidential, 3 March 1938, TNA.
95 Note dated 1 April 1938 in G.O. 8, Revenue Confidential, 4 January 1939, TNA.
96 Note by Bezwada Gopala Reddi dated 20 March 1939 in G.O. 2214, Revenue, 28 August 1939, TNA.
97 Note dated 22 August 1939 in ibid.

3

A Study of Land Transfers in Mau Tahsil, District Jhansi

DIRK H. A. KOLFF
University of Leiden

The purpose of this article is, firstly, to draw attention to the manuscript settlement records in the record rooms of U.P. districts as a source of social and economic history and, secondly, to present, as an example of their contents, a short study of all transfers of *zamindari* rights that took place from early in the nineteenth century until 1889–90 in the Mau *tahsil* of the district of Jhansi. Finally, these data will enable us to make certain hypotheses concerning a change in life-styles that accompanied the different pattern of land control emerging during the century under review.

During the second half of the nineteenth century, British civil servants became increasingly aware of the problems of rural indebtedness, fragmentation of ownership rights and land transfer. The relations between debtors and creditors were at the core of a large proportion of official correspondence in the Revenue Department. At this official level the discussion was mainly carried on in the idiom of economics, using as main evidence a vast collection of data on agricultural history, tenancy, size of holdings and debts. True, in the settlement reports much detail is also to be found on the social history of the larger landholding families and on the castewise distribution of land among *zamindars*, but it is significant that in the forwarding letters which the Board of Revenue wrote when sending these reports to Government, information of a sociological nature did not figure at all. Such data seem almost to be banned from the Revenue Proceedings of the N.W.P. Government, where the administrative tradition of Bird and Thomason persisted throughout the century. Only towards the end of the century did an interest in the general rather than the rigidly defined economic condition of the people reassert itself in the printing of district gazetteers and monumental volumes on 'Tribes and Castes'. But these could only have an indirect role in the process of bureaucratic decision-making.

As an example of the kind of information that got into the official correspondence, we may take the village of Bijeygarh in the Mau *pargana* of the Jhansi district. During the first regular settlement of the district, which ran from 1865–6 to 1889–90, one of the largest single transfers of land would occur in this village: 2,151 acres of *zamindari* land. In 1875, M. Pollock, the Jhansi Commissioner, took Bijeygarh as a specimen 'of the condition of more than half the villages in parganas Mau, Garotha, and Mote' of the Jhansi district. Next year, his facts appeared printed in the Revenue Proceedings of Government as they had been quoted by the Board of Revenue in their letter to them: 'In mauza Bijaigarh Rs 175 were first borrowed to pay the mutiny balances and accounts were carried on to the famine year'—i.e. 1868–9—'and again up to the present time when the debts amount to Rs 7,094, of which the mortgage debts amount to Rs 6,148, and the book debts to Rs 946'. Since the time of settlement, cultivation had fallen from 1,040 to 504 acres. The number of ploughs employed had decreased from 42 to 18 in the same period and the rental assets of the village had diminished from Rs 1,713 to Rs 768. Much of the best and richest land had been overrun with *kans* grass, which practically prevented all cultivation, but, though a remission of Rs 260 on the revenue demand had been made for this, the Government demand still stood at Rs 714–4–0, not much less, that is, than the annual value of the village.[2]

Of course, historians have felt the need to break away from the almost exclusive emphasis on quantitative agrarian economics presented by the bulk of official correspondence. They have turned to district memoirs, the 'Tribes and Castes' compilations and, especially, to the settlement reports. The data these volumes yield allow one to go beyond the bare facts of economics and to bring to life the largest estates and the most 'respectable natives' of quite a number of districts.[3] Yet, these printed records do not present anything but the vaguest idea of the history of individual villages. Such village histories, however, were written by nineteenth-century settlement officers for every village they assessed and settled. They were entered, in handwritten form, with the village statistics in the so-called 'Assessment Volumes' that were meant to be preserved among the district records in the English office of the Collectorate.

Let us turn to the handwritten 'Assessment Remark' that W. H. L. Impey, the Jhansi settlement officer, wrote in 1892 on the same village of Bijeygarh that Pollock had reported on in 1875. The old *zamindars*, a mixed body of Kurmis, Lodhis and Ahirs, had 'borrowed from two men who were anxious to obtain the estate: Gangadin Brahman, son of a jamadar of sepoys who had been stationed at Bijeygarh in the Mahratta time'—a fine old fort, Impey observed, built by the Marathas, was still to be seen—'and Diwan Pahar Singh, [the independent Bundela Rajput] jagirdar of Bijna, who had in old times owned the village. Even before 1868 the village had in great part been mortgaged to them.' Gangadin in time acquired fourteen *annas* (i.e. seven-eighths) of the village. He was a well-off man and owned other estates in *parganas* Moth, where his headquarters had been, and Garotha. When he died in 1888, leaving a small child as heir, the management became worse. Occupancy rights were forcibly suppressed and, not surprisingly, the ex-proprietors got into trouble with the new owner.[4] Such descriptive detail, meant for the use of future district revenue officers, rarely found its way even into the printed settlement reports. The imperial bureaucracy demanded that British civil servants, if they desired to win a reputation for themselves, translate their local knowledge into statistics and an analytical idiom that was relevant to decision-making at the legislative level.

A single instance, however, does not establish the relevance of this source material to the questions the modern historian asks. To start with, it must be emphasized that the village statistics which are also given in the Assessment Volumes cannot be dispensed with, but should be used alongside the village histories. The availability of a combination of detailed statistical and descriptive information enables one to make a number of distinctions which are probably fairly accurate. For Jhansi, the Assessment Volumes of 1892, preserved in the English Office, used jointly with the Urdu Village Volumes for 1865–6, preserved in the Revenue Record Room, provide figures for every single transfer of land during the first regular settlement of the district.[5] These figures, as aggregated caste-wise for all 165 *mahals* of the *tahsil* and *pargana* of Mau, are given in Table I. This table presents only net losses or gains during the period under review. Most caste groups, however, both acquired

TABLE I

ACREAGE OF TRANSFERS OF ZAMINDARI LAND IN MAU TAHSIL

Caste	Acreage ±1800–±1820 and % of total *zamindari* land		Acreage in 1865–6 and % of total *zamindari* land		% loss or gain until 1865–6 (column 2, 4)	Acreage in 1889–90 and % of total *zamindari* land		% loss or gain during 1st Settlement (column 4, 7)	% loss or gain during total period (column 2, 7)
1	2	3	4	5	6	7	8	9	10
Thakur (Bundela and allied clans)	41,304	(16.3)	40,708	(16.1)	− 1.4	43,773	(17.3)	+ 7.5	+ 6.0
Thakur (other clans)	71,594	(28.3)	77,649	(30.7)	+ 8.5	66,348	(26.2)	− 14.6	− 7.3
Deccani Brahman	430	(0.2)	2,284	(0.9)	+431.2	52,166	(20.6)	+ 0.7	+ 7.5
Brahman (others)	48,103	(19.0)	49,535	(19.6)	+ 3.0				
Kurmi	39,438	(15.6)	34,034	(13.4)	− 13.7	24,917	(9.8)	− 26.8	− 36.8
Ahir	27,019	(10.7)	26,140	(10.3)	− 3.3	19,735	(7.8)	− 24.5	− 27.0
Lodhi	9,453	(3.7)	8,932	(3.5)	− 5.5	8,106	(3.2)	− 9.2	− 14.2
Kacchi	5,108	(2.0)	3,167	(1.3)	− 38.0	2,780	(1.1)	− 12.2	− 45.6
Ghosi	3,564	(1.4)	3,006	(1.2)	− 15.7	1,689	(0.7)	− 43.8	− 52.6
Bhat	2,347	(0.9)	2,347	(0.9)	—	1,124	(0.4)	− 52.1	− 52.1
Dangi	1,236	(0.5)	1,236	(0.5)	—	1,153	(0.5)	− 6.7	− 6.7

(Continued)

TABLE I *(Contd.)*

1	2	3	4	5	6	7	8	9	10
Kayasth	1,219	(0.5)	1,219	(0.5)	—	4,804	(1.9)	+294.1	+294.1
Teli	918	(0.4)	918	(0.4)	—	505	(0.2)	− 45.0	− 45.0
Muslim	781	(0.3)	781	(0.3)	—	1,413	(0.5)	+ 80.9	+ 80.9
Bairagi	582	(0.2)	582	(0.2)	—	582	(0.2)	—	—
Kalar	—		558	(0.2)	+	469	(0.2)	− 15.9	+
Marwari	—		—			12,453	(4.9)	+	+
Baniya	—		—			7,620	(3.0)	+	+
Chhipa	—		—			924	(0.4)	+	+
Sonar	—		—			257	(0.1)	+	+
Government	—		—			2,278	(0.9)	+	+
	2,53,096	(100.0)	2,53,096	(100.0)		2,53,096	(99.9)		

and lost land; data on acquisitions and alienations are given separately in Tables II and V.

Concentrating first on purchases and in general on those who acquired land, we can distinguish two categories of transferees, non-agriculturalists—given in Table II—and agriculturalists—given in Table V. The first mentioned category is defined as directly and demonstrably connected with non-local capital or influence. If we ignore all transfers that were the result of inheritance, 22.6 per cent or 57,150 acres out of a total *zamindari* area of 2,53,096 acres was subject to transfer during the first regular settlement, i.e. between 1865–6 and 1889–90. Of this transferred land 29.5 per cent or 16,874 acres represents 'local' transfers among Thakurs, as clans pretending

TABLE II

ACREAGE OF TRANSFERS TO NON-AGRICULTURALISTS DURING THE FIRST REGULAR SETTLEMENT (1865–6 TO 1889–90)

Caste	Alienations	Acquisitions	Net gains or losses	Net gains or losses (percentages)
1	2	3	4	5
Thakur (Bundela and allied clans)	3,768	6,349	+ 2,581	+ 6.3
Thakur (other clans)	11,791	—	−11,791	− 15.2
Brahman	6,025	5,123	− 902	− 1.7
Kurmi	8,265	—	− 8,265	− 24.3
Ahir	6,043	—	− 6,043	− 23.1
Lodhi	659	—	− 659	− 7.4
Kacchi	329	—	− 329	− 10.4
Ghosi	740	—	− 740	− 24.6
Bhat	1,223	—	− 1,223	− 52.1
Dangi	83	—	− 83	− 6.7
Kayasth	196	3,988	+ 3,792	+311.0
Teli	413	—	− 413	− 45.0
Muslim	390	1,022	+ 632	+ 80.9
Kalar	351	262	− 89	− 15.9
Marwari	—	12,453	+12,453	+
Baniya	—	7,620	+ 7,620	+
Chhipa	—	924	+ 924	+
Sonar	—	257	+ 257	+
Government	—	2,278	+ 2,278	+
	40,276	40,276		

to Rajput status are preferably called here, and people who at first sight appear to be mere agriculturalists, including a fair number of Brahmans. The remainder, involving a change of property of 40,276 acres, or 70.5 per cent of all transfers, belongs to the first mentioned non-local category; this is presented in Table II.

Data on landholding and transfers are presented in the tables caste by caste. This seems at least partly justified by the result of distinguishing transfers of a local from those of a non-local character: certain groups, especially Marwaris, Baniyas, Kayasths and peasants like Kurmis and Ahirs are obviously capable of only one of these two categories of acquisitions. Such a correlation of an ascriptive factor like caste with a certain position on a local/supra-local scale has been a fact generally accepted by anthropologists.[6] The range of different economic positions on the local/supra-local scale which one can expect individual members of some castes to occupy may vary widely, but for caste groups a fairly clear pattern is discernible, as Table III shows.

Column 2 of Table III represents the relative position of the caste groups shown as proprietors of *zamindari* rights. Column 3 gives an indication of the relative importance of small-scale moneylending among *zamindars* (often the *lambardars* of villages), their local influence and the purchases of land which resulted from these factors. As column 4 indicates, only in a minority of cases did these dealings of *zamindars* result in mortgages; only Brahmans maintain themselves at this level. Here supra-local factors often involving contacts with district headquarters had a part to play. The showing of several groups in column 4 is only explained in terms of their performance in column 5, which conveys an idea about access to non-local resources of a more intensive nature. The increased share claimed by Kayasths and Baniyas under this heading indicates access respectively to administrative and commercial income. Marwaris did not improve on their performance as mere moneydealers indicated in column 4. The 15.8 per cent for Thakurs reflects the political protection given by the British Government to some of the larger Bundela Thakurs. Brahmans are at their weakest here: many of them seem to perform best at the level of locality and *tahsil*, represented by columns 3 and 4. Among the castes grouped as agricultural, few families were equipped to deal with pressures outside their localities and almost none gained access to the administrative, commercial, or political resources that made for influence at the district level.

TABLE III

AN INDICATION OF DIFFERENTIAL ADAPTABILITY OF SEVERAL CASTE GROUPS: A SCALE OF LOCAL AND SUPRA-LOCAL DEALINGS AND INFLUENCE

Caste	% of *zamindari* land held in 1865–6	% of agricultural acquisitions of land, 1865–6 to 1889–90	% of mortgages held as mortgagee, 1873	% of non-agricultural acquisitions of land, 1865–6 to 1889–90
1	2	3	4	5
Brahmans	20.5	34.6	29.0	12.7
Thakurs	46.8	38.7	18.3	15.8
Marwaris, Seths and Sonars	—	—	31.6	33.9(a)
Bakkals and Baniyas	0.2(b)	—	9.4	19.6(b)
Kayasths	0.5	—	—	9.9
Agricultural castes (Kurmis, Lodhis, Kacchis, Ahirs, etc.)	31.2	26.6	10.7	—
Muslims	0.3	—	1.0	2.5
Others	0.6	—	—	—
Government	—	—	—	5.7
	100.1	99.9	100.0	100.1

SOURCE: Based on Tables I, II and V (column 3 is based on the figures given in column 3 of Table V); the categorization of caste groups and column 4 are taken from para. 58 of B. W. Colvin, Offg. Commr., Jhansi, to Bd. of Rev., N.W.P., 13 Nov. 1873, N.W.P. Rev. Progs., March 1874.

(a) This includes Chhipas (2.3 per cent; they might, however, be regarded as 'Bakkals' rather than as 'Seths').

(b) This includes Kalars (0.2 per cent and 0.7 per cent respectively).

Admittedly, such geographical expressions of the average range of influence of the different caste groups convey only a very crude indication of actual networks. Though, therefore, a general pattern can be perceived in Table III, a break-down into case histories is called for, particularly with Brahmans and Thakurs. For the sake of presentation the so-called non-agricultural transfers will be discussed first, starting with the most unambiguous groups in this respect, Marwaris, Baniyas, and Kayasths.

Of all moneylending groups, Marwaris seem to have stuck most faithfully to the banking profession. But also among Marwaris, distinctions can be made. Most powerful of all in the *tahsil*, indeed in the district, was the firm of Har Lal Bohri, a Marwari Brahman originating from the village of Kamad in the Datiya State. This man moved to the city of Jhansi after 1857. During the next decades he had dealings with many villages in the west of the Mau *tahsil*, i.e. the part nearest to Jhansi, without, however, having a monopoly there. About 1890, more than one-third of Marwari landed property in the *tahsil* belonged to this urban firm which had dealings in all directions from Jhansi and must, therefore, have been heavily dependent on the choice of its agents in the villages. In 1892, the settlement officer wrote about a village of which the firm had, previous to the first regular settlement, after much dispute with the Bhat *zamindars*, finally managed to obtain possession as mortgagees: 'Bad management by the absentee Marwari's agent. The Bhats are too much for the Marwari who does not get the full value out of the village.'[7] In the same year, though, the settlement officer reported about another village that Har Lal's firm 'has had for many years as agent a Kayasth who is well acquainted with all details, and rents have certainly not been kept down'.[8] Relatively few other town-based Marwaris worked in the villages. In the Orchha State, Jatara seems at one time to have been an important banking centre, but its influence had declined by 1873, owing, among other reasons, to the plunder of some of its banking houses in 1857–8 by Orchha troops. Few Marwaris resided in the town of Mau, but in the villages we find many of them, all of them probably Marwari Baniyas. The Ahirs of the village of Rewan had, about 1840, when their bankers of Madarwas —a village some four miles away—failed, 'invited some Marwaris of the jagirdari village of Tori Fatehpur to take up their abode in Rewan and do a friendly banking business. Rewan thus became the headquarters of four Marwari firms, which have lent money to the zamindars of most of the neighbouring villages.' The Ahirs of Rewan, 'with bad seasons, high interest and extravagant expenditure on marriages, etc. naturally got heavily into the debt of the accommodating Marwaris', of whom two, Pokhar Das and Gopinath, 'have prospered considerably'. The Ahirs' debts, about 1890, amounted to some Rs 40,000, this being about twenty times the yearly revenue of the village.[9] Yet, for a long time, the number of shares mortgaged or sold was small: the Marwari was often happy to leave the management to the *zamindars* and to retain as long as possible his image of the 'accommodating' *saraf*. Shares often changed hands among different Marwaris, in one case even up to three times, but not infrequently they ended up in the possession of an 'agriculturalist' *zamindar*.[10]

While Har Lal worked in all *parganas* of the old Jhansi district, the transactions of the Rewan Marwaris were mainly with *zamindars* living within a range of 5 or 6 miles from their headquarters. The Marwari bankers of the village of Patha lent within a similarly restricted area, but their dealings were also considerable. Apart from these three centres of Jhansi, Rewan, and Patha and a few firms in the town of Mau, there were perhaps a score of Marwaris in the *tahsil* doing banking business and living in as many villages. This rural character of many Marwaris made a number of them into resident landlords. Not counting the two Jhansi-based bankers of whom Har Lal was by far the most important, some 28 per cent of the Marwari *zamindars* were, at the end of the first regular settlement, resident in the villages where they had acquired land. Even then, they remained foreigners and in spite of the powerful connections of many of them over much of north India their position was vulnerable because of it. When, for instance, the resident Marwari of Nota, who owned half the village, died, he was 'succeeded by his brother's widow, who came from Malwa, knows nothing about the property and naturally cannot look after it properly.'[11] Absenteeism, on the other hand, did not always mean bad management. Though the settlement officer reported of one Marwari of Rewan that he was 'not a good landlord' and of another that 'the non-resident Marwari has not exerted himself for the village', he could also point to the village of Sanaura, where an absentee Marwari of Rewan 'advances seed to the *pahikashtkars* as required: the village has greatly improved and is now fully cultivated'. In another village (where *pahis* could only be got with difficulty), an absentee Marwari had 'several ploughs going'.[12] The impression is that in a number of poor villages, particularly those that suffered from scarcity of tenants, distance from a market and perhaps a general social and economic isolation, Marwaris, using their wider networks, had a chance to interfere and sometimes did so to the benefit of the local peasantry. Other, non-Marwari, absentee landlords, for that matter, took similar opportunities in similar villages.[13]

While Marwaris acquired 12,453 acres of *zamindari* land in altogether 33 villages, Baniyas in 1889–90 had purchased 7,620 acres in 26 villages. These Baniyas were of a more urban character than the

Marwaris, at least 17 out of the 26 purchases being made by Baniyas from the town of Mau, whereas a number of others lived in other market centres in the Mau and Garotha *tahsils*. As a result, in only three cases shares were purchased by resident Baniyas, the number of resident Marwari purchasers being six. These Baniyas, all or most of them Gahoy Baniyas, had been occupied for generations in the textile trade of the town of Mau. *Kharua* cloth was produced in the villages along the Betwa and Dhasan rivers and was still exported, through the Mau market, to far-away places all over northern India. *Al*, or madder-root, a plant yielding the red dye needed for this cloth, was still grown around Mau, which may partly explain Baniya interest in the property of land. In the village of Kuan, 'al has occupied as a rule a considerable area and the deep digging has had a marked effect on the kans. The Bania owners have no doubt effected some improvement by this method.'[14] In 1874, Brindaban, one of the two 'improving' Baniyas of Kuan, who was well-to-do and the *chaudhuri* of the Mau traders, obtained all *zamindari* rights of another village, close to Mau. Since then, 'he has done much for its improvement by the foundation of a small hamlet, the construction of a well, the digging out of kans and the growing of al. . . . Brindaban has 5 ploughs going in the village.'[15] It is probably significant that this man, who may well have been the most powerful Baniya in the *tahsil*, was one of the only two 'improving' Baniyas mentioned in the Assessment Remarks, the other being a certain Seth Balaji of Mau. Most of the caste-fellows of these two men were not a success as landlords. Even Brindaban, sometimes, had to let go. He also owned a four-*anna* share—i.e. one-fourth—in a poor village situated in an inferior part of the *tahsil*. Here, it was reported in 1892, he 'has done nothing for the village and has no ploughs at work'.[16] Sometimes, indeed, the new Baniya owners had hardly a chance; in a village adjoining the town of Ranipur two Ahirs, though only a four-*anna* share was left to them, continued to manage the village: resenting the intrusion of outsiders, they largely prevented them from securing any profit. In other villages also, Baniyas found it no easy job to get their rents or even their share of grass and grazing.[17] Also, their town of Mau was reported to have declined since, in 1861, the opening of the Central Indian Railway had offered an alternative north-south route to the old fair weather road from Kalpi via Mau to Sagar. In 1871, the municipal committee reported the failure or departure of many traders as a result of this change.

And in 1888, when four well-known *mahajans* of Mau had become insolvent, the municipality pointed to the opening of the Indian Midland Railway from Kanpur to Jhansi.[18] Another factor in this insolvency may well have been the declining trend of the Mau cloth exports which had set in about 1877.

Another example that seems typical of the Baniya failure to turn the acquisition of land into a paying concern, is presented by the village of Tilera. This village, after having long been mortgaged to two Seths of Mau, passed into their hands in 1873, the former Kurmi and Brahman proprietors remaining as occupancy and ex-proprietary tenants in the large area previously cultivated by them. The new *zamindars* succeeded in ejecting the ex-proprietors to the extent of a six-*anna* share; in the remaining ten-*annas* the ex-proprietors, who were 'a troublesome lot', continued to cultivate at the old low rents recorded against them when proprietors. The Baniyas, therefore, had to allow the tenants to intercept a large share of the profits, but devoted the proceeds they could lay their hands on to religious purposes.[19]

Many Baniyas' networks and resources were geared to urban, commercial pursuits; it was probably only for lack of a better investment that some of them turned to investment in land. Marwari Baniyas, on the contrary, had largely restricted themselves to village moneylending from the very beginning; they were less ill at ease in a rural environment and often must have been appreciated as associates rather than as exploiters in the villages. One does not hear of Baniyas being invited to a village as were the Marwaris by the Ahirs of Rewan. The village of Marwa seems to offer another example of this spirit of association. Here, two Marwaris of the neighbouring village of Rewan had acquired a small share from the Kurmi *zamindars*. The settlement officer, wondering why more land had not changed hands, remarked in 1892: 'With a Marwari banker a co-sharer there is no doubt that others were in debt as well, but matters were apparently settled with the Marwaris.'[20] The impression is that such settlements were more frequent with the ruralized, 'accommodating' Marwaris than with the Baniyas of the town of Mau.

The emergence of Kayasths as landed proprietors is associated with their traditional occupation as government servants, particularly as village accountants (*patwaris*). At the first regular settlement in 1865–6 a few Kayasths had shares in two or three villages, probably the result of their position as *patwaris* in these villages.

During the settlement period, however, members of this caste acquired several thousands of acres more. If we start with their largest single acquisition and end with the smallest, we meet the officials almost in order of precedence. During the 1880s, 2,355 acres were purchased by a Kayasth, who was and until his death would remain *diwan* of the Orchha State, i.e. prime minister of the leading Bundela princely state of Bundelkhand. Next comes the son of a former *patwari* whom we have met above as Har Lal's successful agent in one of that chief Marwari landowner's acquisitions in the *tahsil*; this man was no doubt as 'well acquainted with all details' of his own holdings—situated in villages near to Kachneo, where he lived himself—as he was with those of his Jhansi patron's estate. Then there were the purchases of a number of *patwari* families either in their own or in neighbouring villages. Another Marwari's agent bought a small share as did one Nand Ram Kayasth, a contractor, who was an immigrant to the village where he became one of the *zamindars*.[21]

As indicated above, Brahmans and Thakurs present a more ambiguous picture. As Tables II and III show, about as much land was obtained by agriculturalist Brahmans (to be dealt with later) as by Brahman non-agriculturalists. In the latter category is the largest transfer to any Brahman. It occurred in the village of Bijeygarh, where, as related earlier, 2,151 acres of land went to a 'son of a jamadar of sepoys'. This man was not the only Brahman purchaser connected with government service. Second largest in this category was a series of transfers benefiting two brothers of the town of Mau, Ram Lal and Raghunandan. Ram Lal was in 1892 a retired *kanungo*. He and his brother had acquired shares in some six villages and had, in addition, got hold of a number of mortgages by lending money. They were intelligent and well-to-do men and were, in 1892, though often in conflict with their co-sharers and tenants, continuing in an enterprising spirit. Other purchasing Brahmans included several moneylenders of Mau and of Bijna, an independent princely state on the border of the *tahsil*.[22]

As to the differential opportunity of men of different backgrounds to get a share of non-local, external resources, it is significant that almost all purchasers of *zamindari* rights associated with government service were Kayasths and Brahmans. There are, however, as far as we can see, two exceptions to this rule: a Kacchi road overseer of Mau, whose brother acquired a modest share and 'a well-to-do

Kacchi of Mau, formerly employed in the tanks', who settled in a village where he had bought 142 acres of land.[23] On the other hand, entrepreneurial income invested in land had its origin with Marwari, Baniya and Brahman families. To this latter rule we can again find only two exceptions: that of Behari Ahir who was a well-off bullock broker of the town of Mau, an important cattle market at that time. Backed by a Baniya he bought a three-*anna* share in a village where much grazing ground was available, just south of Mau. After some time, however, he pawned most of it to the same Baniya without even having started to properly manage the estate.[24] The second exception is that of the above-mentioned contractor, Nand Ram Kayasth.

Among those who are mentioned in Table II as having acquired land from outside resources during the first regular settlement, only Thakurs are still to be dealt with. As the figures show, the ancient dominant clan of the area, the Bundelas, were entirely responsible for all Thakur non-agricultural acquisitions of land. Why were Bundelas, as compared to other clans, so much more successful in their resistance to the inroads of Marwaris, Baniyas and others? How did they manage to increase considerably the *zamindari* area under their control? The phenomenon is the more striking as before the year 1865–6 Bundelas lost land, whereas the other clans increased their hold on *zamindari* rights. The explanation seems to lie, firstly, in the recognition by Government of their political importance as the ancient rulers of Bundelkhand and, secondly, though probably only for a short while, in their kinship connections and surviving regional power.

Though quite a few Bundela village *zamindars* were, as we shall see, just as badly off as most non-Bundela brotherhoods, a relatively large number of their families held their own thanks to Government recognition of their *muafi* rights. Several *muafis* were resumed during the century, but until 1892 those of the Bundelas were generally spared. Therefore, in 1865–6, one still finds the Bundela *zamindar* of the *muafi* village of Kadaura living in his fort in a village not very far away, where he had another hundred acres of revenue-free land. Two more Bundelas, the proud sons of Diwan Parichat of Patha, who had been, in the *pargana*, the most powerful man of his generation, jointly owned two full-sized *muafi* villages. Then, there was the estate of Taktoli, which consisted of two adjoining villages, one of them *muafi*, the other revenue paying, having been resumed in 1856.[25] The history of this estate demonstrates that the interest Government took in the fortune of powerful Thakur families sometimes went far beyond acquiescence in claims to *muafi* rights and could prove a vital factor in their favour. In 1872, the *zamindar* of Taktoli died. His widows, two 'pardanashin ladies', being at the mercy of their agents who defrauded them, were deemed by the N.W.P. Government 'females . . . incompetent to manage their estates'. The Court of Wards was, therefore, entrusted with the management of the villages. The Court 'planted many fruit and timber trees and improved a small forest on the bank of the river', found out about the right of succession on the death of the ladies and released the estate in 1886, when its liabilities had decreased from about Rs 8,000 to nil. By then, also, the elder widow had died, which probably added somewhat to the stability of management.[26]

The only other estate in the *tahsil* which enjoyed the benefit—and there need be no doubt that it was a great benefit from the economic point of view—of the Court of Wards' management in the nineteenth century was Katera, also a Bundela Thakur possession and by far the largest property in Mau. The *jagir* was founded in 1543 when a Rani of Orchha, becoming estranged from her husband, came to Katera with her sons. In the eighteenth century it became the bone of contention between Orchha and the Deccani Brahman Rajas of Jhansi, and as late as 1857 the troops of Rao Senapat of Katera joined the Orchha army against the Rani of Jhansi. In 1859, Lord Canning, in recognition of the Rao's services, conferred on him the title of Raja Bahadur and a *khilat* of Rs 5,000 while the Orchha Raja gave him the title of Shamsher Jung.[27] He died, however, soon, and at the first regular settlement the *jagir* was managed for his minor adopted son by the Court of Wards. It consisted of four *muafi* villages, among them Katera itself, three and a half *zamindari* villages and the assigned revenue of two villages which were former Katera *muafis*, but had been settled by the government with local communities of non-Bundela Thakurs as *zamindars*. Altogether the property comprised about eight per cent (22,613 acres) of the *tahsil* area and, though most of its *mahals* were rather poor, it yielded, thanks to the *muafi* rights, a yearly income of about Rs 10,000, government revenue paid. Included in this amount were also the cesses which the Raja collected in the well-frequented market of his town: octroi, weighing fees, a cloth tax, excise, and other dues bringing in about Rs 1,200 per annum. A considerable sum was also received from forest products, e.g. honey, gum (used by the Bundelkhand textile dyeing industry), and *singhara* (water chestnut).

The Court of Wards had taken over management of the estate in 1863 when the adopted son of Raja Bahadur Senapat was about six years old. During the year 1876–7 the marriage of the young Raja was celebrated; the costs amounting to Rs 5,203 were sanctioned and paid by the Court. When the young Raja died of smallpox soon after this, a fierce competition within the Katera family began over the vacant *gaddi*. The government favoured the nomination of one Balwant Singh, but 'owing to the factious opposition of Lachman Singh, the uncle of the late Raja, this has proved impossible'.[28] Other members of the family also raised objections. 'In view of these dissensions the estate was resumed and assessed to revenue. Later, however, the family agreed to the nomination of Sirdar Singh, son of Lachman Singh. Lachman Singh himself was ruled out by Government as he was suspected of having aided the rebel Rani of Jhansi.' The government agreed to the nomination of Sardar Singh as head of the family in 1879, granted him the title of Raja Bahadur and made over the estate to him the next year. At that time the property was unencumbered and the Raja received the disposal of savings amounting to about Rs 25,000. The Court had, during its management, purchased *zamindari* rights to the extent of 2,211 acres and within a few years after the release of the estate, the Katera Raja purchased another 637 acres. The Court of Wards had not only steered the Katera family through a precarious period of its history, but had also notably added to its wealth, a circumstance which enabled the Katera chief to play an important role in Jhansi District Board politics until far into the twentieth century.[29]

But the Court of Wards took an interest only in the larger properties. The resumption of most of the old *muafis* in 1892 and a rapid process of subdivision among heirs reduced a number of Bundela landlords to poverty before the end of the century. Of the two sons of Diwan Parichat of Patha, the longest living, Diwan Jagatpat, kept the two *muafi* villages mostly in his own hands. But after his death, his sons and nephews were entered as sharers. They were on bad terms with each other and, in 1892, the settlement officer thought further subdivision was inevitable. He also found these Bundelas 'notoriously bad landlords', 'too proud and disinclined to exert themselves in the management of the village'. Nevertheless, both villages were resumed.[30] Formerly, clan solidarity would have been a major factor in every Bundela estate's history. But now the interdependence of the clan segments which had been the basis for this solidarity was disappearing fast. Rich men like the Katera Raja and the Phalera Raja, who lived in Orchha territory and also bought some land in the British *tahsil* of Mau, were safe and well without the support of their poorer brethren. This applies even more strongly to the chief of all Bundelas, the Maharaja of Orchha. No village history is a better illustration of this than that of Khakora, the village subject to the largest single transfer of land during the first regular settlement, involving 3,190 acres. Previous to 1862, six Bundela Thakurs had enjoyed Khakora revenue-free. In the early 1890s, it stood in the name of the Orchha Maharaja's son. The homestead then was still inhabited by the former Bundela *zamindars*. Because of serious indebtedness, Act XVI of 1882, the Jhansi Encumbered Estates Act, had been applied 'and the Maharaja of Orchha bought fifteen anna four pie for the high price of Rs 10,600. There are now 6 ex-proprietors, 4 living in the village, one in jail for dacoity and one in hiding, charged with murder: an eight pie share is still left to the man in jail. The Maharaja is said to have purchased the village at the earnest entreaty of his fellow caste-men, the ex-proprietors. Still, one of them murdered his agent in the course of a dispute. The Maharaja can't manage properly in the face of the hostility of the Thakurs; he can afford to let it go to ruin. His agents are constantly being changed.'[31]

This terminates the examination of the transfers to be contributed to supra-local factors. Admittedly, as far as the Thakurs were concerned, these factors were unusual. The figures, given in Table II concerning Bundela Thakurs, reflect a special British regard for two or three aristocratic families and the delay granted to a slightly larger number of *muafidars*. This kind of favour, resulting in almost limitless security for a very few Bundelas, meant certain doom for many others. Bundelas, as well as non-Bundelas, were no longer in demand as the base on which their chief's power was founded. The very principle of Rajput politics, the maintenance of as wide as possible networks of men, clansmen having the most conspicuous roles, had lost its value to the chiefs themselves. Also, Thakurs—with the exception of the better-off Bundela families mentioned above—must have felt particularly ill at ease under the regime of regular settlement. Not surprisingly, they caused irritation with Impey who frequently described Thakurs with phrases like 'unsatisfactory landlords, indolent, quarrelsome and of expensive habits', or simply 'a thriftless and impecunious lot'.[32] No doubt the Thakur way of life demanded a more profuse expenditure on marriages, other festivities and retainers; many of them still found it politically harmful to work in the fields themselves. Yet, the lack of sympathy from the side of the authorities must have contributed to their difficulties under the rule of law.

Very few men in the *tahsil* enjoyed the same degree of security as the Orchha and Katera Rajas, who could afford to let their kinsmen or allies 'go to ruin' and to ignore their 'earnest entreaties'. Indeed, in social relationships, the principle of interdependence remained for some time as active as that of abandonment. Perhaps one could say that, in medieval India the principle of the friendly association of different groups in the village had been indistinguishable from the phenomenon of exploitative intrusion. Even the role of intruders like Kayasths, Brahman moneylenders, and Marwaris, as pointed out, was not always negative. To explain this in some more detail, the period before the first regular settlement (1865–6) should be considered more closely.

An example is offered by the village of Hati. Here, Kurmis were the original managers, but, at some time before 1838 one-fifth of the *mahal* had been ceded to Khangar Thakurs 'whom the Kurmis called in to protect them in times past'.[33] Such a 'gift' may sometimes have been a necessity to survive and may well have been typical of many other eighteenth and early nineteenth century land transfers, particularly in villages managed by peasants, who stood in need of links with the outside world. It is indeed striking that, in 1865–6, Kurmis, the typical peasants of the area, shared *zamindari* rights with other castes in as many as 19 villages while owning only 13 villages wholly, whereas the total number of shared villages, at that time, was far less (42) than the number of villages managed by just one community (123) (see Table VI). Another case of such early invitations was that of the Ahirs of Rewan who, around 1840, called in a Marwari banking family. The history of the village has been discussed already. Here, a cession of land was not part of the deal. But whether or not *zamindari* rights changed hands in such cases, what was essentially happening was the association—as a result of gift, barter, or invitation—of groups of relatively localized peasants in need of political, economic, and financial security with other parties having the disposal of protection and violence, labour, or access to a money market. Such deals, which remind one of *jajmani* relationships, were part and parcel of a peasant political culture that could only be maintained by dint of the regular renewal or even the continuous rearticulation of relationships and associations. Now, peasant society used to express and articulate the modified political, social, and economic balance at which it, from time to time, arrived in a variety of idioms. Among these idioms the economic one of rights in land was only one. Others were those of abscondence and settlement (demographic domain), sectarianism and shrine building (religious domain), boundary definition and a judicious use of violence (political domain). These idioms did not provide hard and fast rules of expression and behaviour. They were of a diffuse character, the idiom of landed rights, e.g. using a multiplicity of terms that were not distinctly related to each other, though each had its own connotation, like *malguzari*, *zamindari*, and *milkiyat*, or *muafi*, *inam* and *belagan*. The essence of the Thakurs' role was to try and preside over the rearticulation of power and relationships in as many of these social idioms as they possibly could. To the extent that they succeeded in this, they were not merely managing estates, but acting as agents of state formation as well. But in the nineteenth century both the plurality of idioms and their undefined character were interfered with.

After the British had, in 1838, temporarily occupied the Jhansi State of which Mau was a part, their ideas as to revenue settlement were introduced and these remained in force when the State was returned to its Raja in 1843. The all-important change introduced by British rule was not to confer the right of property, but to supplant the inflexible, legal idiom of *zamindari* right for the diffusion that was bound up with a medieval, dynamic political culture. The government now insisted on dealing only with one kind of brokers, whom they called *zamindars*. To many it became necessary now either to get hold of these newly defined *zamindari* rights, or to cease to count in the region. For Thakurs, no doubt, the situation was most frustrating. The regional dominance exercised by them since the sixteenth century was very inadequately rendered to them in the *zamindari* rights—almost exclusively of the villages in which they resided—now granted to their chiefs and brotherhoods. The rigid system now imposed meant an end to the tradition of adaptation and negotiation, described above, in which Thakurs had played the major role and had often been the arbiters. But as a certain right of brokerage—however circumscribed—was implied in the new *zamindari* rights and as political brokerage was the very essence of a Rajput's role in society, the Thakurs were amongst the most active in the scramble for these rights that followed the introduction of the new system.

In the course of this fight, they seem to have ventured into finance more actively than they had done before, taking upon themselves financial loads that were beyond their ability to bear. Space does not permit me to go further into this financial aspect. Suffice it to mention that, as late as 1865–6, of more than 30,000 acres mortgaged in Mau *tahsil*, 10,000 acres were mortgaged to some of the larger Thakur landlords in the area, viz. the *jagirdars* of Katera, Bijna, and Alipura. The chiefs, however, were soon replaced as creditors at the village level by others, mainly immigrant Marwaris. As Table III shows, in 1873, Thakurs held only 18.3 per cent of mortgages in the *tahsil*. But in their struggle to maintain as much as feasible of their former regional dominance and to have this power recognized in as many *mahals* as possible, they had other means at their disposal. A word has already been said about the declining importance of kinship ties. A more lasting and irrepressible asset of nineteenth century Thakur politics was the carefully weighed use of physical violence. How effective this could be is shown by a case taken from the 'Time of Troubles' in Bundelkhand. When, during 1857 and 1858, the troops of the Orchha *Darbar* invaded the Jhansi territory that had once belonged to its *Raj*, every Thakur who had the means started his own war of independence. Indeed, only the Thakurs had a good chance to prosper in such years. In the village of Pachwara, which was said to have originally been held rent-free, the rights of the Bundela Thakurs 'were restricted in more recent times to bighas 1350 held on an ubari tenure, first at Rs 550 and then at Rs 300.' The *zamindari* rights of the village were granted to Brahmans and Kurmis, who fell into arrears, and previous to 1857 the village was transferred to an outsider. But, 'during the rebellion, the Bundelas took forcible possession of the whole estate, driving out the zamindars and looting and ruining the village. After the restoration of order the zamindars returned', but they never asserted themselves against the Thakurs: 'the arrears could not be realized and the village was held under direct management from 1859 to 1861: the jama being Rs 2,601 plus Rs 300 payable by the ubaridars.' In 1861 the Board of Revenue sanctioned restoration of the village to the *zamindars* at a reduced *jama* of Rs 1,200. But during the settlement operations of 1862, 'the Settlement Officer settled the whole mahal with the Bundelas on a low jama of Rs 886 . . . in order to allow the village to recover. The Bundelas have, therefore, fared well.'[34] Few people except Thakurs could have prospered like this during these years of turmoil in Bundelkhand.

It is obvious that the transfers before 1865–6 as shown in Table IV do not represent 'gains and losses' of the same kind as those of Tables II and V. The fact of an 8.5 per cent increase in the *zamindaris* of Thakurs (other clans) conceals an enormous loss of Thakur influence. The figure may at the most be interpreted as indicating that these Thakurs succeeded in wresting from the new government, in a limited number of cases, legal recognition in terms of *zamindari* rights of their ancient informal control which had now become increasingly difficult for them to exercise openly. This can hardly be called success: they could do very little to prevent the introduction by the British of *zamindari* 'village republics' that shook the very foundation of Rajput political culture. The performance of the Brahman category according to Table IV should be seen in the same

TABLE IV

ACREAGE OF TRANSFERS PREVIOUS TO THE FIRST REGULAR SETTLEMENT (1865–6)

Caste	Alienations	Acquisitions	Net gains or losses	Net gains or losses (percentages)
1	2	3	4	5
Thakur (Bundela and allied clans)	5,448	4,852	− 596	− 1.4
Thakur (other clans)	2,790	8,845	+6.055	+ 8.5
Brahman	1,061	4,347	+3.286	+ 6.8
Kurmi	6,465	1,061	−5.404	−13.7
Ahir	879	—	− 879	− 3.3
Lodhi	521	—	− 521	− 5.5
Kacchi	1,941	—	−1.941	−38.0
Ghosi	558	—	− 558	−15.7
Kalar	—	558	+ 558	+
	17,541*	17,541*		

* 2,122 acres have been deducted from this total because of one village having been transferred twice during the period.

light. Mainly responsible for Brahman 'gains' is a large purchase by a Deccani Brahman, a member of the old administrative elite of the Jhansi state. It would be ludicrous to suppose that such a purchase could even partly make up for the dramatic loss of Deccani influence that took place when the British ousted them from the Jhansi administration after 1838. In the same vein, it may be argued that the loss of *zamindaris* suffered by peasant castes previous to 1865–6, represents a reality different from seemingly similar losses after that year. Villages had been granted not on the basis of local and regional influence, but on the basis of what the British took for actual possession. Many peasants did not have the resources and leverage to turn to advantage their new legal status, but even if they lost this status again, the decline of Thakur regional dominance may have relatively improved their situation. After 1860, Thakurs were no longer 'invited' by peasants to settle in their villages, nor did they easily impose their brokerage on them, though now outside creditors like Marwaris, to much the same effect, offered their kind of exploitative security.

Yet, the impression is that irregular and violent methods could be successfully adopted even after the 1850s, though the change of name for such actions in nineteenth century Bundelkhand from *bhumiyawat* (struggle for land) to the Anglo-Indian term of dacoity with its criminal connotation is significant. The reduced scale of such activities is perhaps reflected in the not very remarkable figures for 'agricultural' transfers after 1865–6 as shown in Table V. A few case histories, illustrating this table, deserve to be quoted. One Aman Singh of Uldan, for instance, was the chief of a small group of Bhadauria Thakurs, who had obtained possession of an uninhabited *mahal* in a somewhat irregular, though not necessarily violent, manner.[35] He then made some purchases in an adjacent, small Ahir *mahal*, helped by the money he received when a certain property he had held as mortgage on account of a very old debt was released under Act XVI of 1882, the Jhansi Encumbered Estates Act. Although, in 1892, Aman Singh was on bad terms with the Ahir ex-proprietors and had difficulty obtaining tenants, he was 'well-known, astute and powerful'. The *mahals* were of 'poor and insecure' quality, bullocks and manure were equally scarce and, after the inroads of *kans* grass in 1873, Aman Singh's home *mahal* had been almost deserted. He was not very well-off, but, having some holdings in other *mahals*, he succeeded in carrying on, using his great authority in the neighbourhood to keep his fields under the plough.[36]

TABLE V

ACREAGE OF 'AGRICULTURAL' TRANSFERS DURING THE FIRST REGULAR SETTLEMENT (1865–6 TO 1889–90)

Caste	Alienations	Acquisitions	Net gains or losses	Net gains or losses (percentages)
1	2	3	4	5
Thakur (Bundela and allied clans)	64	548	+ 484	+ 1.2
Thakur (other clans)	5,496	5,987	+ 491	+ 0.6
Brahman	4,598	5,848	+1,250	+ 2.4
Kurmi	3,769	2,915	− 854	− 2.5
Ahir	1,218	856	− 362	− 1.4
Lodhi	167	—	− 167	− 1.9
Kacchi	550	492	− 58	− 1.8
Ghosi	805	228	− 577	−19.2
Kayasth	207	—	− 207	−17.0
	16,874	16,874		

The chief purchasing Thakur of the *tahsil* was a Gaur Thakur called Raghunath Singh. Unlike Aman Singh he had the advantage of working in an agriculturally better equipped part of Mau. Perhaps this is why he seems to draw nearer to the model of an agrarian capitalist. As, about 1865, there had been no Gaur Thakurs among the *zamindars* of his village, Ragunath Singh may have been the daughter's son and heir of one of the local Payak Thakurs. In his own as well as in nearby villages, he lent money to many Kurmis and to a number of Thakurs, of whom at least some were his relatives. In a number of cases, he obtained decrees against his debtors and got hold of shares either as owner or as mortgagee. Sometimes, he took over cultivation, having several ploughs going in his new possessions and generally improving his holdings. Together with a relative, he owned, in the early 1890s, close to one thousand acres, mostly good land, and possessed many fields as mortgagee, while a number of *zamindars* and occupancy tenants were in his debt.[37]

Both Aman Singh and Ragunath Singh seem to have enjoyed a certain degree of independence from village politics. Aman Singh's family of Bhadauria Thakurs had no *zamindari* rights in the large village of Uldan where they lived and the field of their activities was formed by some small neighbouring *mahals* where the influence of other Thakurs was slight, the Uldan Payak Thakurs being occupied in a protracted fight with the local Kurmis. Raghunath Singh, as argued above, may have been an immigrant, perhaps having at his disposal outside resources other than those based on estate management. The village of Dhawakar provides yet another instance of a Thakur who, starting from a somewhat independent position, was able to invest in a new way and prosper. This was Ganpat Singh, a Parihar *lambardar* of that village, who with his family owned the neighbouring, uninhabited *mahal* of Tungarwara. Here he cultivated a considerable area himself and succeeded in preventing the accrual of occupancy rights by constantly changing the fields leased to tenants—a practice typical of robust, Thakur estate management.[38] Under Act XVI of 1882, two *annas* of the village (i.e. one-eighth of the *zamindari*) were sold by auction to him for a high price. Strangely, however, the large community as a whole, consisting of some fifty Parihar *zamindars*, could not get around to what seemed to be urgently called for from the point of view of estate management. Large areas of jungle had been brought under the plough in the *mahal* since the first regular settlement. In the original holdings, therefore, much waste had been included. Now, the lump rents were much too low and the *zamindars*, though quite alive to the fact, did not agree to secure a suitable income from the occupancy tenants. Many of these tenants, chiefly Brahmans and Kurmis, had large holdings. 'They frequently sublet at rents higher than their own.' Others were in debt and had mortgaged their holdings to the Raghunath Singh whom we have met above and who cultivated in this way much land in the village. Most of the co-sharers 'have looked on with indifference at their proceedings'; some of them had borrowed from their better-off brethren, others owed large sums to Raghunath Singh or to the Baniyas of Mau. 'The total debt cannot be less than Rs 15,000. It must be sheer extravagance.' But extravagance was not the whole explanation: 'the lumberdars, especially Chaudan Singh, are intelligent and well acquainted with the patwari's papers. If they had disinterestedly agreed to secure a suitable income from the occupancy tenants much of the debt might possibly have been avoided. Vested interests, however, have proved too strong. The occupancy tenants are a powerful class.'[39] This immobilized estate management seriously endangered the community. Also, in a faction-ridden Thakur village, occupancy rights could, once established, find champions amongst the *zamindars* themselves. Understandably, therefore, strong Thakur leaders tried, time and again, to prevent the growth of such rights, but whereas a man like Ganpat Singh, who owned a small, uninhabited *mahal* where he was a free agent, succeeded in this, Chaudan Singh, too much enmeshed in the vested interests of the village he lived in, failed.

A certain freedom of action because of outsidc resources, servility of tenants, or strong leadership was of the utmost importance in estate management. We find among Thakur purchasers of land a comparatively large number of *lambardars*. These were more often than not the largest landholders in the village where they lived and they were usually powerful chiefs of lineages. A number of them acquired the *pattis* of co-sharers, others bought shares in nearby villages. Commonly also one or two *hissahdars* (i.e. co-sharers) bought fields while their less fortunate relatives had to sell or were in debt: one of the 'thriftless and impecunious' *zamindars* referred to above bought a share in the next village and a sharer in the *mahal* of Mau, who was one of an 'indolent and apathetic body of Thakurs', purchased a one-*anna* share from a fellow co-sharer.[40] Thakurs, of course, were hard to distinguish from other peasants in this respect. In such cases—and they form a large part of the transfers among all castes—changes in the man–land ratio, generally brought about by demographic factors, may often be held responsible. As Berreman wrote about the Pahari village he studied: '. . . the relative wealth of families shifts with time. . . . The more wealth per man, up to a point, the more wealth is accrued. With too little manpower, even land is useless, and in one of these cases wealth came when a man finally acquired a son and a servant to help him work his more than ample lands.'[41]

When we turn to Kurmis and Ahirs, typical peasant categories, we can see that it was largely beyond their means to turn to profit the *zamindari* rights that had been granted to a number of them. Indicative of the limitations to which Kurmi enterprise was subject is the fact that not in a single instance did a member of this caste acquire a share in a village where a Kurmi had not been *zamindar* before. Even so, a limited number of Ahirs and Kurmis turned to moneylending and a few managed to purchase land. In 1892, in the Kurmi village of Siaori only one of the old *zamindars* owned a considerable area. This was Paku Chaudhuri, then a shrewd, old and well-to-do landlord who had shares in several villages where he did much of the cultivation himself, i.e. without the intermediary of tenants, but with the help of labourers and family members. Of a Kurmi purchaser elsewhere it was reported that he greatly improved a village and made large profits.[42]

About the Ahir *zamindars* of one village the settlement officer wrote that 'being Ahirs, they deal in ghi and apparently prefer to keep the land for grazing'.[43] We have already mentioned the single instance of a bullock-broker who purchased some grazing ground, only to get rid of it after a short while. Ahirs probably tended to invest in cattle rather than in land.

Among Brahman peasants we find many of a type we have met before among other caste groups. In several villages, there were a number of large sharers who could afford to lend money and, in time, purchased some fields. The Brahmans of Suhagpura were well-off. Two of them, 'representatives of Gannu Naik and Mangal, deceased, well-known men in the neighbourhood', were the owners of six *annas* of the village and possessed shares in five other villages as well. One co-sharer, however, had become embarrassed through litigation and his two *anna* eight *pai* share (i.e. one-sixth of the villages) was sold under the Jhansi Encumbered Estates Act. His creditors had been the two *lambardars* above-named, who bought in the share. Yet, the prosperity of these Brahmans could not have been the result of aggressive estate management. In 1892, the settlement officer wrote that 'many of the occupancy tenants are Kacchis and some Brahmans, relatives of the proprietors. The zamindars have allowed them to continue to pay the rents fixed of old and have not forced their rent up to the tenant-at-will level.'[44] An explanation may be found in the appellation of 'Nayak' added to Gannu's name, which may indicate service as a sepoy in the British army. A similar remark may, for that matter, be made about the addition of 'Chaudhuri' to the name of the above-mentioned Paku Kurmi: this may indicate that Paku was a contractor as well as an agriculturalist. One more purchaser of *zamindari* rights in the village of Siaori was Qazi Imamuddin, an ex-*muafidar* of this large village, who may have enjoyed some income from the office of qazi.

In the case of the so-called 'agriculturalist' purchases of land, indications that purchasers derived advantage from outside resources, whether government service, the recognition of privilege, non-agricultural entrepreneurship or any other source of income, were found in many village histories. This suggests that a fair number of the 'agricultural' transfers (Table V) are not, after all, very different from the 'non-agricultural' transfers (Table II). This would virtually leave as agricultural transfers, firstly, those which were the result of the periodical changes in the man–land ratio of family farms and, secondly, those transfers which had their origin in the small-scale moneylending by *lambardars* and co-sharers, mostly to family members and occupancy tenants. In other words, one does not find any proof of fields being bought from the proceeds of agriculture, that is, from estate management. Indeed, there is reason to doubt whether, in more than a very few cases, a real profit was ever made from mere estate management in the *tahsil* of Mau. This seems worth recording as, of course, the British system of *zamindari* tenure was designed to allow full scope to entrepreneurial estate management by thrifty rustics concerned with agricultural economics and nothing else. The archival material studied here did not only concern transfers of land, but related equally to that larger part of the *tahsil* that was not transferred to transferees outside the family. The conclusion must be that very few *zamindars* answered the British model. The scramble for non-agricultural resources was general and was perhaps the essential part of what 'estate management' was about.

If, even after the so-called 'regular' settlement of the 1860s, the practice of *zamindari* estate management in the *tahsil* often comprised a number of activities that could never be taken into account in British-led assessment and settlement operations, no perfect case is found either of the kind of lordly Thakur management similar to state formation from which no idiom or domain of activity— particularly not intimidation and the judicious use of violence—was excluded as irrelevant. But the Thakurs of Maleta in the Hamirpur district, who made their power felt also in Mau, provide proof that Thakur politics, as distinct from British-defined *zamindari* economics, could make for success and power. In the beginning of the present century, the *Hamirpur District Gazetteer* gave the following account of the Parihār Rajputs of Maleta: 'The rise of this family to importance has been very rapid. The present head of the Malehta branch is Pertab Singh, whose great-grandfather had no landed property except his ancestral share in Malehta. His sons, Indrajit and Jagatraj, set systematically to work at the acquisition of estates and soon made their family the most conspicuous in the district.'[45] The family, though mainly active east of the River Dhasan, that is just across the *tahsil* border, attracts our attention because of their involvement in the politics of the village of Uldan in *tahsil* Mau. About 1845, a number of Thakurs had acquired this village from the local community of Kurmis, who later on brought a suit against them on the ground that they had mortgaged, not sold the village. The Thakurs had to defend themselves at considerable expense, while the Kurmis 'obtained the aid of the notorious Thakurs of Maleta in the Hamirpur District', as it was put by Impey, who in his handwritten 'Assessment Remark' phrased things less circumspectly than the author of the *District Gazetteer* could afford to do.[46] But it was not only from 'conspicuousness' and 'notoriety' that these Parihars derived their commanding reputation in the area. The village of Maleta had been a textile producing centre. Substantial profits could be made in such villages, not only by the Dhobis and Chhipas, employed respectively in bleaching and dyeing the local *kharua* cloth, but also by the *zamindars*. By 1878, some of the Thakurs of Maleta, where the industry had meanwhile died out, had got hold of most of the shares of Kuchhecha, another village on the Dhasan. Here, ten or twelve Chhipa families possessing twelve dyeing pans were still carrying on a considerable trade. The *zamindars* derived an income from the ravines along the river, which supplied the *dhawai* flower used by the dyers. They also levied a cess of six rupees per sixty *than* (pieces) of cloth sold to the *baiparis*. Then they charged one *anna* daily for each dyeing pan being worked in. Finally the Dhasan *ghat* belonged to the Maleta Thakurs and the fare charged during the rains was one and a quarter *pai* per person.[47]

The rise of the Maleta family may not have been a case of undiluted political entrepreneurship, but a fairly wide spectrum of factors contributed to it, ranging from outright intimidation via the raising of taxes and the management of a river ferry to rent receiving. As far as their activities did not fit the narrowly defined British notion of estate management, these lords moved in the direction of state formation, which we have defined as all-inclusive and encompassing all idioms and models of behaviour and expression recognized by society. Such a medieval dominion over men and crops demanded the association of peasants, moneylenders, artisans and others in the same estate under Thakur, i.e. clan, leadership. It is significant that under 'regular' British rule, one of the most conspicuous successes in the area was achieved by methods which the new *zamindari* system expressly condemned. Gradually, however, Thakurs had to conform. The introduction of the 'regular' settlement

TABLE VI

INCREASE IN THE NUMBER OF *MAHALS* SHARED BETWEEN COMMUNITIES OF DIVERSE ORIGINS

	Mahals entirely owned in 1865–66	*Mahals* entirely owned in 1889–90
Brahman	27	14
Deccani Brahman	1	–
Thakur (Bundela etc.)	18	17
Thakur (other clans)	28	8
Ahir	19	3
Kurmi	13	–
Lodhi	6	5
Kacchi	4	1
Ghosi	3	–
Bhat	2	–
Dangi	1	–
Bairagi	1	1
Total Unshared *Mahals*	123	49
Shared *Mahals* (or integrally sold to outsiders)	42	116
	165	165

had formally excluded Thakurs from interference with about one half of the *tahsil* and, though they still made themselves felt, especially in Kurmi and other peasant villages, the old political culture, now declared criminal, was increasingly difficult to maintain.

In more general terms, the exclusion of Thakurs meant a ban on the Thakur *dharma* or idiom of conspicuous power, wide kinship ties and state formation. In the long term, it meant the effective 'de-Thakurization' of the area: Thakur clans became castes or *gotras* of castes, stressing the endogamous or exclusive principle rather than the exogamous or inclusive and political idiom of the *biradari*. But the period under review was still characterized by the antagonism between the revenue officers of Thomason's school, i.e. the propagandists of the *zamindari* village, and the communities of Thakur brethren for whom they could not find harsh enough words.

Rural society was changed radically by being thus frozen into the crystals of Bird's and Thomason's rules. Yet, as pointed out in the paragraphs dealing with Marwari purchases, the principle of the association of different groups in the village reasserted itself. The security of every estate and village depended on their capacity to transcend local restrictions. Moneylenders during the nineteenth century often dispensed the only means to achieve this and acquired great power as a result. This new challenge to the British ideal of an exclusively agricultural *zamindari* was met with the Jhansi Encumbered Estates Act of 1882 and later, more adequately, with the Bundelkhand Encumbered Estates Act of 1903. In this respect Bundelkhand was similar to the Punjab.[48] Outside resources were a necessity of life to village management and just as 'de-Thakurization' had brought in the Marwaris and other moneylending groups, the imposition of rural 'de-Vaishya-ization'—for as such the Encumbered Estates Acts' ban on transfers to non-agriculturalists may be characterized—created a demand for links with the outside world of yet another kind. Perhaps the entry of urban politicians into the area in the first decade of the present century should be seen against this background.

NOTE ON SOURCES

The data for Tables I, II, IV, V and VI are taken, for 1865–6, from the *khewats* of the first regular settlement, which are part of the Village Volumes of that settlement. They are available in the Revenue Record Room, Collectorate, Jhansi, 1865–6 (1273 *Fasli*) being the year in which these volumes were written. The data for 1889–90 are from the four Mau Assessment Volumes of the second regular settlement; the latter are available in the record room of the English Office, Collectorate, Jhansi, 1889–90 (1297 *Fasli*) being the year of attestation for that settlement. In a number of doubtful cases the *khewats* in the Village Volumes of the second regular settlement were also consulted.

As the first regular settlement *khewats* as a rule do not show the acreages belonging to individual *hissahdars*, *muafis*, resumed or conditional *muafi*, or Government lands, the *anna-pai* division in these *khewats* has been applied to the *zamindari* area of the second regular settlement, the survey preceding the latter settlement being more accurate than the earlier one. The *zamindari* area is, therefore, assumed to have remained the same during settlement and, indeed, *muafis* when resumed remained, at the time, separately entered. The difference between the total area of the 165 *mahals* (2,59,055 acres) and the *zamindari* area used in the tables (2,53,096 acres) is rather small: it consists mainly of the many small (resumed) *muafi* fields met with in most villages.

The information obtainable from the Village Volumes of the Bundelkhand districts of the U. P. is largely similar to that described by Hagen and Yang for Bihar.[49]

NOTES

1 This article is based on material collected during a stay, from 1968 to 1970, in India, financed by the Netherlands Foundation for the Advancement of Tropical Research. I thank the U.P. Government for permission to work in the district archives in Bundelkhand. To the servants of Government stationed in the Jhansi *kachahri* I owe much for their hospitality and forbearance.

2 Secr., Board of Revenue, to Secr., Govt. N.W.P., 17 September 1875, N.W.P. Rev. Progs, 8 January 1876, no. 15.

3 See, e.g., Eric Stokes, 'Traditional Elites in the Great Rebellion of 1857: Some Aspects of Rural Revolt in the Upper and Central Doab', in Edmund Leach and S. N. Mukherjee, eds., *Elites in South Asia* (Cambridge, 1970), and P. J. Musgrave, 'Landlords and Lords of the Land: Estate Management and Social Control in Uttar Pradesh 1860–1920', *Modern Asian Studies*, 6 (1972), 257–75.

4 Jhansi District Kachahri, English Office, Assessment Remark, Second Settlement, Bijeygarh (VII, 41).

5 See also the 'Note on Sources'.

6 Brenda E. F. Beck, 'The Right-Left Division of South Indian Society', *Journal of Asian Studies*, 29 (1970), 779–98. Of course, what might be called the interactional sphere, given on the right in Beck's graph, is here presented on the left, the attributional sphere on the right.

7 Assessment Remark, Second Settlement, Luhargaon Bhat (VIII, 77).

8 Ibid., Kachneo (II, 9).

9 Ibid., Rewan (V, 117).

10 Ibid., Rajgir (VIII, 125); cf. also Dhakarwara (VIII, 39) and Luhargaon Bhat (VIII, 77).

11 Ibid., Nota (VII, 197).

12 Ibid., Bachera (VII, 9); Burai (VII, 49); Sanaura (VIII, 213); Khajraha (VI, 49).

13 See, e.g., ibid., Barora (VII, 33). Cf. also Malcolm Lyall Darling, *Rusticus Loquitur, or the Old Light and the New in the Punjab Village* (1930), p. 75: 'What gives a moneylender power in a tract like this is its inaccessibility'.

14 Assessment Remark, Second Settlement, Kuan (VIII, 57).

15 Ibid., Marha (VIII, 97).

16 Ibid., Basari (VIII, 13).

17 Ibid., Luhargaon Ranipur (III, 73); Basaria (VIII, 17).

18 Nagar Palika Mau, Annual Administration Reports 1870–1 and 1887–8, Mau-Ranipur Municipality.

19 Assessment Remark, Second Settlement, Tilera (VII, 233).

20 Ibid., Marwa (V, 61).

21 Ibid., Parwa (III, 97); Baman Naigawan (VIII, 9); Burhia Bamhori (VII, 53); Bira (VIII, 25); Bhata (III, 21); Siaori (V, 125).

22 Ibid., Jhankri (VI, 41); Tikri (III, 113); Baragaon (VII, 29); Bamhori (VII, 21); Mau (VI, 57); Ratosa (V, 113).

23 Ibid., Jhankri (VI, 41); Chirkana (VI, 17). The government had constructed two lakes in the *tahsil* and repaired a number of others, see D. L. Drake-Brockman, *Jhansi District Gazetteer* (Allahabad, 1929), pp. 49, 60.

24 Assessment Remark, Second Settlement, Kanja (VII, 135).

25 Ibid., Kadaura (III, 57); Bhadarwara (VI, 50); Bhanpura (III, 17); Patha (VIII, 121); Taktoli (VIII, 141); Mailwar (VIII, 93).

26 Annual Reports 1876–7 through 1885–6, Court of Wards in the N.W.P., Jhansi District, Takhtauli Mahalwara Estate.

27 D. L. Drake-Brockman, op. cit., pp. 102, 162, 163. Assessment Remark, Second Settlement, Katera (I, 21); Assessment Remark, Third Settlement, 1940–1, Katera.

28 Annual Report 1876–7, Court of Wards etc., Katahra Estate.

29 See notes 27 and 28.

30 Assessment Remark, Second Settlement, Bhanpura (III, 17); Patha (VIII, 121).

31 Ibid., Khakora (III, 65).

32 Ibid., Palra (V, 85); Sakrar (II, 37).

33 Ibid., Hati (IV, 45).

34 Ibid., Pachwara (V, 65).

35 The family first owned only five *anna* four *pai* (i.e. one-third) of *mahal* Nimgahna; a Kurmi who had a similar share disappeared and a Kayasth lost his third when officials felt persuaded that this share was not held according to law, Jhansi District Kachahri, Revenue Record Room, Village Volume no. 68 (Nimgahna), Khewat of first regular settlement.

36 Assessment Remark, Second Settlement, Lathesura (III, 69); Buraoli (VI, 13); Nimgahna (VIII, 105).

37 Ibid., Khandarkha (VII, 169); Garhwan (VI, 29); Churari (VII, 85); Dhamna Paik (V, 9); Dhawakar (V, 13).

38 See, e.g., ibid., Laron (I, 37), where the Bundela *zamindars* 'appear to have "arranged" that no tenants or rents should be recorded. The whole of the village was recorded as their ser or khudkasht at last Settlement and has been recorded so since. The Kachi cultivators, who have held the same fields for generations, are considered to be either servants or shikmis: when shikmis they do not pay cash rent, but cultivate on the "batai" system. So the patwari, according to the usual custom of this district, has deemed it unnecessary to enter their names at all in the village papers. The Kachis had in many cases houses on their fields and were practically occupancy tenants; they, however, make no claims of any sort and are no doubt afraid to do so, but they appear to be comfortable and contented with their lot.'

Unfortunately, space does not permit to go further into landlord–tenant relationships as they affect estate management, but the additional example given above may suffice to show that the Assessment Remarks give details on this aspect of village history as well.

39 Ibid., Dhawakar (V. 13).

40 Ibid., Sakrar (II, 37); Mau (VI, 57).

41 Gerald B. Berreman, *Hindus of the Himalayas* (Berkeley and Los Angeles, 1963), pp. 54–5.

42 Assessment Remark, Second Settlement, Kotra (VI, 85); Chimadwara (VII, 61); Siaori (V, 125); Hati (IV, 45); Bar (IV, 5); Bagrauni (VI, 1); Satpura (VI, 69).

43 Ibid., Gurha (III, 53).

44 Ibid., Chimadwara (VII, 61); Durgapur (III, 45); Merki (VII, 193); Suhagpura (IV, 117); Siaori (V, 125).

45 D. L. Drake-Brockman, *Hamirpur District Gazetteer* (Allahabad, 1909), p. 85.

46 Assessment Remark, Second Settlement, Uldan (IV, 121).

47 Hamirpur District Kachahri, English Office, Assessment Remark, Second Settlement, by V. A. Smith, Kachhaucha (I, 89) (in Assessment Volumes, Pargana Rath).

48 See Norman G. Barrier, *The Punjab Alienation of Land Bill of 1900* (Duke University, 1966), and N. Gerald Barrier, 'The Punjab Disturbances of 1907: the Response of the British Government in India to Agrarian unrest', *Modern Asian Studies*, 1 (1967), 353–83.

49 James R. Hagen and Anand A. Yang, 'Local Sources for the Study of Rural India: the "Village Notes" of Bihar', *The Indian Economic and Social History Review*, 13 (1976), 75–85.

4

Canal Irrigation and Agrarian Change: The Experience of the Ganges Canal Tract, Muzaffarnagar District (U.P.), 1840-1900

IAN STONE

University of Cambridge

I

In most areas of India the availability of water determines, more than any other input, the nature of agricultural production. Cultivators in regions and localities without sources of water supply to supplement rainfall are constrained in their choice of cropping patterns and have to suffer enforced adjustments when the rains are abnormal, either in their timing or in their quantity. Such insecurity can never be the basis for agricultural development, particularly because potential surpluses, and the investment and expansion opportunities these imply, are normally relinquished in favour of risk-minimization and survival needs. In most areas, therefore, the state of agriculture depends vitally upon the security and flexibility provided by irrigation facilities—a point long recognized in India. It follows, then, that the substantial British activity in the provision of large-scale irrigation systems—begun in the last decades of the Company's rule, and continued, more vigorously, under the Crown—should have been conducive to agricultural progress in the recipient areas.

A substantial amount of this activity was centred in the Ganges–Jumna *Doab* of what is now Uttar Pradesh. Located on the vast alluvial plain of northern India, it was a comparatively simple engineering task to divert the water from the perennial snow-fed rivers into canals which watered the intervening land. The first major work, the Eastern Jumna Canal, was a renovation of an abandoned indigenous work, and was opened in 1830. This was followed, in 1855, by the opening of the Ganges Canal which stretched almost the length of the *Doab*. By the 1870s this system was watering an average of 750,000 crop-acres annually, though 1,078,000 acres had been supplied in the famine year of 1868–9. The Agra Canal and the loan-financed Lower Ganges Canal were opened during the 1870s, and, by the end of the century, the proliferation of channels and distributaries coursing the land between the Ganges and the Jumna annually irrigated around 1,700,000 acres, whilst being able to supply water to 2.5 million in a year of drought. Of the 11.5 million acres normally sown in this tract, 5 million were irrigated in a dry year—a figure shared almost equally by canals and wells.[1]

Though relatively favourable to their construction, the *Doab* in the mid-nineteenth century was not sufficiently protected by wells to render the tract secure from the marked unreliability of the rainfall in the western U.P. Crude estimates suggest that, prior to the opening of the Ganges Canal, only around 15 per cent of the area annually sown in the *Doab* was protected by wells; clearly there was substantial scope for the extension of irrigation facilities in a tract consisting of districts which were 'among the most insecure in Northern India'.[2] It might be expected, therefore, that substantial agricultural progress would have resulted from the subsequent expansion of the irrigated area due to the introduction of the canals. A section in a recent book, however, throws doubt on whether this expected result was actually realized. Dr E. Whitcombe, having considered the impact of the canals on the rural economy of the western U.P., seems to suggest that the canal brought disadvantages which outweighed its advantages, ultimately concluding: 'The canals proved a costly experiment.'[3]

That the canals brought with them unfortunate side-effects has never been in dispute. Contemporaries connected with rural matters were well aware of the canal's faults and official reports abound with references to the drawbacks. Dr Whitcombe brings together the criticisms and observations to be found in the reports. Strung together these outwardly present a formidable case against the canals: waterlogging was experienced in low-lying lands, particularly where drainage lines had been obstructed by water channels, and this encouraged the formation of *reh* (saline deposits) on the soil surface, increased the incidence of malaria, and periodically damaged standing crops; unlined wells fell in as the water-table rose, and cultivators were forced to rely on the canals' uncertain supply; the production of the staple food crops was diminished in favour of the more lucrative commercial crops—a situation felt particularly in years of drought when the canal, heavily committed for cash-crop production, could do little to decrease the ravages of scarcity; over-watering and the encouragement to over-cropping reduced soil fertility; the contraction of wastes made grazing land scarce; petty officials exploited their position of influence over the canal water supplies; and pastoral castes were seduced away from cattle thieving and breeding into more agricultural pursuits, thus reducing the supply of cattle to *Doab* cultivators.[4]

This indictment of the *Doab* canal schemes runs counter to the general view of them, which—with the exception of some rather unconvincing works condemning the canals, published in the 1870s[5] —accepts the existence of side-effects, but would not claim that overall the disadvantages more than balanced the positive effects. It immediately throws up questions. Why, for example, if the canals were unable to provide effective protection from famine and even increased susceptibility to it through diminishing staple food production, did successive Famine Commissions encourage their construction? Why, when the ill-effects were so well-known, did the construction and expansion activities continue throughout the period? Is it conceivable that the canals could be profitable to the rulers while exhibiting negative welfare effects overall? The basis of this unfavourable view of the canal's impact is really a subjective re-evaluation of the observations of contemporaries which have filtered down to us. Unfortunately the quality of Indian statistics—particularly output data—prohibits the kind of cost-benefit analysis of the direct and indirect effects which would allow quantitative precision in the assessment of the impact of canal irrigation. We are left to make the most of a mass of essentially qualitative data, mainly concerned with revenue matters. The important question is, what was the quantitative significance of these drawbacks in real terms? When arrayed *en masse* the disadvantages appear overwhelming, but were they likely, in fact, to outweigh the benefits? What follows is a closer look at the impact of the canal and a re-examination of some of the benefits and problems generally associated with its introduction into the peasant farmer's environment. If we are forced, as often happens, to rely on subjective evidence in examining historical topics, then it is important to place it into some sort of objective framework in order to obtain a correct perspective. The precise benefits and costs of the canal may always remain out of reach, but a careful examination of its effects may help to reconcile the contradictions noted above, as well as the apparent contradiction between the peasant's observed behaviour and peasant rationality.

II

The area upon which attention will be focused is the Ganges Canal Tract in the eastern part of the Muzaffarnagar district, situated in the upper *Doab*. The tract, 34 miles long and between 12–26 miles wide, consisted of 6 *parganas* bounded on the north by Saharanpur district, with Meerut to the south and the rivers Ganges and Kali to the east and west. It is sufficiently diverse in its characteristics to reflect many of the features found throughout the *Doab*: it possessed both rich loam soils and light, sandy *bhur*; it contained *khadir* (valley) areas as well as upland plain; its cultivators included Rajputs and Gujars as well as the industrious Jats. In natural facilities for irrigation, too, it exhibited contrasts. The extent of irrigation prior to the opening of the canal was both limited and unevenly distributed. While the river levels were too low to provide irrigation for the upland region lying between them, the possibilities for well irrigation were over wide areas restricted by the spring level being generally far below the surface, and by the prevalence of an unstable sandy subsoil, which made the low cost *kachha* (earthen) wells impractical. *Pakka* (masonry) wells were both expensive to construct and to work at such depths. E. Thornton's 1841 settlement report revealed a general pattern of pre-canal irrigation: only the south-western portion of the tract was irrigated, and of that an even smaller portion had any real security. To the north and east, where the sub-soil water was from 60 to 110 feet below the surface, irrigation was 'practically unknown'.[6] The situation was clearly not conducive to careful cultivation, as Thornton noted: 'The scarcity of wells leads to there being very few villages, the cultivators being obliged to locate themselves at such a distance from the fields as necessarily has an injurious effect upon the state of agriculture.'[7] This regional variation in access to sub-soil water resources is reflected in Table I, with the well-irrigated areas being largely confined to Khatauli and parts of Jansath and Muzaffarnagar. The irrigated areas contained in the table refer to the land irrigated in the normal course of cultivation, not that irrigated in any one year. Theoretically, land only irrigated in abnormal seasons, such as famine years, was excluded.[8] The general trend, how-

TABLE I

COMPARISON OF 'IRRIGATED' AREAS OVER TIME, GANGES CANAL TRACT (Acres)

Pargana	1841 Well	1872 Canal	1872 Well	1892 Canal	1892 Well
Purchhapar	53	19,997	48	21,192	58
Muzaffarnagar	3,133	19,140	1,522	25,262	306
Bhukarheri	162	23,878	39	25,530	29
Jansath	6,273	21,725	2,520	21,951	2,433
Khatauli	10,812	20,846	3,438	23,077	2,565
Bhuma Sambalhera	1,200	9,077	422	11,816	216
TOTAL	21,633	114,663	7,989	128,828	5,607

SOURCE: Compiled from settlement report statistics.

ever, is clear: total irrigation between 1841 and 1872 expanded six-fold, to some extent at the expense of well irrigation, which continued to decline throughout the period. The spread of irrigation facilities embraced the whole tract, as A. Cadell, the settlement officer, noted in 1872: 'Throughout the whole tract in which thirty years ago wholly dry villages were the rule, there are now hardly any left.'[9]

INNOVATION AND PEASANT AGRICULTURE

What were the repercussions of technical change on peasant production systems? The agricultural setting is probably best described by T. W. Schultz's phrase, 'the equilibrium of traditional agriculture', and is characterized by static technology and by unchanging preferences and motives of the cultivators themselves.[10] In the absence of technical advance, the marginal productivity of investment in additional agricultural factors declines to the point where there is no incentive to save for investment in them. The marginal rate of return to investment is known, and has 'existed long enough for an equilibrium to have become established between savings and investment and between the demand for and supply of agricultural factors as a source of income'.[11] The experience of generations enables the farmers to gravitate towards this kind of optimum solution to resource allocation. It is a state of agriculture typified by a low rate of capital accumulation and a preference for low risk, low return production rather than potentially larger—though less certain—returns to production involving greater production outlays. With little incentive to add to the stock of traditional capital—either because returns are relatively low, or, obversely, where the cost of traditional inputs is relatively high—cultivation is likely to stagnate: a state of affairs stemming from the constancy of the 'state of arts' causing the price of permanent income streams to be high.[12]

Into this stable and familiar setting came the canal—an innovation which, in many ways, was to revolutionize the agriculture of the tract. Its importance, in both the dry and well-irrigated areas, stemmed largely from the fact that it represented a significant departure from the traditional water supply technologies; it marked a break with the constancy in the 'state of arts'. Over large areas, traditional technology was unable to provide an opportunity for the bulk of cultivators economically to avail themselves of the sub-soil water resources. Not only did the canal make available a supply of water, but it required little investment in the actual water-providing process on the part of the recipient; funds could thus be channelled into investments which complemented the new input and thus increased its productivity. In areas which already had an indigenous water supply, resources tied up in well maintenance and operation could be redirected. A completely new cost structure was imposed by the canal, and its impact on perceptions of risk, on yield expectations, and the availability and productivity of factors of production, transformed the production possibilities in the canal tracts. Inasmuch as the canal used fewer resources in the actual provision of water than did wells, it could simply have been substituted for labour, bullocks and capital equipment with no effect on output. Indeed, Dr Whitcombe suggests that this was likely to have been the result.[13] The evidence of both the switch to more intensive cultivation patterns and the response of the Gujar communities suggests otherwise.[14] The evidence strongly supports the contention that the technical advance represented by the canal shifted upwards the labour-input/crop-output schedule sufficiently to raise the level of returns to the requisite additional labour input to attract it into use—although leisure preference may have led family farms to share the gains with hired labour.

As a result of the new production conditions, the long-standing 'automatic' nature of peasant decision-making had to be substantially revised. Although production adjustments reflected the change in the expected rates of return under the new conditions, the changes represented a complex process. No alterations were made in isolation, the repercussions involved the whole range of economic activity on the farm. One of the questions implicitly raised by the critics of the canal is whether this disturbance of equilibrium was not running out of the control of the individual cultivator.

(a) *The more intensive utilization of land: cropping pattern adjustments*

The cash crop *par excellence* in the Upper *Doab* was sugarcane, and the provision of canal facilities was followed by an expansion in the production of this thirsty crop. In the canal tract agricultural operations were then, as now, to a great extent regulated by the arrangements for its cultivation. Wrote Miller: 'It is regarded above all others as the rent-paying crop; and where the tenant has a fixed rent, and is not liable to a high crop-rate, he puts under cane as much land as the available supply of manure and a due regard for the rotation of crops allow.'[15] In terms of percentages of 1872 cultivated areas, settlement statistics show that from around 3–3.5 per cent (4.5 in Khatauli) in 1841, the *pargana* areas devoted to cane had risen, by 1892, to between just under 8 per cent in Purchhapar and upland Bhuma and 12.7 per cent in Khatauli. In all cases the largest increases had been registered before 1872, at which time Cadell noted the existence of canal estates in Khatauli which could boast 20 to 35 per cent of their cultivated area under cane.[16] That this was primarily the result of the expansion in canal irrigation rather than the opening of railway communications is shown by the fact that the great bulk of the sugar trade still followed the old route over unmetalled roads to Panipat and beyond.[17]

The statistics, however, do not adequately reflect the profound effect the canal had on the cultivation of sugarcane in the tract. Prior to the canal, the great bulk of the area had been sown on unirrigated land. This necessitated elaborate and factor-intensive preparation of the soil in order to maximize the absorption and retention of rain water. The field would be ploughed between fifteen and twenty times over the cold season, each ploughing followed by the use of the *merah* to pulverize the soil and protect the concealed moisture from the sun. The canal revolutionized the whole process: the large amounts of water made available by the canal reduced the need for such elaborate moisture-retaining activities, almost halving the number of preliminary ploughings required.[18] The labour and bullock power set free could be devoted to the larger areas under cane. But more than this, the canal had an important impact on yields in both the quality and quantity dimensions, and much of this derived from the adoption of higher-yielding varieties. Soon after the canal had opened, *agaul* cane was imported for the first time into Meerut from Bareilly and acclimatized in Gagual, a village near Meerut city. From there this thick cane spread into Muzaffarnagar where it quickly ousted the thin strain called *daulhu*, which had been 'all but universal' in 1841.[19] The spectacular success of *agaul* was later to be dampened by the repeated appearance of rind fungus, which caused such damage to the crop during the 1890s that cultivators replaced it with local forms of *ukh* cane; even so, the Upper *Doab* was still noted for 'the superior quality of the canes grown . . ., especially the *dhaur* cane, which', noted one investigator, 'is famous for its high outturn'.[20] Larger areas sown with cane along with heavier outturns put pressure—at times severe—on the cane-pressing capacity of the district, and this region was always the first to take advantage of the several developments in cane-crushing technology, which not only increased the extraction and quality of juice, but reduced both labour and bullock inputs.[21]

Along with sugarcane, rice dominated *kharif* irrigation, as Table II indicates, and this crop, too, underwent significant changes following the introduction of the canal. Encouraged by favourable canal rates, the area devoted to rice increased throughout the tract, particularly in Purchhapar where, between 1841 and 1872, it rose from 3.5 to around 10 per cent of the 1872 cultivated area. Like sugarcane, though, the extent of the changes is not fully reflected in the area

TABLE II

AVERAGE AREAS OF CROPS IN THE TRACT IRRIGATED BY THE CANAL
1869–70—1871–72 (Acres)

Sugarcane	Wheat	Rice	Cotton	Other Grains	Total Area Irrigated
14,291	32,017	15,885	814	6,278	70,436

SOURCE: *Muzaffarnagar DG* (1876): compiled from information on p. 483.

statistics. Important improvements occurred in both the quality of the product and its outturn. Fine rice, *munji*, was virtually unknown in the upland region before the opening of the canal; in 1841 rice was normally a dry crop and, except in the river valleys, was a less valuable coarse variety known as *dhan*. As Table III shows *munji* was a valuable commercial crop and—unlike *dhan*—was grown on the best land, always with a full supply of canal water. By 1872, rice grown on irrigated land was almost always *munji*.[22] Its profitability rivalled that of sugarcane, particularly at times of high grain prices when the quickly-ripening *munji* crop could be followed by gram in the cold season.

TABLE III

PRICES AND YIELDS OF MAJOR CROPS[23]

	Sugarcane (*Gur*)	Cotton	*Munji*	*Dhan*	*Bajra*	Wheat	Gram
Produce/Acre (Maunds)	33.9	2.8	21.9	18.2	7.0	16.9	18.7
Average Prices 1861–73 (Rupees per Maund)	2.6	16.0	1.3	1.0	1.7	2.0	1.6

SOURCES: Yield statistics are selected village estimates, A. Cadell, *Muzaffarnagar SR* (1878), p. 21. Market price data are converted figures from ibid., p. xlii and *Muzaffarnagar SR* (1892), p. 43.

The most valuable *rabi* crop, wheat, showed relatively slight progress in area extension—rather surprisingly, when the impact of the canal in other tracts is considered. For the five *parganas* for which data is available,[24] the proportion of area under wheat remains fairly constant, though in fact, when the increase in cultivated area is taken into account, the period 1841–72 saw the area recorded under wheat increase from 50,729 to 63,146 acres; in addition 7,326 acres are recorded in 1872 as under 'wheat and barley', at least some of which must have been subsumed under 'wheat'. Even so, the expansion of wheat was clearly inhibited by the fact that the expansion of cane, rice, and fodder crops limited the availability of good land. Indeed, the 1903 Gazetteer records that it was a sign of 'careful cultivation' that wheat was often found on poorer soils.[25] On such land it was likely to be sown as a mixed crop, whereas one of the features of wheat sown in good soil with canal irrigation was the high proportion sown alone.

A less clear pattern emerges for other crops over this period. Cotton, the irrigation of which was both irregular and relatively unimportant until the early years of this century, remained overall a marginal crop; it was unable to compete with the other major crops for good land, labour and manure. Acreage movements in other crops, the cheaper *kharif* millets, for example, are particularly difficult to gauge, since they were to a great extent sown according to relatively short-term requirements and sowing conditions. Single-season comparisons have to be viewed sceptically at all times, but especially so when dealing with the cheap and flexible crops such as *jowar* and *bajra*. In a general sense, though, it is possible to identify from the information available, movements which are meaningful in the context of the introduction of a canal-orientated system of agricultural production, and which gain substantiation from trends noticeable elsewhere.

The poor *kharif* crops, such as *bajra*, clearly declined—particularly in those areas with larger proportions of good soil and access to canal irrigation. The more developed the *pargana* the smaller the area occupied by rain-crops such as *bajra*. Although the canal rarely watered the poorer crops—irrigation made little difference to their outturn during normal seasons—its effects extended to them nevertheless. Not only were resources diverted to the production of more cash crops, but the area under fodder crops, too, expanded.[26] The more suitable the soil, when cultivated in conjunction with the canal, the more pressure was exerted by these crops on the coarse *kharif* food crops. Their share of the harvest fell, it is true, but in effect the production of coarse food crops was simply switched to that of *rabi*. While the average *bajra* acreage in Khatauli had fallen to 630 between 1877 and 1888, the area under gram and peas had more than trebled, to stand at 5,794 acres, around 11 per cent.[27] As Miller noted, referring to the tract as a whole: 'there has been a decided increase in the cultivation of gram and peas and a decline in that of the less important kharif staples.'[28] The shift indicated is important in itself, since poor *kharif* grains signified careless cultivation and a shift to the *rabi* was indicative of the existence of irrigation facilities and of increased levels of input in the production of a more valuable output. Compare, for example, the price–yield relationship between gram and *bajra* in Table III. The most likely explanation for this shift is to be found in the fact that the commercial crops required substantial factor inputs, and that the switching of the less valuable crops to *rabi* freed factors for the cultivation and processing of the more valuable ones. In this way the demand for factors would be balanced between the seasons; family labour capacity and the seasonal price of hired labour in such tracts would also encourage this balance in decision-making. Moreover, the presence of the canal as a safeguard should the late autumn rains fail, meant that the switch was not a threat to the security of food supplies that the other system may have provided.

These, then, are the essential features of the tract's cropping patterns over the period. The movements occurred within the framework of an increase in the upland's total cultivated area from 221,423 acres in 1841 to 263,997 thirty years later, a growth of 19 per cent. Only 7 per cent of this came from extension into wasteland. 'Cultivable wastes'—land which had either never come under the plough, or had not been cultivated for the previous five years—fell by around 10,000 acres (35 per cent) in this period. The largest contribution came from the reduction in 'recent fallow'—'that lying uncultivated for three years'—which fell from 32,000 acres to 6,000.[30] Marginal land this may have been, but its value must be seen in that it released a portion of the better land from staple food production to the cultivation of market crops. In addition to the expansion in the area cultivated, further output was obtained through an expansion in *dofasli* (double cropped) area. Figures are unreliable on this as far as the early part of the period is concerned, but Cadell estimated that the *dofasli* area had 'at least doubled' since Thornton's time, and that 10 per cent of the upland area, and 20 per cent of the irrigated area, was cultivated the whole year round.[31]

(b) *Re-allocation of resources resulting from risk-reduction*

The aggregate shifts in the cropping patterns obviously conceal a vast array of reactions by cultivators producing under a variety of conditions. What was the mechanism by which individual farmers adjusted to the new conditions? Where all, or a substantial part of, a holding was under dry cultivation, the introduction of canal water would have the effect of reducing yield variability, raising average yields and extending the range of production. Cultivation under the uncertainty of dry conditions is severely constrained by the large proportion of resources required to secure subsistence, and by the risk of losses associated with costly valuable crops which, because of their relatively high moisture requirements, are especially susceptible to rainfall shortages. Under these conditions the full potential of available resources is not realized: production is wasteful because of the overriding need to reduce risk. The main feature of the system is one where future risk losses are converted where possible into currently budgeted fixed costs—in other words, into a variety of indigenous insurance programmes, such as crop-sharing rent systems, substantial reserve maintenance, a high degree of product diversification, and an overwhelming concentration on food crops of low market value. The main cost of uncertainty is, therefore, output foregone.[32]

Broadly speaking, the canal tended to vastly increase the security of investment in the production of valuable crops: an adequate water supply not only increased their yields, in many cases they simply could not be grown without an artificial supply of water. Less benefit accrued to the subsistence crops whose yields benefited from irrigation only in an unusually dry season. Nevertheless, as will be shown, the canal did provide a degree of security to such staple food supplies in times of rain shortage. Given the relative effects of watering the different classes of crops, it is clear that the new production possibility curve facing the cultivator who has just obtained canal irrigation would show a substantial shift in favour of commercial rather than subsistence production. This differential effect was indeed likely to encourage commercial rather than staple crop production, but was it likely to be at the expense of such foodstuffs? The evidence suggests not.

For the individual cultivator, it was not only the enhanced possibilities for the cultivation of commercial crops, but the protective properties of the canal as well, which exerted an important influence over the choice of output mix. Peasant-cultivator utility functions tend to place a high value on self-sufficiency; it constitutes a vital part of their policy of risk-minimization, since insufficient provision of food can be disastrous when—as is likely—food crop shortfalls on the farm coincide with general harvest failure and high grain prices. Generally speaking, therefore, the area devoted to commercial crops is thus limited by the need to ensure subsistence; the farmer who allocates away from subsistence production runs the risk of having to purchase consumption requirements at an unfavourable price ratio. He is thus likely to discount price-relationships between subsistence and commercial crops quite substantially and allocate sufficient acreage to food crops for full farm requirements in a year of below normal yields. The relative unprofitability of his surplus of most years—its market price *vis-à-vis* that of the foregone valuable crop—in effect represents the size of the risk premium for his protection.[33]

The increased security the canal imparted to food supplies through reducing the likelihood of serious shortfalls, meant that fewer resources were required to ensure subsistence output levels. 'Even in a year of plentiful rain, when the canal is not much used, it still performs its role as an insurer', observed H. A. Brownlow, the Chief Engineer of Irrigation, in 1872.[34] The canal's influence, therefore, extended beyond the area normally irrigated, and when F. Henvey observed that 'farmers will only take canal water to save, not to improve, the coarser crops', he was, in fact, observing this mechanism of insurance.[35] More important, though, the canal safeguarded *rabi* sowings. *Kharif* coarse crops were seldom crucial to a cultivator able to make up for a deficiency caused by a dry summer by putting down a large *rabi* area with the aid of canal water. Canal irrigation was important for this crop, to counter the effects of an autumn too dry to permit any sowings, or too scanty to permit a full area to be prepared quickly enough. The cultivator operating in a canal village could therefore generally place more reliance on his food supplies and thus release some of his resources—primarily land—to extend his production of market crops.

How does this square with Dr Whitcombe's pessimism regarding the impact of the canal, particularly in drought years, on staple food supplies? She writes: 'Generally speaking, canal irrigation did, and could do, little to decrease the ravages of scarcity by expanding the sources of staple food supply; indeed its effect tended to be the reverse, to contract them.'[36] For some producers, it is perfectly possible that the high returns to commercial production led them to discount the importance of subsistence outturn: where, for example, a cash crop was rice or wheat, it could be converted to home consumption should normal subsistence crops prove insufficient.[37] On the whole however, the evidence does not support the contention that the staple food supply was prejudiced by the existence of the canal. Detailed analysis of village crop statistics from Aligarh district, derived from the *pargana* handbook, points to the same conclusion:

that the decline in the area under *kharif* coarse food crops is misleading as an indication of the real food situation, since a portion of that category of crops was switched to the *rabi* season where, though more expensive to produce, the yields of gram and barley were larger and their market value greater.

Since it is a feature of peasant farming that priority is given to meeting subsistence requirements, and since the canal enabled commercial crop production to expand substantially without contracting the production of food crops, it is reasonable to contend that the majority of cultivators in canal villages were able to supply their own food requirements, or at least make secure provision for them. The landless labourers and cultivators with inadequate holdings, however, had less control over their food sources, and were the ones most likely to suffer due to a contraction in the supply of foodstuffs. Is there any indication here that the new conditions in the canal tract affected them adversely? It would appear that this was not the case. The spread of irrigation facilities meant that water was no longer the major constraint to reaping a greater return from cultivation; the most important limiting factor was now, in most areas, labour. The resulting high productivity of this resource tended to be reflected in a buoyant demand for the labourer's services, as Miller noted: 'the difficulty and expense of procuring labourers is a frequent subject of complaint amongst well-to-do cultivators.'[38] The increased demand for labour was also more sustained throughout the year. The canal made cultivation less dependent on the dictates of nature and the expansion of labour-intensive crops, particularly sugarcane, gave rise to a large demand for labour, not only for cultivation, but for processing and for transportation. It was, indeed, the western part of the U.P. which was the high real-wage region, as Cadell noticed in 1872: 'The labourer in Muzaffarnagar dresses better than the average petty proprietor of the eastern districts, and wheat now forms a much larger proportion than of old of the food of the poorest classes.'[39] The quotation suggests another reason why the decline in *kharif* food staples was a less disturbing phenomenon than it outwardly appears. The increasing incomes of this period were reflected in changing consumption patterns. W. H. Moreland enquired into this matter in 1901 and concluded that the Meerut division was 'as a whole a wheat-eating tract'.[40] There are very strong reasons for questioning the existence of a contraction in food supplies available either to the cultivating units or their hired labour, while the urban wage levels predictably responded to those of the villages.

A development of this issue concerns the role of the canal in years of drought. Dr Whitcombe is sceptical as to the canal's usefulness in decreasing the 'ravages of scarcity'. Certainly the canal was not employed to raise extensive crops of *kharif* millets when the monsoons failed. Although the canal had advantages over the well in such conditions—wells tended to dry up and bullocks lifting the water suffered severely in the heat—the efficiency of both was limited by the shrivelling effect on the crops of the scorching winds accompanying dry summers, and the cultivators preferred to use canal water on their commercial crops. Canal facilities were, however, invaluable for the autumn sowings, which were of crucial importance when the summer crops failed. If the autumn months were dry, it became impossible, even with wells, to put down a substantial *rabi* area. With canal water at his disposal the cultivator had the capacity to prepare, sow and ensure the germination of a substantial cold-season crop. The drought of 1868–9, when scarcely any rain fell in the district from late July to February, demonstrated this: the rain crops failed in the unirrigated portion of the upland, and the *rabi* sowings were virtually confined to the irrigable area. Whereas in a typical year around 70,500 acres were watered by the canal, in the famine year 91,590 acres were sown with the aid of the canal in the *rabi* season alone.[41] Assisted by rains falling in February, the yields were described as good.

With the development of trade and communications, the nature of 'famine' in simple terms had changed from being a condition whereby the food supply was insufficient to feed the people, to one primarily of acute unemployment due to the cessation of fieldwork which resulted in a large part of the population being unable to purchase food.[42] It was in this respect that the canal's *kharif* performance was important; it gave substantial protection to the labour-intensive cash crops. While the *kharif* crops in dry areas withered or remained unsown, and while the exhaustion of his cattle led many a cultivator to give up using his well and look hopefully to the *rabi*, the canal villages were tolerably secure against the loss of their commercial crops and made large profits out of their surplus food crops.[43] 'The labouring class of this tract', wrote Cadell, 'has the advantage of continuous employment throughout the year . . .; and they are not exposed to the loss, distress, and danger caused by droughts.'[44] Throughout the *Doab*, in fact, far from constituting a weakness in the face of drought, the canal villages were the focus of immigration from unirrigated villages in dry seasons; as evidence for 1868–9, and 1896–7 shows, these villages contained considerable stocks of food.[45] Further testimony to this is provided by an observation by Cadell in *pargana* Muzaffarnagar: 'with one trifling exception the population has fallen off in every village in the pergunnah which is not watered from the canal. The single exception is the little village of Sitherali, situated between two sand hills but surrounded by canal irrigated estates, which in years of drought afford employment and subsistence.'[46]

(c) *The interaction of irrigation technologies: the implications for factor supplies*

The impact of the canal was no less dramatic in areas previously protected by wells than it was in dry areas. This point is important in a wider context, since it was an observed tendency—particularly in the earlier years—for the canals to encroach upon well areas. The general effect of the introduction of the innovation into well tracts was the substitution of canal for well irrigation. Much criticism of the *Doab* canals revolved around the tendency of the enhanced water-tables, which occurred in the vicinity of the canal and its distributaries, to result in the destruction of *kachha* wells.[47] This widespread destruction was less noticeable in the Muzaffarnagar Canal Tract, since not only was water comparatively far below the surface, but the sandy subsoil meant that there was a high proportion of masonry wells. If there are doubts about the exact comparability of the available well irrigation statistics, the dramatic decline is unmistakable: from over 21,000 acres in 1841, the area watered by wells fell to 9,620 in 1860–1, 8,000 a decade later, and by 1901–2 reached 5,476. The substitution was not confined to earthen wells, but the masonry and half-masonry wells fell into disuse, even though the rise in water-level actually added to their working power. The main cause, according to Bulandshahr's settlement officer, of the switch from wells to canals was 'undoubtedly the preference most tenants show for the latter'.[48]

The general preference shown by Muzaffarnagar cultivators for canal water reflected a theme which ran the length of the *Doab*. This reaction was perfectly understandable where, for example, the water supply and hence irrigating capacity was limited to that which percolated slowly into the bottom of the well, or where the well water was brackish and hence unsuitable for the germination of crops, as in Muttra.[49] However for two reasons, the abandonment of good wells in the south-western part of the Canal Tract was outwardly surprising. First, whereas costs associated with well irrigation were largely of the non-monetary kind—involving the use of inputs employed in the normal operations of cultivation and available on the farm—the cost of canal water was a cash payment and it is therefore likely that the cultivator would discount the relative costs in favour of the non-cash technology. Second, evidence suggests that for certain crops the yields were higher with well than canal irrigation—as S. N. Martin observed, 'well water gives much heavier crops than canal water. All the zemindars agree on this point.'[50] Clearly, for some reason the new form of water technology was preferable to the cultivator, sufficiently so to outweigh these disadvantages. Dr Whitcombe seems to imply at times that leisure preference was the force behind the switch from the toil of well irrigation to the canal. There is, however, another interpretation—important from the point of view of our understanding of peasant motivation—which holds that the switch to the canal was a perfectly rational adjustment within the framework of production processes, and independent of leisure preference. It can be shown, in fact, that the substitution had a positive effect on production.

Assuming no effective limitation on the water supply in the well itself, the limited capacity of this form of irrigation stemmed from the inability of the cultivator to lift more water: 'if a farmer has to work his well he cannot sow more sugar and wheat than he has time to irrigate', observed C. H. Crosthwaite.[51] It is from this point of view that it is possible to appreciate why the wholesale switch away from perfectly good wells occurred. The very factors required in the actual raising of water were those which could be otherwise utilized in cultivation operations associated with an expansion in production. Well irrigation, as a form of water technology, competed for the productive resources which could only be used to raise water at the expense either of the quality of, or the area under, cultivation.[52] It was not, in fact, a very efficient way of irrigating: the labour of three men and a pair of bullocks for five or six days being necessary to irrigate an acre, while 'flow' irrigation required only two labourers and 'almost any quantity of land' could be irrigated in a day.[53] Moreover, the factors released by the switch to the more efficient source of irrigation were highly complementary to the new water input. In Khatauli, for instance, the bullock-power released from the treadmill of water-raising on nearly 7,000 acres was 'sufficient for all the work connected with the increased cane cultivation, and for the ploughing of 10,000 acres besides'.[54] The saving in labour—especially important because of the flexibility of its use and its relation to direct capital formation—was unquestionably the reason behind the more largely increased area, and the more generally maintained quality of the cane crop.[55] Cadell's Rent-Rate Report for Khatauli provides a good example: adjoining first class villages of Bhainsi, Sontah and Dudaheri—all quite closely cultivated under well irrigation—there were, prior to the canal, the estates of Raipur Nagli with a small hamlet, and Sherpur and Jahangirpur entirely uninhabited. All three were cultivated extensively, inferior crops being grown. They were carelessly cultivated by tenants who 'however industrious, had plenty to do in their own villages'.[56] When canal irrigation came to be substituted for that of wells in Bhainsi, Sontah and Dudaheri, 'the men and cattle working at the wells were set free, and at once began to improve the cultivation in their own and adjoining townships'.[57] The introduction of the canal raised the irrigated area in the adjoining estates from 10 to 80 per cent of the cultivated area, and within a short time their crop patterns corresponded to those of the hitherto far advanced villages.

Those *parganas* formerly dry responded more slowly to the introduction of the canal; complementary inputs moved equally slowly into line with the new production conditions since there was comparatively little labour displaced from well duty. The population only gradually expanded to meet the increased demand, it was—as Cadell observed in Purchhapar in 1869—'not in a position to make such inroads on the *bhoor* as were effected elsewhere. The Jats and Tagas, notwithstanding the progress they have made, are still merely working on the edges of the sand waste, while the people of Khutowlee have caused *bhoor* to disappear from estates in which it once formed a large area.'[58]

The value of the released productive factors was clearly an important reason—along with his increased involvement with the market and monetization—why the cultivator overcame his aversion to cash outlays for water. In addition to this, once the canal's impact on cropping patterns is considered, it becomes clear why canal water was preferred to that of the well—even though some crop yields could be lower on canal watered land. The high unit costs of water obtained from wells ensured that the supply was carefully applied to the limited area it would cover, and that such land was meticulously cultivated. This meant that this land would have priority over the manure supply; it grew almost invariably the most valuable crops, and large quantities of labour were lavished upon it. Canal water was not paid for according to volume. Its cheapness in terms of quantity encouraged the cultivator both to dispense with the high degree of input intensity he had had to lavish upon his well-irrigated plot in order to obtain favourable returns on the expense—including opportunity cost—of lifting well water, and also to spread inputs over a larger area. With the increased supply of water which was cheaper in terms of resources, the cultivator could expect an acceptable rate of return on land, the intensive cultivation of which would not have been possible when he relied on his well. The cultivator therefore irrigated a larger area than before, though on average he cultivated it less intensively than he had his fields near his well. On balance, he forfeited some of the output he could have expected from his well-watered fields, but gained from the cultivation of better quality crops on land previously only infrequently irrigated, if at all. In other words, the canal enabled the farmer to increase the total product of his holding, and this seems to have been the general response—as reflected in the observation that 'the whole tendency of Jat and Rawa cultivators is to secure a large average produce, rather than the excessive large average of a few fields'.[59] It is to this tendency that the existence of the yield differentials—where they did exist—is to be largely attributed.

III

External Diseconomies—A Closer Look at the Waterlogging Problem

In the area under discussion the problem of excess water breaks down into two parts: (1) the waterlogging afflicting the *khadir* (valley) areas of Bhuma, Bhukarheri and Purchhapar; (2) saturation problems in the upland plain resulting from the percolation from water channels, the tendency of cultivators to make lavish use of a water-supply charged for by crop-area rather than by volume, and insufficient attention to drainage facilities on the part of the canal engineers.

Within five years of the opening of the canal, *khadir* revenue assessments were reduced, and the pattern established for the rest of the century. The effects upon the *khadir* of canal irrigation of the uplands represents, in fact, a classic case of external diseconomies: the level of consumption of canal water by the upland farmers directly harming the interests of the cultivators in the valleys—mainly the Ganges *khadir*. Water lavished on the uplands percolated down into the valley where it exacerbated a natural tendency to saturation in the soil—particularly below the cliffs where *reh* and swamp-land increased. Nearer to the Ganges, where the land was slightly higher, less damage occurred to the soil, the quality of which was similar to that of the plain. Early official attempts to attribute deterioration in the *khadir* to causes other than the canal soon gave way to the obvious reality: 'It seems that as long as the canal is running, two-thirds of the *khadir* can never form other than a precarious, fever-stricken tract where cultivation is not only financially insecure, but is only possible at risk of health.'[60] The *khadir* mirrored in reverse the effects of the new technology on the upland, and the considerable expenditure by the authorities on drainage did little more than slightly slow the decline. All but the highest and sandiest fields below the upland deteriorated and the area under cultivation declined. It is not possible to give an overall statistical impression of the decline, but the fate of a group of villages in the Solani *khadir*, which adjoins that of the Ganges in the north, seems to reflect the general trend. Here the cultivation of wheat, cane and cotton all contracted as the cultivation declined from almost 1,500 acres before the canal to 840 by the 1870s. Cane was by then only to be found in one village, while even rice had fallen—both in area and in quality of output.[61] Over a matter of several thousand acres of lowland in the *khadir*, rents fell as the population thinned and the fertility of the land declined.

It is important, however, that this essentially unfavourable view is not left unqualified, since the canal's impact in this respect was more complex than it at first appears: the tract's deterioration was not entirely due to the canal's encouragement to saturation; nor do the cultivation trends reflect fully the *khadir*'s relative importance in the agriculture of the area. Prior to the introduction of the canal, the adjacent upland areas were often extremely insecure and parts of the *khadir* were, for some villages, the only areas in which 'produce was tolerably assured'.[62] Generally, though, it was 'unfit for residence' and the cultivators often lived in the 'strong populous villages' on the uplands from which they descended into the *khadir* to grow some of their crops—the output here being more certain than on the upland. If the expected output of these *khadir* crops fell with the introduction of the canal, so the yields of their upland crops increased. A perfectly natural reallocation of resources towards the general area of greater returns meant that production in the valleys would inevitably decline—just as the population in the dry villages was observed to decline in favour of the canal villages.[63] At the same time, if the *khadir* became less important for its agricultural produce, its importance as a grazing ground and fuel source was enhanced both by the contraction of waste on the upland, and by the increased demand for bullocks. Through releasing factors to upland cultivation, the *khadir* contributed to the progress of the canal villages at the expense of its own cultivation. The *khadir* had always been considered an unhealthy area in which to live, and that reason alone was sufficient to limit its development potential.

Although *reh* was seldom encountered in the upland tract, certain localities were prone to periodic waterlogging, particularly during the early stages of canal irrigation, before the importance of the crucial technical requirement—that the alignment of irrigation channels should follow the watersheds—became fully recognized. The extensive remodelling of the *rajbaha* (water channel) system during the 1870s and after had as its aim the correction of a situation whereby, at first, 'distributary after distributary was run out without regard for the drainage of the country, and . . . there was no practical admission of the necessity of allowing waterway under the irrigation channels'.[64] The abandonment of the original Jansath *rajbaha* occurred as part of the attempt to correct some of the original design defects of the system. Funds gradually filtered through, too, to enable drainage channels to be dug, and the Kali river to be straightened and deepened. These measures greatly improved the situation, though they cannot be said to have removed all the waterlogging problems which accompanied the canal. The engineers 'learnt by doing', even if the improvements were only slowly and imperfectly put into practice.

Indications as to the acreages affected by waterlogging in the tract are not available, and would be of limited use if they were, since it is the *degree* of the problem which is the most important from the agricultural viewpoint. For example, abnormal rains in the 1880s caused a great deal of waterlogging, but although this was felt by Miller to have affected the productiveness of the soil, it was only in low-lying places that this had occurred to a 'serious extent'.[65] Elsewhere, waterlogging was observed to prevent *kharif* cultivation, but leave the soil sufficiently moist to allow *rabi* sowings without the aid of irrigation.[66] Clearly the effects of waterlogging varied considerably; they were not always negative. It was quite usual for saturated fields to be devoted to cattle, since they provided water and forage of some kind;[67] furthermore, where *kharif* fields under sugarcane became waterlogged for a time, it was likely that the crop would not suffer serious injury.[68] It seems that, as with other disadvantages and changes, the cultivator adapted to the particular characteristics of the saturation tendencies in his land in accordance with the rates of return and risk associated with its various uses. This adaptation is probably reflected in Miller's observation that the evidence of rent movements was 'against the view that there has been any serious deterioration', and in the remark contained in the 1903 gazetteer that a full supply of canal flow-irrigation was the most valuable quality land could have, and that it commanded a high rent 'even where there is danger of saturation'.[69] The resilience of sugarcane, the suitability of rice cultivation, and the ability to sow *rabi* crops without irrigation are three important reasons why the 'test of competition rents [was] against the theory of deterioration' in the tracts prone to saturation.[70]

In part, too, the problem of saturation was one brought on more by prosperity than by the design faults of the canal system. Increases in product prices and the expansion of population induced farmers to cultivate land which, at the time of the canal's construction, had been much less in demand. Some of the land brought into cultivation during the three decades following 1841 was land which made up the wide margins left around ponds and depressions in Thornton's time; only in seasons of exceptional rain did the flooding of the cultivated areas cause much damage. The encroachment of such lands made flooding likely with less than exceptional levels of rainfall, and Cadell noticed a tendency to blame the canal for what was only '. . . a natural result of the increased value of land which thirty years ago was allowed to lie waste, while it now swells the profits of the landlord in a dry year and intensifies the outcry against the [canal] department in a year of plentiful rain.'[71]

IV

The introduction of canal irrigation into eastern Muzaffarnagar set off a complex series of repercussions which left virtually none of the region's inhabitants untouched. Both dry and canal villages were affected, as all agricultural groups, from the landless labourers to the landowning *zamindars*, from the small cultivating tenants to the sturdy peasant-proprietors, and from the industrious Jats to the law-abiding Gujars and the lowly Chamars, adjusted their activities to suit the rates of return associated with the new production conditions. The overall impression is of a substantial contribution to wealth and security, and the larger returns to, and demand for, factors of production—particularly that most vulnerable section, farm labourers—meant that it was unequal gains, rather than actual gains and losses, which accrued to rural society's component groups. As in all periods of economic change, some groups benefited more than others from the adjustments, and our knowledge of the institutional framework leads us to expect that not only would rich peasants be able to benefit most by directly employing the new technique, but that it would also provide them with further opportunities to extend their influence and control within the village community. It was to labour's advantage, though, that an innovation which had the effect of making labour a comparatively scarce input was not accompanied by the kind of labour-saving complementary technology which has been available in the era of the Green Revolution.

What emerges from this brief glimpse of these six *parganas* is an impression of an energetic response to the new production conditions. Far from being helplessly buffeted by the uncontrollable force of change applied indiscriminately from without—as the deterioration of the *khadir* and the destruction of wells would tend to suggest—cultivators had more control over circumstances than many critics recognized. A close examination of the observed adjustments suggests that they conform to a pattern which our knowledge of peasant motivation and rationality would predict. Peasants, in fact, did not suddenly forget the importance of securing their food supplies—and there is ample evidence that their reluctance to use canal water on coarse autumn food crops during drought years was entirely consistent with the provision of the family's subsistence. Nor did they allow simple leisure preferences to dictate their choice of irrigation technology. Good cultivators, I would argue, did not suddenly become careless ones when they brought canal water to their fields, as many contemporaries implied. It is entirely rational for a cultivator to 'over-water' his crops, for example, if there exists uncertainty over the timing of his next supply of water; perhaps a definition of what 'over-cropping' actually entailed should precede any indictment of the cultivator for following such a practice. It is vital in examining such issues to understand the conditions under which production decisions were made by the various classes of cultivators. It has been the aim of this paper to point out that contemporary comment, when used outside a basic theoretical framework, can result in a misleading impression. Once the qualitative evidence is set into perspective, a more favourable view of the canal's impact—and of peasant adaptability—emerges.

NOTES

The research for this paper was financed by the Social Science Research Council, in the form of a doctoral studentship. It has benefited from the helpful comments of Dr Clive Dewey and Dr W. J. Macpherson, neither of whom is responsible for the views advanced.

1 *Report of the Indian Irrigation Commission 1901–3*, *Parliamentary Papers* [hereafter PP], 1904, LXVI, p. 182.

2 Ibid. The proportion of well protection is calculated from the statistics of R. Baird Smith, *Report on the Famine of 1860–61 in the NWP of India*, cited in E. Whitcombe, *Agrarian Conditions in North India* (Berkeley, California, 1972), pp. 67–8.

3 Whitcombe, *Agrarian Conditions*, p. 91.

4 Ibid., pp. 64–91.

5 A. F. Corbett, *Climate and Resources of Upper India* (London, 1874). Corbett believed that all irrigation was unnecessary and urged deeper cultivation as the key to agricultural advance. W. T. Thornton, *Indian Public Works* (London, 1875), commented upon this on p. 128: 'it is all the more to be regretted that Col. Corbett should have damaged a good case by exaggeration, and that he did not content himself with putting forward his proposals as supplementary to, instead of substitutes for, irrigation.' See also A. K. Connell, *The Economic Revolution and the Public Works Policy* (London, 1883), pp. 121–4 for further criticisms of the canals.

6 A. Cadell, *Muzaffarnagar Settlement Report* (*Ganges Canal Tract*) [hereafter SR], (1878) p. 67.

7 Quoted in ibid., p. 67.

8 The average area actually watered by the canal between 1863–4 and 1870–1 was 77,530 crop-acres. In the drought year, 1868–9, the figure rose to 128,203 —around half the total cultivated area.

(Throughout, unless otherwise indicated, all statistics are taken from settlement reports.)

9 SR (1878), p. 67.

10 T. W. Schultz, *Transforming Traditional Agriculture* (New Haven, 1964), pp. 30–2.

11 See H. Singh, 'Resource Allocation and Enterprise Combinations—A Case Study of UP Farms', *Agricultural Situation in India*, December 1967, pp. 987–96.

12 See P. Panikar, 'Capital Formation in Indian Agriculture', *Indian Journal of Agricultural Economics*, 24:4 (1969), 31–44.

13 Whitcombe, *Agrarian Conditions*, p. 80. She writes: 'Far from firing [the cultivator] with the much-heralded spirit of industriousness which increase was assumed to bring, canal irrigation required less by way of labour than his well had demanded.'

14 'With the less industrious castes . . . increased certainty of the result gives the required incentive to industry, and both on the east and west side of this district there are many Rajput and Gujar communities which have been, comparatively speaking, reformed by what appears to be the most effectual civilizing agent at our disposal—canal water given flush. It is at all events curious to notice the comparative oblivion into which once notorious communities have passed since their estates came under irrigation from the canal, while their neighbours of the same clan, and the same old habits, but without any fresh inducement to adopt an honest life, have more than upheld their ancient evil reputation.' E. T. Atkinson, ed., *Statistical, Descriptive and Historical Account of the NW Provinces of India*, Volume III (Allahabad, 1876) [hereafter *Muzaffarnagar DG*], p. 708. Even the weavers, smiths, carpenters, barbers, *purohits* and *fakirs* substituted agricultural for their former pursuits, finding it 'more paying than hereditary callings'. J. Miller, *Muzaffarnagar SR* (1892), p. 48.

15 SR (1892), p. 27.

16 A. Cadell, 'Rent Rate Report, Pergunnah Khataoli' (1871), p. 65. Uttar Pradesh State Archives, Lucknow [hereafter UPSA], Board of Revenue Records [hereafter BR], 'Different Districts', Muzaffarnagar, File 35, Box 8.

17 A. Cadell, 'Rent Rate Report, Pergunnah Jansath', (1872), p. 9. UPSA, BR, 'Different Districts', Muzaffarnagar, File 29, Box 5.

18 See SR (1878), pp. 19–20 for additional details.

19 S. M. Hadi, *The Sugar Industry in the UP* (Allahabad, 1902), p. 52. The same widespread adoption of superior varieties was noted in neighbouring Meerut where, by the early 1870s, it was recorded that 'the cane that was most generally grown in 1807 is now everywhere considered the most inferior of all the four sorts cultivated in this district'. *Meerut DG* (1876), p. 226.

20 S. M. Hadi, op. cit., p. 110.

21 See J. F. Duthie and J. B. Fuller, *Field and Garden Crops of the NW Provinces and Oudh*, Part I (Roorkee, 1882), p. 58.

22 SR (1878), p. 20.

23 These figures are subject to all the reservations concerning agricultural statistics. They do, however, reflect in a general sense the pattern of yield-price relationships.

24 Crop figures for Bhuma were not included in the 1841 settlement report.

25 H. R. Nevill, *District Gazetteers of the United Provinces of Agra and Oudh*, Vol. III, Muzaffarnagar District (Allahabad, 1903), p. 40.

26 *Jowar*, normally planted thick as *chari* for fodder, also competed for inputs in the *kharif* season. Its area increased significantly between the reports of Martin and Cadell—up to a level of 10 per cent of the cultivated area in Khatauli—and continued afterwards. Dr Whitcombe is critical of the expansion of cultivation into the waste lands reducing fodder supplies: this was just one aspect of the ecological revolution which the canals helped to bring about and which 'most farmers' techniques were not adapted to deal with' (op. cit., p. 90). The evidence, however, suggests otherwise: 'The spread of cultivation . . . rather increases than reduces the fodder supply', observed the Director of Agriculture and Commerce. Fodder derived from crops was more valuable than the grass of uncultivated lands, and the *Doab* in particular was not favourable for the growth of grass. Moreover, this grass tended to fail everywhere in times of drought. Far from being forced into stall-feeding, the cultivator benefited from a change whereby the new possibilities for irrigated cultivation on the good soils made the marginal land, on which useful food and fodder crops could be raised, far too valuable, through their ability to release better land from food production, to be left underutilized. See North Western Provinces & Oudh [hereafter NWP&O] Revenue Department Proceedings, Part A [hereafter Rev Progs], October 1885, p. 15.

27 L. P. Varma, 'Handbook of Pargana Khatauli', (1892), pp. 22–3. U.P. BR Library, Lucknow, Class IVc(7).

28 SR (1892), p. 42.

29 The increase thereafter was slight: 269,738 acres was the figure for 1892.

30 SR (1878), pp. 63–4.

31 Ibid., p. 21.

32 See R. Schickele, 'Farmers' Adaptations to Income Uncertainty', *Journal of Farm Economics*, 32:3 (1950), 356–74.

33 See J. Mellor, *The Economics of Agricultural Development* (Ithaca, N.Y., 1970), p. 201.

34 *NWP Irrigation Revenue Report* [hereafter IRR] 1871–2 (Allahabad, 1872), p. ii.

35 F. Henvey, *Narrative of Drought and Famine* (Allahabad, 1871), pp. 113–14.

36 Whitcombe, *Agrarian Conditions*, p. 75.

37 Cultivators on very small holdings, who survive by hiring out their labour in addition to farming their own plot, often exhibit a high proportion of cash crops in their cropping patterns, due to their dependence on the market to provide circulating capital. See K. Bharadwaj, *Production Conditions in Indian Agriculture* (Cambridge, 1974), pp. 62–3.

38 SR (1892), p. 23.

39 SR (1878), pp. 17–18. This was noticeable in other canal tracts; see, for example, H. Le Poer Wynne, *Saharanpur SR* (1870), p. 138: 'Such is the call for labour, that I have met instances of a high-caste proprietor—even a Rajpoot, associating with a chumar in partnership with himself in his seer holding, on the condition that the latter should enjoy an aliquot portion of the profits.'

40 Commissioners Office, Meerut, Scarcity Department, File No. 2 of 1900–1, p. 1.
41 *Muzaffarnagar DG* (1903), p. 56. See IRR 1896–7, pp. 12–13 for a brief description of the role of the canal when the rains ceased in late August in 1896. With regard to these irrigated areas, it must be remembered that *rabi* crops were often sown in land still moist from *kharif* irrigation, and their areas are not included in the statistics of irrigation.
42 W. H. Moreland, *The Agriculture of the UP* (Allahabad, 1910), p. 25.
43 For example, in *pargana* Muzaffarnagar in the famine of 1860–1, 'those proprietors whose estates border on the canal have been making, during the last year of distress, . . . large but temporary profits', reported the settlement officer S. N. Martin in *Muzaffarnagar SR* (1866), p. 60.
44 SR (1878), p. 18.
45 See F. Henvey, op. cit., p. 15, and *Further Papers Regarding the Famine and Relief Operations*, PP 1898, LXII, No. V, pp. 120–1.
46 A. Cadell, 'Rent Rate Report, Pergunnah Moozuffurnugger', (1872), para. 36. UPSA, BR, 'Different Districts', Muzaffarnagar, File 29, Box 5.
47 See, for example, R. S. Whiteway, *Muttra SR* (1879).
48 T. Stoker, *Bulandshahr SR* (1891), p. 47.
49 *Muttra SR* (1879), p. 18.
50 SR (1866), p. 59.
51 *Etawah SR* (1875), p. 16.
52 See K. Singh and J. Hrabovszky, 'An Economic Analysis of Bullock Labour Use on Delhi Farms', *Indian Journal of Agricultural Economics*, 20:4 (1965), 17–28. While bullock-use on the farms was nearly identical in January and February, the study showed that bullocks were watering wheat on well-irrigated land and preparing the fields for sugar on the canal-irrigated farms.
53 IRR 1873–4, pp. cvi-cvii.
54 SR (1878), p. 71.
55 Ibid.
56 A. Cadell, 'Rent Rate Report, Pergunnah Khataoli', (1872), pp. 35–6.
57 Ibid.
58 NWP Rev Progs, June 1870, p. 47.
59 *Muzaffarnagar DG* (1876), p. 545.
60 The discussion over the cause of the *khadir*'s deterioration is summarized in SR (1878), Appendix XII. The quotation is that of the settlement officer of neighbouring Gordhanpur *pargana*, made in 1899 and cited in *Muzaffarnagar DG* (1903), p. 5.
61 *Muzaffarnagar DG* (1876), pp. 477–8.
62 Ibid., p. 478.
63 SR (1878), p. 78.
64 *Muzaffarnagar DG* (1876), p. 476.
65 SR (1892), p. 10.
66 IRR 1873–4, pp. 1A–2A.
67 IRR 1880–1, p. 16A.
68 IRR 1873–4, p. 20A.
69 SR (1892), p. 9 and p. 53.
70 Ibid., p. 9.
71 SR (1878), p. 5.

5

Trends in the Agricultural Performance of an Indian Province: The Bombay Presidency, 1900–1920

NEIL CHARLESWORTH
University of Glasgow

The great debate over the performance of India's agricultural economy under British rule rages on. Recent provincial studies[1] have given the discussion both greater sophistication and a more solid empirical base. Yet their failure to discern many similar trends is conspicuous. This in itself has suggested an interpretation which is fast becoming the new orthodoxy: that in the late nineteenth and early twentieth centuries, the performance of Indian agriculture varied dramatically from province to province, district to district, incorporating in different localities buoyant expansion, the stagnation of changelessness and crisis-laden involution. How else can we assimilate the situation in Dewey's Punjab with its possible 105 per cent increase in gross output over 50 years[2]—a rate of growth far faster than the current wisdom on Meiji Japan—and in Rajat Ray's Bengal where apparently population increased by 10.8 per cent between 1901 and 1921 at a time when the cultivated acreage was actually contracting?[3]

Even so, it is no great surprise to find confirmed a substantial disparity between Bengal and the Punjab. In these two provinces, as Dewey points out, a major divergence of agricultural performance was evident from Blyn's pioneer use of the statistics.[4] What of the provinces, a large number, where the trend was less decisive? The Bombay Presidency is a prime example here.[5] Its established position is of middling neutrality along the Bengal–Punjab spectrum. This, however, is simply the result of ignorance. In Blyn's study, Bombay, as the author admitted, was the least satisfactorily treated of any of the provinces: statistical problems forced him to combine the Presidency proper with Sind in an uncomfortable amalgamation of the two distinct agricultural, climatic and cultural patterns.[6] Nevertheless, for Blyn, 'Bombay-Sind' is one of the vital, mainstream provinces where a fundamental unfavourable disparity between population growth and changes in foodgrain output emerged at some time around the First World War.[7] At the same time Bombay is likely to be, *par excellence*, a province of considerable local variations. Its overall performance in the non-food crops, on the 'untreated' agricultural statistics, was good enough for Blyn to date the turning-point in per capita all crop output as late as around 1931–2, ten years after the U.P., the Central Provinces and Greater Punjab.[8] This may not mean much for mass consumption because the Blynist statistics suggest, as the Thorners pointed out, that 'increase in commercial crops was achieved largely at the expense of food crop production'.[9] But was any, possibly marked, expansion in cash crop output concentrated mainly in one or two regions whilst a per capita decline in foodgrain production occurred elsewhere? Bombay Presidency contained, for example, Gujarat, traditionally associated even with the Punjab as an agricultural pacemaker, and the central Deccan, where serious famine had struck in both the late 1870s and the late 1890s. In these ways, the province provides a microcosm for the study of British Indian agricultural performance.

This paper, then, seeks to examine some of the overall trends in Bombay agriculture between 1900 and 1920. The choice of dates is dictated by both pragmatic and intellectual considerations. The tantalizing mountain of acreage and output figures only begins to pile up late in the nineteenth century and Blyn's study starts at 1891. Yet, also, the early twentieth century arguably provides in chronology what the Bombay Presidency offers regionally: a case study testing ground for wider views about Indian agricultural performance. By the mid and late 1930s the range for argument will have considerably diminished: we are then in a world of indisputably rising population pressure and falling per capita output in most districts. However, was this the acceleration of a long-term decline or the abrupt reversal of a fundamentally buoyant trend? An examination of the first two decades of the twentieth century might suggest some answers to this.

Even so, our enquiry is circumscribed by the now notorious problems of the agricultural statistics. The comprehensive general reservations expressed by Dewey about the Punjab statistics[10]—the incompetence of the primary reporting agencies, the inaccuracies of crop cutting experiments and so on—are clearly valid for the Bombay figures also. Here too, as Heston convincingly demonstrates,[11] the crop yield assessments are subject to particular error. Crop yields in Bombay were estimated by modifying a 'standard yield' through a 'condition factor', determined mainly by annual climatic and ecological variations. However, local officers' assessment of the quality of each season affected, for them far more significantly, their population's land revenue charges as well as the 'condition factor' for the benefit of the agricultural statistics. By the First World War the Bombay land revenue system was under attack from strong nationalist pressure. After the Bardoli campaign of 1928 the government effectively abandoned all new fully-fledged revision surveys but well before then it was politic for local officialdom to find ways to nullify the impact on the ground of any upward revisions. Not surprisingly, therefore, reported 'condition factors' were pessimistic, typically bringing the annual crop yield estimates down below the 'standard yield'.[12] Overall, the Bombay crop yield estimates, from period to period, probably tell us more about the current political strength or weakness of the local administration in the countryside than about the actual performance of the province's agriculture.

However, the attack on the statistics can, perhaps, be made too sweeping. It is easy to revel in a nihilism defended by statistical inaccuracy but all evidence on so impressionistic a subject as agricultural performance is necessarily controvertible. Are, say, the comments of local officials decisively more reliable? In Bombay current views, where any consensus existed, about economic development in the countryside tended to swing between extremes of pessimism and optimism, often simply according to current climatic patterns. Around the middle of the twentieth century's first decade, orthodoxy was pessimistic, considering that events had 'reduced the capital of the cultivators and diminished the number of their cattle':[13] but between 1904–5 and 1907–8 only in one year were rainfall and climatic conditions even fair. Gloom, in this era, was shared at the Government of India level. Instructions for the drawing up of the annual Season and Crop Reports, issued to the provinces in January 1907, demanded the inclusion in future reports of a new section entitled 'Agricultural Deterioration'.[14] Yet after about 1910 the pendulum swung back strongly. 'Agricultural Deterioration' was last featured in a Bombay *Season and Crop Report* in 1913–14, and by 1917 the *Report* was exuberantly talking about the 'generally prosperous condition of the people':[15] by then there had not been a poor season since 1911–12. The report writer, then, is not necessarily a more stable guide to long-term trends than the statistic gatherer with his sins of commission and omission.

In fact we can gain most from all sources by treating them with a healthy sense of pragmatism. Sometimes the statistics, the official reports 'feel right': at other times they seem impossible to square with other established aspects of the situation. The most fundamental criticism of Blyn's conclusions is not statistical but their basic lack of correlation with acknowledged characteristics of the inter-war period outlined by Macpherson: 'falling mortality, the relative absence of famines until the Bengal, war-complicated disaster of 1943, and rapid population growth . . .'.[16]

The real problem with the statistical material has been the use made of crop yield estimates. The demolition of their reliability is surely now complete. They can never again be used as conclusive evidence without the careful handling and correction possible only with the smallest geographical unit. Yet a mass of other material exists. Predominantly, there remain the figures on the cultivated area —the total land under tillage, lying fallow and available for new cultivation, and the amount growing each crop—at province and district level. Now, of course, these statistics suffer from many of the same limitations as the crop yield assessments. They were compiled by the same possibly conniving, possibly inefficient village officers. The estimates of 'cultivable waste' land must be treated with extreme caution: as Farmer has recently argued,[17] they typically represent an over-sanguine view of future agricultural opportunities. However, for the bulk of the statistics on actual existing cropped land nothing like so many value-loaded judgements were involved as with yield estimates. The amount of land and the type of crop a man cultivated was far more widely known, much less open to the chicanery of political expediency at every level than his specific annual harvest performance. To discover the general fluctuations in the overall cultivated acreage and the pattern of crops grown is a reasonable question which we can justly ask of these statistics.

The answer is, also, of supreme relevance. Increasing agricultural output has always everywhere been a slow, expensive and unspectacular process: the effects of new technology, of better seed varieties, of improved fertilizer only slowly and unevenly show up on the production sheet. Typically, it is fluctuations in the cultivated area, bringing new land under the plough or failing to match the pressure of a growing population, which produce change in total per capita output most conspicuously and most quickly. Admittedly, expanding cultivated acreage with a static technology is a 'once and for all' process, which is apt to lose momentum. Even so, in the short term it can provide a crucial, sudden boost to agricultural income. How many 'agricultural revolutions' are caused fundamentally by a marked expansion in land in use relative to numbers? In Japan, for example, the overall Tokugawa heritage of extensive land reclamation coupled with slow population growth may be more critical as the base to expansion than the much vaunted Meiji performance.[18]

In Bombay Presidency the nineteenth century had unquestionably witnessed a substantial increase in the extent of land under cultivation. Land Settlement reports of around 1840 frequently argued that under half of the potential arable land was then actually being cultivated: those on Bhimthari *taluk* of Poona District in 1838 and on Bunkapur *taluk*, Dharwar of 1846, for example, made such comments.[19] Probably this was partly the result of high land revenue demand, and, as the Wingate settlements of the 1840s and 1850s reduced the pitch of assessment, the cultivated area grew substantially. As early as 1852 Wingate was claiming that his surveys had already brought over a million acres of formerly waste land under the plough in just the four districts of Poona, Ahmednagar, Sholapur and Dharwar.[20] Thereafter the Presidency's total cultivated acreage continued to mount steadily up to 1900, apart from minor setbacks in the famines of the late 1870s and late 1890s. From 1880 the Gazetteer enquiries began to provide patchy statistics and they revealed some probable marked jumps in the 1880s. In Bijapur District, for instance, the cultivated area as a proportion of the total area investigated rose from 68 per cent in 1880–1 to 77 per cent by 1890–1.[21] In the Deccan especially, forest and waste land was being steadily cleared throughout the late nineteenth century: in the vast, and before 1850 largely untilled, northern district of Khandesh a genuine frontier situation existed, with the steady advance of cultivation and settlement.

The fluctuations in the pattern of growth of cultivated acreage closely matched the probable general trends in agricultural performance. The expansion of the 1850s arguably paved the way for the American Civil War cotton boom of the following decade: it made available land for new cash crop cultivation without decreasing the overall acreage of foodgrains. Again, the 1880s growth marked an era of extending commercialization in many districts as local railways spread and cash crop prices in the localities remained buoyant. These changes in the overall cultivated area should tell us something about the critical period after 1900. Most important, the varying distribution of crops grown, given in the acreage figures, provides valuable evidence. If Bombay, or an individual district's agriculture was becoming involuted in the early twentieth century one would expect obviously an increasing concentration on foodgrains, particularly the millets, at the expense of the dominant cash crops, especially cotton. Again, an expansion, for instance, of crops grown specifically to provide fodder for animals might suggest serious pressure on spare grazing land.

However, even the crop acreage statistics require careful treatment. Firstly, they are not comprehensive. In 1904–5 out of a total of about 23,000 villages in the British territories of Bombay Presidency, cultivated acreage figures were unavailable for over 2,000.[22] At this time the Bombay Government's central revenue department simply made guesses about the situation in these villages and forwarded the results separately to the Government of India: no information about the villages appeared in the early Season and Crop Reports. And these defaulting villages were widely spread. Although only Ratnagiri District by the early twentieth century provided no information for a majority of its villages, in most districts returns for a steady four or five per cent were missing. In 1904–5 only three out of 18 districts—the Panch Mahals, Sholapur and Kanara—boasted complete registers.

Of course the statistical coverage was being steadily extended. The 1904–5 situation represented a substantial improvement on that twenty years before. For example, Poona District by the turn of the century provided information for over 3.3 million acres, over a million acres more than in 1880.[23] By 1900 many of the villages for which statistics were still unavailable were either *inam* villages (held revenue free)[24] or those held on some non-*ryotwari* overlord tenure like the *Khoti* tenure in Ratnagiri, where simply no British land survey had yet taken place. As surveys of *inam* villages were carried out and records compiled for the first time, the area providing statistical information steadily rose, though not at the spectacular rate of the 1880–1900 period. By the end of the First World War, another third of a million acres had been drawn in since 1904–5.[25] In 1915–16, too, a procedural change attempted to strengthen the statistical evidence. District officers were now required to submit estimates for the areas without detailed statistics and these appeared separately in the *Season and Crop Reports* from 1915–16.

The changing statistical coverage obviously requires attention to compare like with like. It was not consistently upwards, for sometimes villages might temporarily drop out as two Poona ones did in 1907–8 when fire destroyed their survey accounts. Nevertheless the general trends can be computed easily over time, particularly at Presidency level. Taking the period 1904–5 to 1921–2,[26] the statistical area of the Bombay Presidency rose from 44,199,635 to 44,557,546 acres, an increase of 0.81 per cent. At district level big changes over this period were confined to four districts. In Khandesh, Nasik, Satara and Ratnagiri new surveys substantially increased the statistical coverage. Elsewhere at district level we shall only have to make the smallest, easily calculated allowances for statistical changes. If we do this (and for safety's sake ignore the guesses made for the areas without statistics both before and after 1915–16),[27] then we should be able to say something about the overall pattern of agricultural change.

The crucial first question is obviously the general availability of land and the relation between its expansion or contraction and demographic trends. Had western India run out of land or was the tilled acreage—or the amount of land double-cropped—still capable of significant expansion to meet any population rise?

Appendix 1 demonstrates that the total cultivated acreage was clearly still rising steadily in early twentieth century Bombay. Apparently a full eighth as much land again, even taking into account the statistical expansions, was under cultivation in the post First World War period compared with the early years of the century. This must have meant an overall increase in average land per capita between these two periods, for the census recorded only a 4.1 per cent rise in Bombay's population between 1901 and 1921.[28] The expansion in the gross cropped area seems to have been entirely the result of new land being brought under the plough: double-cropping was apparently still insignificant throughout western India.[29]

Nevertheless, many objections remain to making simple-minded sanguine assumptions about overall agricultural performance from these figures. The population increase was compounded of leaps followed by stagnation and decline rather than an even pattern of very slow growth, so that population pressure on land may still have built up severely at certain times. Klein, too, reminds us that apparent population stability in pre-1920 India was typically the product of high mortality, of the poverty and disease which continually threatened the Indian masses.[30] Can there be any possibility of genuine agricultural buoyancy here? Certainly the population levels recorded in the 1921 census had been brought down by relatively recent high mortality. Yet the character of that mortality—the influenza epidemic of 1918–19—did not automatically suggest a population succumbing through agricultural decline and distribution. Influenza had devastating effects in the industrial West as well as in India in the last year of the war and the first year of peace. And in no part of Bombay was there serious famine between 1901 and 1921.

Even so, it is clear that population growth would have seemed to be more rapid if the census had been held in 1917 and not in 1921. However, cultivated area would still probably have been running ahead of the simple increase in numbers: gross cultivated acreage stood at 26.98 million acres in 1916–17, only 0.16 million acres below the average for 1919–20 – 1923–4 quoted in Appendix 1. The major expansion in land in use had come in the first two-thirds of the century's second decade. The motivation and mechanics of this expansion are clearly important. Was new land brought under the plough at times of hardship as part of an urgent quest to find more land for food or in times of buoyancy as the product of profit maximizing expansionism? The Bombay *Season and Crop Report* for 1907–8 implied the former, arguing that 'cultivation has extended in some parts of the Presidency' as a consequence of 'a series of bad years'.[31] Yet the annual fluctuations in the recorded statistics hardly bore out this thesis. Contrary to the Report's statement, gross cropped acreage in 1907–8 was actually lower than in three of the five previous years. Overall, during our period, it is striking that years of favourable climate and harvest witnessed the short-term increases in land in use: a run of three good years from 1914–15 to 1916–17 produced an expansion in the cultivated area of over two million acres. The poor years climatically—1907–8, 1911–12, 1918–19, and 1920–1—saw perceptible declines. By and large, the Bombay peasant, in making decisions about the extent of cultivation, was apparently reacting according to the opportunities for high output. This, we might tentatively suggest, indicates a motivation mainly fuelled by expansionism rather than a desire to maintain living standards under population's threat.

However, the major qualification about the value of simple growth in the cultivated acreage remains: was the new land marginal and therefore far less productive? The 1907–8 *Season and Crop Report* considered that the extensions involved 'poor lands which will hardly ever yield a good crop and will frequently fail to produce anything'. The *Report* believed what has often been asserted since: that 'much of the labour, which is wasted on these poor lands, might be more profitably applied in giving better cultivation to the good lands.'[32] The issue of the availability of new land and its quality is extremely difficult to decide. Assertions are freely available on each side. Many have argued that the expansions in land use in pre-1920 Bombay by no means exhausted the possibilities for the future. In 1920, for example, Keatinge, the Director of Agriculture, estimated that, even discounting five million acres for natural and man-made obstacles and seven million acres of forest land, a full seven million acres of land in Bombay lay immediately available for cultivation, and waste-land, capable of clearance, occupied another one million acres.[33]

Nevertheless, persuasive evidence that land supply was not everywhere unlimited was provided by the growing problem of grazing land. Cattle needed a large amount of grassland for grazing: an ancient rule was that there should be one acre of grazing land to every ten of cultivated. Throughout the nineteenth century this ratio had apparently always been maintained. By the 1920s, however, 'the area available for common grazing, or for grazing by paying a small fee to a private owner has been reduced in almost every part of the Bombay Presidency.'[34] The result was that crops had to be specially grown for fodder. In 1907–8 a new category of 'fodder crops' appeared in the Bombay agricultural statistics, and this was by no means simply the result of changes in crop-reporting technique. Harold Mann reported in 1920 that, although crops, of course, had sometimes eventually been used for fodder, 'the growing of crops specially and only for the sake of their fodder value is almost a new thing in Western India.'[35] By the end of the First World War the reported acreage of 'fodder crops' in the Bombay Presidency had reached over 1.5 million acres. Certainly this needs to be deducted from any 'increment' to Bombay agriculture caused by the expansion of the cultivated area: it was a wasteful side-effect of the process.

Even so, there must have been a limit to 'fodder crop' needs: their development provided little threat to long-term foodgrain supply, because neither cattle numbers nor demand for plough animals was rising substantially between the late nineteenth century and the 1920s. Bombay's cattle stock, greatly depleted by the famine of the last years of the nineteenth century, had recovered its 1890s numbers by the mid 1920s, but not much more.[36] It was often argued that the optimum cattle requirement for basic cultivation was now reached. Arguably, the fodder problem was a minor by-product of the thirsty quest to expand tillage, not a justification to challenge its importance. Over half the growth of the cultivated area remains unaccounted for. And the comments on the development of purely fodder crops at least serve as confirming documentary evidence about how steadily the land under tillage was expanding in the early twentieth century.

Initially then, one might venture, the steady growth in the cultivated acreage suggests an overall firm buoyancy in the Presidency's agricultural performance in our period. Yet there may still have been substantial regional variations. For much of the nineteenth century, the spectacular additions to the cultivated area had come in the north Deccan districts of Khandesh and Nasik and now, clearly, the major expansions may have been limited to a minority of districts. Certainly attempts to calculate the district by district population/cropped acreage ratios suggested that land availability varied widely throughout western India. Patil's estimate for 1914–15 found only about half an acre per head as the norm for the Konkan compared with nearly three acres and more in east Deccan districts like Ahmednagar, Sholapur and Bijapur.[37] These distinctions largely followed ecological and climatic differences. Far more land per head was needed in the east Deccan, with millet cultivation on arid land enjoying unreliable rainfall, than in the intensive wet-crop Konkan. Yet incongruities remained. The food crop productivity per acre of, say, Dharwar District, where two acres per head was Patil's average, was probably not greatly less—although different crops were involved—than that of much of the Konkan.

However, these were long-standing differences. The Konkan was traditionally the most intensely peopled part of Bombay Presidency and the variations from districts like Dharwar would have been at least as great for most of the nineteenth century. One of the most striking features of Bombay's agricultural history in our period is that the distribution of the cultivated area's expansion by district correlated firmly with the localities' different rates of population growth: fastest growing numbers meant fastest increasing tilled acreage.[38] The result was that in, apparently, no district was the land–population ratio significantly worsening. Thus, if we take the period between 1914–15 and 1924–5,[39] only in Ahmednagar and Bijapur Districts did the gross cropped area fall. But in these two districts any population growth was occurring at rates much below the norm. In Ahmednagar, hard hit by influenza, the population actually fell substantially from 838,000 to 732,000 between 1901 and 1921, against the Presidency-wide trend of 4.1 per cent rise: even by 1931, after that decade of quickening population growth, Ahmednagar's numbers had risen less than 5 per cent on the 1911 level.[40] In Bijapur the lack of acceleration of population increase as the twentieth century wore on was even more marked. The rise here between 1911 and 1931 was under 1 per cent: at Presidency level it was over 11 per cent.[41] Elsewhere, excluding the four districts mentioned earlier where calculations are difficult, the trend in the gross cultivated acreage, even for the short ten year period, was clearly up, allowing for the statistical changes. The relationship between expanding land use and growing population was close enough for the balance of traditional regional variations in land–population ratios not to be changing radically. Yet, our impression is that in general, in almost all districts, the pressure for change came from prior growth of the cultivated area providing the occasion for population increase.

Nevertheless, there are more than hints here of large regional disparities. In Ahmednagar and Bijapur declining population and land use suggest a stagnant agrarian economy. Elsewhere traditionally low land–population ratios may have become more harsh and oppressive in the conditions of the early twentieth century. Economic forces were changing land's position. It was acquiring a much higher market value. It was becoming subdivided into much smaller units, perhaps partly as a result of greater demand caused by that enhanced value. The differences between regions with less people and most land and those, *par excellence* the Konkan, with most people and traditional limitations on land expansion, may now have been much more important. Taken together, the population and cultivated acreage statistics do suggest clear regional trends. The greatest buoyancy was in Gujarat. Population rose in the 'Northern Division' of Bombay[42] by nearly 9 per cent between 1901 and 1921 and by over 13 per cent in the period 1911–31: the equivalents for the whole Presidency were 4.1 per cent and 11.3 per cent respectively.[43] Here, too, were among the biggest expansions in cultivated acreage. Surat's, for instance, on the same statistical coverage, rose spectacularly from 515,000 to 786,000 acres between 1914–15 and 1924–5.

In the 'Southern Division', in contrast, total population fell between 1901 and 1921 and the rise from 1911 to 1931 was under 7 per cent.[44] In addition, the cultivated acreage trend in the Konkan, taking into account some important increases in the statistical area, was largely static. For example, in Kolaba District the 9,000 acre increase in the gross cropped area between 1914–15 and 1924–5 barely exceeded a 7,000 acre expansion of the area providing statistics. Surprisingly perhaps, the relative stagnation of the Konkan seems to have been shared by the three Southern Maratha districts of Belgaum, Bijapur and Dharwar. Bijapur's stagnant performance is explicable in historical terms: in the east, it had always been firmly in the region of variable rainfall and famine. Yet Dharwar, traditionally a substantial cotton-growing district, followed similar trends. The area under the plough here, on a stable statistical area, went up only marginally—by less than 3 per cent—between 1914–15 and 1924–5. Here, too, was the familiar concomitant of population decline over 1901–21, and the rise between 1911 and 1931 was by no more than two-thirds of the Presidency norm. On these criteria, the Deccan districts varied between the poles represented by the south and north, without any clear inter-regional pattern emerging. Sholapur, for example, in the south-east famine belt, was apparently more expansionist than Poona District in the west. In the former population was rising more quickly and so too was the cultivated area: by 4.5 per cent compared with under 3 per cent in the decade 1914–15 - 1924–5.

These simple cultivated acreage statistics suggest some initial general hypotheses about changing agricultural patterns in Bombay Presidency. Buoyancy was shifting to the north; stagnation was setting in throughout much of the south. Stagnation in the Konkan might be explained in terms of communications problems and failure to create a wider market. Into this region of indented coastline no local railways came and coastal shipping remained the basic organ of commerce.[45] Yet this sort of explanation hardly fits a district like Dharwar, served by the Southern Maratha Railway. The Southern Maratha districts, major participants and beneficiaries of the American Civil War cotton boom in the 1860s, had come to lose their buoyancy after 1870, if McAlpin's impressions for the late nineteenth century can be added to ours for 1900–20.[46] Initially, some long-term climatic and ecological change seems at work here.

However, general cultivated acreage statistics can only hint at the broadest regional variations, and, at every level, increases in the tilled area *per se* would not mean much if the wrong crops in terms of output and price were being grown. So, what crops were being cultivated on the Presidency's expanding farmland?

The basic foodgrains, in Bombay substantially the millets, *bajra* and *jowar*, with some wheat in the north and some rice on the coastal south, maintained an overall dominance. In the early years of the twentieth century cultivation of all cereals and pulses hovered around the 18 million acres mark, about three-quarters of the total tilled acreage. However, the statistics suggest that in the next twenty years the cultivation of these crops did not extend especially, certainly not on a scale commensurate with that 13.8 per cent rise in land usage. In the early 1920s the recorded acreage for 'all cereals and pulses' ranged from a low of 16.7 million acres to a peak of 19.4 million acres. Of course this is forgetting the rise of the fodder crops, which were not categorized under cereals and pulses but involved the same mode of dry crop cultivation. Yet even counting their early 1920s average of 1.8 million acres the increment in this type of grain crop would be below the norm at around 10 per cent.

The solidest gains in cultivation do appear to have been made in the cash crops. Cotton was the success story of early twentieth century Bombay, continuing the expansion of the late nineteenth century. Its total area, averaging just under 3.5 million acres in the years 1902–3 – 1906–7, had risen over the 4 million acres mark during the first half of the 1920s, an increase of more than 15 per cent. By 1925 cotton had firmly replaced *bajra* as the Presidency's second crop after *jowar*. Looked at over the whole period since 1880, when cotton resumed its climb after a decade of depression, this steady and continuous growth in Bombay cotton cultivation appears far more meaningful and even spectacular than the much discussed American Civil War boom. Even in the peak year of 1869–70, then, the cotton acreage of Bombay Presidency had never reached 2 million acres.[47]

Foreign demand played a vital part in this early twentieth century cotton boom. The First World War era saw the explosion of Japan onto the world stage as a major cotton goods manufacturer and exporter. The value of Japanese exports quadrupled between 1910 and 1920,[48] and cotton manufactures were the fastest growing sector. Exports of cotton cloth went up by 185 per cent between 1913 and 1918 alone.[49] This Japanese industrial success was founded, substantially, on Indian raw cotton. By 1898 India had become Japan's most important raw cotton supplier,[50] and she maintained this position unchallenged throughout Japan's first export boom until rivalled by American produce in the 1930s.[51] With such demand in export markets, the price of western Indian raw cotton increased considerably. Official reports during the First World War spoke of 'exceedingly high prices for the raw material'.[52] According to all-India statistics, average prices of raw Broach cotton, standing at Rs 215 per candy of 784 lbs in 1901, had reached Rs 303 per candy by 1910 and then Rs 461 in 1917.[53] These price levels were maintained and even rose again into the 1920s. Whilst many agricultural produce prices were beginning to fall consistently by 1922 or 1923, raw Broach cotton prices were at a peak of Rs 582 per candy as late as 1924.[54]

Other cash crops did not enjoy the world-wide buoyancy of cotton. But still, to judge from the cultivated acreage statistics, they were, at lower absolute levels, experiencing expansion up to 1920. Tobacco is an obvious example here. Its average total acreage between 1902–3 and 1906–7 stood at 68,100. By 1919–20 – 1923–4 this had reached nearly 100,000 acres. Sugarcane experienced a marked boom during the First World War, though its cultivation fell off sharply after 1919 as the price fell. From an average of just above 50,000 acres at the beginning of the century the mean for the war years reached nearly 70,000 acres.

The real importance of the extension of such crops' cultivation was not simply that they were sold on the market at increasing price levels. Many might question whether the bulk of these growing returns reached the peasant cultivator, without being siphoned off by middleman, landlord or moneylender. Even so, most export crops, as Macpherson argues, 'had higher yields per acre and per man'.[55] One Agricultural Department Bulletin in 1914 argued that, even viewed as a subsistence food crop, sugarcane performed better than *jowar* and *bajra:* 'from 7,000 to 8,000 lbs of human food is obtained per acre and . . . this is far greater than can be obtained by any grain-crop'.[56] The same source suggested that profits on sugar, on the canal irrigated lands of the Deccan, varied from Rs 100 to Rs 200 and more per acre, when even cotton cultivators could not expect profits much above Rs 30 per acre.[57]

But how widespread were these super profits? Sugar, always well under 100,000 acres in extent, was obviously very much a minority interest. It required reliable irrigation and a large capital investment at the beginning of the season: the Bulletin's estimate of Rs 100–200 net profit was based on an assessment of total costs as high as Rs 597.[58] The climatic and soil requirements of cotton, sugar and tobacco were each highly individual, making most conditions in most districts unsuitable for their cultivation. None of these three, for instance, particularly suited the Konkan. So the regional distribution of the extending cash crop cultivation was crucial.

What, first then, of cotton? This was much the most important cash crop in terms of area, and, apart from those in the Konkan, every Bombay district had some tradition of its cultivation. In 1914–15 there were three major and one minor regions of cotton growing. The major were Gujarat (where nearly 43 per cent of Surat's cultivated area and 25 per cent of Ahmedabad's was under cotton), Khandesh (with 34 and 47 per cent in West and East respectively) and the Southern Maratha Country (Dharwar and Bijapur had each around a quarter of their land growing the crop). The minor region was the central Deccan,[59] where about five per cent of the cultivated acreage produced cotton.

Yet the rates of expansion in the different regions already varied decisively. In the next decade, up to 1924–5, the Presidency's total cotton acreage went up by well over half a million acres, but the increment was regionally concentrated. By now the whole of the Deccan was very much less significant in cotton cultivation: in all the central districts, there had been clear absolute decline in cotton acreage and Khandesh had merely stood still. Against that, the expansion of cotton in Gujarat had been marked. In the five districts[60] the cultivation of cotton apparently extended from 718,000 acres in 1914–15 to over 1,200,000 acres by 1924–5. Even allowing for some additions to the statistical area (of around 8–10 per cent in Kaira and 4–5 per cent in Ahmedabad) this was a substantial increase. In the three Southern Maratha districts, the expansion of cotton cultivation was not as spectacular as in Gujarat, but certainly marked enough to query our initial impression of relative stagnation in this region. In Belgaum and Bijapur, the growth of the cotton area in the decade 1914–15 - 1924–5 amounted to 29 per cent and 24 per cent respectively.

Cotton, as much the most extensive cash crop, is the most helpful crop indicator of regional performance. The distribution of other commercial crops depended often on special factors. Sugar's expansion was almost confined to the canal-irrigated schemes and here the central Deccan was the major beneficiary: 23 per cent of the sugarcane acreage was in Poona District and a further 19 per cent in Satara over the period 1908–13.[61] Nevertheless, the distribution of expansion in the minor cash crops does tentatively support the regional pattern which is beginning to emerge: Gujarat the pacemaker, the Konkan the laggard, the central districts jostling in between. Tobacco was the most buoyant of the lesser cash crops and it was certainly mainly a Gujarati product. The leading area of its cultivation was the southern and eastern subdivisions of Kaira District, the main bulwark of support for Gandhi's Kaira satyagraha in 1918.

We could continue at considerable length outlining precise regional variations in cropping patterns in the early twentieth century. But let us stop here and discuss the general suggestions which emerge from this short preliminary review of land and crop acreage statistics. Firstly the cultivated land area was expanding steadily in all regions of early twentieth century Bombay. Furthermore, up to 1920 this increase seems to have 'led' population growth. Unless output per acre was declining markedly, the production of foodgrains per capita must have been at worst maintained at an even level, probably in every district. In addition, cash crop production expanded; in the case of cotton, boomed, reacting to a world demand. The development of the cash crops did not 'rob' foodgrains in most areas. The one conspicuous exception here occurred in parts of the Southern Maratha Country, especially Bijapur District. In Bijapur the acreage of the foodgrains was dropping absolutely during our period whilst the cultivation of the major cash crop, cotton, was extending steadily. Within a pattern like this, considerable internal variations seem likely. Throughout the Southern Maratha districts the split was probably widening between west and east: the west with better soil and climate and more efficiently linked, in terms of communications, with the rest of the Presidency; the east, particularly the east of Bijapur, living in serious danger of famine and more remote from the central regions of Bombay. The differences and the stratification in performance were clearly here most conspicuous within the region rather than between regions.

In the most pacemaking areas of Gujarat there was some tendency by 1920 for the expansion of cash crop production to prove so dynamic as to convert some localities into food importers. Bardoli *taluk* of Surat District, later scene of the famous 1928 no rent campaign, was one of the leading cotton-growing areas. By 1923–4 over 40,000 acres in the *taluk* were growing the crop, more than twice the area producing *jowar*, the major foodgrain.[62] As a result 'people have largely to import their food-stuffs from outside the Taluka.'[63] Yet this only occurred, even by the 1920s, in a few small areas, and these were entirely subdivisions, like Bardoli, with long-established patterns of local commerce with neighbouring areas which produced the grain. In the conditions of the pre-1920 period in no sizeable area, except parts of Bijapur, did the expansion of cash crops seem to threaten the stability of that area's food supply.

Nevertheless, agricultural 'improvement' was clearly spread extremely unevenly throughout the Presidency. What was happening was that cropping patterns, particularly in the commercial crops, were becoming more 'rational', more closely determined by local climatic and ecological factors. The American Civil War period of the 1860s had produced a rambling expansion of the cotton-growing area throughout much of the Presidency. Then, in the 1870s, cotton cultivation receded in many districts, not simply due to price changes but because of frequent problems of soil unsuitability. After 1880, there was, in western India, a more coherent response to the resumed growth of world demand for cash crops. In our 1900–20 period cotton cultivation was extending rapidly on the most suitable soils; declining absolutely in less favoured areas.

Yet this created stratification between regions. Gujarat's performance probably, unless the output of the new lands and crops was poor, matched that of anywhere in India. Its coincident emergence on the political stage, particularly with Gandhi's campaign in Kaira in 1918, can be no surprise. The Konkan districts, in contrast, have featured little in our analysis. Here the land–population ratio was traditionally low, much lower than elsewhere in the Presidency. Consequently, the dependence on food crop cultivation was high throughout the region: in Kolaba District, for example, over 95 per cent of the cultivated area providing statistics in 1914–15 was growing cereals and pulses.[64] It is hard to see that this was changing at all, certainly in the districts south of Bombay City. By 1924–5 most of a 9,300 acre expansion in the total cultivated area of Kolaba District was accounted for by a 7,000 acre increase in the area providing statistics: and the proportion of foodgrains was still nearly 96 per cent. This might not yet have meant any decline in per capita performance, for population increase was so limited: in Kolaba, as well as Ratnagiri, population declined over 1901–21. This—a more common phenomenon in India before 1920 than 'involution'—was agricultural stagnation, a performance which influenced the need, particularly among Ratnagiri's population, to supplement incomes in the Bombay mills.

And yet, our overall thesis—that in most Bombay districts cultivated acreage was expanding successfully ahead of population growth up to 1920—hardly marries well with widespread official comment about alleged intense subdivision and fragmentation of land. Throughout the 1910s Keatinge and Mann, Bombay's leading agricultural experts, were increasingly perturbed by evidence that peasants' holdings, and the separate plots into which most holdings were divided, were decreasing markedly in size. The problem was a major theme of Keatinge's two books[65] and highlighted by Mann's study of one Deccan village, Pimpla Soudagar, published in 1917.[66] In the latter, by 1914–15, a total of 156 holdings, of which apparently only two were larger than 30 acres, were subdivided into as many as 718 distinct plots, some as small as 0.05 acres.[67] Presidency-wide statistics suggested that the number of holdings of under five acres more than doubled between 1904–5 and 1916–17.[68] The evidence collected genuinely seemed indicative of crisis in the agricultural economy.

Despite Pandit's timely challenge,[69] the orthodoxy about alleged subdivision and fragmentation throughout India remains that of early twentieth century Bombay officialdom: that the phenomenon was caused by population pressure wedded to inheritance procedure.[70] Yet the point made by Pandit's case studies in South Gujarat—that in practice the members of the family to be allocated land remained relatively constant—surely must have been true for most districts of Bombay between 1900 and 1920: the evidence that population was not rising much over the period is both statistical and documentary. Arguably the main force behind subdivision and fragmentation has been totally misunderstood. Interestingly the strongest pressure appears to have been not in the stagnant or problematic areas like Bijapur but often in the pacemaking regions. Land in the canal tracts of the central Deccan was greatly subdivided by 1920. In the sugarcane producing areas of Haveli *taluk*, Poona District, 'the land is much sub-divided. In the area around Sinhgad and Khadakwasla Tank few cultivators pay as much as ten rupees land revenue.'[71]

Why was this? The market price of agricultural land had increased substantially throughout western India in the late nineteenth and early twentieth centuries.[72] By the First World War period the demand for land, particularly that growing cash crops, was intense, and prospective cultivators were typically prepared to accept the smallest unit of the best land. Thus in one Deccan village boasting irrigated land growing valuable vegetables, the land was 'tremendously cut up' because 'it seems to be the ambition of everybody in the village to own about a guntha of irrigable land'.[73]

Hence fragmentation, the dividing of holdings into small separated plots, was at least partly the result of market demand: the enthusiasm of potential agricultural entrepreneurs to acquire the tiniest units of land. Subdivision—the concept that each individual's total holding of land was diminishing—is a problem more fundamental. But how much alleged subdivision was really fragmentation? To observers like Keatinge and Mann the decline in size of land units seemed alarming. Yet what was happening probably (up to 1920 at any rate) was that an individual's total landholding was not falling but becoming split into smaller and more geographically separated plots. Often, perhaps, some plots would be held in different and sometimes distant villages, particularly where the land was valuable. In these villages' records such smallish pieces of land held by the relatively unknown outsider would inevitably be delineated as 'holdings': more often than not they were really 'plots'. As market opportunities grew, as agricultural performance stratified and as the price of land increased, agriculturists fought both on the market and within the extended family to obtain what they could of the most productive land. Of course, as Keatinge argued, fragmentation made effective tillage more difficult. But, like the development of specialist fodder crops, it was, at first, a by-product of agricultural buoyancy not decline.

Our concern, throughout this paper, has been solely with aggregate trends in agricultural performance. The issue of the social distribution of the products of agriculture remains outside our purview on this occasion. Even so, one factor might be briefly mentioned, particularly in view of McAlpin's recent comments on income distribution in the cotton-growing areas in the late nineteenth century.[74] McAlpin's findings—that labour was sometimes relatively scarce and hence, arguably, able to secure a stake in any growing returns from cotton cultivation—can be applied to our period too. In the 1900–20 era, the steady expansion of relatively labour-intensive crops like cotton and sugarcane produced a thirsty demand for labour, and many official commentators argued that labour wages in agriculture were now rising noticeably in real terms. The phenomenon was particularly marked in a year of slight but perceptible general price rises, like 1924–5: 'prices for articles produced by the people for their own use remained steady or slightly advanced but the rates of wages rose considerably while scarcity of labour was felt in many areas.'[75]

Interestingly, the onset of the agricultural depression and a decline in cash crop prices from the early 1920s, in the short term intensified the process. Faced with this crisis, most cotton producers aimed at first to expand operations and increase output to maintain incomes. So, demand for labour grew. The *Season and Crop Report* for 1922–3 (the first year of general fall in prices) heralded, it thought, a new social order 'the exact nature of which it is difficult at present to forecast': 'the general result seems to be a rise in the prosperity of the labouring classes in the rural areas', but 'the farmer producing market crops and employing labour largely in his work has suffered badly.'[76] Even as the agricultural depression set in firmly, cultivator employers may well have been unable to force down labour wages to match the general price decline. As late as 1930–1 it was claimed that 'for labouring classes earning cash wages, the year under report has been an especially good one. For, while prices have greatly fallen the reduction in the rates of wages has been relatively small.'[77] By then, of course, opportunities for labour employment had probably been considerably reduced, so this advantage may have accrued to relatively few. Even so, the evidence is growing that labour in agriculture offered a valuable source of by-employment in the Bombay village by the early twentieth century and one which, at times, probably secured an increasing return in real terms. This needs to be considered when judging the effects of agricultural performance in the 1900–20 period. It is more likely than not that cash crop cultivation left at least a backwash of benefits among the rest of the village apart from growers and marketers.

This paper was born out of the author's perplexity about apparent contradictions in Bombay's agricultural development in the period between 1900 and 1920. Keatinge and Mann tell us that land was under strong pressure from population and that the size of units of cultivation was falling steadily. Yet the most cursory glance at the census material shows that population was never rising substantially in Bombay before 1920. In addition there was no major famine in the Presidency in our period. In fact, the crop and total acreage statistics indicate genuine buoyancy in most regions up to 1920. This, admittedly, was based not on a technological breakthrough but on the once-for-all process of expansions in land in use. Even so, there is no reason why this could not have been used to sponsor long-term rises in per capita income or even structural changes in the rural economy. Of course it did not. After 1920, population began to rise substantially. By 1931, as Appendix 2 shows, the total Presidency population had risen by 13.4 per cent since 1921. The cultivated acreage had continued to expand steadily but it could not match this pace of growth: its increase was by 7.1 per cent in an equivalent period. Social patterns of land use—notably the fragmentation of land—which had emerged in a less difficult period now imposed a straitjacket making it extremely difficult for agriculture to increase productivity to ameliorate declining land availability per head. Probably, there was an extremely sharp turning point in per capita agricultural performance somewhere in the mid or late 1920s. The overall agricultural performance of the Bombay Presidency hence moved towards the fate charted by the pessimists. And in the end the unspectacular but sound expansion of 1900–20 had gone simply to pay for more mouths.

Even so, one might wonder whether Bombay agriculture could possibly have accommodated the population increase of the 1920s if the wider economic climate had been more favourable. The onset of the agricultural depression, enforcing a decisive downturn in cash crop prices after long years of buoyancy, was a major blow at the Bombay rural elite. Since 1850 the large cash crop cultivator had, arguably, proved the main beneficiary of agricultural change in most regions.[78] Now, the situation intensified by the labour wage levels, he was the very one most hurt. By the late 1920s it was clear that 'the class of the agricultural population which has suffered most is the big cultivator employing hired labour on a large scale in producing his crop; and especially . . . the Deccan Canal Irrigator and the cultivator of commercial crops.'[79] It may be possible from this situation to argue that the strategy of rural economic development through commercial agriculture selling for export was not necessarily a failure in Bombay Presidency: it did not have a full chance. The impact of world demand on Bombay agriculture only had its greatest effect in the period we have been discussing. In cotton cultivation, for example, it was only the 'take off' in the Japanese cotton industry which provided a consistently expanding demand for the raw material in the Indian countryside. Western cotton industries had never regarded the Indian product as more than a poor second-best and the demand and price levels they had created had always fluctuated substantially. Yet the new opportunities which emerged after the 1890s lasted for only a short period. By the mid 1920s the prices of all the major cash crops were slumping in the Bombay countryside. Exogenous factors—the crucial turn in world terms of trade—by destroying the confidence of the agricultural elite, as much as anything ushered in the age of declining per capita agricultural performance in Bombay Presidency.

APPENDIX 1

Changes in Population/Land Ratio in all Bombay Presidency, 1901–1921

A: Population

1901	18,530,315
1911	19,650,101
1921	19,291,719

Percentage change 1901–1921: 4.1%

B: Gross Cultivated Area (Figures in acres)

1902–3	24,374,000
1903–4	24,181,000
1904–5	23,697,000
1905–6	22,401,000
1906–7	24,552,000

Average of the five years 23,841,000

APPENDIX 1 *(contd)*

1919–20	27,719,000
1920–21	25,126,000
1921–22	27,599,000
1922–23	27,743,000
1923–24	27,511,000

Average of the five years 27,140,000
Percentage change 1902/7–1919/24: 13.8%

SOURCES: *Census of India, 1931, Vol. 8, Part 2. Bombay Presidency,* Imperial Table 2. *Season and Crop Reports*, years stated.

APPENDIX 2

CHANGES IN POPULATION/LAND RATIO IN ALL BOMBAY PRESIDENCY, 1921–1931

A: Population

1921	19,291,719
1931	21,879,123

Percentage change 1921–1931: 13.4%

B: Gross Cultivated Area (Figures in acres)

1919–20	27,719,000
1920–21	25,126,000
1921–22	27,599,000
1922–23	27,743,000
1923–24	27,511,000

Average of the five years 27,140,000

1928–29	28,958,000
1929–30	28,718,000
1930–31	29,132,000
1931–32	29,372,000
1932–33	29,155,000

Average of the five years 29,067,000
Percentage change 1919/24–1928/33: 7.1%

SOURCES: *Census of India, 1931, Vol. 8, Part 2. Bombay Presidency,* Imperial Table 2. *Season and Crop Reports*, years stated.

NB Periods for gross cultivated area statistics in both appendices have been selected for containing, so far as possible, mainly 'normal' years.

NOTES

1 I have found the following the most interesting and important of these: Rajat Ray, 'The crisis of Bengal agriculture 1870–1927—the dynamics of immobility', *The Indian Economic and Social History Review*, 10:3 (1973), 244–79; Ira Klein, 'Population and agriculture in northern India, 1872–1971', *Modern Asian Studies*, 8:2 (1974), 191–216; Clive Dewey, 'The agricultural output of an Indian province: the Punjab, 1870–1940', unpublished seminar paper.

2 See Clive Dewey, op. cit.

3 Rajat Ray, op. cit., p. 249.

4 See George Blyn, *Agricultural Trends in India, 1891–1947; Output, Availability and Productivity* (Philadelphia, 1966).

5 Here, and subsequently, the area covered by this term is the British administrative unit of the Bombay Presidency, excluding Sind.

6 For Blyn, the undesirable pairing of Bombay and Sind was forced on him by the combined reporting of the two as one unit in his all-India statistics between 1921 and 1932. See George Blyn, op. cit., p. 81.

7 'In Madras and Bombay-Sind the disparity in trends started about midway during 1911–21; in United Provinces, Greater Punjab and Central Provinces the turning point was about 1921.' Ibid., p. 100.

8 Ibid., p. 247.

9 Daniel and Alice Thorner, *Land and Labour in India* (London, 1962), p. 103.

10 See Clive Dewey, '*Patwari* and *Chaukidar*: Subordinate Officials and the Reliability of India's Agricultural Statistics', Clive Dewey and A. G. Hopkins, eds., *The Imperial Impact* (London, 1978), pp. 280–314, 381–93.

11 See Alan W. Heston, 'Official yields per acre in India, 1886–1947: some questions of interpretation', *The Indian Economic and Social History Review*, 10:4 (1973), 303–32.

12 By the period 1946–54 reported yields were below the 'standard yield' in all of 59 cases investigated by Heston: in 26 of these they were even under 70 per cent of the 'standard yield', Alan W. Heston, op. cit., p. 313.

13 *Season and Crop Report of the Bombay Presidency 1907–8* (Bombay, 1908), para. 11.

14 See *Season and Crop Report of the Bombay Presidency 1906–7* (Bombay, 1907).

15 *Season and Crop Report of the Bombay Presidency 1916–17* (Bombay, 1917), para. 15.

16 W. J. Macpherson, 'Economic Development in India under the British Crown, 1858–1947', A. J. Youngson, ed., *Economic Development in the Long Run* (London, 1972), p. 137.

17 See B. H. Farmer, *Agricultural Colonization in India since Independence* (London, 1974), Chapter 2.

18 Since all participants in the Meiji debate now accept that the early Meiji harvest figures are to some degree underestimates, it is clear that agricultural performance in Japan was relatively good in 1868. What had brought this about? Hanley and Yamamura's comments are interesting: 'the 1873 survey put the total arable land at 4,126,771 cho of paddy and upland fields. If we compare this figure with the oft-cited estimate of about 2.06 million cho for

the beginning of the Tokugawa period, we can conclude that the amount of land reclaimed during the Tokugawa period doubled the size of the total arable area.' At the same time 'the annual average rate of growth of the population for the entire (Tokugawa) period was under one-fifth of 1 per cent.' Susan B. Hanley and Kozo Yamamura, 'Population trends and economic growth in pre-industrial Japan', D. V. Glass and Roger Revelle, eds., *Population and Social Change* (London, 1972), pp. 473, 485.

19 See *Selections from the Records of the Bombay Government, New Series, No. 151, Settlement Report on Bhimthari* taluk, *Poona District* by A. Nash, 2 November 1838; and *Parliamentary Papers 1852–53*, vol. LXXV, *Official Correspondence on the system of revenue survey and assessment in the Bombay Presidency, Settlement Report on Bunkapoor* taluk, *Dharwar District* by G. Wingate, 29 September 1846.

20 School of Oriental Studies, Durham University, papers of Sir George Wingate, Box 293/8, G. Wingate to H. Green, 31 July 1852.

21 *Gazetteer of the Bombay Presidency, vol. 23B Bijapur* (Bombay, 1905), Table VII, p. 9.

22 *Season and Crop Report of the Bombay Presidency 1904–5* (Bombay, 1905), Statistical Table 1. All subsequent agricultural statistics, where no reference is given, are taken from the appropriate *Season and Crop Report.*

23 *Gazetteer of the Bombay Presidency, vol. 18B Poona* (Bombay, 1904), Table VII, p. 10.

24 Even in the early twentieth century over 2,000 whole villages out of a 23,000 total in Bombay Presidency were *inam*, quite apart from the existence of some *inam* land in many of the other villages. See *Season and Crop Report of the Bombay Presidency 1903–4* (Bombay, 1904), Statistical Table 1.

25 After 1904–5 no further statement of the overall 'area for which statistics are available' at Presidency and district level exists in the official reports of the next twenty years. This figure, and subsequent similar ones, were compiled simply by totting up the yearly fluctuations recorded in each *Season and Crop Report.*

26 1921–2 has been chosen as a 'baseline' year, as fairly standard climatically. It also allows direct comparison with the demographic material of the 1921 census.

27 Though Maddison claims that 'the areas not covered by statistics were generally on the margin of cultivation and may have had a more steeply rising trend than the average area covered', Angus Maddison, *Class Structure and Economic Growth: India and Pakistan since the Moghuls* (London, 1971), p. 52. There may be something in this for the districts, notably Khandesh, where lack of easy accessibility rather than tenurial deviation was the main reason for failure to collect statistics.

28 See Appendix 1.

29 The stability of the amount of land recorded as cropped twice—at around 0.5 to 0.75 million acres—throughout our period may, obviously, be a result of statistical unreliability. It looks suspiciously as though district officers simply recorded figures of the same sort of magnitude year after year. However, in the predominantly dry-crop Bombay, with its relatively small percentage of irrigated fields, it is unlikely that double-cropping could have

been important. Quite possibly the practice did expand slowly, and the increment was hidden from or ignored by local officials. This would simply add another, perhaps, 50,000 acres or so to the growth of the gross cultivated area in our period.

30 See Ira Klein, 'Population and agriculture in northern India, 1872–1971', *Modern Asian Studies*, 8:2 (1974), p. 193.

31 *Season and Crop Report of the Bombay Presidency 1907–8* (Bombay, 1908), para. 11.

32 Ibid.

33 Quoted in P. C. Patil, *The Crops of the Bombay Presidency. Their Geography and Statistics*, Bombay Department of Agriculture Bulletin No. 109 of 1921 (Bombay, 1922), p. 63.

34 L. B. Kulkarni, *Improvement of grazing areas in the Bombay Presidency*, Bombay Department of Agriculture Bulletin No. 112 of 1923 (Poona, 1923), p. 1.

35 Harold H. Mann, *Fodder Crops of Western India*, Bombay Department of Agriculture Bulletin No. 100 of 1920 (Bombay, 1921), p. 1.

36 The census of agricultural stock, held every four or five years, revealed more or less identical total cattle numbers for 1895–6 and 1924–5.

37 Patil, *The Crops of the Bombay Presidency. Their Geography and Statistics*, p. 21.

38 McAlpin's work on the cotton-growing regions in the late nineteenth century suggests that this pattern was no new phenomenon. In the period 1870–1900 her 'interior cotton belt' saw increases in total cultivated land roughly commensurate with population growth: in her 'Carnatic' region and in Gujarat both population and cultivated acreage remained relatively stable. See Michelle B. McAlpin, 'The effects of expansion of markets on rural income distribution in nineteenth century India', *Explorations in Economic History*, 12 (1975), 289–302.

39 I have chosen these years, rather than the earlier longer-term comparison, because they provide about the most satisfactory comparison for all regions at district level. Not the least difficulty of finding benchmark years is the inevitable considerable regional variations in climate in a given year: one year may be good in Gujarat but poor in the Deccan and another vice versa. 1914–15 and 1924–5 were both satisfactory and even years climatically, with adequate falls of rain well spread, but overall 1914–15 was still a slightly better year and the comparison understates rather than exaggerates differences.

40 *Census of India, 1931, Vol. 8, Part 2, Bombay Presidency*, Statistical Table No. 2.

41 Ibid.

42 This included the north Deccan districts of Khandesh and Nasik as well as Gujarat.

43 *Census of India, 1931, Vol. 8, Part 2, Bombay Presidency*, Statistical Table No. 2.

44 Ibid.

45 For further discussion of the effects of the pattern of communications improvements on the Konkan and other regions, see my 'Agrarian society and

British administration in western India, 1847-1920' (Cambridge Ph.D., 1974), Chapter 4.

46 McAlpin claims that there were no major increases in cultivated area or population in the districts of Belgaum, Dharwar and Bijapur between 1870 and 1900: in Bijapur in fact population fell and in Dharwar such population increases as occurred came at a faster rate than the expansion of the cultivated acreage. See Michelle B. McAlpin, op. cit., pp. 296–7.

47 Peter Harnetty, 'Cotton exports and Indian agriculture, 1861–1870', *The Economic History Review*, 2nd Series, 24:3 (1971), p. 416.

48 G. C. Allen, *A Short Economic History of Modern Japan* (revised edition, London, 1972), p. 98.

49 W. W. Lockwood, *The Economic Development of Japan* (expanded edition, Princeton, 1968), p. 38.

50 S. J. Koh, *Stages of Industrial Development in Asia* (Philadelphia, 1966), p. 141.

51 Ibid., p. 145. Even then 'from the Indian point of view, Japan was still the principal market for raw cotton until the end of the 1930s.'

52 *Season and Crop Report of the Bombay Presidency 1916–17* (Bombay, 1917), para. 15.

53 *Index Numbers of Indian Prices, 1861–1926* (Department of Commercial Intelligence and Statistics, Government of India, 1928), Table V, p. 7.

54 Ibid. Higher prices had been recorded, briefly, in 1918 and 1919, but otherwise this was the highest Broach raw cotton price to date.

55 Macpherson, 'Economic development in India under the British Crown, 1858–1947', p. 154.

56 J. B. Knight, *Sugarcane, its cultivation and gul manufacture*, Bombay Department of Agriculture Bulletin No. 61 of 1914 (Bombay, 1914), p. 1.

57 Ibid.

58 Ibid., p. 33.

59 i.e. the four districts of Poona, Ahmednagar, Satara and Sholapur.

60 i.e. Ahmedabad, Kaira, Broach, Surat and the Panch Mahals. The latter peripheral, less highly cultivated north-eastern district shared much less in the expansion.

61 J. B. Knight, *Sugarcane, its cultivation and gul manufacture*, p. 3.

62 *Selections from the Records of the Bombay Government, New Series, No. 648, Settlement Report on Bardoli taluka, Surat District* by M. S. Jayakar, 30 June 1925, para. 11.

63 Ibid.

64 Patil, *The Crops of the Bombay Presidency*, p. 24.

65 See G. Keatinge, *Rural Economy in the Bombay Deccan* (London, 1912) and *Agricultural Progress in Western India* (London, 1921).

66 See Harold H. Mann, *Land and Labour in a Deccan Village, No. 1* (London, 1917).

67 Ibid., p. 47.

68 In the whole Presidency including Sind holdings up to five acres in size apparently comprised 425,037 out of a grand total of 1,405,134 holdings in 1904–5; 991,234 out of a 2,179,045 total by 1916–17, India Office Library, Bombay Land Revenue Proceedings, vol. 11330, Feb. 1923, p. 65. Note by

the Deputy Secretary to Bombay Government, Revenue Department on 'Proposals to check excessive sub-division and fragmentation of holdings'.

69 Dhairyabala Pandit, 'The myths around sub-division and fragmentation of holdings: a few case histories', *The Indian Economic and Social History Review*, 6:2 (1969), 151–63.

70 See, for example, Macpherson, 'Economic development in India under the British Crown, 1858–1947', p. 163.

71 *Selections from the Records of the Bombay Government, New Series No. 577, Settlement Report on Haveli taluka, Poona District* by R. D. Bell, 7 March 1916, para. 23.

72 For details see my 'Agrarian society and British administration in western India, 1847–1920' (Cambridge Ph.D, 1974), Chapter 6.

73 India Office Library, Bombay Land Revenue Progs, vol. 11473, June 1925 A, p. 441. Report by F. G. H. Anderson, Settlement Commissioner, 6 April 1925, para. 8.

74 See McAlpin, op. cit.

75 *Season and Crop Report of the Bombay Presidency 1924–25* (Bombay, 1925), para. 34.

76 *Season and Crop Report of the Bombay Presidency 1922–23* (Bombay, 1923), para. 24.

77 *Season and Crop Report of the Bombay Presidency 1930–31* (Bombay, 1931), para. 44.

78 I have discussed these issues and the question of rural stratification in my 'Rich peasants and poor peasants in late nineteenth century Maharashtra', Clive Dewey and A. G. Hopkins, eds., *The Imperial Impact* (London, 1978), pp. 97–113, 392–6.

79 *Season and Crop Report of the Bombay Presidency 1930–31* (Bombay, 1931), para. 44.

Part II

TRADE AND FINANCE

6

Markets and Traders in India during the Seventeenth and Eighteenth Centuries*

K. N. CHAUDHURI

The School of Oriental and African Studies, University of London

In the development of long-distance trade the subcontinent of India has played a major role throughout history. Within its own geographical or political frontiers an active interregional commerce made it possible to sustain a fairly advanced form of economic specialization. This in its turn enabled the local political authorities or imperial governments to maintain public expenditure at a high level, drawing the envious attention of warrior rulers living in less fortunate circumstances. To Jean Baptiste Tavernier and many other contemporary European observers, the Mughal Emperor was the most powerful and the richest monarch in Asia. He was elevated to this status by the wealth, fertility, and the populousness of the territories over which his rule extended.[1] The productive capacity of Hindustan was commented upon by Babur himself, who described his latter years in Kabul as a 'harsh school of poverty'.[2] Within three generations the descendants of the dispossessed Turani prince had established in India an imperial and economic order which probably surpassed anything the country had previously experienced. There is no question that the Mughal political and military strength in India largely rested on its agricultural wealth. In 1624 Pietro della Valle wrote in his travel diary while he was in Goa that the king of India was an exceedingly rich prince whose income came mainly from his lands and not from the sea ports. The naval superiority which the maritime nations of Europe were able to exercise in Asia lost a great deal of its strategic advantage in the eyes of della Valle because of Mughal indifference to trade.[3]

However, there is ample evidence to show that the customs revenue derived by the central and provincial governments from seaborne or inland trade was by no means negligible.[4] The meticulous care with which imperial officials in Surat, Hugli, or Balasore recorded in writing the exports and imports of the respective ports is only one indication among many of the Mughal administrative preoccupations with matters of trade.[5] The high degree of centralization achieved by the Mughals in government had a strong financial and monetary base, which was fostered by a long tradition of banking and commercial exchange. It is inconceivable that the state machinery dealing with even land revenue could have functioned properly without financial intermediaries and an active market mechanism. The loss of Mughal state papers and lack of private commercial records has meant that much of this interaction between trading activities and government policy is hidden from our knowledge. But there is little doubt that the Indian economy of this period contained a prosperous and enterprising commercial community responsible for the distribution and marketing of both the products of agriculture as well as industrial handicrafts. Although direct evidence is often lacking, some light can be thrown on the nature and character of India's foreign and internal trade from the historical information contained in the papers of the European chartered companies. In setting up their trading organization in India the European companies made extensive use of the existing indigenous commercial institutions, and their relationships with the Indian merchants provide important insights into different forms of economic behaviour.

While there are many studies that deal with a descriptive account of Indian trade, few attempt to provide an analytical treatment of its form and content. A theoretical analysis of Indian markets and traders in the pre-modern period must begin by raising a number of fundamental questions. We are concerned here with mainly non-local trade, and a critical assumption in the analysis of its character is the conceptual and spatial separation of the buying and selling markets. The linkage between these can take a number of different institutional forms which are determined by local conditions and practices. It is not a necessary condition of economic exchanges between widely separated markets that their character should be identical or even similar. Trade between unequal partners, between societies with different rates of growth and development, is a common historical phenomenon. But such differences call for a considerable flexibility in commercial techniques on the part of merchants and traders whose task it is to connect the buying and selling markets. The appearance of north European traders in India during the early years of the seventeenth century brought a new dimension to the contemporary commercial practices. For they were organized on the basis of a bureaucratic institution acting as a central distribution agency in the selling markets of Europe. But the markets in which the Dutch and the English East India Companies made their purchases were still the traditional ones with a large number of individual merchants offering their services to the customers and trading in commodities that were the products of peasant and artisan labour. Even in the European selling markets, once the East India goods had been sold in the annual auctions, their distribution and retail sales were in the hands of non-corporate traders. The economic innovation which the joint-stock organization of the East India Companies represented lay in the latter's attempt to impose some form of unified decision-making on markets that were traditionally decentralized and fragmented.

If the pre-modern trade of India or Asia lacked the continuity and the regularity later created by the Industrial Revolution, we have to determine still the degree to which markets and traders were influenced in their commercial decisions by uncertainties and an incapacity of consumers to absorb the economic surplus of the exporting areas on any substantial scale. But, before the investigation of this problem is taken any further, we need a definition of the term market. Theories on markets can be arranged into several categories, all of which incorporate the necessary assumption that the term involves an exchange of some kind. A market may be defined first of all as a form of economic behaviour. It is also a locus in space where the physical process of exchange takes place. A corollary of the spatial definition of the market is its dynamic features. Time is an important second dimension in its measurement. Finally, a market can be taken as a sociological phenomenon, in which various social groups perform differentiated functions. The relationships between political rulers and merchants, between merchants and brokers, or the pedlars and householders, all fall within the last category and such relationships, apart from raising purely economic issues, also involve wider questions of power and social stratifications. The most explicit examination of these ideas on trade is to be found in the paradigm propounded by Karl Polanyi.[6] He made a fundamental distinction between trade which was conducted through economic calculations and that which was an expression of political or social will. As an institutional definition trade was a method of acquiring goods which were not available locally. But Polanyi defined market trade as a double movement of goods in opposite directions passing through a supply–demand price mechanism. The movement was regulated by prices, and these in turn were the function of the market. But institutional trading was independent of such a market. The chief, or the king who acted for the community, acquired the goods through a command system and distributed them according to customary practices. The whole process of exchange included considerable ceremonial and ritualistic elements. Out of these ideas came Polanyi's well-known concept of market-less trading.[7]

It is clear that the long-distance commerce of Mughal India, with which we are concerned here, falls in the category of market trading. But it is equally evident that the operation of the price system in premodern markets may be highly imperfect, and it is necessary to examine the historical evidence carefully to see how the market mechanism was differentiated by several gradations of economic behaviour. Even in this area of study historical theories are not lacking. In his classic description of the trading world of Asia in the early seventeenth century, J. C. van Leur stressed the function performed by the small trader and the pedlar in the distribution of commercial goods.[8] Although he carefully distinguished between small peddling trader and large wholesale merchants to be found in India and China during this period, his sociological scheme of Asian trade was characterized by extreme fragmentation, multiplicity of markets, and unstable prices. To support his view of a highly volatile market, van Leur quoted a series of extracts from the records of the Dutch East India Company. The following example is a typical one. In 1621 the Dutch factor in Mocha reported that 'the big ship that comes each year from Suez has not come yet, that is long overdue and is a great loss for all the ships lying here, for by lack of buyers they have to give their goods so cheap that they cannot stand it. . . . At the moment there are nothing but sellers here and each one seeks only to get rid of what he has in order to leave here with the monsoon and not stay over. . . . They cannot collect the debts they have, however diligently they may try; it all is waiting for the coming of the ships from above.'[9] The point which van Leur draws from the above passage is of course the disruption in the normal trading activities of the port due to the non-arrival of the Suez ships. It is perfectly true that the letters written by both the Dutch and the English merchants in later years show that the entrepôt trade of this great Red Sea port and the price of coffee, its sole export, were strongly influenced by the timing of the Suez and Jedda fleets.[10] These ships brought large quantities of bullion to Mocha, and a failure in the supply of this essential lubricant to trade could have serious repercussions stretching out to Surat and the weaving towns of Gujarat. But the question to which the historian must address himself is whether the cause-and-effect relationship between money supply and the velocity of economic transactions was unique to Asia or India as a manifest expression of its primitive, small, and decentralized markets. The answer must surely be in the negative, and if van Leur had searched the Dutch records describing the European markets for the Company's products he would have found no difficulty in identifying similar situations.

The truth is that all pre-modern trade whether in Europe or Asia was painfully dependent on a smooth flow of bullion supplies which determined to a great extent the level of monetary circulation. The commodity market, on the other hand, was particularly susceptible to rapid fluctuations in prices due to the irregularities in supplies. The effect of a severe credit crisis on the personal liquidity of merchants can be seen very clearly from the English East India Company's account of the crisis following the collapse of the South Sea Company in 1720. In February 1721 the Court of Directors informed the Madras Council, 'When we took up in August last the large quantity of shipping before mentioned, it was upon the prospect of our Trade being carryed on with its usual currency, but some little time after that a General Stagnation of Credit overspread all these parts of Europe. Holland, France, Spain and Italy, as well as Britain have felt the sad effects of it, each countrey affecting the others, insomuch that bullion was not to be gotten, though we thought we had made a sufficient provision for it. The merchants abroad were afraid of parting with their ready money (for bullion is such). This was heightened by many and very eminent merchants being run upon beyond what they were able to answer, having their effects abroad, and the same evil has befallen several . . . bankers in this and the neighbouring countreys.'[11] Even in the institutionalized market for East India goods in London a single ship was capable of making a considerable difference in prices. In 1722 one of the Company's homeward-bound ships, the *Addison*, was lost at sea, and the Directors wrote to their Bengal officials that had the news of the shipwreck arrived before the auction sales were held, prices would have risen to the point at which the entire loss could have been recovered.[12]

The imperfect knowledge which we possess on the structure of Asian markets may lead us to conclude, if we are not careful, that the ordinary entrepreneurial character of this trade was a sum of peddling activities. The views of van Leur have recently been revived by Niels Steensgaard in his study of the overland caravan trade in the early seventeenth century. He admits that the peddling trade could make use of fairly sophisticated commercial methods, but he concludes, 'Nevertheless, the ordinary entrepreneur operates on the pedlar level, and there is nothing in the sources to indicate the existence of comprehensive coordinated organizations—of an Armenian, Turkish or Persian version of a Fugger, Cranfield or Tripp.'[13] The operations of the Middle Eastern merchants have not been studied in sufficient depth from the original sources, Armenian, Turkish, or Persian, for us to believe uncritically in such a categorical statement. In 1697 the English East India Company described the Armenians who at that time traded between Europe and the Levant as 'the most ancient merchants of the world' and their trade in woollen cloth as one which 'they have been possessed of ever since any cloth was made in the world'.[14] Is it possible to believe that men to whom such a homage was paid by one of the largest business institutions of the time conducted their trade on a level no higher than that of pedlars? Steensgaard has referred to the detailed journal of the Armenian merchant, Hovhannes, who travelled in the 1680s all the way from Isfahan, through India to Lhasa, and his business transactions reveal very small-scale sales and purchases.[15] For India there is Tavernier's description of the itinerant trade of the grain dealers, the *Banjaras*, travelling with upward of 10,000 pack oxen. They carried grain and salt right across the country and lived a completely nomadic life.[16] But even the evidence from the records of the European trading companies would prove that the existence of the *Banjaras* or men like Hovhannes does not justify the conclusion that the interregional trade of India or the Middle East was conducted solely at the peddling level. The actual structure of the Asian markets and trade, as we hope to demonstrate, was much more complex.

The first point which must be noted in any analysis of the pre-

Industrial Revolution market is its small scale and dimensions. There was a considerable element of speculation in it also, because large differences in prices between one regional market and another gave the merchants the opportunities for making large profits and compensated for a high degree of risk. As the cost of transport, even in the case of high-valued goods, was a substantial item in total variable costs, a certain margin of price differentials was a necessary condition of trade. If we start with the assumption that the pre-modern trade was independent of the economies of scale and that instability of prices was a feature of the best regulated markets, it is not difficult to understand the reason for the coexistence of small traders and pedlars with merchants whose wealth and power compared favourably with territorial princes. It is possible that the small trader never really accounted for the cost of his own labour. Theoretically, he was the commercial equivalent of the peasant farmer. In India the true pedlars were those who were engaged in mostly local trade. They went from village to village with their pack bullocks, buying pieces of cloth from individual weavers and retailing their ware in the same fashion.[17] The Armenian traders, on the other hand, were in quite a different category. They were a group of highly-skilled arbitrage dealers who were forced through historical circumstances to develop very flexible and geographically mobile forms of commerce. The Armenians were prepared to deal in any commodity that offered the prospect of making a profit, and their uncertain political and national status bred a sense of ethnic solidarity that was independent of the place of residence. An ability to measure the risks of overland trade and a readiness to vary the size of commercial transactions were the special services which the Armenians brought to the trading world of the Middle East, India, and even Europe. But there were, among them, also merchants whose status was equal to that of the most successful merchant of London and Amsterdam. In the early eighteenth century Khwaja Surhaud of Bengal enjoyed so much power and influence that he even interceded on behalf of the East India Company at the Imperial Court in Delhi. At the time of the Revolution of Plassey, one of the most eminent merchants in Bengal was another Armenian, Khwaja Wazid, who was given the title of *Fakhr-ut-tujar* or the chief of the merchants. As the head of the Dutch Factory reported in 1755 he was truly the maintainer of the riches of the rulers in the court of Nawab Alivardi Khan. He gave the Nawab rich presents willingly rather than under compulsion and the Dutch

Chief recommended that Wazid's friendship should be cultivated as he could prove very useful to the Company.[18]

The European trading companies traditionally dealt with merchants in India who were able to handle a large volume of trade. In the 1660s and 1670s, for example, the records of the English Company contain numerous references to the great South Indian merchant, Cassa Verona; he was the only Indian partner of the Company whose death was commemorated with the firing of 30 gun salutes.[19] In Surat there was Virji Vora whose reputation was even more legendary. The concentration of economic power in his hands had become so great by 1636 that the English Council felt obliged to point out the if Virji Vora wished to deal in a particular line of goods no other merchant in Surat would be bold enough to challenge him. Even the Company's broker who had the least dependency on his good will refused to come to the English Factory with alternative buyers for the Company's imports.[20] Two years previously, the fine coral was sold to a merchant other than Virji Vora, because the Factory had thought it opportune to try and break the great merchant's monopoly of the market. But the purchaser of the coral in the end did not dare to collect it and the consignment remained languishing in the Company's warehouse.[21] This was a situation in which the market for the Company's export goods was completely predictable as a result of the monopolistic control exercised by a single merchant. Steensgaard has summarized in his work the views of P. W. Klein on the role of monopoly in the Dutch market. As he puts it, in Klein's opinion 'the risks attached to stock formation would discourage the entrepreneurs under the non-transparent conditions of the market if they did not have the possibility of controlling the market by means of a monopoly or a quasi-monopoly. The monopolistic tendencies reduced the risk and thereby the transaction costs, and thus, far from being disturbing elements, they fulfilled an important function in the concrete, pre-industrial market.'[22] If the operation of the monopolistic market forces in Holland was an advance over primitive market forms, its presence in Surat as exemplified by Virji Vora's business dealings seemed to have been unwelcome to European merchants familiar with these higher commercial techniques. It should not be thought that a man like Virji Vora was exceptional in the commercial life of Surat. Although the family lost its pre-eminence after his death, the business enterprise founded by Abdul Gafur in the last quarter of the seventeenth century lasted for more than four generations. Alexander Hamilton, who knew Surat and its merchants intimately at around the turn of the century, specially singled him out in his *A New Account of the East Indies*. 'Abdul Gafour, a Mahometan that I was acquainted with,' Hamilton wrote, 'drove a trade equal to the English East-India Company, for I have known him fit out in a year, above twenty sail of ships, between 300 and 800 tons, and none of them had less of his own stock than 10,000 pounds and some of them had 25,000; and, after that foreign stock was sent away, he behoved to have as much more of an inland stock for the following year's market.'[23] Even in 1742 his great-grandson, Mulna Fakir-uddin, was described as a great *saudagar* of the city.[24] To these examples, it is possible to add others, and a proper examination of the sources may reveal that Asian business houses headed by merchants such as the members of the Gafur family were not after all very different from a Fugger or a Cranfield able to undertake comprehensive and coordinated commercial ventures.

If the emphasis placed by Steensgaard on the pedlar is an exaggeration in the context of contemporary Asian trade, the same criticism attaches to his acceptance of van Leur's second characterization of Asia's international commerce: the existence of 'as many markets as there were towns and ports, each one with its own money, its own weights, its own measures, its own customs'.[25] Of course the multiplicity of money and weights, and even government fiscal regulations, was a constant feature of pre-modern trade. The English Channel marked the separation of two distinct systems of commercial institutions, those of France and England. The provincial mints of the United Republic of Holland each issued different types of coins. The merchant's almanac with long conversion tables for a multitude of separate currencies was an indispensable business tool of every reputable foreign-exchange dealer in Europe. In their weekly correspondence with the English East India Company, the Amsterdam banking and merchant firm of George and Isaac Clifford regularly included the rates of exchange between half a dozen different European monetary units.[26] The independence of economic institutions between trading centres does not necessarily point to complete market autarchy, otherwise trade would not have taken place at all and prices would have remained unaffected by supply factors, which is a theoretical absurdity. In relation to Asian trade, it will not take long to show the active operation of the law of market areas. Perhaps the most perfect example in our period was the coffee market of Beit el-Fakih and Mocha in the Yemen, where the daily prices of coffee during the trading season were fixed by those prevailing in the intermediate markets of Jedda, Cairo, and Alexandria, and the entire mechanism was compared by a servant of the English Company to the fluctuations in a stock exchange in Europe.[27]

The successful conduct of long-distance trade depends crucially on several interrelated factors, such as transport costs, the temporal pattern of demand and supply, the ability of merchants to hold stocks, price elasticities, and finally, the political or natural hazards to trade. If merchants and traders are not able to establish some sort of equilibrium between and within each of these different variables, trade would be characterized by a random mix of commodities, sudden appearances of excess supply or demand leading to violent price movements, and rapid rise or decline of particular markets. The history of pre-modern world trade contains numerous examples of such disequilibria, but the question which we have to resolve is how far were these conditions the rule. Let us first of all take the problem of transport costs. The means of conveyance, and the associated system of communication, determines the distance scales over which goods are carried for sale, and in addition it also fixes the commodity composition. If transport costs rise monotonically with distance, high-valued goods of course yield higher profits than bulky low-valued commodities. But it would be unjustified to conclude from such a theorization that the pre-modern long-distance trade was composed solely of rich goods. It is important to make a distinction between water and land transport, if we are to understand the economic mechanism which determined the balance of commodities exchanged between different regions. There can be little doubt that a high volume of international commerce both in Asia and in Europe was carried in boats and ships. But the technology of shipping required the transport of rich as well as bulk cargoes. The former reduced the fixed overhead costs of transport, while the latter provided essential ballast for the ships and stabilized them during long voyages. No contemporary merchant would have willingly laden his ships with rich commodities alone because of the high risk of shipwreck. The vessels belonging to the European trading companies always carried mixed cargoes and their value was not permitted to exceed a predetermined limit. That this was the practice followed by Indian merchants also we know from a letter written to the Bombay

Council by the Court of Directors in 1759: 'It is clearly our interest to encourage the import of bullion from Mocha to Bombay and as plain that merchants will always divide their risk whenever it is in their power, and if there is but one bottom to freight upon, it follows that silver intended for Bombay may frequently be carried to Surat.'[28] With overland transport, of course, there was no equivalent technological compulsion to combine rich and bulk goods. But the system of travelling in caravans with a large number of wheeled vehicles or pack animals protected by armed guards meant that merchants had to meet a certain amount of fixed costs which could be minimized by varying the composition of goods. Even bulky commodities such as grain, indigo, and coffee were transported on pack animals in large quantities. In the Yemen upwards of 80,000 bales of coffee were moved in one trading season between the inland market and the ports of shipment. The exact costs of camel-hire were available in the English Factory Records from Mocha, and the Court of Directors could easily calculate from these the economics of transport in their coffee trade.[29]

The fact that, in overland caravan trade, goods are moved in small units does not necessarily mean that these are retailed in the same way. The scale of pre-modern Asian trade cannot be taken as fitting into one particular type alone. The number of buyers and sellers and the size of their transactions varied according to the nature of the markets. The evidence compiled by van Leur seems to show that the Indian trade to South East Asia in the seventeenth century was conducted by a very large number of individual traders operating on a minute scale. The presence of south Indian Chuliar pedlars in Bantam and their trading methods were noted by the Fort St. George Council in the 1670s.[30] The Dutch copies of Surat or Hugli shipping registers also contain lists of cargo in odd packs and bales, obviously the property of small consigners.[31] As against this evidence, we can easily produce examples of large-scale wholesale dealings undertaken by Indian merchants whose operations extended from Mocha to China. We have already mentioned the family house of Abdul Gafur. In the middle of the eighteenth century, when John Henry Grose visited Surat, he saw stolid Hindu merchants who would singly buy up the entire cargo of a European ship with half an hour's bargaining and prompt cash payments.[32] The English Factory Records from Mocha are quite illuminating on this point. In 1735, for example, out of a total of 42 traders in Beit el-Fakih supplying coffee to the Company there were 5 whose share came to 77 per cent of the quantity. The coffee market of the Yemen was in fact dominated by a group of oligopolistic traders, though there was also a large number of very small sellers.[33]

The existence of a similar market structure for the subcontinent of India can be illustrated in relation to other commodities, pepper, saltpetre, or indigo. The English Council in Surat during the seventeenth century frequently purchased Malabar and Kanara pepper in the town itself, though the practice was disliked by the Company. In 1625, the Company's broker, who was sent to the Deccan to buy pepper, found himself unable to secure any supplies as a result of Virji Vora's offer of a higher price made to the local traders in pepper. The decision to send the broker to the inland markets was secretly made in order to avoid having to deal with Virji Vora in Surat. For the Factory had earlier entered into negotiations with him, and found that he was not only demanding a high price, but had also engrossed all the pepper brought in by the 'Decannee merchants' who were not permitted to sell it to anyone else. In the end, Virji Vora's willingness to lower the terms slightly and the fear of Dutch competition—they had recently received large funds from Holland—induced the Council to close with him.[34] In the second half of the century, spot market pepper purchases in Surat were quite common, in spite of the fact that several factories were maintained on the Malabar coast for pepper investments. Later on, during the eighteenth century, the Tellicherry Factory almost always purchased pepper in the local bazars when the season opened, and the prices were fixed by those being offered at the bigger ports such as Calicut.[35] Speculative stock-holding by Indian merchants in anticipation of rising prices was common not only in the pepper trade, but also in that of saltpetre and indigo.

In Bengal, the Court of Directors were continually urging the Calcutta Council not to incur the expense of keeping a separate establishment at Patna for its saltpetre purchases, but to try and obtain the supplies in Hugli. In 1718 Fort William bought up the whole quantity of 10,000 bags which had been imported by the Hugli merchants because the Council had heard that no further supplies were likely to come down that year.[36] However, spot market transactions in saltpetre were generally rare events for the English and the Dutch Companies, and their local servants in Bengal preferred instead to buy in the interior market of Patna, Chapra, and Singhiya.

The reason for resorting to the producing market, as given by Alexander Hume, the Chief of the Osten Company from 1726 to 1730, was an interesting one. Saltpetre occupied a vital position in the trading arrangements of the European Companies in the form of ballast cargo for the homeward-bound ships, and without it no return voyage from Bengal was possible for European shipping. As Hume found out from his own experience, unless advance contracts were made for its delivery at the right time, the Hugli merchants with speculative stocks in their hands enjoyed an iron monopoly, and it was in their power to put the success of a voyage at risk.[37] For indigo there were two separate markets, one in Surat where it could be bought from intermediate dealers, and the other in the producing districts such as Sarkhej or Biana. From the famous account left by Francisco Pelsaert of the indigo trade at the beginning of the seventeenth century, we can see that prices were determined by both spot market conditions as well as forward dealings. Pelsaert's advice to his masters, the Dutch East India Company, was quite explicit on the method of purchasing indigo. 'When the yield is plentiful . . . one or two experienced men should be sent in the end of August or the beginning of September to Chanowa or the adjoining villages, and should buy whatever is really good; but if the crop promises to be short, it is better to remain quietly in Ghanowa, and buy only from the substantial Hindu or Moslem merchants, who live there and have been many years in the trade, and who have made advances against indigo some months beforehand, binding the debtors to sell to no one else. These merchants would rather deal with us at a small profit than with other buyers.'[38] The presence of large dealers helped to stabilize prices, and the contracts made by leading merchants such as Mirza Sadiq and Ghazi Fazil of Biana even acted as price leaders. The export of indigo to the Middle East or Europe was not emphatically organized at the peddling level nor was it completely at the mercy of unpredictable market forces. Traders could and did anticipate price movements. In 1670, for example, Bhimji Parrack advised the Surat Council to make their contracts for indigo with the Agra agent, because they were informed 'by the lately arrived Bussora ship that the esteem and price of said commodity is much risen there, which news will certainly encourage the merchants here to buy up great quantities and then the price will also rise'.[39]

Any observer of the practical aspects of international trade is familiar with the leads and lags which influence the day-to-day movements in the market. But merchants engaged in long-distance trade strive to minimize these disturbing effects through arbitrage operations and stock-holding. Neither of these two remedies can work effectively unless the buyers and sellers have access to fixed locations where the transactions can take place. Peddling trade is geographically mobile, and, from the consumers' point of view, offers little choice because of its discontinuity. On the supply side, if the producers are dependent on the pedlars alone for the off-take of their goods, one must assume that either trade is a very marginal activity or that the rhythm of production itself is highly haphazard. The interregional or seaborne trade of Mughal India passed through three different types of spatial markets. If a functional hierarchy is constructed, at the apex would appear the great sea port markets. Surat, Masulipatam, and Hugli, along with Jedda, Mocha, Gombroon, Malacca, Achin, and Canton, can be placed in such a hierarchy. In the second category were the regional or provincial commercial towns which also served as entrepôts for a smaller hinterland or area of influence. We can have no difficulty in recognizing these places for India, they were Patna, Benares, Agra, Burhanpur, Lahore, Multan, and many other towns of lesser fame. The third type of market was not located at a particular place or town but was rather a collection of small towns and villages forming a single unit and producing a single export commodity. By way of examples one can name Biana and Sarkhej for indigo, the Chapra district of Bihar for saltpetre, the raw silk producing areas of Kasimbazar, the Dacca district for fine cotton textiles, and so on. There are many functional distinctions which can be drawn between these three basic types of markets in India. The great sea ports are best described as primate nodal markets able to offer a wide variety of services and goods to resident or visiting traders. Once the concentration of skills had grown beyond a certain point, they acted as a magnet for further agglomeration. The initial locational advantage which had probably brought them into prominence also tended to become less important. In Surat goods from all over India, Asia, and even Europe were brought for sale, irrespective of transport costs. The central place functions were performed in the inland markets also, but these were much more sensitive to catchment areas and the configuration of trade routes. The single producing market was of course completely specialized, and the decision of the traders to go there was influenced by the fact that such markets offered considerable price advantages.

Our three-fold division of Indian markets is based on their spatial and functional features. From the point of view of commercial methods and techniques, it is possible to make further generalizations. Every large sea port, the secondary interior towns, and the single-product areas included three types of markets, a purely local market serving the needs of the resident population, a wholesale spot market which supplied both the retail trade, the bazar and interregional commerce, and finally, the latter's offshoot, a wholesale forward market. The price formation in each of these three different markets would be a separate process, following different degrees of risks and economic motivation. In the bazar, competition among sellers as well as among buyers and sellers would presumably fix the level of prices at which the market would be cleared.[40] The distinguishing mark of bazar transactions is their minute scale and not the nature of their participants. For example, a large proportion of the bazar customers may be final consumers, but they could equally well be pedlars and small middlemen from neighbouring local markets who prefer to use the retail trade of a large town in order to secure a wider choice of goods and keener prices.[41] No European traveller visiting India in the seventeenth century failed to describe the great bazars of Surat, Ahmedabad, Burhanpur, or Lahore. Fryer's account of the crowded cloth market and the peddling stalls of Surat can be supplemented by the description of Ahmedabad left to us by Pietro della Valle. On Shrove Tuesday 1623, della Valle wrote in his diary, 'walking in the morning about the town, I saw a handsome street, strait, long and very broad, full of shops of various Trades: they call it *Bezari Kelan* (*Bazaar-i-kalan*), that is, the Great Market, in distinction from others than which this is bigger.'[42]

The determination of prices in the wholesale spot market was a more complicated process than in the retail market. The exact mechanism varied according to the different types of commodities offered for sale, and price fluctuations could take place as a result of both speculative motives as well as a genuine intermixture of supply and demand factors. Some idea of the operation of the wholesale spot market can be gathered from the East India Company's coffee purchases in Surat during the 1670s. The President of the Factory informed the Company in November 1670 that the price of coffee in town had varied unaccountably during the previous four months. It was selling at Rs 22 per maund before the Red Sea fleet returned from Mocha, but with the arrival of new supplies the price had come down to Rs 10–11 and currently it was Rs 12–13.[43] Two years later there was another extended discussion in Council about the state of the coffee trade in Surat and the extent of its interconnection with the markets of the Middle East. The first sign that the very large orders received from the Company (500 bales) were causing some anxiety to the President, came from the consultation held on 9 August when the broker was asked to bring in samples of coffee. There were apparently about 1,000 maunds of last year's coffee left in town which were selling from Rs 8.5 to Rs 9. This was a price lower than usual for many years, particularly at the end of the trading season while the ships were still away in the Red Sea. It was feared that the news from the Yemen might raise the price when the merchants learnt that the actual state of affairs in the coffee market was different from that in India. As the ships began to arrive in port from Mocha towards the end of the month, by a strange coincidence this apprehension turned out to be true. Coffee was particularly dear in Mocha that year and the price had risen to 45 Spanish dollars per bahar 'by reason of the great quantities . . . transported thence to Bussora and other parts of Turkey'.[44] At this price there was little inducement to the Surat merchants to import it, and, out of the total estimated amount of 3,300 maunds brought back, no less than 2,000 were in the hands of a single seller. But the merchant refused to take advantage of the prevailing scarcity, and after 15 days of negotiations over the price the Factory bought the entire amount at Rs 11.22 per maund. The English Council thought that the deal left him with very little profit.[45] One can only surmise what reasons had impelled him to sell. A single seller in possession of nearly two-thirds of the total supplies was obviously in a strong position to bargain. Equally, his risk was much greater than that of merchants holding smaller stocks and prepared to gamble on the prices rising with the arrival of the Europe ships and the opening of the roads up country after the rains. The seventeenth century merchant is known to have attached great importance to quick turnover as it increased the velocity of a limited metallic currency, and in this case it may well have been one of the explanations. But it is also possible that a more complex factor was at work. The Surat merchants trading to the Red Sea made their main profit on the sale of Indian exports and usually remitted the proceeds in bullion and coins. By importing coffee, and selling it at a relatively low profit, the merchants may have maximized the total sales revenue from the voyage. It was certainly a better alternative than importing money.

From this particular example, and similar instances to be found in the records of the trading companies, it is possible to state that the level of prices in the Indian wholesale spot markets adjusted according to the normal interaction between supply and demand current at the time of the transactions, according to the information available to the buyers and sellers, and the merchants' experience of the past behaviour of the market. However, one of the main instruments for stabilizing prices and reducing the risks associated with spot bargains in commodity markets, is the method of forward dealings at agreed prices. In our period the selling side of a particular Asian commodity was not so concentrated that the suppliers could always influence prices at will. But whatever risk there was for such an occurrence could be minimized through advance contracting. Much has been written about the Indian advance payment system, under which merchants received a down-payment on the signing of a formal contract, and they in turn undertook the prior financing of the producers. A whole nexus of credit relationships permeated Indian economic life and it was an important instrument of social control, in addition to being a source of capital for workmen too poor to provide just more than their own labour. But no one has pointed out that the system was essentially a form of forward dealing. If a willingness to hold inventories is a precondition of the emergence of a spot wholesale market, forward transactions are a means of reducing price fluctuations and the instability of the market arising from a disequilibrium between supply and demand. For the European traders it had the added attraction of ensuring a certain measure of standardization. The Indian system of advance payments has been interpreted by some historians as a kind of European 'putting out' system of production. But this is quite wrong. Merchants who gave advances, seldom did so in raw materials as was customary in Europe, and they were much more interested in contracting for the services of the artisans in order to secure prompt and firm deliveries at agreed prices. The origin of the advance system as it was practised in Mughal India can perhaps be traced to the ideas of Islamic jurisprudence. The law of *sillim* sales, for example, derived its authority from the Koran itself and signified a contract involving a prompt delivery in return for a distant delivery. In the language of the law, it meant a contract for sale, causing an immediate payment of the price, and admitting a delay in the delivery of the wares. According to Hanifa a *sillim* sale was valid only if, among other conditions, it specified the period of the delivery and the rate of the capital advanced. It is also specifically mentioned in the *Hedaya* that 'articles bespoke from the manufacturer, in a contract of Sillim, are considered as entities . . . and that a contract for workmanship is a sale and not merely a promise.'[46]

Was the institutional character of Asian markets and merchants in the seventeenth and eighteenth centuries very different from their European counterparts? It can be seen, taking the evidence of European sources alone, that the Dutch, the English, and later the French East India Companies traded in Europe and Asia following the same basic commercial methods. They did not bring new techniques to the purchasing markets of Mocha, Gombroon, Surat, Hugli, Bantam, and Canton. They did not, and could not, command the local markets. As Gerard Aungier, the President of the English Factory in Surat, wrote to the Company in 1677, 'We take the due notice of what you advise touching the low price of pepper in Europe and your orders to bring down the price here also; wherein we have not been wanting to use our best endeavours; but without success. For there is so great a consumption of pepper in these countries and so many dealers therein, who transport it to foreign parts, as well that of Deccan as of Malabar, that it is impossible to lower the price to the rates you limit.'[47] Similar instances of the operation of the market mechanism forcing up or down prices in London or Amsterdam can be easily compiled. What is needed at the moment, is a much more careful study than has hitherto been attempted, of the different types and forms of market structure in pre-modern trade classified by functions rather than geographical area.

NOTES

* For a more detailed discussion and treatment of the ideas presented in this paper, see the author's forthcoming work, *The Trading World of Asia and the English East India Company 1660–1760*, to be published by the Cambridge University Press.

1 *Travels in India by Jean-Baptiste Tavernier*, ed. V. Ball and W. Crooke, 2 vols. (London, 1925), I, p. 260.

2 *The Babur-nama in English: Memoirs of Babur*, translated by A. S. Beveridge, 2 vols. (London, 1921), II, p. 525.

3 *The Travels of Pietro della Valle in India*, ed. E. Grey, 2 vols. (London, 1892), II, pp. 417–19.

4 In 1716 John Surman was able to examine the Surat Customs Registers in Delhi and he was surprised to discover just how much the English private traders paid to the Imperial exchequer. See Bengal Public Consultations, 14 March 1716, vol. 3, p. 177.

5 These copies will be found in Koloniale Archieven Oost-Indie, Algemeen Rijksarchief, the Hague.

6 See Karl Polanyi, C. M. Arensberg, and H. W. Pearson, eds., *Trade and Markets in Early Empires* (New York, 1957); and Polanyi, 'Traders and Trade', in J. A. Sabloff and C. C. Lamberg-Karlovsky, eds., *Ancient Civilization and Trade* (Albuquerque, New Mexico, 1975).

7 For a discussion of Polanyi's work, see G. Dalton, 'Karl Polanyi's Analysis of Long-Distance Trade and his Wider Paradigm', in Sabloff and Lamberg-Karlovsky, *Ancient Civilization and Trade*.

8 J. C. van Leur, *Indonesian Trade and Society: Essays in Asian Social and Economic History* (The Hague, 1955), p. 132.

9 Ibid., p. 217.

10 For an example, see India Office Records, Surat Factory to the Court of Committees, 30 November 1683, Original Correspondence, vol. 43, No. 5001, p. 4.

11 India Office Records, Despatch Book, 24 February 1721, vol. 100, para. 77, pp. 520–1.

12 India Office Records, Despatch Book, 21 December 1722, vol. 101, para. 17, p. 367.

13 N. Steensgaard, *Carracks, Caravans, and Companies: the Structural Crisis in the European-Asian trade in the Early Seventeenth Century* (Copenhagen, 1972), p. 30.

14 India Office Records, Despatch Book, 1 September 1697, vol. 92, para. 8, p. 608.

15 L. Khachikian, 'Le registre d'un marchand Arménien en Perse, en Inde et au Tibet (1682–1693)', *Annales, Économies, Sociétés, Civilisations*, 22 (1967), 231–78.

16 Tavernier, *Travels in India*, I, pp. 32–3.

17 India Office Records, Fort St. George Factory to the Court of Committees, 30 November 1676, Original Correspondence, vol. 37, No. 4215, para. 17, p. 11.

18 Memorie of Jan Kersseboom, 14 February 1755, The Hague, Koloniale Archieven 2791.

19 *Records of Fort St. George: The Diary and Consultation Book of 1680–81*, 28 March 1680, p. 20.

20 *The English Factories in India 1634–1636*, 28 April 1636, p. 218.

21 Ibid., 8 April 1634, p. 24.

22 Steensgaard, *Carracks, Caravans, and Companies*, p. 15; P. W. Klein, *De Trippen en de 17e eeuw* (Assen, 1965).

23 Alexander Hamilton, *A New Account of the East Indies*, ed. W. Foster, 2 vols. (London, 1930), I, p. 89.

24 India Office Records, Factory Records Surat, 29–30 September 1742, vol. 27, pp. 34–5.

25 van Leur, *Indonesian Trade and Society*, p. 214.
26 For a collection of these letters written in 1708, see India Office Records, Miscellaneous Letters Received E/1/1, part 2, Nos. 11–19.
27 India Office Records, Factory Records Egypt and Red Sea, 4 July 1733, vol. 2, No. 324, para. 8, p. 253.
28 India Office Records, Despatches to Bombay, 24 November 1759, vol. 996, para. 55, p. 709.
29 India Office Records, Factory Records Egypt and Red Sea, 20 July 1721, vol. 1, No. 29, paras. 13–25, pp. 54–7.
30 India Office Records, Original Correspondence, 23 July – 6 August 1676, vol. 37, No. 4215, paras. 66–7, p. 11.
31 As the Dutch records do not indicate ownership of cargo but only that of ships, it is difficult to make any estimate of the size of individual shipments.
32 John Henry Grose, *A Voyage to the East Indies* (London, 1757), pp. 159–60.
33 India Office Records, Factory Records Egypt and Red Sea, vol. 2, No. 342, p. 324; No. 348, p. 342; No. 356, p. 361; No. 372, p. 389.
34 *The English Factories in India 1624–1629*, 10 July 1625, p. 90; 24 September 1625, p. 94.
35 See, for example, *Records of Fort St. George: Letters from Tellicherry 1733–1734*, 8 April 1734, p. 43.
36 India Office Records, Bengal Public Consultations, 6 December 1718, vol. 3, p. 606.
37 Memorie of Alexander Hume, 1730, Stadsarchief Antwerp, Generaal Indische Compagnie (The Ostend Company), 5769.
38 *Jahangir's India: The Remonstrantie of Francisco Pelsaert*, ed. W. H. Moreland and P. Geyl (Cambridge, 1925), p. 16.
39 India Office Records, Factory Records Surat, 10 May 1670, vol. 3, p. 65.
40 On this point, see C. Geertz, *Peddlers and Princes: Social Change and Economic Modernization in Two Indonesian Towns* (Chicago, 1963).
41 For a similar motivation on the part of the sellers, see India Office Records, Factory Records Java, 30 January 1671, vol. 4, p. 74.
42 *The Travels of Pietro della Valle*, I, p. 96.
43 India Office Records, Surat Factory to the Court of Committees, 20 November 1670, Original Correspondence, vol. 31, No. 3515, p. 16; Factory Records Surat, 9 August 1672, vol. 3, p. 11; ibid., 16 September 1672, vol. 3, p. 16.
44 Ibid.
45 Ibid.
46 Charles Hamilton, *The Hedaya or Guide: A Commentary on the Mussulman Laws*, Second Edition (London, 1870), pp. 299, 302, 308.
47 India Office Records, Surat Factory to the Court of Committees, 22 January 1677, vol. 37, No. 4258, pp. 5–6.

7

Bombay Merchants and Structural Changes in the Export Community 1850 to 1880

MARIKA VICZIANY
University of Melbourne

It is a commonplace observation in the books written on the economic history of the subcontinent that the development of Bombay differed greatly from that of Calcutta because the indigenous entrepreneur played a much more important role in the trade and industry of western India than did his counterpart in Bengal.[1] However, the evidence presented here suggests that this difference has probably been exaggerated, and that in the colonial port-city of Bombay there were forces at work in the nineteenth century which facilitated the growing commercial dominance of foreign business houses. This paper is a case study of the raw cotton export trade of Bombay in the period 1850 to 1880. In the light of recent research on the process of indigenous capital formation in 'backward economies', one need hardly emphasize the importance of establishing the identity of those business interests which controlled the export of India's leading cash crop. The criteria for 'control' or 'dominance' is the ownership of raw cotton at the time of its sale in an overseas market: more specifically, this paper shows that after 1870 a growing proportion of the profits earned in the raw cotton export trade went to foreign firms, whereas in the previous decades the greater part of these profits had been earned by the indigenous merchants. The timing of this change had important long-term implications because after 1870 the declining value of the Indian Rupee meant that foreign firms were reluctant to hold rupee assets. But there is a second sense in which the European firms 'dominated' the cotton trade even before they came to 'dominate' as actual shippers. Their presence was felt through the modern institutions which handled banking, shipping and insurance in Bombay, because in addition to business on their own account the European firms acted as agents for Indian shippers.[2] Prior to 1870 the bulk of native consignments was channelled through the agency houses. This method of trade was called the consignment system. The 'dominance' by the European firms cannot adequately be explained in terms of their superior capital or financial resources, for, on the basis of the limited evidence which is available, it appears that the European agency houses borrowed extensively from local Indian merchants.[3] Nevertheless, there can be little doubt that the European firms were more skilled in pooling resources and better at collating market information from overseas.

There are two parts to this paper: the first deals with a statistical survey of the number of Bombay cotton shippers and the degree of concentration in the export trade, and the second attempts to explain the structural changes outlined by the survey. It needs to be stressed that the present study is limited in its aims. The multifaceted character of India's international trade in the mid-Victorian era has been greatly simplified. Here we will only be dealing with one major cash crop,[4] with only the port of Bombay from which the bulk of it was exported,[5] and with only one overseas market, that of Liverpool, to which the greater part of Indian raw cotton was shipped.[6] For various reasons, the conclusions put forward are tentative. First, the interpretation of the Export Manifests of Bombay (the statistical sources used here) awaits the scrutiny of more readers. Wherever possible the accuracy and reliability of this data was tested against other sources of information. But this procedure was not very helpful when one was confronted with the haphazard way in which the port officials transliterated vernacular names into English. The following survey was compiled from the names of exporters listed in the Export Manifests and because translation was not standardized,[7] the name of Haji Ghulam Hussain for example could be written in many different and often grotesque ways. In the present paper an arbitrary convention was used in assuming that the various renditions of a similar sounding name referred to one and the same person. This modifies our conclusions by suggesting that the statistical survey probably underestimated the number of small, indigenous firms which participated in the export trade. The problem of identification does not arise in the case of the larger and better known firms. Second, access to the histories, records, journals and account books of both the European and Indian business houses is at present too limited to allow anything but the most superficial comments regarding the organization of individual firms. Our understanding of the entrepreneurial decisions made, and the motives involved, is virtually limited to speculative guesses.

I The Survey

Table I was compiled from a detailed survey of the daily Export Manifests of the port of Bombay.[8] These documents give the name of each shipper (that is, the owner of each consignment), the name of the overseas consignee, and the type, weight, bulk and value of each individual shipment. The data were collected and arranged to answer two basic questions: first, what was the degree of concentration in the cotton export trade and second, were there any significant changes in this during the period 1850 to 1880? Table I is an abstract of the results of these enquiries.[9] The survey involved the three sample years 1851, 1861 and 1875. These were selected because, amongst other things, they roughly spanned the three crucial decades which witnessed a rapid expansion in India's foreign trade.[10] After adding together the day by day exports of each shipper, the merchants were grouped according to the size of their annual shipments. From this it was possible to calculate the total exports of each group and the percentage share of each category of shippers in the total trade of each sample year.

In Table I the most noticeable aspect of the cotton trade was that the bulk of the merchants operated on a very small scale. Hence, in all three samples, Group VI was numerically very large but had the smallest share in the total trade. The survey also suggests a decline, from the 1850s onwards, in the relative importance of the smaller merchants—namely those whose annual shipments averaged less than 500 bales. This distribution of shipments amongst the lower categories was matched by a small number of large-scale firms in the first two categories who, in all three sample years, controlled well over half of the exports.

This general characterization of the cotton export trade obscures a number of important structural shifts which occurred in the years under review. The first thing to note is that in the 1851 sample there were no firms which shipped more than 10,000 bales. If firms operating on such a large scale existed at all, they were possibly exporting

TABLE I

A SUMMARY OF A SURVEY ON THE NUMBER OF BOMBAY MERCHANTS EXPORTING BALES OF RAW COTTON TO LIVERPOOL IN THREE SAMPLE YEARS 1851, 1861 AND 1875

GROUP		Total Number of Shippers	Total Amount Exported	Average per Shipper	Percentage share in total of each Group
1851					
I	10,000 + bales	—	—	—	—
II	5–9,000 „	4	25,449	6,363	31
III	1–4,999 „	12	22,255	1,854	26
IV	500– 999 „	17	11,668	686	13.9
V	100– 499 „	95	19,164	202	22.7
VI	1– 99 „	100	5,627	56	6.6
TOTAL		228	84,163		
1861					
I	10,000 + bales	12	270,625	22,552	35
II	5–9,999 „	25	165,918	6,639	21.5
III	1–4,999 „	97	226,087	2,330	29.3
IV	500– 999 „	76	55,254	721	7
V	100– 499 „	222	47,607	214	6.2
VI	1– 99 „	116	5,423	47	1
TOTAL		548	770,914		
1875					
I	10,000 + bales	14	340,131	24,295	62
II	5–9,999 „	10	65,747	6,574	12
III	1–4,999 „	40	71,768	1,794	13
IV	500– 999 „	35	24,541	701	4
V	100– 499 „	173	37,514	217	7
VI	1– 99 „	149	8,338	56	1.5
TOTAL		421	548,039		

to the China market which until 1860–1 attracted about one-third of India's cotton shipments. The appearance of Group I of exporters in the 1861 sample reflected the expansion in India's foreign trade with Europe—a growth which can be traced to the stimulus of the Crimean War. The majority of shippers in this category were Indian firms (see Table III) who had a long history of trade with the Far

East. A comparison of 1861 with 1851 further suggests that in the 1860s the export trade was becoming less concentrated: in 1851 only 16 firms exported 57 per cent of all shipments but ten years later 37 firms exported an equivalent percentage. This coincides with information in the market reports of Bombay which convey a picture of overall prosperity and competition in the commerce of the late 1850s and early 1860s. It was this environment which attracted both large and small merchants, and therefore accounts for the greater number of total shippers to Liverpool in the 1861 sample. The combined effect of the expansion in the volume of trade and the appearance of large operators to the Liverpool market, however, was to reduce the relative share of the smaller merchants in the export trade. This remained a permanent feature from 1861 onwards.

Though limited to changes in the topmost bracket of exporters, the contrast between 1875 and 1861 was even more dramatic. The trend towards growing concentration in this period is unmistakable. Despite the contraction in the total volume of shipments to Liverpool in 1875, the merchants in Group I greatly expanded their share in the trade both in terms of absolute shipments and their relative share of annual exports which rose to 62 per cent. Nor were these changes accompanied by any great expansion in the number of merchants belonging to Group I, for, compared to 1861, only two more firms had joined that rank by 1875. The middle range of merchants was severely affected by these shifts. The number of merchants in Groups II, III and IV was drastically reduced and so, too, was their total volume of exports and their percentage share of annual shipments.

These structural shifts warrant a closer inspection of the composition of Group I. The following graph illustrates the growing concentration of trade within that category. In 1861 Ritchie Steuart and Co.,[11] the largest exporter, shipped 66,000 bales to Liverpool and this was roughly three times the size of average shipments in Group I. However, by 1875 a relatively new firm, that of Gaddum and Co.,[12] shipped more than 100,000 bales and this was almost five times the average in that group. The difference between the largest exporter and the smallest firms in Group I grew much more rapidly than this comparison with average shipments suggested.

The results of an additional survey involving those firms which shipped cotton to the European continent in 1875 (Table II)[13] provides further proof of this growing concentration. With the opening

GRAPHS SHOWING THE DEGREE OF CONCENTRATION IN GROUP 1 OF THE COTTON EXPORTERS IN THE SAMPLE YEARS 1861 AND 1875

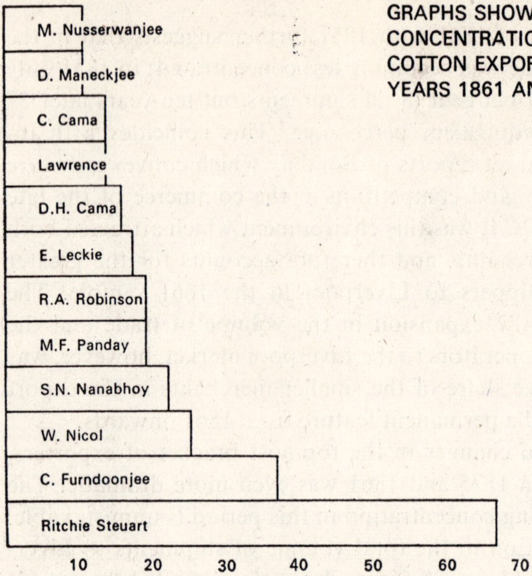

(a) Shipments in thousands of bales : 1861

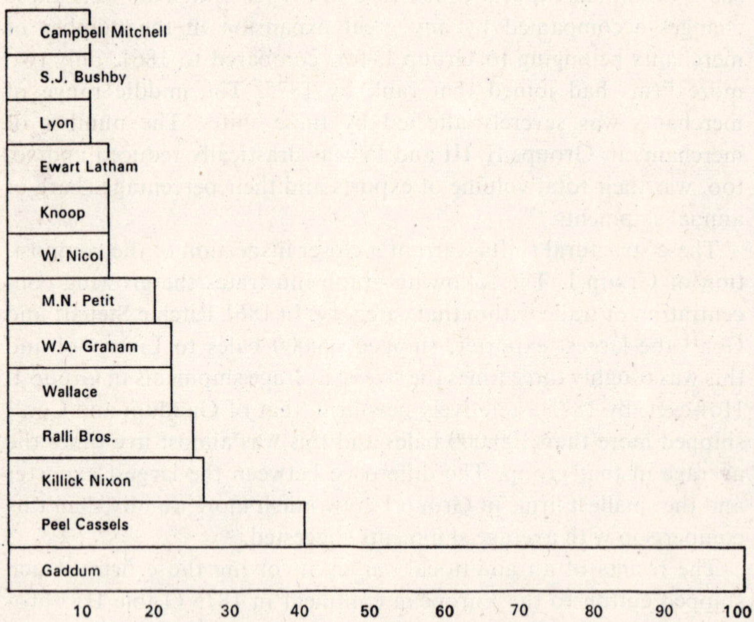

(b) Shipments in thousands of bales : 1875

of the Suez Canal a direct trading route between Bombay and the continental ports replaced the old practice of transhipment from Liverpool. The changing direction of trade after 1870 could have been reflected in the contraction of shipments to Liverpool and shifts in the relative importance of certain categories of merchants. The evidence in Table II, however, not only supports the general argument of a growing concentration of ownership in the export trade, but also suggests that exports to Europe were even more concentrated than those to Liverpool. Of the 12 firms which shipped 86 per cent of Bombay cotton to the European ports the majority were already well established in the British markets. Once again, Gaddum and Co. emerged as the largest operators. Taking this firm's total exports to both the European continent and Liverpool, Gaddum and Co. 'controlled' 20 per cent of the cotton export trade of Bombay in 1875.

TABLE II

A SUMMARY OF A SURVEY ON THE NUMBER OF BOMBAY MERCHANTS EXPORTING BALES OF RAW COTTON TO THE EUROPEAN CONTINENT IN 1875

GROUP	Total Number of Shippers	Total Amount Exported in bales	Average Exports per Shipper in bales	Percentage share of each Group
I 10,000 + bales	12	267,452	22,288	86
II 5–9,999 ,,	3	24,469	8,156	8
III 1–4,999 ,,	6	12,682	2,114	4
IV 500– 999 ,,	4	2,555	639	1
V 100– 499 ,,	15	3,129	208	1
VI 1– 99 ,,	9	332	37	—
TOTAL	49	310,619		

Until now we have limited the discussion to the basic structural changes which occurred in the cotton export trade and have concluded from the evidence that this sector of Bombay's foreign commerce was becoming concentrated in the hands of a few, large-scale firms. The second important transformation in the period 1850 and 1880 was in the ethnic character of the merchant community. Table III summarizes the relative share which the Indian and European shippers had in the total annual exports of the three sample years.

TABLE III

THE RELATIVE SHARE OF EUROPEAN AND INDIAN MERCHANTS IN THE RAW COTTON EXPORT TRADE OF BOMBAY TO LIVERPOOL IN THREE SAMPLE YEARS 1851, 1861 AND 1875

GROUP	*Number of Shippers*			*Quantity Exported in Bales*		
	Total	Indian	European	Total	Indian	European
1851						
I						
II	4	1	3	25,449	8,115	17,334
III	12	5	7	22,255	6,233	16,022
IV	17	14	3	11,668	9,335	2,333
V	95	90	5	19,164	17,588	1,576
VI	100	98	2	5,627	5,554	73
TOTAL	228	208	20	84,163	46,825	37,338
1861						
I	12	7	5	270,625	128,799	141,826
II	25	17	8	165,918	109,561	56,357
III	97	78	19	226,087	176,190	49,897
IV	76	72	4	55,254	52,625	2,629
V	222	216	6	47,607	46,022	1,585
VI	116	115	1	5,423	5,373	50
TOTAL	548			770,914	518,570	252,344
1875						
I	14	1	13	340,131	19,617	320,514
II	10	2	8	65,747	10,689	55,058
III	40	34	6	71,768	56,448	15,320
IV	35	32	3	24,541	22,517	2,024
V	173	165	8	37,514	35,329	2,185
VI	149	145	4	8,338	8,114	224
TOTAL	421	379	42	548,039	152,714	395,325

Until the 1870s indigenous merchants had a considerable stake in total exports but by 1875 the European firms had superseded, though not entirely replaced them. We begin by examining Table III of the exporters to Liverpool. In Group I of 1875 all except one of the merchants (the Indian firm of N. M. Petit)[14] were European. N. M. Petit was in the middle range of the exporters in Group I but his operations in 1875 (19,617 bales) were well below the average for that Group (which was 24,295 bales). Nor did the position of the indigenous firms improve in Group II: of the ten firms only two were Indian houses and their sum consignments amounted to only one-sixth of the Group total. The bulk of traders in Groups III to VI were indigenous and they also exported the greater part of shipments in those categories. But as has already been pointed out, the relative importance of these lower Groups had declined drastically by the 1870s. Thus growing concentration in the cotton export trade implied an increasing control by European firms. This conclusion is supported by the distribution of shipments to the European continent. Table IV shows that not a single Indian firm appeared in Group I or Group II, the combined totals of which accounted for about 94 per cent of all the consignments to Europe.

TABLE IV

THE RELATIVE SHARE OF EUROPEAN AND INDIAN MERCHANTS IN THE RAW COTTON EXPORT TRADE OF BOMBAY TO THE EUROPEAN CONTINENT IN THE SAMPLE YEAR 1875

GROUP	*Number of Shippers*			*Quantity Exported in Bales*		
	Total	Indian	European	Total	Indian	European
1875						
I	12	—	12	267,452	—	267,452
II	3	—	3	24,469	—	24,469
III	6	1	5	12,682	1,200	11,482
IV	4	1	3	2,555	504	2,051
V	15	11	4	3,129	2,029	1,100
VI	9	7	2	332	286	46
TOTAL	49	20	29	310,619	4,019	306,600

By comparing 1875 to 1851 and 1861 in Table III of exports to Liverpool we see striking differences in the involvement of Indian merchants. Although the majority of large-scale operators in 1851 were European firms and they shipped the bulk of the consignments in Groups II and III, the overall share of the Indian merchants exceeded that of the Europeans' because the total volume of exports was distributed more evenly between the Groups. As a result the small shippers (Groups V and VI), most of whom were Indian, had a considerable interest in the export trade. Furthermore, the one

Indian firm in Group II (that of Kimchund Moteychund) was the largest shipper in 1851. To sum up: in 1851 Indian merchants exported well over one half of the annual shipments of Bombay. In the 1861 sample the importance of the Indian traders was even greater than this—the quantity shipped by them in that year was roughly double the consignments of the European houses. Table III shows that except for Group I this 'dominance' applied to all categories both in terms of the number of indigenous traders and their aggregate shipments. In Group I there were 7 Indian and 5 European firms, the total exported by the latter being slightly larger than that of the former. The leading Indian firm, that of Khurshetjee Furdoonjee Parekh,[15] was also the second largest operator in that year—the largest being a European house.

The three sample years used in this survey were widely dispersed in time and therefore can only act as signposts which outline the changing composition of Bombay's export community. But there was other information which helped in identifying the early 1870s as the crucial years of transformation. In addition to encouraging the heated debates amongst merchants about the proper conduct of Bombay's foreign trade, the local newspapers themselves compiled and published statistical tables which showed the very rapid growth of European ownership in the export of cotton.[16] Against this background we can conclude two things from the above survey: first, that until the 1870s the bulk of Bombay's raw cotton export trade was in the hands of Indian merchants and second, that the trend of growing concentration in the export sector was characterized by European firms acquiring a position of dominance as the owners of export consignments. By 1875 the relative roles and importance of these two sections of Bombay's merchant community had been reversed. Until the turn of the century the European firms continued to dominate Bombay's export trade while the indigenous merchants were limited to inland commerce.[17] In contrast to Calcutta, it was the good fortune of Bombay that the growing dominance of the European firms occurred after a long period during which the Indian merchants had participated in foreign trade. This experience enabled many of the most prominent Indian merchants to acquire the capital and commercial skills which facilitated the transfer of their ability from foreign trade to local industry.

II Interpretation

In the second part of this paper we turn to consider the complex of factors which caused or contributed to the structural changes described in the preceding section.

Vernacular newspapers such as the *Jam-i-Jamshed* complained of an element of unfair competition which fostered European dominance in Bombay's export trade. It was reported that the native merchant had been driven from the field[18] and that the European firms, supported by an alien imperial government, now monopolized the export of raw cotton. There is no doubt that some European houses profited from their connections with the Bombay government, and that even the most well established Indian firm never enjoyed comparable advantages. Nicol and Co.[19] was the most blatant example of such a well connected business concern. In 1869, as managers of the Elphinstone Land and Press Company, they sold that company's reclaimed lands to the local government at vastly inflated prices. The affair created the widespread impression that a formidable private interest was bearing on the government,[20] and this aroused the hostility of the other European merchants. But as this particular example shows, government patronage was highly selective and thus it could not adequately explain changes in the structure of an export trade which involved so many diverse and competing European firms. More importantly, influence in government circles was not only secondary to, but indeed flowed from the strength of a firm's financial connections. Through the Fleming family of Glasgow, Nicol and Co. of Bombay had access to the considerable credit resources of the City of Glasgow Bank. When this bank failed in 1878 it was disclosed that for a token deposit of 5 lakhs the Bombay firm had received advances amounting to 82 lakhs.[21] Unrestricted credit facilities eventually ruined both the City of Glasgow Bank and numerous associated business houses, but not before Nicol and Co. had grown, at the expense of its weaker competitors, into one of the most ambitious and aggressive firms in western India.[22]

Mr Hamilton Maxwell, a partner of Nicol and Co., had been President of the New Bank of Bombay in the 1870s. His discretionary powers were probably instrumental in securing favourable credit terms for his firm because in 1878 it was discovered that despite the warning provided by the tragic history of the old Bank of Bombay[23] the new presidency bank had given Nicol and Co.

Rs. 510,000 credit without demanding any security or guarantee.[24] This type of privilege was not restricted to the head office of the presidency bank; nor was it exclusive to this one European firm. Upcountry branches of the Bank of Bombay had liberal lending policies in their dealings with important European merchants. A newspaper correspondent reported in 1878 from the market town of Amraoti:[25]

It has always been a matter of surprise to me how our Bank gives large 'cash credits' to the European trading class in Berar who make a living ostensibly on the 'cash credit system' as the capital they are known to possess, in proportion to the advances they are allowed, is no security whatever.

When dealing with the modern banking institutions of Bombay the European firms enjoyed many obvious advantages. To this extent the complaints of the vernacular newspapers were justified. However, the vernacular press itself did not explain or analyse the causes of the disabilities suffered by the Indian merchants: the complaints were bitter but superficial. In all probability the familiarity of the European merchants with the methods of modern banking and the personnel managing these institutions meant that they were less of a credit risk. But a modern banking structure was only one ingredient in the commercial environment of the 1870s and so the skewed nature of the credit facilities could not explain the growing dominance of the European firms.

Reflecting the opinions of their compatriot traders, the English newspapers of Bombay argued that the changes in the export sector after 1870 were brought about by the 'superior business aptitude displayed by the European merchants in the special circumstances of the present time'.[26] In a strictly literal way, the 'superior business aptitude' of the European merchants was not a convincing explanation because it ignored the substantial contribution of the indigenous merchants to Bombay's early development. But, in a much wider sense, there was some truth to this assertion. After 1870 new methods of conducting long distance trade were rapidly replacing the old ways and it was the European business houses which took the lead in making the necessary adjustments.

i. The Consignment System

The consignment system was the first victim of the revolution in international transport and communication which epitomized the post-1870 era. To appreciate why this was so, it is necessary to review the way in which the system worked. Bombay merchants and firms who did not have overseas contacts (head offices, branches or correspondents) shipped produce to foreign markets through agency houses. The agents assumed all the responsibilities for managing the export operations. This allowed exporters who did not have any specialized knowledge of the cotton trade, who did not speak English or any other foreign tongue, and above all, who did not possess substantial capital of their own, to engage in long distance trade. The existence of a consignment system suggests that until the 1870s the export trade of Bombay was not very specialized. More significantly, it also indicates that the European firms in their capacity as agency houses played a 'dominant' role in India's foreign commerce long before they came to 'dominate' as shippers on their own behalf.

The consignment system evolved from the East India Company practice of giving advances to private traders of up to two-thirds on the value of any shipment.[27] The value of a consignment (its anticipated selling price abroad) was determined on inspection by a government official. After 1851 the Company discontinued this practice and agency houses and exchange banks substituted for the Company's role. From then on the consignment system was a much more elaborate process. A multifaceted trade pattern which involved many intermediaries (see diagram) replaced the vertical flow of goods which had previously been channelled through the East India Company.

The consignor now obtained an advance from the Bombay agency house either directly through the agent's consignment department or indirectly through an independent consignment broker.[28] As before the money advanced was calculated on the basis of the anticipated proceeds but the actual proportion of the advance to the total value of the goods fluctuated with the degree of competition between the agency houses.[29] The company's practice of inspection was abandoned and instead the consignor now needed the 'good word' of a guarantor. In short, the consignment system came to be based on the principle of *Shah*—the ancient Indian custom of doing business only with persons of good character. The guarantor could be either a well known Bombay firm or the Bombay agent of an important upcountry trading concern. Guarantees for the quality of the consignment were given verbally to the manager of the agent's consignment department, but after the notorious Aurora Frauds (1870)[30] it became more common to demand a written guarantee.[31]

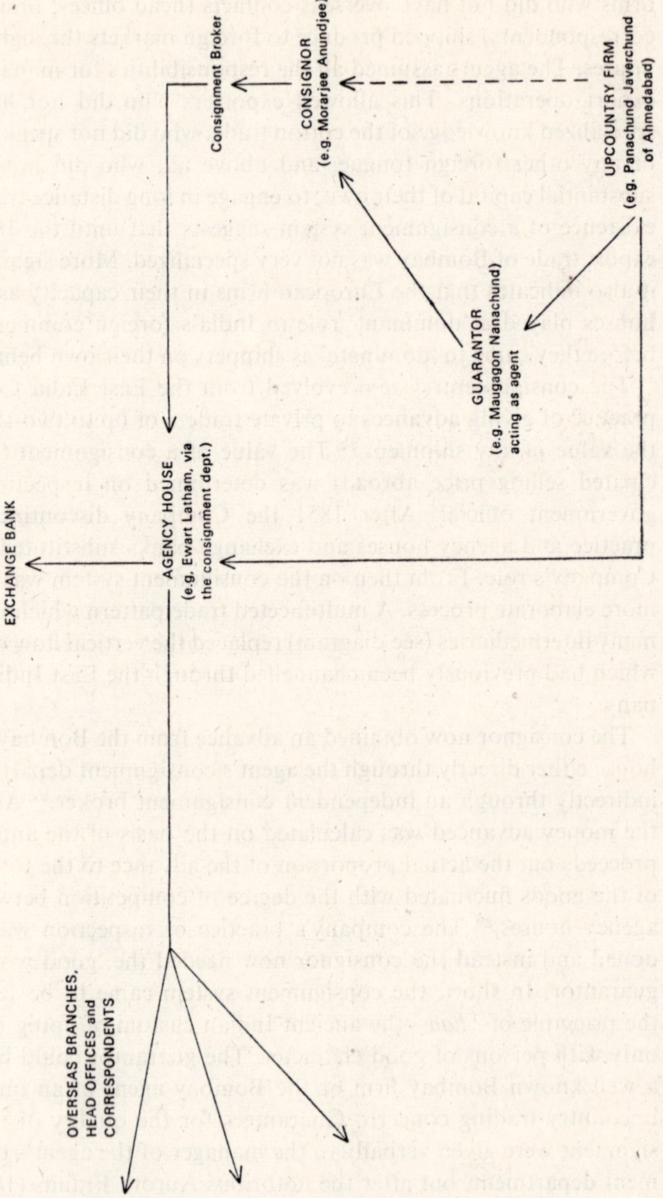

DIAGRAM ILLUSTRATING THE PRINCIPAL INTERMEDIARIES
INVOLVED IN THE CONSIGNMENT SYSTEM AFTER 1851

The consignment system relied upon a battery of intermediaries not only at the export end but also on the purchasing side. In the diagram for instance,[32] the consignor purchased raw cotton through his *shroff* (banker, money changer) who in turn purchased the goods from a larger firm—often a firm for which the *shroff* was acting as a Bombay commission agent. The *shroff* was not only the consignor's purchasing broker but also his guarantor. Sometimes the firm with which the *shroff* was connected acted as the guarantor. Apart from the conflict which could arise from this intermeshing of interests, the noteworthy point about the system was that the consignor's sole function was to issue instructions to various middlemen. If instructions could be given promptly, it was possible for the consignor to minimize his capital investment by using the advance from the agent to pay for the raw cotton he had purchased.[33] Could it be that the consignment system was one of the reasons behind the highly speculative character of the cotton trade in the 1850s and 1860s?

Shipping cotton through an agency house was not unlike mortgaging property—with the difference that accounts were settled after the consignment had been sold abroad. Once an agreement had been reached between the shipper and the agent, the former drafted a Bill of Exchange which was then discounted by the agency house. Often this Bill was rediscounted by the agent with a local exchange bank. If the consignment realized a profit, the difference between the proceeds and the advance was remitted to the consignor. If the proceeds fell short of the advance, a redraft demanding payment of the difference was presented to the shipper.[34] The remission of profits (or losses) to the Bombay exporter is the criterion for determining the ownership of Bombay's export staples.

In both its domestic and international aspects the consignment system had obvious weaknesses. For the agent the security of a verbal guarantee was not always sufficient because it was difficult to establish what exactly the guarantor had promised. Even written guarantees were inadequate protection if a serious disagreement arose between the agent and the guarantor about the quality and value of a consignment. Then there was the possibility that the guarantor himself had an ulterior interest in securing an advance on the consignor's behalf. One such case occurred in 1870 when the shipper used his advance to pay off his largest creditor, the Ahmedabad firm of Panachund Javerchund.[35] The guarantor, Maugagon Nanachund, had also been acting as Panachund's agent. A third type of risk arose if a Bill of Exchange was discounted before the goods were loaded on ship. This provided the exporter with an opportunity of substituting the intended consignment with inferior goods.[36] But fraud of this sort was very rare. The exporter, on the other hand, was at risk when a Bill of Exchange was discounted by the agent at an exchange bank. The Bombay banks had no interest in the identity of the actual consignor. According to Otto Müller, manager of the Comptoir d'Escompte de Paris in Bombay, the exchange banks looked to the credit and respectability of the firm managing the shipment because the 'consignors were often men of straw and we never look to them'.[37] From statements such as these, it appears that the principle of *Shah* had been adopted by the modern financial sector of Bombay. Thus, when an agency house failed, the exchange bank appropriated all the property tied to those unmatured Bills it had discounted. When, for instance, Tyabji and Co. went bankrupt in 1866, their creditor, the Comptoir d'Escompte de Paris, refused to settle accounts directly with the clients of this agency house.[38] The wealthier shippers could challenge this procedure in the High Court, and at least one Indian merchant had his property returned in this particular instance.[39]

In its international aspect the most common complaint by the agency houses was the difficulty of ascertaining the identity of the Indian partners involved in joint ventures. When a redraft was due it was in the interest of those persons who wanted to escape from their financial commitments to say that they did not belong to the firm concerned, or that they had no share in that particular venture.[40] In the absence of any system of registration,[41] and given the multiplicity of ephemeral partnerships and the general lack of information about the composition of indigenous firms, the agency houses often had difficulty in obtaining restitution from the more anonymous business firms.

But the consignment system displayed its greatest weakness in matters of personal judgement. The problem was that once the shipment had left the shores of western India the consignor had virtually no control over the vital decisions made in the disposal of his goods. In realizing the value of the consignment the shipper was totally dependent on the good faith, good sense and accurate judgement of the overseas agent. Hence it was the custom to meet a redraft only on the understanding that the agent had exercised all due skill and caution on his client's behalf.[42] If negligence could be established the redraft was rejected on the basis of a breach of contract. In times of great economic uncertainty there was every possibility that the overseas agent and the Bombay shipper would differ not only in their assessment of the present and anticipated condition of the market but also in the appropriate course of action. One illustration should suffice to clarify this point. In 1864 the firm of Ramkrishna Sazba rejected a redraft from Lawrence and Co. alleging that the overseas agent had failed to understand the developments in the American Civil War:[43]

> If peace in America had been re-established and dreading the consequence they had sold our cotton we would not have grudged to accept their Bills; but on the contrary, it was a time when it was believed by the English public that Lincoln stood almost every chance of re-election and when symptoms of money becoming easy were apparent. We must respectfully state that we do not think that Messrs. Lawrence and Co. paid regard to our interest.

To this the agent replied:[44]

> We can assure you that opinions were very much divided on the subject (of the course of the war) and as to any prospect of money becoming cheaper, we think that it was generally believed that it would become still dearer.

Even when the Bombay exporter and the foreign agent communicated regularly, ultimately it was the agent's responsibility to decide when and how much cotton to sell. This method of long distance trade placed the Bombay exporter in a weak and disadvantageous position. The agent for his part began to take, from the mid-1860s onwards, measures to secure his position by rewording the Letter of Hypothecation. This document set out the conditions of the advance and gave basic instructions for the insurance and sale of the consignment. It also included a clause which said that all redrafts would be accepted by the exporter *provided* that the transactions had been conducted in good faith. By the inclusion of a new clause the agent relieved himself of this constraint and in future the consignor was compelled to accept all redrafts unconditionally.[45]

Despite the inherent weaknesses in this method of trade the consignment system was not breaking down of its own accord. The agency houses and exporters were aware of the risks attached to this type of business activity and adjustments on both sides were continually being made to eliminate the worst defects. Also it is important not to exaggerate the element of conflict which was involved. The Civil Proceedings of the High Court of Bombay, from which most of the information on the relationship between the agency houses and the shippers was collected, dealt only with the litigious aspects of Bombay's commercial life. The principal threat to the consignment system probably came from Bombay's 'Share Mania'.[46] The financial crisis of the mid-1860s not only destroyed the leading Indian firms,[47] many of which had acted as guarantors for the smaller shippers, but it also severely shook the confidence of Bombay's trading community and thereby ushered in an era characterized by excessive caution and distrust. The 'Share Mania' had damaging repercussions. Even so, the combination of these external and internal pressures would not have sufficed to doom the consignment system to extinction. The real challenge came from the changing international environment in which long distance trade after 1870 was conducted, and the novel demands this made on those firms which wanted to trade in Indian staples.

ii. The International Environment

With the end of the American Civil War the United States gradually regained its position as the world's leading producer of raw cotton. From 1866 onwards this was reflected in the long term decline in cotton prices, from which India was the first to suffer because the short staple she produced had a limited and irregular market unlike the medium and long staple substitutes grown by her competitors. For the Bombay shipper the export trade became extremely risky. By comparison, the European importing firm was in a much better position to assess fluctuations in demand on the basis of which it could then place specific orders in Bombay:[48]

> If importers at home who should know exactly the wants of the consumers on the spot, send out their letters of credit with orders for cotton to be sent overland, our merchants will no doubt be glad to do such business with all possible despatch. But as to shipping cotton around the Cape on the responsibility, either directly or secondly, of merchants here, that we take to be out of the question for anyone who looks fairly at the present position of the market and the rapidly increasing stocks.

Some European firms had already established branches in Bombay in the early 1860s, and after 1866 the role of these in forwarding produce to their head offices became more important. Reliable telegraphic communication[49] also increased the preference of the European based firm to import cotton on its own account. Everything now depended on speed, promptitude and precision.[50] By contrast, the consignment system became cumbersome and outmoded and it was unable to adapt to the development of international future trading. Rather than ship blindly to Liverpool in the hope of selling cotton after arrival, telegrams enabled the Bombay merchants to trade by 'firm offers'. Shippers now cabled 'offers' to Liverpool and these were accepted 'if they were at such prices as would enable the house . . . to sell "futures" against them at a profit'.[51] Many indigenous merchants who survived the 'Share Mania' faced bankruptcy in the late 1860s and early 1870s;[52] according to the Bombay newspapers this happened because they had not resorted to the new business methods.[53]

As distant markets were brought into closer and more frequent contact with telegraphic communication, the opening of the Suez Canal and the growth of steam shipping, the price differences between goods in these markets tended to diminish. In such a situation profits margins in long distance trade were bound to shrink.[54] Profits could be maintained only if measures were taken to reduce the costs of inland transport and foreign shipping. The new technology of the 1860s and 1870s made this possible, but it was up to the individual firm to take the necessary measures to streamline its trading operations. As economies of scale became increasingly important in this process of adjustment, the larger firms came to dominate Bombay's foreign trade.

Economies were first effected in the inland transport of raw cotton. The European firms in Bombay sent their representatives to the upcountry market towns as soon as these had been linked by the railway lines to Bombay city.[55] The inland agents not only purchased supplies but also ginned and pressed cotton. Before the coming of railways, cotton reached Bombay city in loosely packed bales called *dokra.* This form of packaging was unsuitable for railway cartage and the Great Indian Peninsular Railway Company introduced a graduated freight rate which penalized *dokras* and encouraged the movement of half-pressed, and especially full-pressed bales.[56] Those merchants who wanted to avail themselves of the advantage of railway transport therefore had no choice but to full-press cotton in the hinterland.[57] This development in packaging might have appeared trivial, but it had far-reaching consequences. After cotton had been full pressed upcountry, it was ready for immediate export on arrival in Bombay. Full-pressing in the hinterland eliminated a wide range of charges incurred by the inspection, repacking, storage and cartage of unpressed cotton and half pressed cotton on the Bombay market. But, because a full-pressed bale was never inspected or opened, the success of this system depended on the use of standard cotton classifications from Liverpool. Unfortunately, for reasons not entirely clear to us, the indigenous merchants both in Bombay city and the upcountry towns were slow in adapting to this practice and as a result they forfeited a large part of the inland trade to European business houses.[58] By moving into the hinterland the European firm integrated and simplified a marketing process which had involved various Indian middlemen, each with a distinct function. It was the large-scale firm which benefited most from this transition.

Equally important was the reduction in shipping costs between Bombay and Liverpool. But this was not feasible until the opening of the Suez Canal which greatly enhanced the advantages of transport by steam ship. First, a steamer could be loaded in under ten days, but a sailing ship required up to five weeks.[59] As a result, steamers reduced the costs of storage and fire insurance on the Bombay foreshore. Second, although the freight rates for shipment through the Canal were higher than those for the old route around the Cape of Good Hope,[60] the shorter duration of the voyage lowered the cost of marine insurance and reduced any deterioration in the quality of the goods.

Shipping by steamer through the Suez Canal created new problems for the small-scale operator. The accelerated speed of long distance transport allowed Indian cotton to reach Liverpool earlier in the year—in the months of June and July. It was during this same period that the bulk of American cotton came to the British market. As a result, after 1870, Indian cotton competed more directly with the American supply.[61] What prevented the Bombay exporter from spreading his shipments more evenly over the whole year? It was the monsoon. Until the construction of proper dock facilities in the 1880s, Bombay's shipping season was limited to the first half of the year. The monsoon rains of late June not only disrupted international shipping, but also coastal transport which remained an important method of conveying the cotton from Gujarat and Kathiawar even after the railways had linked the northern provinces to Bombay city. The monsoon climate, combined with the uncertain demand for Indian cotton in the short term, made the costs of storage in Bombay city or in the upcountry markets prohibitive. Poor storage facilities meant a deterioration in the quality of the fibre and hence its market value, whilst the additional expense of warehousing, without the certainty of a better selling price at a later date, was a risk which the Indian merchant could not easily undertake. The alternative of storing cotton in Liverpool or Manchester for an indefinite period was not a feasible proposition for the Indian shipper who had no foreign warehouses and who was dependent on his agent's judgement in timing the sale of his goods. Furthermore, after 1870, when the usance on Bills of Exchange was reduced from four to three months,[62] the Bombay shipper had less time in which to realize the value of his shipment. Although we do not know much about the financial resources of the large British and European firms it seems improbable that their trading operations were seriously restricted by considerations such as the usance on foreign bills. Also, the Bombay house which had its head office in Liverpool, Manchester or London was more likely to possess the management and financial resources necessary for carrying stock.

iii. The European Firms

Not only were the international conditions favourable to the rise and spreading influence of the European firms, but also within India itself the growth of modern transport helped foreign firms to achieve the position of 'dominance' which was discussed earlier. This section of the paper examines the activity of the European firms in the Bombay hinterland.

Although the opening of the Suez Canal increased direct trade with the European continent, only a few new firms were established in Bombay. There had already been a great expansion in the number of foreign business houses. Three main stages of growth can be distinguished. Following the gradual abolition of the East India Company's trading privileges, a number of Scottish firms were set up in the 1820s and 1830s.[63] The abolition of the Navigation Acts further broadened the sphere of private trade,[64] and for the first time continental firms like Volkart Brothers[65] were attracted to the trade of the east. Then in the 1850s and 1860s branches of Manchester and Liverpool houses were established. These were motivated by the prosperity of India's foreign trade and the new opportunities created by the growing commercialization of India's agricultural production. It was the largest of these firms, Gaddum and Co. and Ralli Brothers,[66] which came to dominate the cotton trade of Western India.

The European firms of Bombay were not a homogeneous group:

they had been established at different times for different reasons, they represented many nationalities, and they were engaged in a diverse number of commercial ventures. But transcending all these differences was their attempt to achieve some vertical integration in their cotton export business. Since the 1840s the European firms of Bombay had expressed the desire to eliminate the Indian intermediaries who purchased cotton in the agricultural districts, transported it to Bombay city and then resold it to exporters. The first attempts by Europeans to place their agents in the upcountry markets were not successful.[67] But with the construction of the major railway lines European firms rapidly established their presence in the hinterland in the form of upcountry purchasing agents and upcountry ginning and pressing companies. The leading European houses of Bombay city promoted and managed the companies: for example, Nicol and Co. managed the Mofussil Press and Ginning Co.;[68] Volkart Bros. were associated with the United Press Co.;[69] and Gaddum and Co. controlled the Berar Co.[70] The companies owned factories in the hinterland markets: in 1875 for instance the Berar Co. owned ginning factories at Budnaira and Khamgaon and pressing factories in Julgaon, Khamgaon, Akote and Amraoti.[71] The European managers were usually shareholders in these companies, had representation on the Board of Directors, and derived their income from both commission on management and dividends as part-owners. Although most of the ginning and pressing companies represented joint ventures between European and Indian capital (as evinced by the mixed character of the Boards of Directors), it seems that the involvement of indigenous business interests did not go beyond the motivation of a good investment. By contrast, the European managing firms viewed these companies as tools for their own advancement in the export trade of western India. In turn, the financial success of these companies was directly linked to the fortunes of the European managers. The struggle between Macauley and Co. and Gaddum and Co. for control of the Mofussil Press and Ginning Company in 1878 demonstrated this point. The shareholders eventually elected Gaddum and Co. to replace Nicol and Co. as managers for the following reasons.[72] First, because Gaddum and Co. were the largest buyers of cotton in the mofussil, it was expected that as managers Gaddum would bring a large proportion of their cotton to be cleaned and packed at this company's factories. Second, Gaddum and Co. were prepared to buy shares in the Mofussil Press and Ginning Company, thus bringing in new capital and forging a direct identity of interest between the company and its manager. Finally, Gaddum and Co. were already managing the successful Berar Co., and this demonstrated the firm's managerial ability. It is also probable that the Mofussil Press and Ginning Co. envisaged definite advantages from Gaddum and Co. acting as the manager of the two largest, and hitherto most competitive, companies in the hinterland.

Those European firms which were not involved with upcountry factories were nevertheless well served by the facilities provided by those which were. Ralli Brothers, for example, did not extend their business activity into this quasi-industrial field until the turn of the twentieth century.[73] However, from the mid-1860s onwards, this firm did establish purchasing agencies in the major upcountry markets. It was the responsibility of these agents to fill orders despatched from Bombay, ensure that the cotton was properly ginned and packed into full pressed bales, and expedite the arrangements for transporting these bales to the port of Bombay with the least possible delay.

In the districts where the European firms established agencies, branches and factories they developed new trading networks which partially replaced, or at least circumvented, the old channels of trade via Indian middlemen. The penetration of the European firms into the hinterland stemmed in the first instance from the changes in the export trade. In the previous section we saw that from the mid-1860s the Bombay shippers were under great pressure to effect economies in their trading operations. By integrating the procurement of supply with their export business the Bombay firms were able to meet this challenge. The desire to eliminate the Indian middlemen had existed from the beginning of private trade in India, but it was not until railways provided new economic opportunities that this became practicable or profitable. By the mid-1870s, almost one half of the raw cotton which reached the port of Bombay arrived as full pressed bales, and most of this belonged to the European houses. But it is difficult to conclude from this that the European merchants had established a monopoly of the cotton trade of western India. Even in the Central Provinces and Berar, where the foreign merchants had their deepest roots, it is doubtful whether even the largest firm controlled the supply of any one of the producing districts. The impact of the European firms rarely extended beyond the large inland market towns. Moreover, if they wanted to procure supplies from

Gujarat, Kathiawar or Dharwar they had to enter into contracts with Indian importers and middlemen.

iv. The Indian Merchants

The way in which the European merchants responded to the changing circumstances of commerce in the 1860s and 1870s is only one aspect of a complex process. It is equally important to ask ourselves what happened to the Indian merchants who played such an important role in Bombay's foreign trade before 1870? To answer this question we need to differentiate between three basic categories of Indian shippers: the 'men of straw' or the small-scale amateur operators; the importers who specialized in the upcountry trade; and finally the large exporting firm which traded in a number of commodities.

The small-scale, unprofessional shippers (Group VI in Table I)[74] persisted as a feature of Bombay's export trade throughout the period 1850 to 1880. It is difficult to say who these 'merchants' really were because the bulk of them were individually insignificant and therefore remained anonymous.[75] Many of them were probably small shopkeepers, clerks or petty dealers who shipped produce only occasionally as a speculation. No doubt they often acted on the advice of their better-connected friends. Often their export operations were motivated by the need to raise a short term loan and when things went wrong they normally ran off to their home villages. In these circumstances anyone, even a child,[76] could become a 'merchant' overnight. Although the operations of these amateurs annoyed the agency houses and professional merchants, they had only a marginal effect on the condition of the trade.

The Indian importer represented a completely different interest. The volume of cotton he exported in any one year varied with the quality of each season's output and the condition of the Bombay spot market.[77] The large-scale Indian and European shippers tended to export the better quality cotton, and this often left the importer to ship the remaining, less valuable stock. From various petitions and reports it has been possible to establish the identity of the leading firms in this category.[78] Many of them belonged to the *bhattia* caste. It is difficult to say to what extent the importing of cotton overlapped with the business of export in any one of these firms. But we do know that Jivraj Balloo,[79] without doubt one of the largest firms, was also an important exporter of raw cotton. Other merchants, like Mooljee Jeatha, who was the biggest buyer of cotton in the Khandesh district,[80] preferred to concentrate on the import trade. Goculdass Tejpal[81] and Luckmidass Khimjee[82] were two firms which shipped large volumes of cotton as part of their general trade. Although they were known primarily as cotton exporters and piecegoods merchants, given the extent of their inland business connections it is probable that they also imported raw cotton and other commodities from the hinterland. The merchants of this class of exporter were eminent men within their own castes, and well known and respected by the European community of Bombay.

Indian merchants who specialized as raw cotton importers did not have the international networks of the larger firms, and hence they shipped produce through agency houses. But this line of business gradually lost its attraction. With the revival of cotton production in America the market for the inferior staples which the importers had shipped in previous years declined. More significantly, the expansion in the number of Indian cotton mills[83] increased the internal demand for cheaper varieties of fibre. In supplying a local market the importer no longer needed to bother about ginning and pressing. In brief, the evidence suggests that the Indian importer was lured from the export trade by the better alternatives available in inland commerce.

Finally we come to consider the Indian firms which in their size and eminence ranked with, and even surpassed, the leading European houses. The majority of these were Parsi and in the first half of the nineteenth century they accumulated massive fortunes in the China trade.[84] It was characteristic of these firms to have numerous overseas branches in Britain and the Far East and this enabled them to act in the dual capacity of merchants on their own account, and commission agents. The financial panic occasioned by the crises on the cotton market in 1865 and again in 1866 ruined the best of them.[85] Two of the important firms which survived, that of Dinshah Manakji Petit[86] and Merwanji Framji Panday,[87] were extensively involved in industrial ventures such as promoting cotton mills. After 1866 these firms, like the Indian importers, turned their attention to supplying the internal market. But past assessments of the 'Share Mania' have exaggerated its detrimental effects on the Bombay business houses. The shrewder and more solvent Indian merchants benefited from the collapse in property values by buying valuable estates at depressed prices.[88] The claim made by a contemporary observer,[89] that every creditor was a debtor and every debtor a creditor, can mislead the reader, for when all the accounts were ultimately settled a handful of Bombay firms clearly emerged as creditors.[90] Nevertheless, the 'Share Mania' had important repercussions on the export trade because it eliminated, with few exceptions, the large-scale Indian shipper.

Conclusion

The eclipse of the Indian merchants as the owners of Bombay's raw cotton export crop can be attributed to many overlapping factors, Some business houses were ruined by the financial crisis of the mid-1860s. Those firms which remained, or re-established themselves after clearance by the Insolvency Court,[91] shifted their interest from long distance overseas trade to the commerce of the interior and the promotion of nascent industries. But it would be inaccurate to assume that these adjustments were made in a smooth or voluntary fashion. Technological innovation, a catalyst of changes in this era, was not always ethnically neutral in its effect. In theory all the merchants of Bombay city should have benefited from the introduction of the railway, but in practice the evidence clearly shows how the railway promoted, to the detriment of the Indian shipper and importer, the designs of foreign firms. In a similar way, the complexion of the international environment from the mid-1860s onwards favoured the large-scale European firm. But of course, we need to know much more about the experience of individual European and Indian firms before the evidence on this point can be accepted as conclusive.

The question, to which there is no immediate or simple answer, is whether the transformation described in this paper was beneficial to the development of Bombay—or more generally India. It is tempting to argue that it was more important for Indian capital to develop indigenous industries capable of generating employment and technological change in new directions. But the contribution which foreign trade is capable of making to a country's economic development should not be underrated. Can it be that the 'engine of growth'[92] was not beating audibly in the Indian environment of the last quarter of the nineteenth century because the country's export crops, especially raw cotton, were the property of foreign firms?

NOTES

1 See, for instance, Morris D. Morris, *The Emergence of an Industrial Labour Force in India, A Study of the Bombay Cotton Mills 1854–1947* (London and California, 1965), p. 15, note 28.

2 Some prominent Indian firms which had agents in London also acted as consignment agents for the Bombay merchants. A list of these is given in the *Times of India*, 2 March 1867, 3 at a time when the rate of commission was increased from 2.5 to 3.5 per cent. It is difficult to say what proportion of the Bombay consignment trade these Indian firms attracted. The impression is that the European houses handled the bulk of this sort of business because (a) they had wider business networks in Britain and Europe and (b) they were more familiar with the market and had better access to credit. In any case, after the 'Share Mania' most of the Indian agencies disappeared.

3 See the Balance Sheet of Nicol and Co. on their bankruptcy in 1878. One quarter of that firm's 'unsecured liabilities' were classified as 'Native Loans': *Times of India*, 9 October 1878, 3. Meetings of the creditors confirmed that Nicol and Co. owed a lot of money to Indian investors: ibid., 5 October 1878, 2; 9 October 1878, 3. The *Times of India* reported on 11 October 1872, 2 that Nicol's failure had shaken 'native trust in Europeans'.

4 The percentage share of raw cotton in the total value of Bombay's foreign trade in the nineteenth century was: 1800–10: 91.0; 1811–20: 85.7; 1821–30: 42.9; 1831–40: 30.0; 1841–50: 21.5; 1851–60: 45.5; 1861–70: 71.8; 1871–80: 55.5; 1881–90: 40.5; 1891–1900: 31.3. (SOURCE: *The Gazetteer of Bombay City and Island*, I, p. 421.) The above percentages have been calculated from the value of exports given in lakhs.

5 Bombay's share of India's total volume of raw cotton shipments in the period 1856 to 1875 was:

1856–57	87.0 per cent	1865–66	65.6 per cent
1857–58	92.0 ,,	1866–67	65.0 ,,
1858–59	94.0 ,,	1867–68	72.6 ,,
1859–60	92.0 ,,	1868–69	70.7 ,,
1860–61	93.0 ,,	1869–70	69.3 ,,
1861–62	86.9 ,,	1870–71	75.0
1862–63	77.2 ,,	1871–72	66.0 ,,
1863–64	73.6 ,,	1872–73	64.8 ,,
1864–65	72.5 ,,	1873–74	77.6 ,,
		1874–75	80.0 ,,

SOURCE: *Bombay, Annual Statement of the Trade and Navigation of the Presidency, 1855–56 to 1874–75*; J. E. O'Connor, *Review of the Accounts of the Trade and Navigation of India for 1874/75 as compared with previous years* (Calcutta, 1876).

6 Liverpool was Britain's major cotton market. The percentage of Bombay's total volume of exports which went to British markets in the period 1855 to 1876 was:

1855–56	76.0 per cent	1865–66	95.8 per cent
1856–57	82.4 ,,	1866–67	94.5 ,,
1857–58	77.0 ,,	1867–68	88.0 ,,

1858–59	76.0 per cent	1868–69	80.7 per cent
1859–60	75.1 ,,	1869–70	80.9 ,,
1860–61	78.4 ,,	1870–71	81.9 ,,
1861–62	93.4 ,,	1871–72	70.9 ,,
1862–63	95.0 ,,	1872–73	72.9 ,,
1863–64	95.4 ,,	1873–74	72.1 ,,
1864–65	94.5 ,,	1874–75	69.4 ,,
		1875–76	64.5 ,,

SOURCE: *Bombay, Annual Statements of the Trade and Navigation of the Presidency, 1855–56 to 1875–76.*

7 The first attempt to introduce some uniformity into the 'chaotic medley of absurd and inconsistent forms of Indian geographical and personal names as written in the English character' was made by Dr. W. Hunter of the Statistical Department of the Government of India. By Government Order of April 1868 Hunter's system was adopted by the Post Office, the Telegraphic companies and the Railways: *Times of India*, 15 February 1872, 3. But the Customs House of Bombay was unaffected by this and remained insensitive to the problem of transliteration.

8 For an account of the way in which the Bombay Customs House collected this information see: A. W. Elliott (Assistant Collector of Customs), *The Rules and Practice of the Bombay Customs House and the Bombay Customs Code* (Bombay, 1843), pp. 39–53. The Export Manifests of the port of Bombay exist in three forms:

(a) as the original documents in the present Customs House. But these are unsorted and hence difficult to use.

(b) in the private publications of certain individuals, but I have not succeeded in locating any of these: see (Maharashtra State Archives), Revenue Dept. 1854, CLXII, Collector of Customs, 28 January 1854.

(c) as daily reports in the columns of the *Times of India* under the heading 'Journal of Commerce'. This was the source used in the present study. For an account of how the data were collected see my doctoral thesis: 'The Cotton Trade and the Commercial Development of Bombay, 1855–75' (University of London, 1975), pp. 186–9.

9 For a complete list of the names of all the Bombay exporters and the quantities of raw cotton shipped by each of them in the years 1851, 1861 and 1875 see my doctoral thesis, ibid., Appendix I, pp. 367–84.

10 On the problem of selecting sample years see ibid., p. 187.

11 This was a Scottish firm, which was first mentioned in the *Bombay Kalendar and Register 1820*, pp. 106–7. For a brief history of this firm see the manuscript of a history of Forbes, Forbes and Campbell of Bombay (2 vols.) in the possession of Mr. F. H. Kemple of the same firm in Bombay. Forbes and Co. and Ritchie Steuart and Co. amalgamated in 1903.

12 Gaddum and Co. established a Bombay branch in *c.*1865. J. K. Bythell, the firm's local manager, became a prominent man in that city. For a fascinating account of the background to the Gaddum family see: P.W.G., *Henry Theodore Gaddum, His Forebears and his Family: A Revision and a Continuation of H.E.G's. The Gaddum Family* (Manchester, 1973, private circulation only).

13 This survey was conducted in exactly the same way as the sample of exporters to Liverpool.

14 For a short history of N. M. Petit see *Times of India*, 25 April 1873, 3.

15 H. D. Darukhanawala, *Parsi Lustre on Indian Soil* (Bombay, 1939), pp. 90–1, 'C. F. Parekh (1819–1896)'. Parekh failed during the Bombay Share Mania in 1866: *Times of India*, 3 July 1866, 3 and John Lawrence Collection, India Office Library and Records, London: MSS. Eur. F. 90/45, Sir B. Frere to J. Lawrence, 7 July 1865, Poona.

16 For a complete list of the leading exporters in the years 1870 to 1875 see my doctoral thesis, op. cit., pp. 199–200; *Times of India*, 3 August 1875, 2; *Bombay Gazette*, 17 July 1872, 2.

17 This separation of interest was seen in the composition of Bombay's two major merchant associations: 25 per cent of the members of the Bombay Cotton Exchange Limited (an Indian organization formed in 1890) were exporters, the rest importers. But 75 per cent of the subscribers to the Bombay Cotton Trade Association (a European organization formed in 1875) were exporters and only a quarter were importers. M. L. Dantwala, *A Hundred Years of Indian Cotton* (Bombay, 1948), p. 65.

18 Extract from the *Jam-i-Jamshed* in *Times of India*, 4 June 1873, 3.

19 One of the early Scottish firms set up in Bombay. It was first mentioned in *Bombay Kalendar and Register 1824*, p. 87.

20 *Reports from the Select Committee appointed to Inquire into the Finance and Financial Administration of India*, *Parliamentary Papers*, II, 1873 (194) XII, Evidence of J. M. Maclean, 2629, 2486, 2487, 2488.

21 *Economist*, 26 October 1878, 1256; 23 November 1875, 1372–3; *Times of India*, 5 October 1878, 2; 9 October 1878, 3; 11 October 1878, 2.

22 *Times of India*, 11 October 1878, 2.

23 The best account of this is in the *Report of the Commission on the Failure of the Bank of Bombay*, *Parliamentary Papers*, 1868–9 (4162) XV.

24 Extract from the *Rast Goftar* in the *Report on Native Newspapers*, 19 October 1878, 12.

25 *Times of India*, 12 October 1878, 2.

26 Ibid., 24 October 1872, 2.

27 For the conditions relating to the hypothecation of goods by the Company see: *Report from the Select Committee on Indian Territories, with Minutes of Evidence*, *Parliamentary Papers*, 1852 (533) X; Appendix 2, pp. 311–55.

28 Bombay High Court [hereafter BHC], Justice Charles Sargent's notebook [hereafter Sargent], vol. XXII, No. 257 of 1871, pp. 24–36, Evidence of Heerjeebhoy Hormusjee (consignment manager of Forbes and Co.); pp. 42–3, Evidence of Panachund Jadowjee (consignment broker to Forbes and Co.).

29 *Proceedings of the Council of the Governor of Bombay, 1869*; 21 October 1869, Mr A. H. Campbell (of Ritchie Steuart and Co.), p. 217.

30 On the Aurora Frauds see: *Times of India*, 20 July 1870, 3–4; 1 August 1870, 5–6. These frauds were perpetrated by the leading *European* freight broker house of Bombay.

31 BHC Proceedings on the Original Civil Side [hereafter Proceedings], No. 257 of 1871, Forbes and Co. *v.* Ootoomchund Heerjee, Statement of Plaintiff.

32 This illustration is based on information gathered from numerous cases in

the High Court of Bombay. A good example of an Indian shipper who lacked any expertise in the cotton trade is to be found in: BHC Sargent, vol. XXII, No. 257 of 1871, 9 December 1871, pp. 70–3, Evidence of Latiff Noor Mahomed (the shipper); pp. 51–6, Evidence of Mohunjee Bhimjee (guarantor). Latiff N. Mahomed was a timber broker by profession and on his own admission, could not tell the difference between one type of cotton and another.

33 Sometimes consignment business was more blatantly resorted to as a method of raising short term finance. Once the money had been obtained many of these 'merchants' absconded: *Times of India*, 29 July 1872, 2; 18 February 1867, 2; 14 November 1866, 2; *Bombay Gazette*, 25 May 1871, 3.

34 BHC Proceedings, No. 105 of 1865, Passmore and Co. *v.* Jetha Megjee, Statement of Plaintiff.

35 BHC Sargent, vol. XXI, No. 585 of 1870, pp. 118–20, 122–6, Evidence of Sorabjee Nowrojee (consignment manager of Ewart Latham and Co.); ibid., vol. XXII, 585 of 1870, pp. 44, 49–63, Evidence of Girdhur Dalsook. The names of the parties involved in this case were used as illustrations in the diagram.

36 In 1872 Dewsee Jairaz and Nursey Lilladhur were convicted of attempting to cheat Ewart Latham and Co. by shipping cotton waste and sweepings instead of old Dholera and New Kutch cotton: *Times of India*, 3 July 1872, 4. A more controversial case which also involved an internal caste dispute was that of Govind Girdhur: BHC Sargent, vol. XV, No. 252 of 1867, Trustees of Govind Girdhur *v.* Macdonald Twedie and Co., pp. 8–9, Evidence of Govind Girdhur; pp. 21–3, Evidence of Mooljee Thackersey (Mukaddam to Twedie). But a firm which was really desperate for finance would not even bother to ship produce once an advance had been obtained: see *Times of India*, 8 February 1871, 5 and 14 March 1871, 3, regarding the fraud by Eduljee and Pestonjee Shapoorjee. As the Chamber of Commerce pointed out, the only solution was in European firms not signing Bills of Lading until the goods had been placed on board ship: *Report of the Bombay Chamber of Commerce, 1869–70*, p. 21 and Appendix R.

37 BHC Sargent, vol. XIII. No. 786 of 1866, Hajee Suffer Misky *v.* Gustave Pietsch, pp. 81, 85, 87, Evidence of Otto Müller.

38 BHC Proceedings, No. 786 of 1866, Hajee Suffer Miskey *v.* Gustave Pietsch, Statement of the Defendant.

39 BHC Sargent, vol. XIII. No. 786 of 1866, p. 87, Judgement.

40 For example see: *Times of India*, 7 May 1873, 3, Judgement of Mr Justice Green; BHC Sargent, vol. XXIX, No. 343 of 1876, Henry Maxwell *v.* Pudumsey Luckumsey, pp. 76–8, Evidence of Shamjee Sozpal; pp. 69–72, Evidence of Rodger Sedgwick; BHC Proceedings, No. 343 of 1876, Statement of the Defendant.

41 The Chamber of Commerce's request for the compulsory registration of Indian partnerships had been rejected by the Government of India as impracticable and unsuited to Indian conditions: *Report of the Bombay Chamber of Commerce, 1867–68*, pp. 132–3, J. Taylor to the Secretary to Government Judicial Department, 24 January 1868, Bombay; ibid., *1874–75*, pp. 491–5. The request was repeated in 1878: ibid., *1878–79*, pp. 439, 447–9.

But the Chamber withdrew its demand because the task of drawing up a draft Bill proved too difficult: ibid., *1878–9*, p. 336.

42 BHC Sargent, vol. XIII, No. 1779 of 1866, Roper Price *v.* Assaria Poonsey, p. 101, Evidence of Assaria Poonsey.

43 BHC Proceedings, No. 113 of 1865, Lawrence and Co. *v.* Ram Krishna Sarzba. Exhibit F, Sarzba to Lawrence, 16 December 1864.

44 Ibid., Exhibit G, Lawrence to Sarzba, 17 December 1864.

45 BHC Proceedings, No. 1779 of 1866, Roper Price *v.* Assaria Poonsey, Statement of Defendant and Exhibit of the Hypothecation Document.

46 For an account of this financial crisis see: R. S. Rungta, *The Rise of Business Corporations in India 1851–1900* (Cambridge, 1970), pp. 72–93.

47 For a list of the major Indian firms which failed in the 1860s see my doctoral thesis, op. cit., Appendix VI, pp. 395–7.

48 *Times of India*, 2 May 1867, 2; also 29 August 1867, 2.

49 In 1864–5 the average time of transit for a telegram between Britain and Karachi via the submarine cable was 5 to 6 days: *General Report on the Administration of the Bombay Presidency 1864–65*, p. 171 and Appendix VI. By the mid-1870s the time of transit had been reduced to a maximum of four and a half hours via Teheran and 23 hours via Turkey: *Indo-European Telegraph Department Administration Report 1875–76.*

50 *Times of India*, 24 October 1874, 2.

51 T. Ellison, *The Cotton Trade of Great Britain* (London, 1886), p. 280. Ellison's comment was a general one, though it also applies to Indian trade.

52 *Times of India*, OS, 25 December 1869, 1, *re* failure of Goculdass Lilladhur, Dyal Khimjee and Mukundass Morarjee.

53 Ibid., 10 January 1870, 2; 3 February 1870, 3. But without access to the records of these Indian firms, we cannot be sure of the business methods used by these houses.

54 *Bombay Gazette*, 1 January 1872, 2.

55 For an account of the development of Bombay's railway lines and their effect on inland trade see my doctoral thesis, op. cit., Chapter 6.

56 The amount of railway freight saved by full pressing cotton into bales of 400 lbs. each, rather than transporting an equal weight in *dokra* form, was calculated to be in excess of Rs 7 per bale: *Bombay Builder*, 5 December 1866, p. 122; also see *Times of India*, 12 October 1866, 3.

57 For a discussion of the early problems of rail transport see: *Railways in India 1865–66, Parliamentary Papers*, 1866 (3696) LII, pp. 605, 613, 619; *Native Opinion* in the *Times of India*, 7 May 1866, 3; *Report of Mr H. Rivett-Carnac, Cotton Commissioner for the Central Provinces and the Berars, On the Operation of his Department for the year 1867, Parliamentary Papers*, 1868–9 (289), XLVI, pp. 75–8, 90–2.

58 J. K. Bythell (Gaddum and Co.) before the Annual General Meeting of the Bombay Chamber of Commerce: *Times of India*, 15 March 1872, 3.

59 *Times of India*, 5 August 1874, 2.

60 See reports on the freight market in the 'Journal of Commerce', *Times of India* from 1870 onwards.

61 Ibid., 5 August 1874, 2.

62 *Bombay Gazette*, 11 July 1870, 2. The usance on foreign bills had already

been reduced from six to four months sight in 1866 (*Times of India*, 11 July 1866, 3; 23 August 1866, 2; 27 July 1866, 2) and the native merchants had complained of the hardship which this occasioned (*Indu Praksh* extract in *Times of India*, 19 July 1867, 3).

63 *Bombay Times*, 8 March 1852, 226.

64 The double duty on imports and exports in foreign bottoms had worked prejudicially on Bombay's foreign trade with the European continent: *Third Report from the Select Committee (of Sess. 1847) on the Navigation Laws, Parliamentary Papers*, 1847–48 (7) XX, Part I, F. C. Brown, 3820–1; P. Colquhoun, 3951.

65 For a history of this Swiss firm see: H. Peter, Solomon Volkart (1816–1895), in *Schweizer Pioniere der Wirtschaft und Technik* (Zürich, 1956) No. 6, pp. 59– ; G. Reinhart, *Volkart Brothers, In Commemoration of the Seventy-Fifth Anniversary of the Foundation* (Winterthur, 1926).

66 For the background to this Greek business house see: *Ralli Brothers Limited* (London, 1951); J. Gennadius, *Stephen A. Ralli, A Biographical Memoir* (London, 1902); B. G. Orchard, *Liverpool Legion of Honour* (Liverpool, 1893), 'N. Paspati'.

67 See my doctoral thesis, op. cit., Chapter 6, pp. 247–59.

68 *Times of India Directory 1870*, pp. 491–4.

69 This company was formed in 1873 with the amalgamation of factories in Tuticorin, Berar and Kathiawar. In 1873 an 8 per cent dividend for 6 months was declared (*Times of India*, 16 September 1873, 3).

70 *Times of India Directory 1875*, p. 385. By 1880 they also managed the India Press Co., ibid., 1880, p. 792.

71 *Times of India Directory 1875*, p. 385.

72 *Times of India*, 24 October 1878, 3; 2 November 1878, 3; 6 November 1878, 2.

73 *Ralli Brothers Limited.*

74 This is only a rough approximation. Not all the shippers in Group VI could be regarded as 'men of straw'; some of them were well-known firms which had decided not to deal in raw cotton in those particular years. Nor were all the trade's amateurs confined to this category. Depending on personal wealth, the combined resources of an extended family or a sudden and sizable inheritance, it was possible for an amateur to deal on a much larger scale.

75 An example of this was the frequent confusion of names and identities. A certain Bhimjee Canjee narrowly escaped imprisonment by proving that another man by the same name (deceased at the time of the enquiry) was the correct party concerned: BHC Sargent, vol. XXIV, Notes pertaining to Bhimjee Canjee, pp. 22–4 for evidence of various witnesses. Adding to the confusion and enhancing the anonymity of these petty merchants was the custom of trading under assumed or fictitious names: BHC Sargent, vol. XXX, No. 528 of 1877, Dayabhoy Jugjeewandass *v.* Wallace and Co., p. 88, Evidence of Luckmidass Khimjee; pp. 107–8, Evidence of Motechund Hurruckchund.

76 BHC Proceedings, No. 133 of 1865, Jamnadass Balkisondass *v.* Govindass Vurjeewundass, Statement of Defendant. At the time of purchasing the raw cotton the defendant was 16 years old and a student of Elphinstone College.

77 For an account of the intricate market mechanism which influenced the decisions of the Indian importers see my doctoral thesis, op. cit., Chapter 4, pp. 123–32.

78 Ibid., Appendix V, pp. 393–5; *Times of India*, 15 August 1876, 3, *re* meeting of Indian cotton merchants to oppose the rules of the Bombay Cotton Trade Association; ibid., 27 July 1874, 3, *re* a petition of Indian cotton merchants 1 July 1874 expressing dissatisfaction with the old contractor of the Railway Carting Agency.

79 R. F. Vacha, *Mumbai-no-Bahar* (Bombay, 1874), p. 112, gives a history of how the family came from Kutch to Bombay and amassed a fortune.

80 *Report of the Commissions to Inquire into the Working of the Cotton Frauds Act* (*IX of* 1863) *with Minutes of Evidence* (Bombay, 1873), Evidence of C. Wilkinson, Cotton Inspector for Khandesh, pp. 88–93.

81 R. F. Vacha, op. cit., p. 124, records how his uncle first came to Bombay from Kutch and worked his way up from walking the streets as a hawker, to acting as a night watchman, to trading as a merchant along the western coast. Goculdass's father began as a stamper of cotton bales and later joined his brother in the coastal trade. When Goculdass Tejpal died in 1867 he left behind 37 lakhs: BHC Proceedings, No. 601 of 1870, Shamavahoo, widow of Goculdass Tejpal *v.* Dwarkadass Vussonjee.

82 R. F. Vacha, op. cit., p. 118. This firm were guarantee brokers to the European agency house of Wallace and Co.

83 Morris D. Morris, op. cit., Appendix I, p. 213: between 1870 and 1876 the number of Bombay Textile Mills increased from 10 to 29.

84 Christine Dobbin, *Urban Leadership in Western India: Politics and Communities in Bombay City, 1840 to 1885* (Oxford, 1972), pp. 9–13. Kharshedji Furdonji Parekh was a typical case. As the son of a wealthy *Parsi* merchant he went to China in 1835. After his father's death in 1841 he returned to Bombay and became a partner in Jamsetji Jijibhoy and Sons. When this firm was dissolved in 1850 he began to trade on his own. His personal fortune was immense. D. H. Darukhanawala, op. cit., pp. 90–1.

85 On the failure of K. F. Parekh: *Times of India*, 3 July 1866, 3; on B. H. Cama: ibid., 19 May 1865, 3; 22 May 1865, 3; 13 June 1865, 3; on S. N. Nanabhoy: ibid., 22 May 1866, 3; on Luckmedass Hunsraz: ibid., 8 August 1866, 3; 1 October 1866, 3; on Cursondass Madhowdass: ibid., 31 May 1866, 3.

86 Christine Dobbin, op. cit., p. 156.

87 H. D. Darukhanawala, op. cit., p. 430.

88 For instance, Morarjee Goculdass, who had been one of Bombay's leading piecegoods merchants, purchased the George the Third Jute and Wool Mill Co. which he converted into a cotton Mill: *Times of India*, 18 October 1880, 2.

89 D. E. Wacha, *A Financial Chapter in the History of Bombay City* (Bombay, 1910), p. 219.

90 For example, creditors like Jivraj Balloo had to write off a large proportion of their loans as bad debts. But judging from the reports in the Bombay newspapers this firm, like a number of others, recovered a good percentage of their outstanding loans and was therefore in an enviable position com-

pared to the plight of many business houses: *Times of India*, 2 June 1866, 2; 22 May 1866, 3.

91 For example, in late 1867 S. P. Framjee applied to the Court for permission to commence trading (*Times of India*, 12 August 1867, 3). However, it is very difficult to trace the career of most firms which went bankrupt but eventually recommenced business. The names of the firms were changed, different partners joined and new capital was absorbed.

92 W. Arthur Lewis, *Aspects of Tropical Trade 1883–1965: Wicksell Lectures 1969* (Stockholm, 1969), p. 10. Also see his *Tropical Development, 1880–1963, Studies in Economic Progress* (London, 1970), edited by W. Arthur Lewis.

8

Monetary Policy and Economic Development: The Rupee Ratio Question 1921-1927

B. R. TOMLINSON
University of Birmingham

The rupee ratio question of the early 1920s was not simply a matter of the ratio of the rupee. Underlying the often bitter controversy between government officials and the spokesmen for the most advanced sector of Indian industry over the interests of native manufacturers and foreign importers, of rich peasants and landless labourers, of producers and consumers in India and of industrial capitalists and the proletariat was a clash of opposed notions on the correct role of government policy and its links to the agricultural and industrial development of the colonial economy. Those who argued so passionately for a 1s. 6d. or a 1s. 4d. rupee were not merely quibbling about exchange rates, the issue was that of the purposes of monetary policy as a whole. As a government official reported at the height of the storm:

> The absence of demand for [cotton] piece goods is generally attributed [in Bombay] to the effects of the currency and exchange policy of Government. . . . [T]he better informed do not object so much to the high exchange as to the monetary policy which has crippled the buying power of the peasantry by restrictions imposed on the normal expansion of currency. The majority . . . contend that the present position has been brought about by Government's policy and that it is up to Government to come to the aid of the industry in meeting a situation brought about by its own action.[1]

To understand the issues at stake in this debate we must first trace the history of monetary policy since the time India was placed on a gold-exchange standard in the 1890s. The two committees which had then considered the problem of India's relationship to the international economic system (the Herschell Committee of 1893 and the Fowler Commission of 1898) had both recommended as an ideal solution that India be placed on the international gold standard with a gold currency. Had this policy been implemented, India's balance of settlements with the rest of the world would have been settled by the import or export of gold. Gold brought into the country in payment of India's export credits abroad would have been presented to government mints and turned into coins; thus an export surplus would lead to an automatic expansion of the currency. To balance an import surplus, gold would have to be exported and hence the level of currency contracted. The automatic regulation of the Indian economy would have been assured by the operation of the quantity theory of money. In practice, however, the conservatism of the Indian peasantry and the suspicions of the British Treasury combined to frustrate the Government of India's attempts to introduce a gold currency. In any case, the most economically sophisticated of the members of the Government of India and the India Office saw that in the special circumstances of India there was no need for a gold coinage or a full gold standard. India's major link to the international economy was via London—most of India's foreign trade was financed from London, the silver bullion for her silver coinage could best be bought there and the largest single transaction in her international balance of settlements was the remittance of the home charges to the Secretary of State. When India had a balance of trade surplus, as she normally did, it was thought to be needlessly inconvenient and expensive to force purchasers of Indian goods to send gold to India when that gold would then have to be shipped back to London by the government to enable the Secretary of State to buy the silver bullion necessary to coin rupees and expand the currency. If India had a balance of trade deficit, then her creditors would have to be paid in a gold-based currency not in silver rupees; it would be cheaper for them, and hence less debilitating of Indian reserves, to be paid in London rather than in India. In these circumstances it made more sense for London rather than Calcutta or Bombay to be the place at which the equalizing transactions in India's international balance of settlements were carried out. To transfer money from Indian revenues to London to meet the home charges the Secretary of State had always offered Council Bills, sold for sterling in London which the government met in rupees in India. Between 1898 and 1913 this system was simply extended and although some of India's trade surplus was met by the import of treasure most of it was balanced by the sale of Council Bills.[2]

The 1914–18 war destroyed both the international gold standard and India's gold-exchange standard. War conditions changed the nature of the real world from that on which the basic assumptions of classical economics were based. The Council Bill system tended to move funds from India to London and the level of currency in India could only be maintained and expanded by the return of silver bullion to be coined into rupees. During the war the price of silver rose and the difficulties of supply and of shipping increased. At the same time, the Government of India's need for funds grew greater because of heavy sales of Council Bills needed to meet the large surplus of raw materials vital to the Allied war effort. The Government of India also had to finance a large amount of 'imperial' war expenditure out of its own resources—the money to pay for this being reimbursed by the War Office in London which did not help liquidity problems in India. To ease the strain, Council Bills were rationed and exchange controls introduced in 1917. To create new currency without silver bullion the note issue was increased against British Treasury Bills bought by the Secretary of State and against Indian Treasury Bills issued by the government in India. Also in 1917 the rising world price of silver resulted in the bullion value of the 1s. 4d. rupee being greater than the coin's token worth. Thus the exchange rate was forced upwards, reaching 2s. 4d. in January 1920. By the end of the war the interdependence of the exchange value of the rupee with the level of currency in India—the essential basis of the pre-1914 monetary system—had been shattered. The exchange rate was now determined by the sterling price of silver and the level of currency in India was largely influenced by the government's need for cash.

In 1919 a new expert committee (the Babington–Smith Committee) was appointed to find a solution to these problems: its report proposed a gold standard with a gold coinage and an exchange rate of 2s. gold. The selection of a high rate for the rupee was thought by the expert committee, and by the currency authorities in India, to have several advantages; an important one would be to facilitate the contraction of currency and the deflation of the economy. The Babington–Smith Committee's recommendations were put into effect in January 1920 and the government prepared to support the new exchange rate by the sale of Reverse Councils, which were also a means of contracting the currency. Unfortunately, events proved that

1920 was not a suitable year in which to attempt to reform Indian currency and the new ratio had to be abandoned in September.[3]

From September 1920 to October 1924 the monetary authorities in India consciously refrained from any action to influence the rate of the rupee exchange, which fell initially to 1s. 3d. sterling in early 1921 and then slowly rose to 1s. 6d. in late 1924. But eschewing influence on exchange did not mean that the authorities could do nothing at all. The imperatives of internal governmental finance and of remitting funds to London to meet the Secretary of State's expenditure necessitated action which affected the level of currency circulating in India. Because of the world trade depression the Secretary of State was not able to sell any Council Bills in London until January 1923, yet his expenditure still had to be financed. This was managed in several ways: by raising loans in London, by using the recoveries from the War Office from 'imperial' war expenditure and, most importantly for Indian conditions, by cancelling currency notes in India to release capital from the currency reserves in London for revenue purposes. During the war the Government of India had evolved several new techniques for meeting its short-term needs for cash. The most important of these was the issue of Treasury Bills in India both as short-term loans from the public and as backing in the Paper Currency Reserve to allow extra notes to be issued in India. By 1919 this floating debt represented 63 per cent of the government's total revenue.[4]

The end of the war did not magically remove the government's liquidity problems. Its revenue was decreased by the trade slump while its expenditure was raised by renewed hostilities in Afghanistan. The floating debt could only be reduced in two ways—bills held by the public could be paid off and bills held in the currency reserve could be cancelled by the withdrawal of currency notes. Officials realized that the existence of this vast amount of floating debt made the government's financing uncertain and too closely tied to fluctuations in the Indian money market, while the created securities in the currency reserves meant that a large proportion of Indian paper money was virtually unbacked.[5] Thus from 1921 onwards the government attempted to whittle down this floating debt as and when it could by cancelling currency notes and the created securities issued to support them, paying off treasury bills and converting short-term debt into long-term debt. This policy was made difficult to implement by the fact that the Government of India's budget was in deficit from

1918–19 to 1922–3, by a total of nearly Rs 100 crores, but the re-establishment of a budgetary surplus in 1923–4, thanks to severe tax increases and retrenchment, enabled the government to redeem all Treasury Bills in the hands of the public by July 1924.[6]

The Government of India managed to contract the currency by almost Rs 52 crores between January 1920 and March 1923, while consistently denying that it was 'engaging upon some policy of deflation on doctrinaire grounds and with some notion of bringing down prices or artificially raising exchange'.[7] Officials were very well aware of the dangers of squeezing Indian credit too hard, for the sake both of their own loan programme and of the financing of trade. The point was frequently made that the imperfect nature of the Indian money market and credit institutions made monetary and credit control extremely difficult and risky. The level of economic activity in India was not constant throughout the year but fell into a distinct 'busy' and 'slack' season.[8] The internal economy was financed mainly by actual movements of cash rather than by transfers of credit, cash crops were purchased by sending rupees up-country to pay the cultivator and these rupees only returned to the trade centres when they were spent on commodities. Banking in the *mofussil* hardly existed, most agriculturalists holding their savings in silver bullion, jewelry or hoards of coin, so a considerable amount of currency went out of circulation every year and never returned to the banks. Thus governmental activity in the short-term loan markets and the contraction of currency by withdrawing it from the government balances held by the Imperial Bank had a disproportionately intense reaction on the financing of trade.[9]

The monetary authorities in India were ill-equipped to take decisions about the optimum level of circulating currency. The official in charge of expanding and contracting the currency was the Controller of Currency in Calcutta, aided by a deputy in Bombay. To estimate whether money was likely to be too tight or too slack at any given moment, these officials had to make guesses about the character of the next monsoon, assess the probable world demand for Indian exports and the Indian demand for imports and make assumptions about major stock market trends. The lack of machinery for automatically contracting the currency was seen as one of the weaknesses of the pre-war gold-exchange system,[10] and with the rupee floating there were not even any guide-lines for officials to follow. The Finance Department was aware of the weaknesses of this arbitrary system—as Sir Basil Blackett pointed out to the 1926 Royal Commission, 'you cannot accurately gauge whether deflation is needed by the country by any method whatever'[11]—and they were alive to the dangers of contracting the currency too much. Even when Reverse Councils had been on sale in 1920 the government had felt unable to contract the currency by the full amount of Reverse Councils sold (Rs 47,14 lakhs were received for reverses but only Rs 36,68 lakhs worth of notes cancelled) because of fears of creating too great a stringency in the Indian money market.[12] The Babington–Smith Committee had stipulated that to reduce the amount of 'created' securities in the Indian Paper Currency Reserve the interest accruing from such securities should be used to pay off as many as possible each year, with a corresponding contraction of currency. The Finance Department officials took up this scheme in 1920 but in March 1922, rather to their relief, the Legislative Assembly amended the budget to divert this interest to revenue.[13]

Between 1921 and 1924 attempts were made to solve the problem of the fluctuating seasonal demand for currency by setting up an automatic system of expansion and contraction against trade bills. Following another suggestion to the Babington–Smith Committee, the Government of India announced in February 1922 that it would issue currency notes to the Imperial Bank against internal trade bills held by the bank, these notes to be withdrawn and cancelled as the bills were paid.[14] Initially this arrangement was implemented for Rs 5 crores of notes when the bank rate reached 8 per cent, but during 1923–4 the amount was increased to 12 crores to be issued in instalments as the bank rate rose from 6 to 8 per cent and in 1925–6 it was decided to issue the whole amount when the bank rate reached 7.5 per cent. However these provisions for emergency currency never worked properly; the amounts involved were too small and the scheme of issuing currency against *hundis* was inefficient since most Indian internal trade was financed by the far cruder instruments of cash credits and advances on demand promissory notes.[15]

From 1921 to 1927 the Government of India was without a clear-cut or theoretically sound monetary policy. Remittance needs required some currency deflation and the stringency that this, and the government's equal need for loans, caused in the credit market was offset only by partial palliatives. Officials were agreed that the only solution to these problems was for the rupee to be re-established on an exchange standard and to be linked, preferably directly, to the international gold standard.[16] 'You cannot have an automatic currency until you have got your rate fixed',[17] but the traumatic experience of attempting to maintain the 2s. gold rupee in 1920 had taught that India could not go it alone. The rupee could not be stabilized until other major currencies, notably sterling, had returned to the gold standard.[18]

In the winter of 1922–3 Indian trade revived to an extent which made it possible once more to make remittances by selling rupee exchange for sterling. Improvement in trade and a slow rise in world prices pushed exchange up from 1s. 4d. sterling in 1923 to 1s. 6d. sterling in October 1924. Officials now began to be haunted by another memory of the 1920–1 crisis, the way in which a sudden rise in exchange followed by an even faster fall had caused disruption in the import trade by creating massive price fluctuations in imported goods. Determined now to remove any uncertainty, the government proposed to London a *de facto* policy of purchasing enough sterling exchange to prevent the rate going materially above 1s. 6d. In November 1924 the Secretary of State gave his consent, although stressing that this was simply a temporary measure which should in no way prejudice an eventual decision on the exchange rate.[19]

The Government of India managed to hold the Secretary of State to this position when exchange hardened again in the busy season of 1925–6, but, once a new currency commission had been appointed, exchange began to weaken again as rumours that the rate would be lowered to 1s. 4d. encouraged remittance and speculation. The currency had been expanded in 1924–5 and 1925–6 by a net amount of Rs 15 lakhs partly to facilitate trade and partly to restrain the rise in the exchange.[20] When exchange broke in March 1926 it was decided that the 1s. 6d. ratio should still be maintained until the Royal Commission's report was issued, again to prevent the disruption to trade that a fluctuating exchange would produce, and that the best way to secure this object was by contracting the currency. An unsigned, undated note (probably by Blackett in mid-April 1926) defended this policy of holding exchange steady as the only logical one and pointed out that since the currency had been expanded in the previous busy season by the purchase of British Treasury Bills in London for the Paper Currency Reserve from the Secretary of State's treasury balances, rather than by issuing emergency currency, this contraction was merely the equivalent of the automatic deflation that would have taken place as the emergency currency was withdrawn.[21] The net contraction of Rs 31,25 lakhs between April and December 1926 was considerably more than the expansion of the two preceding years,[22] but this was not thought to be evidence that the rupee was over-valued at 1s. 6d. The contraction was seen as having been necessitated by the return of rupees from hoards in payment for bullion and by the growth of banking and credit institutions, while the recovery of exchange to 1s. 6d. later in the year offered 'conclusive evidence that prices have in the main adjusted themselves to a 1s. 6d. ratio'.[23]

Indian monetary policy had always been the target of attacks from within India and in the period 1924–6 these reached a new intensity. The most powerful section of Indian commercial and business opinion, that grouped around the Bombay cotton magnates, had always advocated a cheap money policy to stimulate industrial growth and welcomed currency inflation as a method of easing credit and raising internal purchasing power. Ever since the 1890s, Bombay propagandists had attacked the government's monetary policy for not expanding the currency sufficiently. The gold-exchange standard was seen as a means of 'draining' India's resources to Britain and obstructing the formation of native capital; the currency contractions of 1920–6 were seen as a plot to stunt India's industrial growth and open up the internal market to artificially cheapened British imports. The post-war industrial boom and the slump of the early 1920s had had dramatic effects upon Bombay. A survey of 75 of the 85 mills in Bombay in 1923 estimated that 26 had made a profit in the previous year, 43 a loss and 6 had broken even.[24] The unusually high price of raw cotton in 1923–4 pushed up production costs, while a slump in cotton prices in 1924–5 disturbed the up-country market for Bombay's goods.[25] By May 1925 unsold stocks of cotton goods were piling up in Bombay and there were increasingly loud protests about the currency policy which was seen as responsible.[26]

A Royal Commission on Indian Currency and Finance (Hilton–Young Commission) was appointed in 1925 to advise on a currency system for India and an exchange value for the rupee. The Bombay school's attack on government policy now concentrated into a lobby to fix the rupee at 1s. 4d. The main thrust of this campaign was directed not against the implications of a high exchange for foreign trade but against the contraction of currency, tightness of credit and fall in internal prices that were the results of the new rate. While the government argued that prices in India had already adjusted to the higher exchange, and that therefore any increase in the currency would lead to socially disruptive price inflation, most Indian witnesses before the Commission tried to show that prices were already too low to sustain a healthy amount of internal commercial acitivity and that they would fall still further if the 1s. 6d. rate was maintained. Both the Finance Department and its critics in Bombay were agreed that once the internal economy had adjusted to the new level of prices then it did not matter, within very broad limits, what that new level was since both outputs and inputs would conform to it. The argument over adjustment was focused on two points—the level of wages in the Bombay cotton mills and the price of raw cotton and certain food grains, notably pulses.

During the massive price inflation of the war years and the immediately post-war boom, the wages of mill hands in Bombay had soared. According to Sir Victor Sassoon, who represented the Bombay Millowners Association before the Royal Commission, wages had risen from a base of 100 in 1914 to 231 in 1926.[27] The official figures showed a rise in nominal wages of only 87 per cent in the same period, equal to a real rise of 68 per cent taking increases in the cost of living into account.[28] Everyone was agreed that the wage problem was peculiar to western India, industrial wages in Bengal having increased by less than 50 per cent, but agreement was not so universal about what relevance this fact had for the formulation of monetary policy. To Sassoon the 'stickiness' of wages in adjusting to the now-declining price level demonstrated the damage that deflating the economy could do to Indian industrial enterprises and was therefore a major indicator of the need for inflation:[29] to Blackett this was an internal problem for the mill-owners and not one with which government policy ought to be concerned.[30]

The controversy over the level of prices of agrarian produce was more wide-reaching. To the mill interest, narrowly defined, the relatively lower prices of the major cash crops of western India compared to pre-war levels was a cause for concern in that they caused a depression in the up-country market for their produce.[31] More generally, some of the Indian economists who appeared before the Commission argued that the lower prices of exportable cash crops impaired the profits of the most advanced sector of agriculture, pulled down prices of crops produced for the internal market and intensified the burden of debt on all classes of agriculturalists.[32] The official reply to this case was to point out the full implications of the quantity theory of money. With a lower price level what was important was not the amount of money which a peasant received for his produce, but the amount of commodities (or gold) which he could purchase with his surplus. Both the commodities sold and those bought would be cheaper by the same proportion and although the gold cost of debts incurred before 1917 would be higher their rupee cost would remain the same.

This debate revealed two very different and equally over-generalized conceptions of the Indian rural economic scene. The British and their supporters chose to assume that Indian agriculture ran on a fully cash-based marketing model: the Bombay school postulated a rural society in which everything except cloth and bullion was produced on the spot and in which any surplus was turned into cash. Thus while the government and its supporters thought that any agrarian adjustment to a new price level would produce no long-term changes, their critics maintained that the higher the internal price level the better since the peasantry sold much more than it bought.[33] The discussion of this issue before the Commission revealed some remarkable conceptions of the nature of the agrarian economy, epitomized by the surreal exchange between Prof. C. N. Vakil and Sir Rajendranath Mookerjee over whether the peasant would rather have enough to eat but till his fields naked, or clothe his body so that he could beg his food.[34] It is not surprising that the government never accepted the claims of the mill industry and its advisers to speak with the real interests of the peasantry at heart. More interestingly, nationalist politicians, the self-appointed spokesmen of the masses in this period, shared this scepticism. As late as January 1927 the Currency League thought it necessary to despatch a long letter to the All India Congress Committee setting out their case,[35] while Motilal Nehru, leader of the Congress group in the Legislative Assembly, reported to Thakurdas, his patron, that he was not convinced in favour of 1s. 4d.[36] Both the government and its critics were in fact projecting the view of rural society which was necessary to support the rest of their case. The official view, as we will see, was determined by their wish to allow the 'natural forces' of the world economy to transform Indian agriculture, while the arguments of the Bombay school only really applied to the rich cotton growers of western India with whom they dealt so closely.[37]

The report of the Royal Commission did not concern itself with the question of the ideal interests of Indian agriculture, contenting itself with demonstrating that internal prices had largely adapted to the 1s. 6d. rupee and therefore recommending that rate. Similarly, the minority report of Sir Purshottamdas Thakurdas in favour of 1s. 4d. limited its argument to demonstrating that prices had not yet so adjusted. Both reports based their respective cases on an examination of the index numbers of Indian prices, in which neither claimed any confidence as adequate statistical data. The majority report seems to have had the better of this sterile argument; in any case, as Blackett pointed out in the debate on the Currency Bill in the Legislative Assembly, even if prices were not completely adjusted to the 1s. 6d. ratio they were certainly not adjusted to the 1s. 4d. one.[38]

The most interesting of the many questions raised by the controversy over the rupee ratio between 1921 and 1927 is that of the role that the government saw for its monetary policy in the development of the Indian economy. The Bombay interest claimed that the government wanted a high exchange to cheapen its remittances to London and give a boost to imports. Unfortunately there is no evidence for these allegations in the many discussions on the ratio within the Finance Department. Given their belief that Indian prices had already adjusted to the new ratio, officials did not expect any significant increase in imports as a result of fixing the exchange at 1s. 6d.: they did argue that a lower ratio would increase the government's expenditure during the new period of adjustment, but saw this in terms of the interests of the Indian tax-payer, interests which they were hard at work defending against the Secretary of State in a contemporary battle over effecting remittance by purchasing sterling in India.

The most important difference of attitude between officials and their critics was over the role that the government could and should play in the economic development of India. In keeping with their position since the question was first discussed in the 1890s, officials advocated a higher rather than a lower exchange rate in the interests of the consumer over the producer although they had little idea of, and little interest in finding out, what these neatly polarized categories really represented. Their experience since the collapse of the gold-exchange standard in 1917 had convinced officials that monetary policy ought to be passive rather than active; no amount of concern for the interests of Indian commerce nor provision for emergency currency could produce a monetary policy as efficient as what would result from linking the Indian currency system up to the world economy through a gold standard.

The idealized official picture of agrarian life as based around a sophisticated cash-orientated market economy reflected the official model for Indian development. The problems of industry and agriculture could best be solved by the fostering of credit institutions, a stable exchange and an expansion of the cash economy: these prerequisites could only be established by integrating India fully into the world economic system and keeping government interference to a minimum. The prices of agrarian produce might be relatively lower in the 1920s than they had been before the war, but that, it was thought, was a worldwide phenomenon about which government could and should do nothing.[39] The attitude of government was encapsulated in the comment of a Legislative Department official in 1927 on the mill-owners' case:

> It has been suggested by Sir Victor Sassoon that the lowering of the ratio will increase the prices of agricultural products and consequently the purchasing power of the agriculturalist, and the result will be increased profits to mills and to trade all round. This is a remarkable statement to make. If it were easy to create wealth by manipulating exchange, why do not other nations adopt it and where is the limit?[40]

Only four years later many other nations were seeking to do just this.

The advocates of the 1s. 4d. rupee claimed to speak for the whole of India but in fact represented a strong sectional interest. The Government of India in supporting the 1s. 6d. ratio also claimed to speak for the whole of India but in fact represented nobody. At the heart of the government attitude to monetary policy lay a political problem—active attempts to change the framework of colonial societies make imperialists too many enemies and not enough friends. The real case for 1s. 6d. was very simple: government had to abdicate control of monetary policy in favour of an automatic system to ensure 'confidence',[41] and since prices had already adjusted to 1s. 6d., that ratio represented the status quo. Therefore a gold standard system regulated by a central banking institution could be established more quickly if the ratio were not altered again. Blackett was aware of Keynesian ideas of regulating exchange to secure an optimum internal price level, but he thought the notion impractical because it 'leaves the Government in the same invidious position as they were in before the exchange was temporarily stabilised at 1s. 6d. and open to violent criticism from every quarter in every conceivable contingency'.[42] The government won the battle of the rupee ratio when the Central Legislative Assembly passed the Currency Bill early in 1927. However their position had been dictated by their weakness not their strength. Over the next five years, as officials in Delhi and imperial policy-makers in London struggled to cope with the problems caused by the slide of world commodity prices into depression, it was brought home to them just how weak their position really was.

NOTES

1 D[emi] O[fficial] Deputy Controller of Currency to Secretary, Government of India Finance Department 25.5.25 Government of India Finance Department Proceedings [hereafter IF], 64-Finance [hereafter F], 1925.

2 See J. M. Keynes, *Indian Currency and Finance* (Revised Edition, London, 1971).

3 See H. Stanley Jevons, *Money, Banking and Exchange in India* (Simla, 1922), Chapters XIII to XV.

4 *Statistical Abstract of British India*, 1901–11 to 1919–20, Tables 44, 76, 89.

5 See, for example, note by E. M. Cook 5.7.22, IF Accounts & Finance Branch [hereafter A&F], April 1923, 522C.

6 *Reports of Controller of Currency*.

7 DO Secretary, Government of India Finance Department to Financial Secretary, India Office 12.4.22. IF (A&F), May 1923, 60–123A.

8 The 'busy' season ran from August to October in Calcutta, from August to April in Rangoon, from August to May in Lahore, from October to May in Cawnpore, from November to May in Bombay and from December to May in Madras.

9 See, for example, Viceroy (Finance Department) to Secretary of State no. 2205½-F 20.10.22 and DO Officiating Secretary, Government of India Finance Department to Controller of Finance, India Office 31.822 IF (A&F), May 1923, 60–126A. For figures of Imperial Bank and Government cash balances see *Reports of Controller of Currency*. Government balances generally made up from 40–60 per cent of the Imperial Bank's total cash.

10 *Royal Commission on Indian Currency and Finance 1926* [henceforth *Hilton–Young Commission*], vol. II, Appendix 5, Memorandum on a Gold Standard for India by H. Denning, para. 2.

11 Ibid., vol. IV, Minutes of evidence by Sir Basil Blackett 7.1.26 no. 10481.

12 *Report of Controller of Currency 1920–1*, para. 20.

13 Ibid., 1920–1, 1921–2; Viceroy (Finance Department) to Secretary of State no 785-F 13.3.23 IF (A&F), June 1922, 47–74A.

14 This system was, in fact, a good deal more advanced than that proposed by

the Babington–Smith Committee, which had recommended the issue of emergency currency only against external trade bills.

15 *Hilton–Young Commission*, vol. II, Appendix 3, Memorandum giving the History of the Indian Currency System, submitted by A. C. McWatters paras. 19–23.

16 This was the main purpose of the proposals put to the Hilton–Young Commission by the three top officials of the Finance Department, Blackett, McWatters and Denning.

17 *Hilton–Young Commission*, vol. IV, Minutes of evidence of Sir Basil Blackett 7.1.26 no. 10487.

18 Note by Sir Basil Blackett 1.8.24, IF 46–11–F 1924.

19 See telegraphic correspondence reprinted in *Hilton–Young Commission*, vol. III, Appendix 98.

20 Unsigned note 2.4.26; marginal note by C. N. Chackroburty 4.4.26 IF 86-F 1926; note by H. Denning 10.3.27 4-XI-F 1927.

21 IF 86-F 1926.

22 Note by H. Denning 10.3.27 IF 4-XI-F 1927.

23 Note by B. P. Blackett 4.1.27, ibid., 8(IX)F 1927.

24 Survey by A. Fergesson & Co. for Bombay Millowners' Association 5.3.24 quoted in DO Secretary Bombay Millowners' Association to D. T. Chadwick, Department of Commerce no 890/25A of 1924 4.7.24, ibid., 105-F 1924.

25 Unweighted index numbers of average prices (1874 = 100):

	Raw Cotton*	Cotton Manufactures T Cloth	Cotton Yarn
1913	121	114	95
1919	249	276	250
1920	197	305	294
1921	127	274	196
1922	201	259	208
1923	196	212	176
1924	228	228	208
1925	180	203	170
1926	136	160	137
1927	116	139	117

*1873 = 100

Index Numbers of Indian Prices 1861–1931 Table VI

26 See letters from Deputy Controller of Currency to Secretary, Government of India Finance Department, May 1925 IF, 64-F 1925.

27 *Hilton–Young Commission*, vol. IV, Minutes of evidence of Sir Victor Sassoon 11.12.25 nos. 5014–20.

28 Ibid., vol. II, Appendix 46.

29 Ibid., vol. IV, Minutes of evidence of Sir Victor Sassoon 11.12.25 nos. 5014–53.

30 Ibid., Minutes of evidence by Sir Basil Blackett 7.1.26. nos. 10427–9.

31 See, for example, ibid., Minutes of evidence of Sir Victor Sassoon 11.12.25 no. 5041.

32 Ibid., Minutes of evidence of Prof. C. N. Vakil 9.12.25, B. M. Madan 8.12.25, Dr. Balkrishna 14.12.25.

33 Ibid.

34 Ibid., Minutes of evidence of Prof. C. N. Vakil 9.12.25 nos. 4050–4. A government offical, A. Ayangar of the Legislative Department, referred in 1927 to the growing popularity of motoring in rural areas as proof of the wealth of the peasantry IF 8-1-F 1927, Appendix II to Notes.

35 Honorary Secretary Indian Currency League to General Secretary All India Congress Committee 19.1.27 Thakurdas Papers 55 (ii).

36 Sir Purshottamdas Thakurdas to Sir Phiroze Sethna 13.2.27, ibid.

37 The limitations of the Bombay model of the agrarian economy were brought out strikingly in the examination of D. P. Khaitan before the Hilton–Young Commission. Khaitan failed to argue convincingly that a high exchange would affect the wheat producer as he was forced to admit that most Indian wheat was not exported and that much of it never entered the cash economy at all (*Hilton–Young Commission*, vol. IV, Minutes of evidence of D. P. Khaitan 29.12.25 nos. 8153–9). The case of the cotton cultivator was ideal since cotton was an inedible entirely cash crop hit by a fall in world prices. Jute could have provided as good a base for the anti-government case, but jute prices were still high in 1925.

38 *Legislative Assembly Debates 1927*, p. 2555.

39 *Hilton–Young Commission*, vol. IV, Minutes of evidence of Sir Basil Blackett nos. 16–19, 117, 122, 9931–4, 10480–7, 10431–3, 10246.

40 Note by A. Ayangar (undated, January 1927), IF 8-I-F 1927, Appendix II to Notes.

41 *Hilton–Young Commission*, vol. IV, Minutes of evidence of Sir Basil Blackett 6.1.26 no. 9981–4.

42 *Legislative Assembly Debates 1927*, p. 1753.

Part III

INDUSTRY AND LABOUR

9

The Government of India's 'New Industrial Policy', 1900-1925: Formation and Failure

CLIVE DEWEY
University of Leicester

Between 1900 and 1920 the Government of India gradually acquired a new industrial policy.[1] There was no point of decision: no particular date on which a new policy can be said to have been adopted (or abandoned) by a particular body of men. Nor was the policy, at least at first, a very definite set of proposals. Like any complex economic policy with an ambitious goal and numerous components, it changed over time; and at the same time, too, it meant different things to different people. It began with piecemeal initiatives at the centre and in the provinces, each intended to encourage industrial growth, but not adding up to much. Then, slowly, these haphazard measures were sifted, coordinated and augmented, until they formed a comprehensive industrialization programme. The outstanding characteristic of this programme was the sheer amount of state intervention it comtemplated: a degree of intervention which distinguished the new industrial policy from the *laissez faire* that had come before, and the neglect that was to follow.

The official mind identified five leading constraints on development.[2] Indian entrepreneurs—like entrepreneurs throughout the underdeveloped world—were supposedly ignorant of the full potential of western technology, and certainly encountered difficulties when they tried to adapt western methods to Indian conditions. Indian labour, if cheap, was inefficient; there were shortages of technologists, supervisors, and skilled artisans. Indian capital was not so much in short supply as shy of new ventures; it preferred traditional investments in trade, or land, or moneylending. Indian demand for

15

manufactured goods, especially producer goods, was limited by low purchasing power and competition from imports. Finally, there was no ubiquitous source of cheap power.

All these problems, the new industrial policy implied, could be solved through state intervention. The Government of India was to provide the kind of information would-be industrialists needed by systematically disseminating 'commercial intelligence'. An entire cadre of consultants was to answer specific enquiries and give expert advice on particular projects; while a similar 'service' of industrial chemists would undertake research on issues of general concern, and problems brought to them by firms too small to employ their own research staff. 'Pioneer factories' capable of demonstrating the profitability of new products or processes in India, and the kind of adaptations required, were also to be set up. The shortage of technologists was to be overcome through a vast expansion of technical training, and reforms intended to make technical education much more responsive to industrialists' felt needs; skilled artisans were to be trained through a reformed apprenticeship system. Capital was to be provided by state-aided and state-supervised industrial banks which would enjoy the investing public's confidence; in specially deserving cases the state might supply capital direct. The inadequate home market was to be augmented through protection; through agricultural development, which would raise the purchasing power of the mass of the population; and through the systematic deployment of government orders, centralized in a new Indian Stores department. As for power, officials pinned their faith in hydro-electricity—which the state was to develop as a public utility alongside irrigation.

The definitive statement of the mature policy was the report of the Indian Industrial Commission, published in 1918.[3] Contemporaries who instinctively compared the Commission's recommendations with the general run of Indian economic policy between 1858 and 1947 rightly regarded them as a radical and prescient departure. But it is possible, indeed necessary, to view the new industrial policy in two perspectives. If one employs a different frame of reference—if one looks at the policy in the light of eighteenth century mercantilism or the comprehensive economic controls adopted after independence —then the radical new departure shrinks into an ephemeral qualification of a classical market system. Attempts to evaluate the policy are, in consequence, inevitably ambivalent. Considering how little was known of state-led industrialization in underdeveloped areas when the new industrial policy was formulated, the Industrial Commission's report—the culmination of a chain of administrative thought stretching back some twenty years—was an extraordinarily interesting exercise in applied economics. Their programme rested on a series of pragmatic insights into the needs of Indian industrialization, and perceptive hypotheses about the process of industrialization, superior to those of any contemporary economics text. An awareness of aspects of development like the role of forward and backward linkages, the implications of a dual economy, or the choice between 'balanced' and 'unbalanced' growth, which had to be rediscovered by the development economists of the 1950s, informed the official analysis of the obstacles to industrial growth and the steps that had to be taken to overcome them. It seems doubtful if any other country—Germany and Japan not excluded—had so impressive a blueprint for growth. But no economist would now read the Industrial Commission's report for the sake of the 'anticipations' sandwiched between swathes of bureacratic platitude and administrative minutiae. In comparison with the most sophisticated five year plan, the Commission's report is a crude and conservative document.

An advance on the past, an imperfect approximation to the future: the new industrial policy was both these things at once. And which facet of the same stone one chooses to hold to the light depends largely on whether one wants to explain the policy's adoption or its failure. The first part of this paper is a study of the evolution of a set of practical and plausible proposals which made up in shrewdness what they lacked in theoretic rigour. Politically articulate Indian opinion was massively behind them; the Government of India endorsed them *en bloc*; the Secretary of State raised no objections. They should have been effective as a means of promoting industrial expansion, if not an industrial revolution. Yet they failed. Industrial growth in the 1920s and the 1930s was spasmodic. The few spectacular success-stories—steel, say, or sugar—were heavily dependent on a single form of government encouragement: protection. There was no coordinated development of inter-dependent industries; little change in the relative importance of the industrial and agricultural sectors; no real increase in the proportion of the population employed in agriculture. So the programme's limitations—deficiencies both of formulation and execution—decisively influenced India's inter-war development, and are the subject of the second part of this paper. As one of the earliest—if not the earliest—attempts to industrialize a profoundly impoverished subcontinent, the conception and abortion of the 'new industrial policy' has a relevance extending beyond the Indian experience: it has implications for the economic history of twentieth century colonialism as a whole.

The Adoption of the New Policy

However variable the new industrial policy may have been, the factors favouring acceptance of the principle of state intervention to encourage industrialization remained remarkably constant. Their relative importance fluctuated, but with one major exception—the impact of war—the 'causes' of the new policy were the same in 1920 as they had been in 1900. First and foremost was the inherent momentum of the bureaucracy itself. Even in a country like nineteenth century England, where the central civil service was weakly developed compared with politics and local government, a 'revolution in government' has been attributed to the initiatives of administrators responding to administrative imperatives, and in particular to their desire to meet the objectives set them with ever-increasing effectiveness.[4] In early twentieth-century India, where administration subsumed local government and politics alike, and the civil service was dominated by a small, tightly-knit *corps d'élite*, policy formation was far more likely to be influenced by administrators' felt-needs. The topmost echelons of the Indian bureaucracy were deliberately freed from the routine of day-to-day decision making so that they could discharge their principal function: a continuous review of the working of the entire state apparatus. The senior civilians who could analyse the defects of branches of the administration and push through workable reforms were the men who won their contemporaries' respect, and 'left their mark on India'. This process of bureaucratic introspection and initiative was normally inhibited by inertia, especially intellectual inertia; by financial stringency; or by political interests. If ever these constraints were removed or ignored—as they were during Curzon's viceroyalty and the first world war—surges of administrative creativity followed.

The most spectacular example of the administrators' desire to fulfil a traditional function effectively leading to the evolution of wholly new policies was the hotly-contested partition of Bengal. The same process underlay the formation of the industries departments and the appointment of the Industrial Commission: the two basic changes in the way industrial policy was formulated, which made the new industrial policy possible. The new industries departments were the creation of Curzon's viceroyalty. It is possible to exaggerate the importance of a single individual, even a viceroy, in a policy formation; but in a hierarchic, authoritarian bureaucracy like the unreformed government of India, the personality of the viceroy could be as crucial as the personality of a medieval monarch to his kingdom. Curzon, moreover, was an outstanding administrator: perhaps the greatest administrator India has ever known. No one who has read the economic policy files of his viceroyalty and compared them with the records of his predecessors and successors can fail to be impressed by the galvanic effect of Curzon's remorseless determination to define and resolve every problem confronting the Government of India for which an administrative solution could be found. The first principle underlying his government, Curzon claimed, was 'the recognition that for every department of the State . . . there must be *a* policy instead of *no* policy . . . based upon accepted premises . . . and laid down in clear langugage, understood by the officers who have to apply it and intelligible to the people to whom it is applied'.[5] Called upon to sum up his policy in a single word, Curzon chose the word 'efficiency'.[6]

It was this similarity of outlook and ability, more than any bonds of personal sympathy, which made Curzon an effective leader of the most talented imperial secretariat of the age. The councillors and secretaries who collectively created the new industries departments—first at the centre, then in the provinces as they rose to become lieutenant-governors—were characterized by high intellectual ability, outstanding career success, and a common determination to vindicate British rule through dedication to their work. It was these men who were so affronted at the fiasco the Government of India's industrial policy had become, because it reflected on their professional competence. In 1900 the Indian state already accepted some responsibility for the provision of technical education, commercial intelligence and patronage. Internal inquiry showed how badly it provided all these things. A report by Sir Edward Buck—the driving force behind the department of revenue and agriculture set up in 1881 to do for agriculture what the department of industry and commerce was subsequently intended to do for industry—and the discussions at the Simla Education Conference summoned by Curzon to reform the Indian educational system exposed the divorce between industry and the government's technical institutions.[7] Curricula were simply not adapted to the manpower needs of local industrialists; and classroom conditions did little to accustom pupils to conditions in the workshops where they would actually have to employ their skills. The standard of instruction was low: teachers were badly trained, poorly paid, and oppressed by a sense of their own futility. The *volume* of instruction, also, was minute. So, in a country where factory owners constantly complained of the shortage of skilled artisans, pupils of the government's industrial schools were unable to find work.

The quality of official commercial information also attracted complaints from the business community, who resented the delays they encountered in trying to extract information from government departments which only they could give.[8] The demand for information was growing. As India entered the international economy as a major exporter of primary produce and an importer of manufactures, expatriate traders found their profits were directly dependent on their knowledge of the *mofussil*; while Indian entrepreneurs, eager to exploit the potential of western technology, wanted expert advice in adapting it to the Indian environment. They also wanted state patronage. Since 1875 the Government of India had bought pig iron from the one modern iron works in India—the Bengal Iron and Steel Company's plant at Barakar.[9] But they had made no systematic attempt to use the three great spending departments' combined purchasing power to encourage industries of special strategic or artistic value. The stores purchase rules directed requisitioning officers to buy items of the required quality as cheaply as possible; and this meant, in practice, that they bought British, not because British goods were necessarily cheaper, but because the India Office had a proper stores department staffed by expert inspectors who accepted responsibility for the quality of the stores they supplied, something individual requisitioning officers in India were unable or unwilling to do.[10]

Workable solutions for these administrative blemishes were hard to find. An 'expert' committee was appointed to devise a new system of technical education; it proved—after inordinate delay—hopelessly incompetent. Curzon asked the provincial government's advice; their replies oscillated 'between bored indifference and futile suggestion'.[11] The commercial bureau which was to play the part of an Indian Board of Trade foundered amongst the *laissez faire* prejudices of the

India Office officials; the journal it produced was denounced as 'either hopelessly bald or deadly dull . . . the flotsam and jetsam of the Statistical Department'.[12] The revision of the stores rules directing requisitioning officers to satisfy themselves that Indian goods were not available before they indented on London, and to allow Indian goods a 5 per cent preference, had no effect because no stores department was set up in India.[13]

By 1903, accordingly, there was a general realization inside the imperial secretariat that piecemeal reforms were unlikely to produce results. Something always went wrong: reforms were not pushed hard enough, were not based on the necessary knowledge, were not coordinated. At base it was the attempt 'to run an empire with a staff that would be deemed inadequate in a second-class European kingdom' that was at fault; and the remedy was specialization: recourse to 'special departments and special men . . . instead of allowing technical subjects to be dealt with at the end of a day's work by a tired out (generalist) civilian'.[14] A committee of secretaries carved out a new department of industry and commerce from the work of the existing departments; and Curzon's council justified the new departmental system to the Secretary of State on purely administrative grounds. 'The great and still unarrested increase of public business' was what made it necessary—not a *new* policy, but the execution of old established functions in a changing world. Nowhere else, the Government of India argued, was so much work transacted 'by a body of high officials so small in numbers or so habitually overstrained. Indeed no comparison is possible for nowhere else in the world are the affairs of nearly 300 millions of people administered, according to the standards of western civilisation by a single . . . executive body.'[15] The argument that any government 'must be constantly pressing forward in the direction of reform, if a decline in the quality of the administration is to be avoided' had a universal appeal for professional administrators; and the very officials at the India Office who vetoed the extremely modest proposals for a commercial bureau accepted the far more ambitious department of industry and commerce—as a 'purely administrative measure'.[16]

The same desire for the effective implementation of existing policies underlay the establishment of the first provincial industries department. The official who was more than any other responsible for the creation was Alfred Chatterton. Chatterton started out as a professor at the engineering college at Madras. Depressed by the futility of the 'industrial schools' the local government administered, he set out to devise a more efficient way of disseminating new skills and techniques. A man who could 'make things happen', Chatterton first concentrated on the depressed handicraft industries; but the handicraft industries, which seemed well advanced on an irresistible decline, offered too little scope. If the pupils of the government technical institutions were to find employment, it was necessary to start more modern industries to employ them. It soon became apparent that Chatterton's innovations, above all his 'pioneer factories' run on commercial lines to demonstrate the profitability of new products and new processes to local industrialists, had run far beyond the competence of the education department which employed him; and the obvious solution was the creation of an entirely new department—of 'industrial advice'.[17]

Ten years later the appointment of the Industrial Commission exemplified the same transition from a quest for efficiency to the assumption of new functions. The Commission was the immediate outcome of initiatives taken by the commerce and industry department in 1914–15; and the argument in favour of appointing a commission which the industry member and his secretary cited at the beginning of all the notes they wrote was the need to formulate a clearer, more authoritiative policy before the department could operate effectively. They wanted to assess practices which had grown up in the provinces; to find out how the most interesting experiments of all—the pioneer factories—had turned out; to discover just what industrialists did want by way of technical education; to appraise the loans and subsidies given a few selected concerns; and so on. They were conscious that everything that had been done so far had been done haphazardly, without coordination; and they were uncertain, even, as to what they were permitted to do. Three successive secretaries of state had sent different sets of instructions amplifying, qualifying or contradicting their predecessors. The department wanted to be told what it was supposed to be doing, and how to do it; the Industrial Commission was their answer to an institutional 'crisis of identity'.[18]

So the bureaucracy's own imperatives were one source of the new industrial policy; but initiatives taken by isolated civil servants, or even localized groups of civil servants, would have come to little in an unfavourable environment. There were forces for administrative stagnation, as well as administrative change; and if there were good reasons for action, there were often better reasons for abstention. Men's thoughts and actions ran in customary channels: it was habit, above all, that made it necessary to present potentially radical innovations as mere adjustments intended to maintain historic equilibria. '*Laissez faire*'—indeterminate as the term may be—was a serious obstacle to official acceptance of the new industrial policy. There was no question of policy-makers applying a sophisticated model of development through the free market, hedged about with qualifications and exceptions in the manner of Mill. What stuck in their minds was a series of inflexible axioms: the *reductio ad absurdum* of a great intellectual heritage. The central canon of this creed was abstinence from interference with private enterprise—on the theoretic ground that state intervention only distorted the market's 'perfect' allocation of resources to their most productive uses, and the empirical ground that whatever the state could do private enterprise could do better. The taboo of non-intervention was constantly invoked by the new industrial policy's opponents; and under a like-minded or complaisant Secretary of State it often carried the day.

The converse was also true; officials with a wider notion of the state's legitimate functions were irritated by the Government of India's failure to do what it was obviously obliged to do. Curzon had just such a concept of the state: he publicly rejected *laissez faire* as irrelevant in India, and obsolescent even in the country of its birth. 'The days are gone by,' he told the imperial legislative council, 'when Government can dissociate itself from the encouragement of . . . enterprise. There used to be a sort of idea that business was an esoteric thing, to be conducted by a narrow clique, who were alone possessed of the oracles of wisdom, and with whom Government were hardly supposed to be on speaking terms. That was an absurd theory at any time. It is additionally absurd in a country like India, where the Government . . . builds and works railroads . . . controls the sale of opium and salt . . . maintains giant factories . . . and . . . is the largest employer of labour . . .'[19] Unfortunately for Curzon's plans the India Office was 'the only part of the empire where pure political economic doctrines still prevail'.[20] There were some councillors and secretaries who shared his conviction that 'no industry would ever start into being if the political economists were allowed to watch over its birth';[21] usually the younger men, who had been civilians in India and had just returned to Whitehall, often in mid-career. They were contemporaries of the councillors and secretaries who were running the Government of India; they were naturally tolerant of policies they had had some part in formulating; and they shared the same mental horizons. Such men, however, were outnumbered by home civil servants who had never been to India and elderly civilians who had retired years before; and found themselves out of sympathy with the younger generation in India, busily overturning their own cherished administrative arrangements. 'There is probably no country in the world,' the financial secretary noted, almost exactly inverting Curzon's words, 'where an extension of Government activity is more to be deprecated than it is in India; and . . . it would probably be impossible to choose a more unsuitable time than the present at which to inaugurate such a policy, even if the policy itself were suitable to India.'[22] The real leader of the opposition to Curzon's commercial bureau was an outsider: an archetypal late Victorian entrepreneur. Sir James MacKay, subsequently Lord Inchcape, was a Scot born into obscurity who went out East to make his fortune, got a clerkship in an expatriate house, rose to control the Peninsular and Orient Line, acquired an earldom, built a Scottish baronial mansion, and bequeathed a business empire to his heirs. The rugged individualism of his economic thought matched the uninhibited aggression of his career. He was the solitary member of the English Commercial Intelligence Committee of 1898 to oppose the establishment of a department of commercial information to encourage British trade; and as the representative of 'commerce' on the Council of India he denounced 'anything that would impair the value of the information already obtainable by private enterprise, or . . . induce manufacturers and traders to rely on the state, rather than on their own efforts . . .'[24] Defeated in Whitehall, he succeeded in India. There was no one at the India Office to stand up against him, Curzon commented, 'since they are all children in business'.[25]

The same contrasting sets of ideas came into conflict over the Madras industries department. The pioneer factories which Chatterton ran on commercial lines to prove their profitability lay at the heart of the dispute. At the 1908 Ootacamund Industrial Conference spokesmen for the Madras Chamber of Commerce repudiated the government's attempts to 'encourage' them. The British business community regarded Chatterton's factories as unfair competition calculated 'to drive private enterprise from the field'. Their fundamental objection, the chairman of the Chamber of Commerce explained, was 'based on the general principle that Government should confine itself to governing'.[26] This was a principle that found subscribers at the India Office. Chatterton's appointment as 'director of industrial and technical inquiries' had been approved with some reluctance. 'I have the strongest doubts as to whether . . . intervention . . . in industrial development is justified,' one member of the India Council said, 'I regard it as a waste of money and wrong in principle. I don't believe as a rule in attempts to create industries . . . and the probabilities are that the lethargy of . . . Madras . . . is due to causes beyond the reach of State effort.'[27] But Chatterton was exceptionally well-qualified to make a success of intervention; and in Mackay's absence it was decided to allow the Government of Madras to make an experiment for a term of years. In 1910 Chatterton's time was up, and the local government applied for sanction for a permanent department. The apparent success of Chatterton's factories in establishing new industries—chrome tanning and aluminium hollow-ware were cited—coupled with the support given his work by local politicians won over the departmental secretaries. Two India councillors were already actively committed to intervention: the educationalist, Sir Theodore Morison and the solitary Indian member, K. N. Gupta. But Sir James Mackay was back, and Mackay had the Secretary of State's ear:

> I think it is a dangerous and likely to be a mischievous interference with private enterprise and individual initiative to . . . [start] Government factories with the idea of educating the natives and passing on these factories to native capitalists. The whole thing is economically unsound. We may take it as an axiom if any industry is likely to prove profitable . . . in India, capital . . . will speedily be found to start it. There is nothing more calculated to frighten private enterprise and the investment of capital in a new enterprise than the probability of Government interference . . . officials should confine themselves to producing statistics. . . . How can a man like Chatterton possibly teach men who have all their lives been engaged in seeking for enterprises which are likely to be remunerative? The thing is absurd. . . . This man Chatterton, who can have no business or practical experience of factories, [is on] a salary of £1,200 p.a. with a lot of highly paid assistants to fool about with model childish factories which will never earn a sixpence. . . . This is how money is frittered away in India—men seeking soft billets for themselves and getting round those who are responsible for the Government by gulling them into . . . silly schemes.[28]

Arguments like this were irresistible to Morley.[29] A septuagenarian set in his ways, his economic thought was at heart the thought of Bright. Beginning his political career as a journalist vulgarizing the

Gladstonian liberalism of the 1870s, he accepted, by 1910, that welfare considerations might moderate the operations of the free market. The state might intervene to improve the equity of *distribution*: had not J. S. Mill drawn the great distinction between the laws of distribution, which were man-made, and the laws of production, which were eternal? But how could the state intervene effectively to increase productivity? It was still unthinkable that a bureaucracy could perform the market's functions better than the market: especially when the bureaucracy was the Indian civil service. Morley's distrust of intervention was reinforced by his distrust of Indian civilians. As Secretary of State he found them embarrassingly obtuse. They were unimaginative and careless, and never appreciated that actions unpalatable to left-wing MPs meant embarrassing questions in the House: questions which might tarnish Morley's reputation as a guardian of liberal values—the reputation on which his career as a politician and his retention of cabinet office depended.[30] Thus biased, Morley was anxious to believe any tale brought to him about his official subordinates by interested outsiders, provided it was to their discredit. Frittering money away, creating soft billets for themselves, being gulled by adventurers like Chatterton—these were just the kind of things the Indian civil service did, unless a vigilant Secretary of State caught them out.

The despatch which Morley drafted—or caused to be drafted—repeated Mackay's arguments in more seemly periods. The Government of Madras was instructed to restrict itself to 'industrial instruction': 'So limited, interference with private enterprise is avoided, while there still remains an ample and well-defined sphere of activity. The limit disregarded, there is the danger that the new state industry will either remain a petty and inefficient plaything or will become a costly and hazardous speculation.'[31] Chatterton was demoted to be Superintendent of Industrial Education, working under the Director of Public Instruction; the separate department of industries was abolished. Political protests followed, and when Crewe succeeded Morley the Madras Government resolved to try its luck again. They found that Mackay's spirit lived on. 'India believes still,' a councillor advised,

> that it can defy natural laws and protection of particular industries by artificial means will be beneficial. So too Indian opinion would sally to the side of religious intolerance and other exploded ideas. But I firmly believe the good of India requires a wise adherence to the abstention of Government from commercial

undertakings and to the limitation of its functions to the providing of equal opportunities for all enterprises. Trade does not move into new channels without fructifying the fields through which it passes, and every loss to a cramped or moribund industry means a greater gain and vitality to healthier industries. The support of the Indian Government does not alter natural laws. . . .[32]

The argument from natural law was difficult to refute in kind. There was no equivalent theory of beneficent state intervention which could neutralize the free market model of economic development; no body of interventionist axioms commanding instinctive acquiescence. The advocates of pioneer factories and all the other forms of government aid might have a pragmatic case to make out: actual industries initiated in the way they approved. But when it came to general principle, they were perpetually on the defensive. They shared too many of Mackay's premises; they were too apologetic when they suggested his 'natural laws' might be set aside, under exceptional circumstances. Always, they were concerned to minimize the amount of state intervention. The pioneer plants, in particular, were pared away to limit the 'evils' intervention was supposed to cause. Even as they approved Chatterton's appointment, Curzon and the Government of Madras placated their opponents by announcing that only a handful of factories would be set up, to be sold off or closed down immediately they had made their point.[33]

The advocates of intervention were inhibited, also, by genuine uncertainty over the correct development strategy for India. It was far from universally acknowledged that industrialization was the only means of permanently improving living standards. Contemporary commentators differed over the relative importance of the economic benefits brought by factory industry, and the social costs that followed in its train. The growing inequalities of wealth, the intensifying class conflict, the material squalor of the cities, the diminished satisfaction men derived from their work, the inferior aesthetic qualities of machine-made goods—all these inspired the late Victorian revulsion against industrialization which first popularized the term 'industrial revolution' and saturated it with unpleasant assocations. What contemporaries did agree on was the poverty of India's factor endowment relative to the West's. Men doubted not only whether industrialization would do India much good, but whether industrialization was an option open at all. Under these circumstances, the right strategy for India might be concentration on agricultural, not industrial development. The yields of Indian agriculture were so low, the techniques so primitive, that the potential for agricultural improvement seemed correspondingly immense. The theory of foreign trade which upheld the free traders' incessant denunciation of protection laid great stress on the exploitation of comparative international advantage and the reciprocal benefits to be derived from exchange. It provided a satisfying justification of the Government of India's existing economic policies, designed to encourage India's participation in an international specialization of functions, exchanging foodstuffs and raw materials for manufactures; each interdependent partner concentrating on the economic activities for which it was best suited, and benefiting from the other partners' similar specialization.[34]

Proponents of industrialization were generally content with state investment in irrigation and communications. Wedded to the market, they believed that state intervention could only inhibit India's development, by misallocating resources or 'frightening' private capital. The price levels which automatically balanced demand against supply were capable, in their view, of ensuring the maximum volume of investment at the optimum points. They confidently expected the commercialization of Indian agriculture would create the preconditions for spontaneous industrial growth. As India's exports of primary produce increased, rising agricultural incomes—they predicted—would generate the necessary purchasing power and savings; the simultaneous commercial revolution would bring into existence financial institutions and a class of entrepreneurs; taxation falling on the land would finance an infrastructure of railways and modern administration.[35]

Even the advocates of industrialization who were dissatisfied with the 'natural' operations of the market were riven by dissension over the kind of industry the state should intervene to encourage. There were many, like Marx, who looked on India's handicrafts as doomed to extinction. They were technologically obsolescent, and the sooner they were displaced by factories capable of exploiting all the economies of scale and modernity the better for the mass of the impoverished Indian wage-earners. 'The ultimate ruin of the native tanner', the Punjab Government's industrial expert advised them, 'is merely a question of time, and the Government can do nothing, nor is it in the public interest to do anything, directly to save him. The only course to follow is . . . to offer every reasonable encouragement to large tanners, and in particular to subsidise a suitable factory.'[36] But this was not the opinion of all the Indian government's natural advisers on matters of industrial policy. Many were more sympathetic to handicrafts than factory industries. Indeed, they tended to see the principal function of industrial policy as the defence of handicrafts, especially 'art industries', *against* the rise of factories. The same movement of revulsion against industrialization which stressed its high social costs rehabilitated 'arts and crafts'. Aesthetic Luddites—led by Ruskin and Morris—spiritualized traditional handicrafts. Just as Pugin looked to Christianity as the source of all that was best in western architecture, so influential Anglo-Indian art critics—men like Sir George Birdwood or E. B. Havell—stressed the connection between Hindu art and Hindu religion: a connection so intimate that no European could properly judge Indian art, because no European—his capacity for 'superstition' forever destroyed—could enter into the mythology which inspired it.[37] There are few more reliable indices of this rediscovery of Indian art than the catalogues of the great Indian exhibitions. The official handbook of the 1864 Punjab Exhibition was unsympathetic to Indian art, especially to the brilliant miniatures of Kangra. Judged by the criteria of a mid-Victorian drawing-master, their technique was hopelessly incompetent: 'The actual work of drawing, the perspective, the method of delineation, and the style of producing "effect" are as a rule inferior; . . . the mere minuteness and delicacy of handling which . . . occur in rendering the separate hairs of a beard, or the pearls on a tiny necklace, are a species of mechanical power intrinsically of a low order.'[38]

The proper goal of art in 1864 was the combination of fidelity to nature with romantic imagination: and the 'conventionality' of Indian art precluded both. Seventeen years later, at the second Punjab Exhibition of 1881–2, the same civilian wrote the official guide. But on this occasion, he remarked on 'the great revival of public taste' which had enormously increased the European market for Indian art, and converted critics to the notion that 'all truly national . . . forms of art . . . are valuable in themselves to be preserved'. Whereas formerly 'manufacturers delighted to depict flowers, animals, birds . . . in their natural form, shaded to give the appearance of solidity, now . . . it has become recognised that all natural forms must be conventionalised, or turned into patterns, before they can be rightly used . . .'[39]

The new saviours of India's artistic heritage—and in particular the principals of the schools of art set up in the 1880s—were easily the most committed opponents of industrial development in India. As Chatterton's predecessor wrote:

It is doubtless the easier way for Indians to throw aside all their artistic traditions as obsolete, to accept blindly the teaching of European commercial experts, to multiply factories and join in the mad scramble for markets which Europe calls civilisation. . . . Will India be freer, happier and wiser when, instead of lacs of village craftsmen, every town has its 'swadeshi' cotton mills . . . and . . . 'swadeshi' music halls and gin palaces . . . ? No-where in India—not even in the direst time of famine and pestilence—is there such utter depravity, such hopeless physical, moral and spiritual degradation as that which exists in the great cities of Europe.[40]

This problem of choice between large- and small-scale industry seriously inhibited the interventionist camp. The officials responsible for the key initiatives that added up to the new industrial policy were never quite sure what they wanted: and their own indecision communicated itself to the supporters they needed to recruit. Curzon, for example, was torn between his love of Indian art and his consciousness that the world was engaged in a race for industrialization in which it would be dangerous for India to lag too far behind:

the expansion of [factory] industries would be valuable insofar as they would give increased employment to an increasing number of workmen and would therefore swell the number of those who are not compelled to depend on agriculture. From this point of view the introduction of factories and mills is equally laudable. But then comes the other or artistic point of view, which appeals, at any rate to me, much more forcibly. I would sooner attempt to revive the rapidly perishing art industries of India, perishing not because a market is not forthcoming for them, but because the already existing market is being lost by shortsighted parsimony and by the indulgence in vulgar and semi-Europeanised designs.[41]

The same ambivalence in the provinces retarded provincial schemes. In Madras Chatterton dissipated his energies between factories and cottage industries, all the time seeking a via media between the 'uneconomic' single family and the impersonal satanic mill, which would avoid 'the hideous concentration of human life . . . in smoke-begrimed cities with unparalleled luxury for the few and squalor of the many'.[42] In Eastern Bengal and the Central Provinces the new provincial departments were departments of cottage industries 'far more suitable to the simple family life of the people, and . . . far more [conducive] to their happiness and comfort than the conditions of organised labour in crowded centres . . .'[43]

These fundamental disagreements—over the best way to encourage industrialization, and the kind of industry to be encouraged—were never properly resolved. They were replicated inside Congress; and they persist today. Yet the 'balance of ideas' was slowly changing, in favour of intervention and large-scale industry, even before the first world war effected a temporary revolution in men's economic attitudes. The force of example was at work. There were the famous foreign precedents: at first Germany, then, increasingly Japan. Constant references to their success created a climate of opinion in which men were more willing to believe that state intervention might engineer an industrial revolution. Knowledge of the exact means by which the German and the Japanese states had brought about their economic miracles was slight. The mechanics of industry-building were obscure; and the obscurity of the whole process weakened the case for intervention. What decision-takers wanted—what they always want—were sure-fire schemes guaranteed to work in a situation in which only experiment was possible.

It was this which made the early experiments—the 'domestic precedents' for intervention—so important. The Madras department captured the public (and the official) imagination. Here was this man Chatterton, a Government official, going out into the *mofussil* and setting up factories that actually worked at a profit. The thing was so unusual, so impossible according to all the rules of political economy, that men were mesmerized and refused to believe it had actually happened. Those who were already committed to intervention acclaimed Chatterton's success; the more doctrinaire adherents of *laissez faire* decried the damage he had done. No authoritative evaluation was possible, at least in the short-term; so men went on interpreting experience in terms of their preconceptions. It was ten or fifteen years before the criteria by which Chatterton's factories could be judged were generally established, and the necessary information became available. By then provisional assessments had already begun to sway officials 'on the margin'; and a trickle of 'conversions' showed that experience was modifying axiom.

The process of evaluating Chatterton's work—and in particular his notorious pioneer factories—began at the Simla Education Conference of 1900 and petered out in the 1920s. It was especially influential at two points: when the provincial departments were being established (roughly between 1905 and 1912), and during the Industrial Commission's appointment. The Government of India and the Government of Madras persistently approved Chatterton's work; the India Office and the other provincial governments remained sceptical. 'The results represent considerable labour and ingenuity, but they are not of a character to remove my doubts as to the utility of state effort' was Morley's verdict.[44] It was difficult to measure the impact of what Chatterton was doing. It might, conceivably, be possible to appraise the demonstration effects on local entrepreneurs; but what of the alleged damage—the deterrent effect on private enterprise? Even if a cost–benefit analysis vindicated the department, still it might only be the exception that proved the non-interference rule. The Madras experiments were on a small scale, limited to a handful of 'lines'; and their apparent success could always be attributed to Chatterton's unusual gifts, a criticism Chatterton himself did little to dispel. He was a former professor of engineering, for whom western technology held no terrors. He was also an entrepreneur *manqué*, with the imagination to envisage lucrative investment opportunities that no other industrialist had tried to exploit. A born publicist and an experienced administrator, he had the 'commercial instincts' (as the Government of Madras termed them) to seek out untapped markets while simultaneously managing a government department on civil service lines.[45]

The Government of India never really knew what had happened in Madras until it had already decided, on other grounds, to adopt the new industrial policy in full. The first world war discredited habitual appeals to past administrative experience. Cut loose from 'settled principles of policy'—and the systems of ideas which supported them—the Government of India stampeded into intervention. 'Abstinence' was abandoned because the free market seemed incapable of attaining the new objective of economic activity. In peacetime it might attain long-term economic development, measured in terms of increasing capital investment; it was quite incapable of mobilizing resources on a sufficient scale to meet the immediate shortages created by war. Merely to maintain the flow of military supplies the Indian Munitions Board adopted, as temporary expedients, virtually the entire range of 'aids to private enterprise' incorporated in the Industrial Commission's recommendations; and it was the chairman of the Munitions Board who was chosen to preside over the Industrial Commission's deliberations.

Satisfying shortages not only accustomed administrators to the exercise of economic power on a vast scale, it impressed on them the potential of intervention in time of peace. The first 'total' war showed the direct relationship between military capacity and the possession of an adequate industrial base. It enormously enhanced the perceived importance of 'strategic' industries directly related to the war effort. When the preservation of a country's territorial integrity came to depend on its ability to produce munitions, the idea of international economics lost its allure, and the goal of national self-sufficiency abruptly took its place. The military necessity of industrialization was hardly thought of in India before the first world war. Apart from a few ordnance factories, more or less complete reliance was placed on British industry for munitions, and on British naval supremacy to transport them to India. Hence the shock when Britain began requisitioning India for vast quantities of military supplies; and submarine warfare and the resultant shipping shortages seriously threatened the sea-lanes to the East. The terrifying possibility of a Japanese attack timed to coincide with Britain's involvement in a European war sent shivers down the imperial secretariat's collective spine.[46]

So peacetime industrial policy was conceived as preparation for the next war. If the war itself was merely the continuation of diplomacy by force, peace was merely the conduct of war by economic means. 'It seems highly likely,' a member of the Government of India said, 'that Japan will seize the opportunity of the disorganisation of European industry attendant on the war to press a policy of peaceful penetration in India and endeavour by subsidised . . . manufactures and artifically cheapened freights to capture the Indian market and oust Indian trade with China and Japan. . . . Germany will also make desperate efforts to recover her position. . . .'[47] It followed that industrial development could not be left to private enterprise. So long as the international economy of the nineteenth century persisted, it was possible for the Government of India to remain inert; once economic nationalism overwhelmed it, it was no longer possible for any state to opt out of the interventionist policies pursued by its rivals. Strategic industries would not attract capital investment at the necessary rates unless governments intervened to make them sufficiently profitable; and strategic industries could not be favoured in isolation. Because of their complex linkages, *all* industries—and commerce and agriculture—were in some degree 'strategic'.

The icepacks of *laissez faire* prejudice broke up during the second year of the war. Morley's 1910 despatch was freely impugned in official circles as 'doctrinaire'; Mackay's axioms were 'as dead as

Queen Anne'. The war did permanently weaken the theoretic case against intervention. But the real heritage of war was political rather than doctrinal. The great majority of politically-conscious Indians always wanted industrialization, and approved state intervention to encourage it. What changed was not so much Indian opinion, as the force which Indian opinion could bring to bear on the decision-takers. This was part and parcel of the general political developments between 1900 and 1920 which culminated in the Montagu–Chelmsford reforms.[48] But there were also distinctive changes in the organization of economic interest groups which enhanced the effectiveness of economic, as distinct from general political, opinion. There was a proliferation of formal economic associations: local chambers of commerce, trade associations, groups of industrialists. This process was especially noticeable—and was noticed by the Government of India—in the two great industrial centres: Bombay and Calcutta. Some lobbies, like the Bombay millowners, represented so large a proportion of a particular economic interest group that they were accepted as national spokesmen. Others needed coordination at the national level, and the annual Industrial Conferences—first organized in 1905—provided a national platform. Held in the same towns and at the same time as the meetings of the Indian National Congress, they added a new dimension to a political movement dominated by politicians who had few direct connections with industry. The *swadeshi* movement showed the extent to which an *economic* programme could mobilize mass support: and both the British and the nationalists were aware that the agitation against the partition of Bengal (from which the *swadeshi* campaign emerged) posed the most serious threat to the continuity of British rule since the mutiny.

So the new industrial policy was to some extent a direct response to mounting nationalist pressure. Perhaps the clearest example of this was the Government of Bengal's reaction to the *swadeshi* movement: an application to the Government of India to approve a provincial industries department which the local government was unable to afford.[49] But the relationship between policy and opinion was rarely quite so straightforward. The first and most adventurous industries department was, after all, established at a time and in a province in which there was virtually no organized public demand for it. And the province—Bombay—in which industrial lobbies were best organized was amongst the last to acquire an industries department or an industrial development programme. This paradox is difficult to explain unless one accepts that much political organization in India was simply adaptation to the requirements of the state. The several governments, provincial and imperial, manipulated public opinion in favour of policies they wanted to adopt, so as to exert leverage on the Secretary of State. From 1908 onwards they launched a campaign—the official equivalent of an 'agitation'—in support of state-aided industrialization. Official industrial conferences were held at Naini Tal, Ootacamund, Dacca and Lahore to get support for new industries departments. Unofficial resolutions in the various legislative councils advocating intervention were welcomed, and government spokesmen made their sympathy clear. A spate of official publications describing the department's achievements and their potential were run off on government presses: probably the most popular were those containing transcripts of speeches or notes by Indian politicians, which showed them acting out roles approved by both their followers and the British. Informal contacts, also, were used to win business leaders over to intervention and produce 'shows' of support. The resultant 'spontaneous' demand for the new industrial policy was then deployed in despatches to the India Office as an irresistible political reason for the expansion of the provincial departments and the appointment of the Industrial Commission.[50]

The fact that so many of the officials responsible for the new industrial policy expected it to have quite different political consequences is a further complication. Some looked to the mere adoption of the policy to act as 'a great sedative of political unrest'. Indian civilians welcomed the chance to defend British rule against constant allegations that the Government of India had deliberately de-industrialized the country, so as to maximize the Indian market for British exports. Of all the criticisms of British rule, this was in many ways the most dangerous. It contained an element of truth; it provided a plausible and extremely discreditable interpretation of British motives on every occasion, however altruistic they may have been; and it undermined the Indian civilians' *amour propre*, by undermining their delusions of beneficence.[51] Other decision-takers saw industrialization as a longer-term placebo. This was especially the case with Bengal: industrialization was the final solution for the *bhadralok* problem. The most popular official interpretation of the *swadeshi* movement attributed it to economic causes. Where once the *bhadralok*—literally 'the better people'—had been able to support themselves in the style to which they were accustomed on their income from rent, moneylending and the professions, the spread of education and the growth of population created educated unemployment—the chief breeding ground of sedition. Comparisons with western India confirmed this analysis. 'Nowhere', Hardinge noted,

> is the political contrast so great as between Bombay, where Indians are commercially in the ascendant, and where their contentment and self-confidence steady and control the unstable elements; and restless Calcutta, where the educated classes can see nothing before them, but the helotry of clerkdom, tempered only by the slender expectation of one or other of the few prize appointments under Government.[52]

But the confident assumption that industrial development would mop up unrest by relieving middle class poverty was far from universal, or even general in official circles. Several of the most prominent supporters of the new industrial policy believed industrialization would only generate new tensions. 'Industrial development', the president of the Industrial Commission warned,

> may . . . increase the wealth of a comparatively small number of capitalists, and will provide useful employment for many educated people who now take to law and journalism. But neither the capitalists nor the educated employees will thereby become more contented and loyal; on the contrary, they will soon forget that the industrial impetus came from Government; they will imagine that the prosperity is due to themselves entirely, and that therefore they are capable of managing their own affairs. It is only the politically discontented commercial and industrial man who can, and does, act effectively with the intention of thwarting British interests; and he also pays the politician.[53]

'Experience elsewhere', the financial member agreed,

> and notably in Russia, has shown that industrial development with the consequent assemblage of bodies of workers in factories, tends to promote political agitation, agitators and seditionists taking the opportunity of exploiting the workers' . . . grievances for political ends. But of course we could not allow any consideration of this sort to stand in the way of our discharging our duty to India by . . . promoting its economic development in all legitimate ways.[54]

A clear majority of the members of the Government of India which recommended the appointment of the Industrial Commission to the Secretary of State believed industrialization would make it more difficult, not less, for their successors to govern India.

An active industrial policy was perhaps too slender a thread on which to hang a solution for India's political problems. It could still, however, be used to outflank protection; and this was how free traders in the Government of India hoped to use it. Fiscal policy was carefully excluded from the Industrial Commission's terms of reference on the advice of the industry secretary; the purpose of the Commission was to formulate a programme of state aid to industry which would secure industrialization without protection. 'The public', the imperial commerce and industries secretary advised,

> have a policy, on the theoretical advantages of which a large section of them are unanimously agreed; which has been tried in many countries and can point to a considerable measure of success; which is already fully formulated in the campaign literature of a powerful political party; but is at the same time believed to be a dangerous policy from the economical, political and imperial point of view. It is incumbent on Government to show that this policy is also unnecessary, by being able to point to other lines of action which have been tried; which have definite and satisfactory results, and offer good prospects, if taken up on a large scale.[55]

But here again there was no agreement: there were protectionists as well as free traders inside the Government of India, who pressed for the inclusion of protection in the Commission's terms of reference, and only gave way for the sake of unanimity against the Secretary of State. In their despatches home there was no hint of these deep cleavages. The Government of India simply claimed that Indian opinion was united behind its proposals; and the India Office accepted its claim as a powerful argument for letting the Indian governments do what they wanted.

The Policy's Failure

It is possible to argue that the new industrial policy was too timid—and too incomplete—to succeed. The 'free market' model of development was never jettisoned, it was only qualified. Conceiving intervention as 'aid' to private enterprise, competition with the private sector, or control over it, was deliberately eschewed. The state could have revolutionized Indian industry by repeating, in the field of heavy industry, the initiatives it had taken fifty years before with railways and irrigation. The Industrial Commission, however, was emphatic that pioneer factories must be sold off as soon as they became profitable; and state ownership of manufacturing industries declined. This in itself weakened one of the most important forms of state control over the economy. Other controls were similarly neglected. Financial and monetary policy were not subordinated to industrialization; they were directed towards other goals. Indian finance members tried to balance their budgets according to the canons of orthodox finance and the imperatives of an unstable political situation. There was no attempt to adjust the tax structure in ways favourable to industry; no attempt to control interest rates or capital issues; and persistent refusal to ease credit through moderate inflation, or encourage exports through devaluation.[56] Deficit spending was dismissed as 'immoral', probably correctly under the circumstances.

The corollary of this abstinence from control was neglect of planning, conceived as a crude process of physical or financial co-ordination, rather than the allocation of scarce resources based on systematic cost-benefit analyses of the full range of alternative schemes. Contemporary economic theory gave little guidance on such matters; and the Indian governments made no attempt to employ professional economists. Instead they applied 'pragmatic' criteria to the central problem of planning: the allocation of priorities. The returns of manufactured imports served as a favourite notional check-list of products for which unsatisfied demand already existed inside India: the volume of imports and the ease with which import-substitution could be arranged were the usual criteria by which industries were chosen from this list. The Industrial Commission was a little more sophisticated. It selected industries for encouragement according to its estimate of their forward and backward linkages in the British industrial revolution.

This process involved three dangerous assumptions. It underestimated the sheer volume of planning required if even a quite small amount of state intervention was to have an optimal effect; and instead of leading to the appointment of a central planning body, it meant that once the Industrial Commission laid down the rough overall strategy, the implementation of that strategy—the preparation of detailed sectoral and project plans—was delegated to the regular departments of state at the centre and in the provinces. Perpetually distracted by routine administration, and largely operating in isolation, the regular departments persisted in thinking in terms of separate, uncoordinated, schemes. Secondly, this method of selection tended to equate development with the attainment of frankly xenophobic objectives. After generations of political subordination, when the terms on which they traded were wholly beyond their control, Indians were suspicious of all international economic contacts as potentially 'exploitative', however beneficial they might be. The British, for their part, regarded economic autarky as a partial corrective for India's extreme vulnerability to Japanese or Russian attack once the sea-lanes to England were cut. Thirdly, the new industrial policy assumed that the order in which different industries developed in the course of the British industrial revolution provided a universal model of industrialization readily applicable to India. It was when India's 'unbalanced' export-led growth was measured against the British example of successful 'balanced' development that it stood condemned: it could never create the preconditions for industrialization.

The actual prescription at which the Industrial Commission arrived by applying the test of autarky and the British precedent was straightforward.[57] The first prerequisite of industrial revolution, on the Commission's interpretation of eighteenth century British economic history, was a mature iron and steel industry. Once iron and steel production was developed, engineering and machine tools followed, causally as well as chronologically. The lighter industries which they serviced (already in existence in India) then created the demand for chemicals and non-ferrous metals. All these industries needed cheap power, which in India—according to the Commission—meant hydro-electricity and its inevitable concomitant, electrical equipment. These were the large-scale industries which the Commission recommended should receive most encouragement. At the opposite end of the spectrum, they also approved aid for cottage industries, on welfare rather than aesthetic grounds. No representative of 'art industry' was allowed a seat on the Commission; but there was a strong vein of *swadeshi* sentiment to placate, whether or not money spent on traditional handicrafts was likely to promote sustained growth. As the symbolic victims of 'de-industrialization' they were undeniable candidates for 'compensation' when the state set out to reverse the process that had ostensibly destroyed them.

The appendices to the Industrial Commission's report told a strangely different story. The industries which featured in the appendices were neither the cottage industries nor the heavy industries intended to enhance India's self-sufficiency: they were medium-scale agro-industries, like tanning, sericulture, sugar and cotton, to some extent import-substituting, but with great export potential. As the inter-war period showed, it was this kind of medium-scale industry processing agricultural produce which was easiest and cheapest to develop in the Indian environment. Compared with the heavy industries they were less capital-intensive; used simpler technology; were more familiar to entrepreneurs; and needed less skilled labour. They had other advantages; they were comparatively decentralized (and so demanded less investment in social overhead capital); they provided more employment, generating mass purchasing power; and they earned/saved more foreign exchange. Compared with the cottage industries which they displaced they were simply far more efficient. Their deployment of modern technology and organization raised labour productivity, cheapened the cost of products to consumers, and put profits in the hands of industrialists who were willing to reinvest them in further expansion. But medium-scale agro-industries were also unfashionable, associated as they were with the agricultural export-led model of development, officially discarded during the first world war; and their economic advantages counted for little beside the glamour of heavy industry and the tragedy of handicrafts. The great powers' race to industrialize, with its compulsive comparisons of heavy industrial output, meant that heavy industry ceased to be a means of raising the living standards of the mass of the population: it was a proof of national virility, and a guarantee of national survival. The lack of heavy industry was evidence of racial inferiority; the possession of heavy industry was the source of patriotic pride. In the absence of a major industrial base, handicrafts served as a *pis aller*. Economically inferior, they were still morally superior; and their preservation became indelibly identified with national resistance to foreign rule. This dual mystique, far more than any appreciation of multiplier effects, was what underlay the new industrial policy's erroneous strategy.

Despite the defects in the formulation of the new industrial policy, it would still have accelerated Indian industrialization substantially had it ever been put into effect properly. It failed to achieve results not so much because it was badly conceived, as because it was never given a chance. The chief culprit was constitutional reform. The Montagu–Chelmsford reforms were what destroyed the new industrial policy, by transferring control over industrialization to Indian ministers in the provinces. This put an end to all prospect of effective central coordination; and it ensured that sufficient resources would not be put into industrial policy to produce any major economic change.

To implement its programme the Industrial Commission relied on two organizations at the centre: the imperial department of industries, and two 'imperial services'—one of chemists, one of engineers. Insofar as the Commission made provision for centralized planning, it was these organizations that were to undertake it. The imperial department and the all-India services were to act as the planners of the future, constantly debating development problems amongst themselves, and gradually evolving solutions. There were to be provincial departments and provincial cadres in addition; but the commission stressed the need for strong central organizations capable of exploiting advantages of scale and coordinating the development efforts of the provinces.[58] An imperial department could arrange for the circulation of information and ideas between provinces; concentrate stores purchase in a central purchasing agency, maximizing the impact of state patronage; afford larger longer-term investments than isolated local governments; and arbitrate between the parties when disputes arose over industries whose markets and materials straddled provincial boundaries. The sheer size of the imperial services meant a far greater range of specialists could be entertained; men equipped with proper laboratories and libraries at central research stations. They would be large enough to support an elaborate career structure, encouraging recruitment, improving professional competence through competition for promotion, and solving the problem of supervision: senior officers were expected to monitor their subordinates' research, a task beyond the generalist administrators of the secretariat.

The imperial department of industries and the two imperial services were flexible concepts, organizations capable of evolution to meet whatever the requirements of planned industrialization turned out to be. But they never came into existence. Approved by the Government of India and the India Office, they ran foul of the Indian politicians on whose collaboration the Montagu–Chelmsford reforms depended. The essence of the reforms was the transfer of power from the Government of India to the provinces, from the British to Indians, and from civil servants to politicians. What the Industrial Commission proposed was an all-powerful central department to control Indian ministers in the provinces, with the aid of two new groups of civil servants many of whom would be British. In the ensuing conflict between the architects of the new industrial policy and the architects of the imminent constitutional reforms, administrative efficiency was sacrificed to political expediency at every point.

The first round was fought over the list of 'functions' to be transferred to the control of the Indian ministers in the provinces. The Functions Committee thought that the development of industries was something, unlike the army or the police, that could safely be entrusted to Indian politicians; the Government of India thought it would doom the new industrial policy to failure. Sir Thomas Holland, the industries member-designate, was almost incoherent with rage: 'It would be wiser,' he wrote to a permanent official at the India Office, 'to create separate provincial armies and hand them over to the control of political ministers. Fancy the Tatas placing their industrial schemes before a temporary political minister with his friendly and family interests in competing concerns. . . . The whole scheme of the Industrial Commission will just fall to pieces.' 'The only alternative to regular services,' the Industries Secretary agreed, 'is casual recruitment . . . and . . . casual recruitment will not only tend to render nugatory . . . the coordinated industrial policy which I hold to be essential but will fail to afford the necessary training ground for Indians. . . .'[59]

In its third despatch on constitutional reform, sent home in April 1919, the Government of India duly demanded that industries be made a concurrent reserved subject, i.e. that it remain under the control of civil servants, principally British civil servants, at both imperial and provincial levels.[60] The arguments for reservation rested on the difficulty of finding Indian ministers with sufficient experience of industry or sufficient longevity in politics to set up a completely new department and implement the Industrial Commission's intimidating programme; on the Government of India's inevitable retention of control over communications, tariffs, foreign trade and minerals; and the advantages of scale and coordination. These could not simply be ignored, and the immediate outcome was compromise. Industries was made a concurrent subject, but in the provinces it was still transferred to the ministers' control.

The basis of this division of authority was a distinction drawn by Holland, who stopped spitting into the wind, between executive and advisory functions. 'For executive functions', he explained, 'decentralise to the fullest extent; prompt action on the spot guided by an intimate knowledge of local conditions must ordinarily be better than deferred action, no matter how perfect be the advice on which it is based. For advisory functions centralisation in a country like this, which is practically devoid of technologists, is more than usually important.'[61] So long as the personnel of the new chemical and industrial services were scientists and engineers of the highest calibre, Holland believed that local governments would ask and take their advice. It would be the best advice available, and not to take it would cost time and money. In this way, Holland hoped to substitute an informal hegemony over the provincial departments of industries for the formal power to sanction provincial projects—which he realized was incompatible with the Montagu–Chelmsford reforms.

The imperial department's ability to influence provincial policy thus came to depend on the two imperial services. Their establishment was sanctioned. Detailed plans were drawn up by the Chemical Services Committee. But they were never brought into effect. Even before the new constitution came into operation local governments gibed at the dilution of their provincial autonomy; and once the industries ministers were appointed they made their unwillingness to employ members of the two imperial services plain. They wanted power: that was what the reforms were all about: and power meant provincial services, firmly under their own control. Holland made repeated attempts to win them over, but they were adamant; and in 1922 plans for the two imperial services were formally abandoned.[62]

Holland himself was the next to go. He had been the real author of the new industrial policy: no man was better equipped to implement it. He was a distinguished scientist and an experienced administrator; a former director of the geological survey, and the man who put Indian industry on a war footing. Chelmsford, the viceroy, regarded him as indispensable, 'Holland', he wrote to the Secretary of State when Sir Thomas went on leave,

> will be a great loss to me. His knowledge of his special subject and his great driving power have enabled us . . . to come through our war effort with success, and I am sure . . . if we are to make a success of industrial development . . . we shall only achieve it through the agency of Holland. He is desperately keen, he is thoroughly sincere and straightforward; and whether men agree with him or not, they recognise him as the man who can put his policy through.[63]

Two years later the one man with the personal authority to maintain the new industrial policy's momentum at the centre at a time of acute financial stringency, and to provide some kind of leadership for the provincial ministers, was dismissed in disgrace by Chelmsford's successor, Reading. Holland ordered the withdrawal of a prosecution against a Bengali company promoter who had swindled the government over some war contracts, because if the prosecution was successful Holland was afraid that the vast industrial empire the man had built up would collapse around him, seriously retarding the industrialization of Bengal. There was an outburst of press criticism over the government's unwillingess to press charges which the Advocate General had foolishly claimed he could prove up to the hilt; the European community in particular resented the government's seeming toleration of Indian corruption; and Reading was infuriated that Holland had not consulted him (as an ex-chief justice) beforehand.[64]

Soon after Holland's departure the imperial department of industries was stripped of all its major functions except the protection of labour. The new stores section atrophied when the army, the railways, and the provincial public works departments persisted in ordering stores directly. Tariffs were given to the commerce department; banking stayed with finance. Initiative passed to the provinces; and the local governments found they lacked both the men and the money to make anything of industrialization. As at the centre, the financial situation in the provinces was deteriorating. It had seemed reasonable, while the war was on, to suppose that peace would lead to reductions in military expenditure; but the postwar modernization of the army and the third Afghan war meant that the cost of defence was higher than ever. Inflation drove up the cost of ordinary administration; capital projects deferred for the duration of the war had to be begun; and the Government of India's credit deteriorated when investors were frightened by the first non-cooperation movement. In the annual scramble for budget allocations, and still more during the great retrenchment of 1922, industries lost out. In Bengal five of the ten senior officials in the department of industries were discharged, and two posts were left vacant; in Bombay the department was first put on a skeleton basis, then abolished, then reconstituted on a smaller scale without a director; in Burma the department of industries became a department of cottage industries engaged in social work.[65]

A number of factors made the industries departments the first victims of retrenchment. The wartime predilection for intervention receded. After the armistice, Queen Anne was dutifully exhumed. The desire to return to 'business as usual' made the free market model and the old prejudices against bureacratic interference respectable again. The strategic importance of heavy industry declined; long-term growth supplanted autarky as the goal of economic policy, and officials once more argued that long-term growth would best be attained by leaving private enterprise alone. In the immediate post-war period foreign example worked against the new industrial policy as well as in its favour; and when the foreign example was British, it bore upon Indian opinion—especially Anglo-Indian opinion—with far greater force. The immense system of war controls gradually built up in Britain—*directly* regulating two-thirds of British industry, almost the whole of Britain's imports, and a substantial part of world trade through inter-allied agreements—was demolished within a matter of months. For all its magnitude and complexity, it had been almost entirely an improvisation. Every additional advance was justified, R. H. Tawney has explained,

> as an exceptional concession to some specific emergency, which, because it was exceptional, raised no question of principle. Thus a collectivism was established which was entirely doctrineless. The most extensive and intricate scheme of state intervention in economic life which the country had seen was brought into existence without the merits or demerits of state intervention being even discussed.[66]

This piecemeal, empirical approach at first facilitated the growth of controls. Opportunities for a frontal collision of principles were reduced to a *minimum:* there was no obvious point at which a stand could be made. But once the war was over,

> what had been a source of strength became a weakness. War collectivism had not been accompanied by any intellectual conversion on the subject of the proper relations between the state and economic life, while it had not lasted long enough to change social habits. With the passing, therefore, of the crisis that occasioned it, it was exposed to the attack of the same interests and ideas as, but for the war, would have prevented its establishment.[67]

The new industrial policy was not an integral part of the Indian system of economic controls devised to deal with the war. In embryo, it antedated the war; the enormous expansion in scope which it underwent during the war *was* accompanied by a sharp, if short, debate over the principle of state intervention which ended with a consensus far more favourable to intervention; and the policy itself was always intended to be brought into operation after the war was over. In the minds of the men who devised it decontrol had no necessary connection with the new industrial policy. But other officials, the business community, and the general public found it difficult to keep the two distinct. Both were tarred with the same brush. The war gave the new industrial policy an immense fillip; and the postwar race to decontrol which brought down the British ministry of reconstruction automatically discredited all forms of state intervention associated with the war, except further instalments of the Asquith ministry's prewar 'welfare' programme.

The transition can be traced in the Secretary of State's correspondence with the Viceroy. What Montagu wrote to Chelmsford in the palmy days of the Industrial Commission was very different from what he was writing to Reading in the summer of 1921. 'Everything', Montagu complained,

> [Lord Chetwynd] tells me reinforces my profound despair about industrial development in India. I don't believe we shall ever get on unless the province is made the unit and unless my Council and your Government will agree to leave to a Local Government questions of provincial development . . . the dead hand of government must be taken off development; and when Lord Chetwynd tells me that the best way of developing Bihar, whose riches he says are almost incalculable, is to promote a Bihar Development Corporation which would have a concession to develop railways, forests, mines and everything, I am not sure he has not got the right suggestion. . . . The new evidence of the inadequate methods of constructing railways by hand labour instead of machinery, the false economies which mean the inclusion of impossible gradients rather than the necessary expenditure of tunnelling and the eternal bandying of letters, telegrams and interviews between various authorities drives me to despair.[68]

The critical link between the resurgence of *laissez faire* in Britain and the subversion of the new industrial policy in India was, once again, Sir James Mackay. He acted as a spokesman for British business in its successful crusade for decontrol; and Montagu—the natural leader of 'all men of goodwill'—appointed him chairman of the 1922 retrenchment committee which reduced the Indian industries departments to skeletons of what the Industrial Commission had hoped they would become.

Thus vulnerable on theoretic grounds, the industries departments had no omnipotent political lobby behind them. It is arguable that political pressure for the new industrial policy was effective only because the Government of India wanted a new industrial policy anyway; and that if the lobby supporting the new industrial policy was not exactly the government's own creation, its principal function was its periodic appearance in despatches to the Secretary of State. The business community was too divided. There was no straightforward racial split. When Sir James Mackay condemned Curzon's commercial bureau, the Bengal Chamber of Commerce—bastion of British business in India—supported it; when he attacked the Madras department of industries, he found the Madras Chamber of Commerce on his side. Managing agencies primarily dependent on international trade were naturally hostile to import-substitution; while managing agencies which thought their prospects of diversifying into industry were good, welcomed all the encouragement they could get. There was no proof—only suspicion—that industrial policy would be used to discriminate against expatriate firms; and many of the qualifications for classification as an 'Indian' concern—rupee capital, incorporation in India, token Indian directors, a certain proportion of Indian employees, technical training for Indian workmen—were already satisfied, or easily satisfied, by British businesses. The greatest split of all was between the old established firm, afraid of fresh competition from any quarter, and the prospective entrepreneur whom the industries departments existed to set up in business. Unfortunately for the industries departments, entrepreneurs yet to be brought into existence were a weak political force. So were the other ostensible beneficiaries of the departments: the craftsmen. Illiterate, impoverished, unorganized, unenfranchised, they were quite incapable of representing their own interests; and the 'virtual representation' of philanthropists was no substitute for the keen cutting edge of self-interest.

The great industrialists who might have been expected to get most out of the new industrial policy were suspicious, like capitalists everywhere, that state aid would lead to state inspection, if not state control: a suspicion reinforced by the traditional secrecy of Indian business, and the 'unorthodox' manner in which so many joint stock companies were run. The provincial departments, rapidly reduced to departments of cottage industries, had little to offer them: the budgets of concerns like Tatas far exceeded the total financial resources of the industries departments in the provinces where Tatas operated. When the Tata Iron and Steel Company ran into a financial crisis, it was to the Government of India, not the provincial departments, that it looked. Other 'national' industries, like cotton, wanted things that neither the provincial nor the imperial industries departments could grant. They wanted a low rupee exchange rate, which was the concern of the imperial finance department; they wanted low local taxation, which meant approaching the local finance departments; they wanted, above all, protection, which meant approaching the imperial commerce department. All the imperial industries department did was enforce labour legislation: not the most congenial form of contact.

Under dyarchy, the natural countervailing lobbies were strong. The new constitution was biased in favour of the landed. The rural members who constituted the majority in the new provincial legislatures wanted money for agricultural development, not industry. The urban members were mostly middle class professional men who wanted money for education and a host of 'nation-building' subjects; while the British civilians still in charge of reserved subjects wanted money for 'security'. The industries departments were too young to have had time to prove themselves, or to become part of the accepted machinery of government; and there was no powerful arbiter left, capable of controlling the competing factions, and reserving funds for new ventures. The fact that provincial revenues—from which the bulk of the new industrial policy was to be financed—were static or declining (while the imperial government appropriated the elastic sources of taxation) only intensified competition for what money there was. Administrative talent, also, always in shorter supply than finance, was diverted to other departments. The rise of nationalism was a great distraction, weakening the governments' ability to carry out any constructive policy whatever. Where once the most brilliant civilians had made high-flying careers by specializing in agrarian problems the men who became secretaries, councillors and governors in the inter-war years were men who had made their reputation as experts in the problem of political containment; and the industries departments were relinquished to technical experts, with little influence outside their own ministry.

So the new industrial policy was in some respects defectively formulated and poorly implemented. But it is important, in considering its failure, to bear three mitigating circumstances in mind. The problem was novel. Before the great war, only a handful of countries were fully industrialized; only another handful were manifestly *en route* to industrialization; only one of the industrializing countries was Asiatic; and none combined India's poverty and complexity with its size. The techniques employed by contemporary states to promote industrial development were crude and uncertain: no one really understood how industrialization, as distinct from a show of growth, could be brought about. Few sovereign states, in the extraordinary circumstances of the 1920s and the 1930s, performed particularly well, least of all the British.[69] Roosevelt, arguably, did more to prolong than curtail the depression; in England Keynes remained a prophet without honour. And where the powers did succeed in increasing an apparent control over their industrial destiny, they tended to succeed by accident or at the cost of appalling sacrifices. The German and the Japanese recoveries can be seen as the adventitious results of militarism; in Russia the resumption of industrial expansion was accompanied by famine, massacre, and dramatically depressed living standards.

The sheer scale of the Indian problem, also, was enormous. There is no need to run through lists of 'obstacles to industrialization' present in India; it is enough to know that if they existed anywhere in the world, they existed in India in exacerbated form. No problem, it has been said, is ever solved; it merely evolves new facets. And there is a limit to the capacity of any society and state for problem resolution. Even if the Indian state had made available a much larger proportion of its resources—even if it had made available all of its resources and more—an industrial policy based on the latest development theory might still have failed to bring about an industrial revolution. It may be—this is the third plea in mitigation—that we overestimate the ability of states to perform economic miracles: that we expect them to do too much. The late twentieth century is as eager to turn to state intervention as a cure for every problem as the nineteenth century was averse, and with no more reason.

This touching faith has been back-projected on our notions of economic history; above all, on our interpretation of the Japanese industrial revolution. The Japanese example has always been used as a stick to beat the Government of India. The Japanese Government intervened, and Japan industrialized; therefore all the Government of India had to do was what the Japanese did, and all that prevented the Government of India doing it was British rule. This view ignores the vast contrast between India and Japan: a contrast so great that all they have in common is membership of the same continent. Even if the Indian government had done exactly what the Japanese government did, we can be certain that the results would have been very different. It may be that the crux of the matter lies in this question of results; of private response to official initiative. Changing historiographical fashions are now bringing the Government of India's and the Japanese government's economic policies closer together. The

Government of India is seen to have done more than it has ever been given credit for; while the Japanese government is seen to have done rather less. Were one to compare the volume and quality of state aid to industry in inter-war India, even after the new industrial policy aborted, with the volume and quality of state aid to industry in the late nineteenth century Japan, the similarities might be more striking than the differences.[70]

The immediate postwar impression of Japanese economic policy—a perfectly-conceived plan, responsive to changing circumstances, implemented in a sustained and coordinated manner, and ultimately irresistible, has lost something of its credibility. Subject to detailed appraisal, much Japanese economic policy looks suspiciously like a package of *ad hoc* expedients constantly falling apart and having to be tied together again: expedients which are not so much optimal measures to promote national development as the outcome of mercantilist conspiracies between cliques of businessmen and politicians to loot the public as taxpayers and consumers. As one group of politicians lost control of the economic ministries, so economic policy turned against their erstwhile business allies, and in favour of their successors' financiers. The more rapid the rotation in office, the more unstable economic policy became; and in the 1880s one sees the Japanese government doing its best to put the leading Japanese shipping line out of business, because the rival Japanese line had better political connections. Again, there are serious reservations about the competence of much of what the Japanese state tried to do.[71] The officials in charge of one of the most famous Japanese pioneer factories, far from encouraging private industrialists to visit it, actually refused permission to inspect the plant because they were afraid that their own incompetence would be exposed. Similarly, of the ten famous sets of spindle units imported from England and sold on hire purchase to become the basis of a Japanese cotton industry, only one was acquired by a really successful concern.

If the *zaibatsus* did more for Japanese economic growth than the economic ministries, it may be that the crucial difference between India and Japan was not what the state did so much as the private entrepreneurs' response to official stimulus. Any programme of state aid to private industry was crucially dependent on the response of indigenous entrepreneurs; and it was precisely in the most backward provinces that the possibility of entrepreneurial failure was greatest.

Chatterton's pioneer factories in Madras disproved, in the Director of Industries' view,

> the belief that the Indian capitalist in industrially-backward provinces has only to see the commercial result of a new venture to come forward with his money. Nothing could have been more disappointing than the attitude of the well-to-do Indians in the Presidency interested in tanning and hide exporting, towards the chrome leather factory, when it came to the question of disposing of it. The Hon. P. T. Chetti assured me that he would have no difficulty in finding an Indian syndicate to take it over at the price at which it was subsequently sold to the Rewala Durbar, but after several months' negotiations nothing tangible resulted. And accordingly, when after 7½ years working, the chrome tannery and its connected boot factory were finally [sold] . . . all that was removable from Sembiam was taken off [to Rewala] . . . while Mr. Chatterton's most accomplished Indian assistants joined the Mysore Chrome Leather Company at Bangalore. . . .[72]

When I asked Sir Gokal Chand Narang, the minister responsible for the second Punjab State Aid to Industries Act, why so little use was made of its provisions for financial assistance to industrialists, he told me simply that besides himself and Harkishen Lal—the minister responsible for the first Punjab Aid to Industries act—there were no industrialists in the Punjab interested in applying for loans.

It may be that these two testimonies should be used as evidence of the disillusionment of the architects of the new industry policy with the Indian entrepreneur, rather than indictments of the entrepreneur *per se*. It will not do to revive the old *canard* that industrialization did not take place because Indians were incapable of managing industries. But neither will it do to replace the old *canard* with another, and to assume that whenever enterprise was required it was automatically forthcoming.[73] The great retardation in late nineteenth century Britain has been attributed to entrepreneurial failure; and if economic historians can conceive of the possibility that the largest, richest, most experienced and confident set of entrepreneurs in the world could fall short of the requirements of the leading industrial power, it is hardly mere bigotry to reopen the question of the adequacy of the Indian business class when confronted with a challenge so immense and intractable.

Whatever their other characteristics, one attribute of the Indian business class was in striking contrast to their Japanese compeers: their relationship with the state. It is not so much that the higher levels of the Government of India were alien and therefore unsympathetic to Indian business: from before the first world war the evidence is rather the reverse. But Indian businessmen were unable to build up permanent alliances with Indian civilians through systematic *douceurs*, or to bring continuously effective political pressure to bear upon them. Few countries have ever industrialized—perhaps no country has ever industrialized—in which entrepreneurs have been unable to corrupt the state, exploiting taxpayers and consumers far beyond the limits set by popular tolerance or public policy statements and the need to uphold formal standards of integrity in public life. Whether covert or overt, spasmodic or institutionalized, so symbiotic a relationship ensures that the state responds flexibly to industrialists' felt needs. It was, perhaps, this element that was missing from the Government of India's new industrial policy; and its presence which explains how India's economy continues to function, despite twenty-five years of post-independence planning.

NOTES

I am grateful to Dr. W. J. Macpherson, Professor W. H. Morris-Jones, and Dr C. Baker for comments on earlier versions of this paper which helped me clarify several important issues.

1 Industrial policy—as the term was used by the Government of India—excluded protection, and this is the sense in which the term is used in this paper. For fiscal policy in this period, see 'The Eclipse of the Lancashire Lobby and the Concession of Fiscal Autonomy to India', in *The Imperial Impact*, ed. C. J. Dewey and A. G. Hopkins (London, 1978), pp. 280–314, 381–93.

2 What follows is based upon the *Indian Industrial Commission, 1916–1918, Report* (Calcutta, 1918), especially Chapter IV; and a number of less complete discussions which preceded the commission's appointment. For example: Proceedings of the Government of India, Commerce and Industries Department, Industries Branch [hereafter ICI-Industries], May 1917, 1–31, Keepwith [hereafter KW], C. E. Low note, 3 May 1915 in the National Archives of India, New Delhi [hereafter NAI]; W. H. Clark note, 12 November 1914, enclosed in a letter to Hardinge of the same date, amongst the Hardinge papers at Cambridge University Library; Proceedings of the Government of India, in the Education Department, March 1910, 53–4, L. J. Kershaw, Secretary to the Government of Eastern Bengal and Assam, to the Secretary to the Government of India, Department of Commerce and Industry, 12 May 1909; India Office Revenue Departmental Papers [hereafter IORDP] no. 8417 of 1915, Despatch of the Government of India to the Secretary of State for India, 26 January 1915; ICI-Industries, April 1916, 1–24, 'Report of the Committee Appointed to Advise on the Possibility

of Replacing German and Austrian Manufactures by Indian Made Articles' (NAI); India Office Judicial and Public Departmental Papers [hereafter IOJ&PDP] no. 1940 of 1906, M. D. Taylor, acting Secretary, Education Department, Government of Madras, to the Secretary to the Government of India, Home Department, 12 May 1905; IORDP no. 2662 of 1911, Dr M. Travers to the Secretary to the Government of the United Provinces, Industries Department, 4 March 1910; *Papers Relating to the Industrial Conference held at Ootacamund* (Madras, 1908); J. G. Cumming, *Review of the Industrial Position and Prospects of Bengal in 1908* (Calcutta, 1908); C. E. Low, *Report on the Industrial Survey of the Central Provinces and Bihar, 1908/9* (London, 1911); A. Latifi, *The Industrial Punjab* (Lahore, 1911).

3 For the motives underlying the decision to appoint the commission, see ICI-Industries, May 1917, 1–31 (NAI); the 'Memorandum by the Viceroy upon Questions Likely to Arise in India at the End of the War' in the Hardinge Papers at Cambridge University Library; and IORDP no. 8417 of 1915.

4 By Oliver MacDonagh, in 'The Nineteenth Century Revolution in Government: a Reappraisal', *Historical Journal*, I (1958), 52–67.

5 *Lord Curzon in India*, ed. Sir T. Raleigh (London, 1906), p. 579.

6 Ibid., p. 564.

7 Curzon Papers, India Office Library [hereafter IOL], vol. 280, 'Technical Education'; IOJ&PDP, no. 661 of 1904; ibid., no. 155 of 1909; *Papers Relating to Technical Education in India, 1850–1904* (Calcutta, 1906); *Report of the Committee on Technical Education* (Calcutta, 1903); *Report on . . . Technical Institutions . . . in India* (Calcutta, 1912); *Parliamentary Papers*, 1913, XLVII, 'Report (on) . . . the System of State Technical Scholarships'; R. I. Crane, 'Technical Education in India Before World War I,' in *Education and Economic Development*, ed. C. A. Anderson and M. J. Bowman (Durham, North Carolina, 1965), p. 8; IORDP no. 3554 of 1902; Proceedings of the Government of India, Finance and Commerce Department, Statistics Branch, January 1903, 16–31 (NAI).

9 See S. K. Sen, *Studies in the Industrial Policy and Development of India (1858–1914)* (Calcutta, 1964).

10 A. G. Clow, *The State and Industry* (Calcutta, 1928), pp. 84ff.

11 Curzon Papers vol. 280, 'Technical Education', Curzon note, 26 July 1903 (IOL).

12 Curzon Papers vol. 279, 'Commercial Bureau and Journal', Curzon note, 22 February 1903.

13 A. G. Clow, loc. cit.

14 *Lord Curzon in India*, op. cit., pp. 277–8.

15 Proceedings of the Government of India, Home Department, Public Branch, October 1903, 1, Despatch of the Government of India to the Secretary of State, 1 November 1903, and Curzon minute, 4 July 1903 (NAI).

16 IOJ&PDP no. 2332 of 1903.

17 Chatterton's activities can best be traced in his publications and a note written by one of his successors as Director of Industries, Madras. See A. Chatterton, *Industrial Education* (Madras, 1905); *Notes on Handweaving* (Madras, 1904); *Note on Industrial Work in India* (Madras, 1905); *Chrome Tanning in Madras* (Madras, 1906); *Lift Irrigation* (Madras, n.d.); *The Salem*

Weaving Factory (Madras, 1907); *Irrigation by Pumping* (Madras, 1908); *Industrial Evolution in India* (Madras, 1912); and *Rural Economies in India* (London, 1927). Cf. ICI-Industries, May 1917, 1–31, KW, C. W. E. Cotton note, 23 July 1915 (NAI).

18 Hardinge Papers, W. H. Clark to Hardinge, 12 November 1914 (Cambridge University Library); ICI-Industries, May 1917, 1–31, KW, C. E. Low note, 3 May 1915, and W. H. Clark note, 11 May 1915; IORDP no. 8417 of 1914, Despatch of the Government of India to the Secretary of State, 26 November 1915.

19 *Lord Curzon in India*, op. cit., pp. 158–9.

20 Lord George Hamilton to Curzon, 24 October 1900; quoted in Edna R. Bonner, 'The Economic Policy of the Government of India, 1898–1905' (University of London MA Thesis, 1955).

21 Curzon Papers vol. 280, 'Bengal Iron and Steel Company', Curzon note, 22 August 1905 (IOL).

22 IOJ&PDP no. 2332 of 1903, L. Abrahams note, 10 November 1903.

23 See Hector Bolitho, *Sir James Mackay* (London, 1936).

24 IORDP no. 2554 of 1902, Sir James Mackay note, n.d.

25 Curzon Papers vol. 279, 'Commercial Bureau and Journal', Curzon note, 7 May 1903 (IOL).

26 *Papers Relating to the Industrial Conference held at Ootacamund* (Madras, 1908), note by A. J. Yorke, Chairman of the Madras Chamber of Commerce, 14 September 1908, pp. 194–6; and minute of dissent by A. J. Yorke, E. W. Orr, and C. B. Simpson, 19 September 1908, pp. 225–6.

27 IOJ&PDP no. 1940 of 1906, notes by W. Lee-Warner, 1 August 1908, and T. W. Holderness, 28 June 1906.

28 IORDP no. 2645 of 1909, minute by Sir James Mackay, 2 April 1910; cf. the notes by Sir Theodore Morison, n.d., and K. N. Gupta, 6 April 1910.

29 Ibid., Morley note, 6 May 1910.

30 This is the burden of many of Morley's letters to Minto in the Minto Papers (National Library of Scotland, Edinburgh).

31 IORDP no. 2645 of 1909, Secretary of State to Government of India, 29 July 1910.

32 IORDP no. 2662 of 1917, W. Lee-Warner note, n.d.

33 *Papers Relating to the Industrial Conference*, op. cit., p. 7.

34 The official 'free trade' development strategy was best expounded by Sir John Strachey (finance member of the viceroy's council and lieutenant-governor of the North-West Provinces in the 1870s), his brother Richard (an engineer who was president of the Indian Famine Commission of 1880), and Sir Louis Mallet (permanent under-secretary at the India Office). See J. and R. Strachey, *The Finances and Public Works of India* (London, 1882); J. Strachey, *India* (London, 1888); and Sir Louis Mallet, *Free Exchange*, ed. B. Mallet (London, 1905).

35 A good example of this outlook is W. W. Hunter's speech during the 1882 Indian budget debate, in IOJ&PDP no. 736 of 1882.

36 A. Latifi, *The Industrial Punjab* (Lahore, 1911), pp. 106–7.

37 See Sir G. Birdwood, *The Industrial Arts of India*, 2 vols. (London, 1880); E. B. Havell, *Essays in Indian Art, Industry and Education* (Madras, n.d. but

c. 1910) and *The Basis for Artistic and Industrial Revival in India* (Madras, 1912).

38 B. H. Baden-Powell, *Handbook of the Arts and Manufactures of the Punjab*, II (Lahore, 1872), p. 342.

39 *Reports on the Punjab Exhibition, 1881–1882: Selections from the Records of the Government of the Punjab*, N.S. XXII (1883), pp. 4ff; and *Gazetteer of the Punjab, Provincial Volume, 1888–9* (Calcutta, 1889), pp. 142ff. The change in taste can also be seen in *Papers Relating to Maintenance of Schools of Art as State Institutions: Selections from the Records of the Government of India, Home Department*, CCCLVI (Calcutta, 1898).

40 E. B. Havell, *The Basis for Artistic and Industrial Revival*, op. cit., p. 8.

41 Curzon Papers vol. 279, 'Art Industry', Curzon note, 21 October 1900 (IOL).

42 A Chatterton, *Industrial Evolution*, op. cit., pp. 22ff.

43 Proceedings of the Government of India in the Home Department, Education Branch, March 1910, 53–4, L. J. Kershaw, Secretary to the Government of Eastern Bengal and Assam to the Secretary to the Government of India, Department of Commerce and Industry, 12 May 1909 (NAI); C. E. Low, *Report on the Industrial Survey of the Central Provinces and Bihar*, op. cit., pp. 16ff.

44 In the despatch cited in note 31 above. Cf. *An Account of the Work and Activities of the Department of Industries, Madras* (Madras, 1926).

45 The most convincing eulogy is in the Cotton note cited in note 17 above. IOJ&PDP no. 1940 of 1906, *passim*.

46 The most urgent exposition of the new situation is in Sir Thomas Holland's minute of 20 October 1916, enclosed in Chelmsford to Chamberlain, 26 October 1916, in the Chelmsford Papers (IOL). Compare the parallel movement in Britain towards 'postwar reconstruction planning' described by P. B. Johnson, *Land Fit for Heroes* (Chicago, 1968); and the British system of economic controls created in the course of the war: E. M. H. Lloyd, *Experiments in State Control* (Oxford, 1924).

47 ICI-Industries, May 1917, 1–31, KW, R. H. Craddock note, 19 October, 1915.

48 See S. G. Robb, *Government of India and Reform* (Oxford, 1976).

49 Proceedings cited in note 43 above.

50 Members of the Governor-General's executive council successfully suggested that they 'doctor' the despatch in which the Government of India asked the Secretary of State to allow them to appoint an Industrial Commission because they thought it would be easier to reverse Morley's 1910 veto on political than economic grounds: ICI-Industries, May 1917, 1–31, KW, C. H. A. Hill note, 16 October 1915 (NAI).

51 Craddock note cited in note 47 above.

52 Hardinge Papers, 'Memorandum by the Viceroy upon Questions Likely to Arise in India at the End of the War', p. 33 (Cambridge University Library).

53 Holland minute cited in note 46 above.

54 ICI-Industries, May 1917, 1–31, KW, W. S. Meyer note, 24 July 1915.

55 Ibid., C. E. Low note, 3 May 1915.

56 See B. R. Tomlinson's paper in this volume, 'Monetary Policy and Economic Development: The Rupee Ratio Question, 1921–1927'.

57 The key chapter in the Commission's report, containing their overall development strategy, was chapter IV. Cf. P. T. Bauer's criticism of excessive investment in heavy industry in the 1950s in his *Indian Economic Policy and Development* (London, 1961), pp. 50–9.

58 The advantages of an imperial department and the imperial services were a constant refrain in all the notes and correspondence in which the Government of India discussed the Commission's recommendations: see, for example, ICI-Industries, June 1919, 7–22 (NAI); and IORDP no. 5340 of 1919.

59 Both quotations are taken from the Keepwith to ICI-Industries, June 1919, 7–22. Cf. the *Report of the Committee . . .* [*on*] *the Division of Functions*, *Parliamentary Papers*, 1919, XVI.

60 The despatch is in the India Office Judicial and Public (Reforms) Departmental Papers, no. 196 of 1919.

61 Quoted in the *Report from the Joint Select Committee on the Government of India Bill*, III, pp. 37–8, *Parliamentary Papers*, 1919, IV.

62 IORDP no. 5340 of 1919; for Holland's attempts to woo the provinces (and his ultimate defeat), see the proceedings of the four industrial conferences in *Bulletins of Indian Industries and Labour*, 1, 5, 18 and 27. Similar constitutional/political wrangles inhibited economic planning in India during the second world war. There is a fascinating account of the discussions in the executive council on reconstruction planning in a letter of Sir John Colville to Leopold Amery, then Secretary of State for India:

Dalal [the new planning member] and his department are in favour . . . of confining State ownership to industries such as ordnance factories and railways, which are already state-owned, and to other key industries for which private capital may not be forthcoming. Ambedkar, with his socialist ideas, is naturally in favour of nationalising as much of industry as possible, and he was supported by Khare . . . the general view was that State ownership should be confined. . . . I think myself that a large excursion into state ownership . . . would be disastrous without more experience of owning industries. Council were in favour of State assistance to industries in a number of forms, and this is not controversial. What, however, is controversial is the subject of licensing. Planning and Development Department want to license all the industries in a comprehensive list of 20 key industries which they propose by legislation to make a Central subject. Constitutionally this can, of course, be done. . . . They would also apparently encourage the Provinces to license in the provincial sphere, which covers the rest of industry. Those with industrial experience and interests, such as Benthall and Srivastava, strongly disapprove of licensing because they fear that the cumbrous machinery will obstruct the development of industry and lead to intolerable graft and corruption. Wylie has pointed out with considerable force that no scheme of industrial development and control can possibly work unless the States come into line. Even state assistance to industries is useless if they are subjected to unfair competition from other industries established under different taxation systems and controls . . . the vast majority of the states . . . will have to be brought into line by the firm use of paramountcy. Muslim Provinces may well hold that nationalisation is pre-

ferable to the encouragement of private industries because state industries would have to give a proportion of the posts to the minorities. . . . Again . . . there is a suspicion that a clique of capitalists will gain control of the Central Government, and that the Provinces should resist any extension of their powers. It is all a very tangled business.
[*The Transfer of Power*, V, ed. Nicholas Mansergh (London, 1974), p. 864.]

63 Chelmsford Papers, Chelmsford to Montagu, 9 June 1919 (IOL).

64 The whole saga can be followed in Reading's correspondence with Montagu between September and December 1921, in the Montagu Papers at the India Office.

65 *Report of the Indian Retrenchment Committee, 1922–23* (London, 1923), p. 212. There is a brief account of the devasation wrought in A. G. Clow, *The State and Industry*, op. cit., especially pp. 30–5. The annual reports of the provincial industries departments tell the same tale in greater detail.

66 R. H. Tawney, 'The Abolition of Economic Controls, 1918–1921', *Economic History Review*, 13 (1943), 7.

67 Ibid.; cf. Susan Armitage, *The Politics of Decontrol of Industry: Britain and the United States* (London, 1969).

68 Reading Papers, Montagu to Reading, 9 August 1921.

69 For a devastating critique of British industrial policy see D. H. Aldcroft, *The Inter-War Economy: Britain, 1919–1939* (London, 1970), pp. 345–9, 295ff.

70 Compare Clow's *State and Industry*, op. cit., or *An Account of the Work and Activities of the Department of Industries, Madras* (Madras, 1926), with T. C. Smith, *Political Change and Economic Development in Japan* (Stanford, 1955).

71 E.g. Kozo Yamamura, *A Study of Samurai Income and Entrepreneurship* (Cambridge, Mass., 1974), pp. 128–9.

72 Cotton note, cited in note 17 above.

73 This seems to me what A. K. Bagchi does in his *Private Investment in India 1900–1939* (Cambridge, 1972). The plain fact is that economic historians have done next to no research worth the name on Indian entrepreneurs, so that we know singularly little about their professional competence or their connections with the state. Economic policy is hardly in better case: the most popular accounts—including Bagchi's—seem to have been written without reading a single government file. In this context, see M. D. Morris' important review article, 'Private Industrial Investment on the Indian Sub-continent: Some Methodological Considerations', *Modern Asian Studies*, 8 (1975), 535–55, which takes Bagchi's 'racial conspiracy theory' to task. It seems to me at least as likely that the Government of India's unwillingness to favour the British business community *enough* was responsible for India's industrial backwardness as any propensity to favour them too much.

10

The Distribution of the Indian Working Force, 1901-1951

J. KRISHNAMURTY
Delhi School of Economics, University of Delhi

A study of changes in the Indian occupational structure is a prerequisite for any meaningful quantification of economic change. Estimates of national income for the period before 1950 are available only at the all-India level and important parts of the national income are estimated by multiplying the number of workers in a particular sector by some net output (or net earnings) per worker ratio. The further back one goes in time the greater is the dependence of income estimates on working force estimates.

We examine below, on the basis of our estimates for undivided India and for the Indian Union, the working force and its distribution between 1901 and 1951. The percentage shares of different broad activities in the working force in 1901, 1911, 1921, 1931 and 1951 have been computed separately for males and for females and have been pooled for persons. Figures were also obtained down to the major group level of aggregation for manufacturing and services. For some major groups in some years disaggregation into minor groups was also possible. The estimates for undivided India for 1951 are not as detailed as those for the Indian Union, for they are obtained from pooling the results of the Census of India and the Census of Pakistan.

Tables 1 and 2 present the percentage distribution of the working force, separately for males, females and persons, for the period 1901–51. The estimates for females must be treated with caution as problems of comparability are serious.[1] The estimates for males are more reliable as their numbers are not so sensitive to conceptual and procedural changes.

1911 might be taken as the base for it was a fairly normal year and the 1911 Census was an efficient one. The 1901 Census has an inflated figure for manufactures because all 'makers and sellers' were included in it.[2] Also, the proportion of 'unspecified' workers was as high as eight per cent, compared to three to four per cent for most other censuses (except 1931 for which it was six per cent). The 1901 estimates are therefore more sensitive to the inevitably arbitrary allocation procedure we have used for distributing the unspecified. The 1921 estimates were affected by the influenza epidemic, the 1931 estimates by the Depression and the 1951 estimates by the partition of India. There are also other reasons for doubting the quality of the 1931 and 1951 estimates.[3]

While the estimates for females for the Indian Union and undivided India are not trustworthy, some trends are discernible and deserve mention. The shares of manufacturing, and trade and commerce declined through the period. We examine in detail later the absolute decline in manufacturing; we show that it was concentrated in lines of production which had been largely traditional, in which female employment within the household had been common and which were being progressively replaced by modern methods using male labour working outside rural households. Similar organizational changes in trade and commerce were probably responsible for the relative decline in female employment in that activity.

Unless specifically stated to the contrary, our analysis relates to male workers only. While this is in conformity with the general practice,[4] it means securing more reliable but less representative results.

The Indian Union

If we regard activities 1, 2 and 3 as constituting agriculture, then the share of agriculture rose from 70.3 per cent in 1901 to 71.7 per cent in 1951 (see Table 1). But the 1951 estimate for livestock, forestry, fishing, etc. was certainly an underestimate and the 1901 figures were not very reliable because of the high proportion of 'unspecified' workers in that census. Instead, we take the 1911 share, 73.6 per cent, regard the 1951 share, 71.7 per cent, as an underestimate, and conclude that the share of agriculture did not vary much over the period. If we define agriculture to comprise only cultivators and agricultural labourers engaged in the production of field crops, then it is not unlikely that agriculture's share rose slightly over the period. For six out of the fourteen Indian states

TABLE 1

THE INDUSTRIAL DISTRIBUTION OF WORKING FORCE IN THE INDIAN UNION, 1901–51 (PERCENTAGES)

Activity (1)	Males/Females/ Persons (2)	1901 (3)	1911 (4)	1921 (5)	1931 (6)	1951 (7)
1. Cultivators	M	49.9	51.8	54.6	50.8	51.8
	F	41.0	41.4	47.9	41.2	45.0
	P	46.9	48.0	52.3	47.8	49.8
2. Agricultural Labourers	M	15.9	16.8	15.3	18.2	17.9
	F	31.6	33.1	28.1	31.5	35.3
	P	21.2	22.8	19.7	22.3	23.0
3. Livestock, Forestry, Fishing, Hunting and Plantations, Orchards and allied activities	M	4.5	5.0	4.5	5.0	2.3
	F	2.8	3.0	3.1	3.6	2.3
	P	3.9	4.3	4.0	4.6	2.3
4. Mining and Quarrying	M	0.1	0.2	0.3	0.3	0.5
	F	0.1	0.2	0.3	0.2	0.3
	P	0.1	0.2	0.3	0.2	0.4
5. Manufacturing	M	10.4	9.5	9.2	8.9	9.7
	F	11.2	10.0	8.7	8.1	7.7
	P	10.6	9.6	9.0	8.6	9.1
6. Construction	M	1.1	1.2	1.1	1.3	1.4
	F	0.8	0.8	0.8	0.9	0.9
	P	1.0	1.0	1.0	1.2	1.2

TABLE 1 (*Contd.*)

(1)	(2)	(3)	(4)	(5)	(6)	(7)
7. Electricity, Gas, Water Supply and Sanitary Services	M	0.5	0.5	0.4	0.4	0.4
	F	0.7	0.8	0.7	0.7	0.7
	P	0.6	0.6	0.5	0.5	0.5
8. Trade and Commerce	M	5.7	5.5	5.8	5.7	6.2
	F	5.3	5.2	5.2	4.7	2.8
	P	5.6	5.4	5.6	5.4	5.2
9. Transport, Storage and Communications	M	1.5	1.5	1.2	1.3	2.0
	F	0.2	0.2	0.2	0.1	0.3
	P	1.0	1.1	0.9	1.0	1.5
10. Other Services	M	10.5	8.0	7.6	8.2	7.7
	F	6.4	5.3	5.1	9.1	4.8
	P	9.1	7.1	6.8	8.4	6.8
TOTAL WORKERS	M	100.0	100.0	100.0	100.0	100.0
	F	100.0	100.0	100.0	100.0	100.0
	P	100.0	100.0	100.0	100.0	100.0

SOURCE: Unpublished tables prepared at the office of the Registrar General, using the Indian Standard Industrial Classification. However, for 1951, estimates for activities 6, 7 and 10 and the unspecified were taken from J. N. Sinha, *The Indian Working Force: Its Growth and Changing Composition* (Delhi, 1972). In both Table 1 and Table 2, general labour and services otherwise unclassified have been distributed *pro rata* between agricultural labour, construction and some branches of other services.

considered, there were clear trends in the share of agriculture. The share fell in Kerala, Madras, Maharashtra and West Bengal and rose in Orissa and Rajasthan.[5]

Employment in mining and quarrying expanded considerably: the number of persons employed more than doubled between 1911 and 1951, Bihar alone accounting for about 44 per cent of the increase. Employment, however, declined by 13 per cent in West Bengal which had accounted for over half the total employment in this activity in 1911.

Male employment in manufacturing fluctuated over the period, but female employment declined absolutely. While total manufacturing employment rose from 11.7 to 12.8 million between 1911 and 1951, this was made up of an increase from 7.5 to 9.6 million for males and a decrease from 4.2 to 3.1 million for females.[6] The increase for males was after 1931 and the decrease for females was mainly before 1931. In Kerala, Madras, Maharashtra and West Bengal manufacturing employment grew rapidly between 1911 and 1951. At the same time, manufacturing employment declined in Bihar, Punjab and Rajasthan and rose somewhat in the remaining seven states.

The share of construction rose slightly over the period, but at no point did this activity have a substantial share in the total working force. Again, in another even smaller branch, electricity, gas, water supply and sanitary services, there was no major change.

Trade and commerce rose over the period, though the increase was mainly after 1931. The rise between 1931 and 1951 was due partly to the effect of the partition on Punjab, resulting in population transfers and economic dislocation.[7] But the increases in West Bengal and Madras were also substantial, possibly reflecting commercialization and industrialization in these states. In transport, storage and communications there was a sustained increase after 1921. All states shared in this increase except Rajasthan, where the capital-intensive railway system replaced the labour-intensive system of transport on camelback. Other services rose after 1921. Significant increases occurred in Madras, Assam, Kerala and Gujarat, and a substantial decline took place in Rajasthan.

We do not find sustained and substantial changes in the distribution of the male working force between ten broad branches of activity. In mining and quarrying, construction and trade and commerce, transport, storage and communications and other services there were increases: in transport, storage and communications, the increase was sustained and significant.

Undivided India

The share of agriculture (activities 1, 2 and 3) in the male working force appears to have remained constant between 1911 and 1951 (see Table 2). Given, however, that the 1951 figure was unduly low (the 1921 and 1931 figures support this contention), there was probably a rise in agriculture's share over the period. The evidence for the share of agriculture (activities 1 and 2 only) is certainly that there was an increase from 68.9 to 70.8 per cent between 1911 and 1951; the increase would probably turn out to be a little larger if the under-enumeration of agricultural workers in 1951 were taken into account.

The share of manufacturing in undivided India in 1951 was no higher than in 1911. The increases in the shares of transport, storage and communications, and construction were at best marginal; the share of trade and commerce rose significantly and that of other services fell. In general the pattern is not dissimilar to that observed for the Indian Union during the same period.

Between 1900 and 1947 for undivided India real output per head rose by about 17 per cent.[8] The exclusion of the government sector lowers the rate to 8 per cent and the exclusion of services lowers the rate to virtually zero. In other words, real goods output per head did not increase between 1900 and 1947, but changes in the structure of output are significant: the share of the primary sector in output declined from 63 to about 47 per cent over the period; the share of the secondary sector rose moderately from 13 to about 17 per cent; the striking increase was in the share of the tertiary sector which rose from 24 to 35 per cent over the period. The real product from agriculture rose by 12 per cent over the period, but declined per head of population, as the latter grew by about 30 per cent over the same period. The real product of the secondary sector doubled over the period while that of the tertiary sector more than doubled.

By comparing the broad distribution of real product and of the working force some useful conclusions can be reached. In 1900 the output per worker in the primary sector was slightly lower than that of the three sectors taken together, while the ratios for the other two sectors were somewhat above the average. This indicates a moderate degree of intersectoral inequality in relative product per worker. By

TABLE 2

THE INDUSTRIAL DISTRIBUTION OF WORKING FORCE IN THE UNDIVIDED INDIA, 1901–1951
(PERCENTAGES)

Activity (1)	Males/ Females/ Persons (2)	1901 (3)	1911 (4)	1921 (5)	1931 (6)	1951 (7)
1. Cultivators	M	53.2	53.5	56.1	49.8	54.4
	F	43.6	41.0	48.1	30.4	45.7
	P	50.3	49.6	53.5	44.3	52.2
2. Agricultural Labourers	M	14.3	15.4	14.4	19.5	16.4
	F	30.2	32.5	28.0	43.8	34.5
	P	19.1	20.8	18.6	26.3	21.1
3. Livestock, Forestry, Fishing, Hunting and Plantations, Orchards and allied activities	M	4.2	4.9	4.1	4.9	2.4
	F	2.9	3.2	3.2	3.8	2.3
	P	3.8	4.4	4.0	4.6	2.4
4. Mining and Quarrying	M	0.1	0.2	0.2	0.2	0.4
	F	0.1	0.2	0.3	0.2	0.3
	P	0.1	0.2	0.2	0.2	0.4
5. Manufacturing	M	9.5	9.1	9.0	8.4	9.1
	F	11.4	10.9	8.4	8.8	7.7
	P	10.1	9.6	8.8	8.5	8.7

TABLE 2 (*Contd.*)

(1)	(2)	(3)	(4)	(5)	(6)	(7)
6. Construction	M	1.1	1.3	1.1	1.2	1.4
	F	0.8	0.8	0.8	0.9	0.9
	P	1.0	1.2	1.0	1.1	1.3
7. Trade and Commerce	M	5.8	5.5	5.9	5.9	6.1
	F	3.5	5.3	5.2	4.8	2.8
	P	5.1	5.4	5.7	5.6	5.2
8. Transport, Storage and Communications	M	1.5	1.7	1.3	1.4	1.9
	F	0.2	0.2	0.2	0.1	0.3
	P	1.1	1.2	1.0	1.1	1.5
9. Other Services	M	10.2	8.3	7.8	8.6	7.8
	F	7.2	5.9	5.7	7.1	5.6
	P	9.3	7.6	7.2	8.2	7.2
TOTAL WORKERS	M	100.0	100.0	100.0	100.0	100.0
	F	100.0	100.0	100.0	100.0	100.0
	P	100.0	100.0	100.0	100.0	100.0

SOURCE: The estimates for 1901 to 1931 were prepared from census data by the author; the estimates for 1951 were obtained by pooling the Indian Union results, reported in Table 1 with figures obtained from the *Census of Pakistan, 1951*, Vol. I, Pakistan, Report and Tables (Karachi, 1953), Tables 12 and 14. Note that electricity, gas, water supply and sanitary services have been included under manufacturing.

the end of the period intersectoral inequality had increased very substantially. The index (as defined by Kuznets) rose from 22 to 58.[9]

As Table 3 indicates, the bulk of the increase in intersectoral inequality is explained by the substantial increase in relative product per worker in the tertiary sector over the period. Such a sharp contrast in the behaviour of goods production and services at so low a level of economic development is indicative not of modern economic growth but of distortions and lopsided growth. It would be illegitimate to infer any significant improvement in living standards from this evidence.

TABLE 3

Sector	*c.* 1900 share in:		Index of Relative P/W (1)/(2)	*c.* 1950 share in:		Index of Relative P/W (4)/(5)
	Work Force (Persons)	Product		Work Force (Persons)	Product	
	(1)	(2)		(4)	(5)	
	%	%		%	%	
Primary	74	63	0.85	76	47	0.62
Secondary	11	13	1.18	10	17	1.70
Tertiary	15	24	1.60	14	36	2.57
Total	100	100	1.00	100	100	1.00

While there was no clear movement away from agriculture towards manufacturing and services at the national level, some trends can be discerned by disaggregation: we examine below employment in the manufacturing sector.

Employment in Manufacturing

In this section all the estimates relate to persons. Within the manufacturing sector of undivided India, employment in factories[10] rose from 0.6 to 2.9 million; employment in the rest of manufacturing, i.e. small scale enterprises, fell from 12.6 to 11.4 million during the same period, 1901–51.

While we have no reliable direct information regarding output per worker in the two sectors, we can make some assumptions and test the results so obtained against available estimates. If we make the extreme (and obviously unrealistic) assumption that output per worker was the same in both sectors in 1901 and did not change over the period, the total manufacturing output must have increased by 8 per cent, since the work force in manufacturing increased by 8 per cent.

But our assumptions can be more realistic and meaningful. Assume (i) that output per worker in the small-scale sector remained constant over the period, i.e. that $An_0 = An_1$; (ii) that output per worker in the factory sector was twice that in the small-scale sector in 1901, i.e. that $Af_0 = 2.An_0$; and (iii) that output per worker in the factory sector was five times that of the small-scale sector in 1951, i.e. that $Af_1 = 5.An_1$. We already have the employment figures for 1901 and 1951 for the two sectors, Ln_0 and Lf_0 and Ln_1 and Lf_1. The outputs of the manufacturing sector in the two years, Q_0 and Q_1 can be obtained in terms of An_0 and the increase over the period can be determined. We have:

$$Lf_0.Af_0 + Ln_0.An_0 = Q_0$$

$$\text{and } Lf_1.Af_1 + Ln_1.An_1 = Q_1$$

So, since we know the values of Lf_0 and Lf_1, and Ln_0 and Ln_1, and since $An_1 = An_0$, $Af_0 = 2.An_0$ and $Af_1 = 5.An_0$

$$0.6\,(2.An_0) + 12.6.An_0 = Q_0$$

$$2.9\,(5.An_0) + 11.4.An_0 = Q_1$$

Therefore:

$$Q_1/Q_0 = 25.9\ An_0/13.8\ An_0$$
$$= 1.88$$

Our assumptions thus give a rate of growth of manufacturing output of 88 per cent over the period. If we had assumed that $Af_0 = 5.An_0$, instead of $2.An_0$, this would lower the growth rate to 60 per cent. As population increased between 1901 and 1951 by about 50 per cent per head manufacturing output increased by at least 10 per cent.

We have deliberately chosen assumptions unfavourable to the expected result, i.e. that manufacturing output increased. Actually with technological progress in the small-scale sector, e.g. handloom weaving (which we discuss later), and the emergence of *modern* small-scale enterprises, output per worker probably rose over the period. A rise in the output–worker ratio in small-scale manufacturing between 1901 and 1951 would tend to raise total manufacturing output by more than 60 per cent, all other assumptions remaining the same. Secondly, while our assumption that $Af_1 = 5An_1$ is perhaps a slight overestimate (being based on a 1961 estimate),[11] the assumption of $Af_0 = 5An_0$ is certainly much more of an overestimate of Af_0. As we have seen, a lower Af_0 would *ceteris paribus* raise the rate of growth of manufacturing over the period. Finally, the Census figure for manufacturing employment in 1901 was an overestimate.[12] A lower figure would imply a smaller decline in small-scale employment and this would tend to raise the rate of growth of aggregate manufacturing output. Since our assumptions have generally been chosen so as to overestimate the 1901 level and/or underestimate the 1951 level of manufacturing output, we suspect that the real increase must have been more than 60 per cent. Sivasubramoniam's estimates, though obtained from a wide variety of sources,[13] are not inconsistent with our lower bound 'estimate'. He finds a 123 per cent increase in the real income produced by the secondary sector between 1900–1 to 1904–5 and 1942–3 to 1946–7.

Detailed figures for different branches of manufacturing are available only for the Indian Union and so the results presented in the rest of this section have necessarily to be limited to the Indian Union. Between 1911 and 1951 employment increased absolutely in beverages, tobacco, jute textiles, miscellaneous textiles, wood and wood products, paper and paper products, printing and publishing, rubber, petroleum and coal, chemicals and chemical products, metals and metal products, machinery, electrical equipment and transport equipment. The increases in beverages and tobacco reflected changed tastes possibly partially associated with urbanization after 1931, while the increase in miscellaneous textiles was largely due to the shift towards stitched clothing. The increase in wood was absolute but not relative: while the demand for wood probably grew fairly rapidly—though possibly losing a little ground to cement, bricks and steel in construction—the advent of saw mills may have operated to reduce employment growth. In the remaining activities their relative novelty and the absence of a pre-existing traditional sector made for rapid expansion: though their share in manufacturing employment doubled from 8.4 to 15.8 per cent their weight in manufacturing employment remained small.

Foodstuffs, cotton, silk, and woollen textiles, leather and leather

TABLE 4

CHANGES IN MANUFACTURING EMPLOYMENT AT THE MAJOR GROUP LEVEL: INDIAN UNION, 1911–1951
(in thousands)

	PERSONS				MALES				FEMALES			
	1911 (1)	1921 (2)	1931 (3)	1951 (4)	1911 (5)	1921 (6)	1931 (7)	1951 (8)	1911 (9)	1921 (10)	1931 (11)	1951 (12)
1. Foodstuffs	2077	1617	1445	1431	749	671	674	862	1328	946	771	569
2. Beverages	20	10	35	182	12	7	29	171	8	3	6	10
3. Tobacco and tobacco products	30	34	114	572	21	22	78	361	9	12	36	212
4. Cotton textiles	3340	2930	3169	3161	2015	1767	2003	2149	1326	1163	1166	1012
5. Jute textiles	229	316	277	397	186	265	242	316	41	52	36	81
6. Wool textiles	170	115	111	108	104	72	67	60	66	43	44	48
7. Silk textiles	123	59	75	80	72	32	55	54	51	28	21	27
8. Miscellaneous textiles	713	765	617	1174	451	499	474	908	262	267	142	266
9. Wood and wood products	1448	1316	1384	1608	1075	1017	1088	1235	374	299	296	373
10. Paper and paper products	4	4	—	35	3	3	—	31	1	—	—	4

TABLE 4 (*Contd.*)

	PERSONS				MALES				FEMALES			
	1911 (1)	1921 (2)	1931 (3)	1951 (4)	1911 (5)	1921 (6)	1931 (7)	1951 (8)	1911 (9)	1921 (10)	1931 (11)	1951 (12)
11. Printing and publishing	43	41	44	130	42	40	43	126	1	1	1	3
12. Leather and leather products	1102	1054	929	750	907	870	808	677	194	184	121	73
13. Rubber, Petroleum and Coal products	—	2	3	32	—	1	2	31	—	1	1	2
14. Chemicals and chemical products	37	25	55	128	25	19	39	106	12	6	16	22
15. Non-metallic mineral products	1128	1124	917	960	726	761	636	709	403	363	280	251
16. Metals and metal products	660	654	639	879	584	569	588	818	76	86	51	61
17. Machinery and electrical equipment	—	—	—	170	—	—	—	167	—	—	—	3
18. Transport equipment	10	15	20	233	10	14	19	228	—	1	1	5
19. Miscellaneous manufacturing	573	568	599	644	536	529	558	592	37	39	41	52
TOTAL	11707	10648	10433	12674	7518	7158	7403	9601	4189	3494	3030	3074

SOURCE: The figures in Tables 4 and 5 were calculated from census data.

TABLE 5

EMPLOYMENT WITHIN SELECTED MINOR GROUPS:
INDIAN UNION, 1911–1951
(figures in thousands)

	PERSONS		MALES		FEMALES	
	1911	1951	1911	1951	1911	1951
1. Milling, dehusking, processing of grain	886	412	71	163	815	248
2. Sugar and syrup production (mills)	42	94	24	91	19	3
3. Indigenous sugar and candy production	incl. in 2	92	incl. in 2	56	incl. in 2	36
4. Slaughtering, preservation of meat and fish; fish canning	125	59	102	51	23	8
5. Bread, biscuits, cake, etc.	376	121	145	83	232	37
6. Butter, *ghee*, etc.	6	124	3	63	3	61
7. Edible oils and fats	539	286	321	212	218	74
8. Other food products (incl. cashew-nut processing)	108	239	85	147	23	92
9. Cotton ginning, cleaning, baling, etc.	248	146	147	116	101	30
10. Cotton spinning and weaving	2750	2884	1715	1941	1035	943
11. Cotton textile processing[a]	112	124	74	93	38	30
12. Earthenware and earthen pottery	884	609	563	434	321	175
13. Chinaware, crockery, porcelain, etc.	2	8	2	6	1	1
14. Glass bangles and beads	93	36	56	33	36	3
15. Glass, glass products and apparatus	21	17	12	16	9	1
16. Cement, cement products and lime[b]	25	27	15	23	9	3
17. Structural clay products like bricks, tiles	88	215	66	170	22	45

Notes: a. Includes bleaching, dyeing, printing of cotton and other textiles. 1961 evidence suggests 90 per cent were in cotton textiles.

b. The 1951 figure excludes lime workers.

products, and non-metallic mineral products declined absolutely. In foodstuffs the decline was mainly in the milling, dehusking and processing of grain and the production of edible oils. In both, mechanical processing resulted in labour displacement, and additionally, vegetable oil was being replaced by kerosene as an illuminant.[14] Butchers, bakers and fish-curers declined for reasons that are unclear. At the same time employment in sugar, milk, butter, cheese and other food products (including cashew-nut processing) expanded. In cotton, silk and woollen textiles the factory sector supplanted the small-scale sector in terms of employment. The substantial decline in leather was due to tanneries, shoe and boot factories competing out the village worker. Also the demand for leather articles like saddles, bags and jars must have shrunk. The decline in non-metallic mineral products was largely due to the massive decline in earthenware and earthen pottery, which lost out to metal, china and glass utensils which flooded the countryside.

The cotton textile industry, which employs over 3 million workers, merits special attention. According to our estimates (Table 6) employment in small-scale weaving declined from 1.9 to 1.8 million over the period, and it is possible that the decline in handloom weaving was in fact more substantial for (a) small-scale weaving establishments using power-looms must have increased over the period; (b) factory employment in 1901 was probably lower than our figures suggest; and (c) the number of hand-spinners in 1951 may have been larger than what we have assumed.

The Textile Enquiry Committee conducted a census of handlooms in 1954 and estimated that employment was 1.5 million for the Indian Union.[15] The Fact-finding Committee on Handlooms estimated that in Pakistan in 1956, 0.4 million workers were engaged in this activity.[16] So about 2 million workers in undivided India and 1.5 million in the Indian Union were engaged in handloom weaving in the mid-1950s. A somewhat earlier, and less reliable estimate was that of the Fact-finding Committee (Handloom and Mills) in 1941.[17] The Committee estimated employment in handloom weaving in 1941 for undivided India to be 2.4 million. Morris cites a much higher figure of 4.7 million based on including many workers with only a very marginal attachment to handloom weaving, who would have been excluded in a working force count, or else classified under some other occupation.[18]

Morris' estimate is crucial to his argument that an industry (hand-

TABLE 6

EMPLOYMENT IN COTTON SPINNING AND WEAVING IN THE INDIAN UNION, 1911–1951
(in millions, persons)

	1911	1951
1. Total Employment	2.75	2.89
2. Factory Employment	0.31	0.69
3. Employment in Hand Spinning	0.51	0.40
4. Employment in Small-scale Weaving (Row 1 *less* rows 2 and 3)	1.93	1.80

SOURCES:
Row 1: Table 5
Row 2: The 1911 estimate is from *Census of India, 1911*, vol. I, Part I, Report (Calcutta, 1912), p. 444; the 1951 estimate is from the Government of India, Labour Bureau, *Digest of Indian Labour Statistics* (Simla, 1960), p. 19.
Row 3: The 1911 estimate is actually the 1901 figure for undivided India available in the census; the 1951 estimate is an assumed one. We know that employment in 1961 was 0.6 million and we assume that it increased between 1951 and 1961 due to the encouragement given to *khadi*, and that it declined between 1911 and 1951.

looms) employing 4.7 million people in the early 1950s could not have been undergoing long run decline in its absolute size. Following Morris let us assume that in 1800 undivided India had a population of 200 million and a work force of 60 million, but that only 2.0 to 2.4 million people worked in the handloom industry. Handlooms then employed 4 per cent or less of the 1800 work force; Morris' estimate would imply a much higher proportion, 8 per cent. Instead, if we were to assume that there were 3 million handloom workers in 1800, the proportion to the work force of that year would be 5 per cent—a not unreasonable magnitude. It is possible, therefore, to visualize a scenario in which the number of handloom workers declined over the 1800–1950 period.

The evidence on handloom output during the period after 1901 is rather weak: much depends on the assumptions one makes and the years one chooses. We believe that handloom output rose from 965 million yards in 1902–3/1912–13 to not less than 1068 million yards in 1930–1/1937–8.[19] The output rose even though employment declined: this was because machine yarn, which replaced hand-spun yarn, was less subject to breakage; also, after 1900 there were important technical improvements in the handloom sector. The introduction of the fly-shuttle attachment to the common pit loom was a major improvement initiated early in this century and by 1940 about 35 per cent of handlooms were fitted with fly-shuttles. There can be no doubt that this raised output per worker considerably, though the benefits may not have accrued to the handloom weaver, but to the middleman who controlled the supply of machine-made yarn.[20]

Conclusions

The change in the overall distribution of the working force between 1901 and 1951 was at best marginal. If we had separate and comparable estimates for rural India, we would probably find a more pronounced shift towards agriculture in rural India, given that the share of the urban sector in the total population rose from 11 to 17 per cent over this period.[21] Comparing trends in the structure of both output and employment we conclude that lopsided development occurred. Within manufacturing, for which the employment figures are more reliable, the factory sector tended to displace the small-scale sector in terms of employment, though output in both sectors probably expanded.

NOTES

I am indebted in particular to Professors K. N. Raj and Dharma Kumar for commenting on many earlier drafts of this paper. I have also benefited from discussions with Professor Morris D. Morris. The defects that remain are entirely mine.

1 For a detailed discussion see J. Krishnamurty, 'The Industrial Distribution of the Working Force in India, 1901–1961: A Study of Selected Aspects', Ph.D. thesis, University of Delhi, 1970 (unpublished), Chapter 2.

2 In subsequent censuses 'makers' and 'sellers' were kept distinct. When reclassifying the 1901 data on the basis of the 1961 classificatory scheme, makers-cum-sellers were included in manufacturing instead of trade.

3 See Krishnamurty, 'Industrial Distribution', Chapter 2.

4 See, for example, the view of the Census Commissioner for 1961, A. Mitra, in *Census of India, 1961*, Paper No. 1 (Delhi, 1962), p. xxv.

5 For a detailed examination of trends at the state level for the Indian Union, see Krishnamurty, 'Industrial Distribution', Chapter 6.

6 The exclusion of the state of Jammu and Kashmir from our estimates for

1951 is unlikely to affect our conclusions as employment in manufacturing in that state could not have exceeded 0.1 million, it being somewhat lower in both 1931 and 1961.

7 As a result of the Partition, many refugees came into Indian Punjab and initially took to trade and commerce prior to moving into other occupations. For details, see Krishnamurty, 'Industrial Distribution', Chapter 6.

8 Product estimates have been derived from S. Sivasubramoniam, 'National Income of India, 1900–1 to 1946–7', Ph.D. thesis, University of Delhi, 1965 (unpublished). The changes relate to the period 1940–1 to 1946–7 compared to 1900–1 to 1909–10.

9 Kuznets defines the index of intersectoral inequality as 'the sum, signs disregarded, of the differences between the shares of sectors in total product and in total labour force respectively'. Using K. Mukherji's product estimates and Alice Thorner's working force estimates, Kuznets concludes: 'In India and Egypt . . . the share of the A sector in the labour force was relatively constant over the long period back to the beginning of the century. . . . This combination of a constant share of the A sector in the labour force and a declining share in product . . . implies that the (I+S)/A ratio was rising, and that product per worker in the A sector was actually falling.' See S. Kuznets, *Economic Growth of Nations: Total Output and Production Structure* (Cambridge, Mass., 1971), pp. 213, 290–5.

10 The definition of a factory changed many times during the period. From 1891 to 1922 it covered all establishments employing 50 or more workers; after 1922, all establishments employing 20 or more workers but using power; and from 1948 all establishments employing 10 or more workers with power or 20 or more workers without power. See S. Sivasubramoniam, 'National Income', pp. 34, 174, 253.

11 In 1961 the gross product per worker in small-scale manufacture was Rs 595 and in large-scale manufacture it was Rs 3247. See Central Statistical Organization, *Brochure on Revised Series of National Product for 1960–61 to 1964–65* (New Delhi, 1967), pp. 36, 31 and 92.

12 For 1901, we have had to include all makers-cum-sellers in manufacturing. See note 2 above.

13 Sivasubramoniam's estimates for the factory sector for each year are based on actual output estimates for eight 'known' industries; he assumes the same output per worker for the 'unknown' industries and multiplies it by the number of workers in these industries. For the small-scale sector, he uses available information on wages and earnings. See Sivasubramoniam, 'National Income', pp. 225, 252.

14 'Kerosene is replacing vegetable oils as an illuminant and the Telis are in consequence generally taking to other pursuits . . .' *Census of India, 1901*, Part I, Report (Calcutta, 1903), p. 212.

15 Government of India, Ministry of Commerce and Industry, *Report of the Textile Enquiry Committee, 1954* (Delhi, 1954), vol. I, pp. 16–17.

16 Government of Pakistan, Ministry of Industries, *Report of the Fact-finding Committee on Handlooms* (Karachi, 1956), p. 21.

17 Government of India, *Report of the Fact-finding Committee* (*Handloom and Mills*) (Calcutta, 1942), pp. 35–6.

18 See M. D. Morris *et al.*, *The Indian Economy in the Nineteenth Century: A Symposium* (Delhi, 1969), pp. 159–65.

19 These figures are calculated using the same data and methods as in S. D. Mehta, *The Indian Cotton Textile Industry: An Economic Analysis* (Bombay, 1953). Mehta's own conclusion is different because he compares 1906–7 to 1908–9 (a triennium with abnormally high output levels) with 1936–7 to 1938–9. See Mehta, op. cit., p. 126, Table 'A'.

20 According to Chatterton, a member of the Indian Industrial Commission, a former Director of Industries of the Madras Presidency and the pioneer of the new loom: '. . . it has been worked out very carefully as to what the advantages are in substituting the ordinary fly-shuttle for the indigenous slay . . . and the average comes to Rs 2/8 [Rs 2.50] a month. In the South of India over 100,000 of these slays have been put in. . . . These 100,000 looms have enabled the weaver to earn another 2.5 lakhs a month.' Government of India, *Report of the Indian Industrial Commission*, Minutes of Evidence, 1916–17, Bombay (Calcutta, 1918), p. 57. Also see the *Report of the Fact-finding Committee* (*Handloom and Mills*), pp. 199–200; pp. 69–70 and pp. 204–5.

21 See Ashish Bose, 'Six Decades of Urbanization in India', *Indian Economic and Social History Review*, 2:1 (January 1965), 39.

11

Social Factors in the Recruitment of the Bombay Millhands

R. K. NEWMAN
University College, Swansea

The workers of the Bombay cotton mills are probably the best-documented section of the Indian industrial labour force, but the information about them is rather limited in kind. Royal commissions and government enquiries have provided many statistics and a mass of evidence on working and living conditions from employers, bureaucrats and functionaries of the trade unions and welfare agencies. This material has been worked over by economic historians and increasingly elaborate constructions have been built upon it. On the other hand, the social organization of the millhands has received very little analysis, partly because there is very little direct evidence to analyse. Nevertheless, the social historian cannot leave his subjects in a void; he must attempt an imaginative reconstruction of the social milieu based upon whatever circumstantial evidence is available. In the case of the Bombay millhands this task has become more necessary because of the studies of modern industrial workers, in Bombay and elsewhere, which are now being provided by anthropologists and sociologists, examples which suggest that a purely economic analysis of the workforce may have led to a distorted view of its social realities. The aim of this paper is to identify these distortions and show how a renewed emphasis on the social preferences of the millhands can clarify some aspects of the development of an industrial labour force.

Jobbers and Their Gangs

The Bombay cotton mills recruited their workers through intermediaries, known locally as jobbers. Little is known about the jobbers' origins. It is usually assumed that they were appointed to bridge the social and linguistic gap between the supervisors and the ordinary workers, for the supervisors were mostly Europeans or urban, Gujarati-speaking Indians, while the workers were drawn from the villages of many regions, especially Maharashtra.[1] The workers also differed among themselves in their religion and caste, their language and dialect and many details of their culture and custom, all of which were potential obstacles to the effective control of the workforce. The jobbers were therefore selected as interpreters, spokesmen and mediators in many technical and disciplinary matters. The first jobbers were probably brought into the mills from the docks, railways or raw cotton trade as established recruiters of labour; later on, jobbers were usually selected from the millhands because personality, intelligence or physical strength had given them an ascendancy over their fellow workers.[2]

A jobber's most important duty was to recruit men into the section of the workforce under his control. If he failed to keep his gang up to strength, he was liable to dismissal by the management and to a loss of power in the economic and political networks outside the factory. In order to establish his control over a supply of labour, the jobber occasionally went out to the villages to recruit, but usually it was necessary only to be known to the villagers so that when migrants arrived in the city they would naturally come to him for help in finding work, lodging and credit.[3] The jobber's patronage in the tenements was essential to his leadership in the mills. 'He endeavours', wrote one observer, 'to acquire an influence over his friends and acquaintances who live in the same or neighbouring chawls. He lends them money, advises them in family affairs and arbitrates in disputes. When labour is required, he uses the influence so gained and is generally successful in procuring hands.'[4] Jobbers lent money on their own account, acted as agents for professional lenders and collaborated with *banias* who provided grain on credit; they also collected money for *tamashas* and for celebrating festivals and marriages.[5] Jobbers were involved in the running of *khanavalis*, where single men clubbed together to obtain meals, and they often controlled gymnasia, where the millhands held wrestling competitions and other sports. They were deeply involved in the politics of the mill area, from gang warfare and demonstrations to canvassing in municipal elections.[6] Through these activities the jobbers were able to achieve a position 'analagous to that of the Patil or Headman of a village'.[7]

To offset absenteeism among the permanent hands, each jobber accumulated a pool of substitute workers, or *badlis*. A crowd of *badlis* usually assembled each morning at the mill gates, waiting for the jobbers to come out and select men to fill vacancies for the day. When this had been done the unsuccessful applicants drifted off to casual employment elsewhere.[8] In spite of its apparently indiscriminate nature, there is good reason to suppose that the supply of *badlis* was selective and a necessary part of the jobber's system. Substitute work was a recognized avenue to permanent employment and *badlis* had an interest in attaching themselves as closely as possible to jobbers who could give them work. The jobbers, for their part, had strong financial and functional motives for surrounding themselves with dependable *badlis* who would keep their gangs at full strength and work with reasonable efficiency.

Inside the mill, the jobber's duties were largely technical and supervisory: he allotted work, granted leave, gave training to the hands, made minor repairs to the machinery and enforced the company's work regulations. The importance of these functions varied from one department to another and depended to some extent on the nature of the work and the personality of the jobber, but they usually gave the jobber considerable influence over the men. By assigning his favourites to work with new machinery or the best quality raw material, he could lessen workloads and, for piece-workers, increase production and earnings. Since the jobber kept the record of workloads and absenteeism he played a significant part in the calculation of piece-wages for individual workers. He also 'gave meaning and content to the formal work regulations' that were framed in general terms by the company.[9] Workers could be fined or dismissed for offences such as late attendance, negligent work, damage to materials, insubordination and other breaches of discipline and although, in theory, the punishments were decided upon by the departmental heads, in practice it was the jobber who reported misbehaviour and inflicted the penalty. For example, an official enquiry showed that fining by jobbers was more common than the rules allowed and gave rise to 'considerable abuse'.[10] Furthermore, offences like insubordination were so broadly defined in the regulations that it was possible for personal grudges and rivalries to be fought out inside the mills. The consequence was that 'mill-hand loyalties necessarily tended to be identified with the jobber rather than with the employer'.[11]

The jobber was therefore a man with considerable patronage, both inside and outside the mill. It was difficult, if not impossible, to secure and retain a job in the mills without his help and approval. The strength of his control is shown by the way that workers tended to enter or leave employment in groups and the way that group identities were preserved in strikes and trade union activities.[12] But the jobber's gang was more than a division of the industrial work-force; it should be seen as a unit of urban society with economic, social and political functions. In many ways the jobber was providing services which the municipality and the millowners were unable or unwilling to provide; migrant workers, newly arrived in a strange environment, found his patronage very opportune.

Inevitably the jobber profited from his position. He took commissions for his agency work on behalf of the Marwaris and *banias*, he received presents and services from people seeking entry to his gang and he took payments—known as *dasturi* or bribes—for appointments to permanent jobs. It has been argued that *dasturi* encouraged the jobber to speed up the turnover of labour in order to increase his income from bribes.[13] But there would have been disadvantages in such a practice. The jobber could not dispense with men who owed him money, he could not risk the unity of his gang by introducing new members too rapidly and, if he was paid according to the output of his men, he could not afford to ignore the comparative inefficiency of raw recruits. It seems more likely that *dasturi* was one of those customary payments, common in many parts of Indian society, which were symptomatic of a patron–client relationship;[14] it is even possible that workers actually welcomed the opportunity of paying *dasturi* in order to place the jobbers under an obligation to give assistance. In any case, there were surprisingly few complaints about *dasturi* from ordinary millhands.[15]

The jobber has also been held responsible for the 'ramshackle discipline' in the mills but this, too, is an exaggerated complaint.[16] A jobber was unwise to pursue his selfish aims to a point where he lost the confidence of supervisors or workers. In practice, this meant that the jobber tried to prevent disputes from becoming too contentious, which could result in his being placed in a situation where he might be dismissed by his employer or disowned and deserted by his followers. To this extent the jobber's interest lay in discipline of a kind, a discipline which promoted his own influence and, at the same time, frequently helped to reduce tension between management and labour. If this was not always consistent with management's idea of discipline it was because of the diffusion of authority among the jobbers and the informal way in which their authority was exercised.

The millowners' attitude to the jobbers was thoroughly ambivalent. It is clear that the owners were often frustrated by their inability to control the workforce directly; hence their interest in proposals for the abolition of the jobber system that were made from time to time. On the other hand, it was difficult to find an alternative way of recruiting compatible groups of workers and ensuring that casual absentees were always replaced. Recruitment through labour exchanges or specially-appointed labour officers still had to be adjusted to the habits and preferences of the millhands, something that jobbers were uniquely capable of doing.[17] Minor modifications of the system were equally difficult. If the jobbers lost some of their powers, their position as a whole was weakened and their usefulness in other areas reduced. The millowners were forced to conclude that the jobber was 'a necessary evil'.[18] His existence was a logical consequence of the heterogeneous nature of the workforce.[19]

The Jobber's Influence on Wage Levels

Most studies of recruitment into the Bombay mills have emphasized the connection between labour supply and the level of wages, but this connection may need to be modified to take account of the jobber's powers. Indian villagers do not usually migrate at random nor do they automatically select the nearest industrial town; they prefer to go to places where they can be sure of having the support of relatives or fellow villagers. Personal contacts are the most common way of finding a job. Recent studies of migration and job selection tend to support the impressionistic historical evidence from Bombay which suggests that the jobber, or the group identity which he represented, was vital in attracting recruits to particular occupations.[20]

One of the most serious difficulties in relating wages to labour supply is the unreliability of the data. The shortcomings of the available statistics have been freely admitted by previous writers but it is perhaps worth asking whether any statistical series based on the wage books of the companies could reflect the involvement of the jobber in the cash relationship between employer and worker. The monthly wage was subject to fines and *dasturi* and possibly to other deductions connected with the jobber's services outside the mill. The wages which the millhands carried out of the compound were not necessarily the wages which the pay clerks had handed over the counter.

Any explanation of labour supply which is based upon wages assumes that the worker will respond to monetary incentives and seek the highest pay. These assumptions need to be qualified for at least the first seventy years of the cotton industry's existence. Wages for particular occupations varied greatly from mill to mill; for example, M. D. Morris has calculated that in July 1926 the difference in average daily earnings between low-paying and high-paying mills was 33.55 per cent for weavers and 72.55 per cent for reelers.[21] Morris argues that this was due to the raiding of skilled workers as the mills expanded and tried to draw experienced men away from their competitors. There is certainly much evidence to support this view, but it does not explain why variations occurred in the wages of unskilled workers (such as reelers) for which there was no competition, nor does it explain why variations were not evened out in periods of economic standstill or decline, as they would have been in a perfectly responsive labour market. The fact is that wage variations cannot be explained without reference to the role of the jobber, for it was he who bargained for wages and other terms of employment with the small number of departmental heads who were known to him personally. In the process of bargaining the jobber would probably have tried to maximize his workers' income, but he could not identify himself so closely with the interests of his men that he was unable to cultivate the relationship between himself and his supervisor, a partnership that was vital to the interests of both. The importance of this partnership is shown by the way in which supervisors preferred to bring their own jobbers into a mill when they were appointed and take them away when they left; indeed, it was not impossible for the replacement of a manager to lead to a complete change of staff throughout the mill, beginning with the departmental heads and ending with the ordinary workers.[22] In practice, therefore, each millhand was part of a limited labour market that operated through personal relationships as well as through a cash nexus, a labour market that was bounded by vertical ties of patronage.

Mobility is the natural consequence of wage differentials in a responsive labour market. The Bombay millhands were constantly criticized for their wandering habits, a result, it was often said, of the lure of higher wages in neighbouring mills. Equally remarkable, however, is the number of millhands who moved rarely or not at all. A survey of long-serving millhands made in 1913 showed that 41 out of 100 had 'changed mills because of improved earning possibilities', leaving 59 who had either not moved or done so for non-financial reasons.[23] A few years later another survey showed that more than half of the sample had worked in only one mill.[24] The most detailed survey, which was published in 1930, showed that 47.7 per cent of the workers had spent their time in one mill and another 21.8 per cent had moved only once. Better wages accounted for only 21 per cent of the moves.[25] The surveys showed that absenteeism led to a smaller permanent turnover in labour than might have been supposed. Although migrant workers went back to their villages from time to time and all workers shared in the custom of taking two or three days casual leave after pay day, most of them could be fairly sure of getting their jobs back when they wished to resume. By attaching themselves to jobbers, the workers lost most of their freedom to move around in search of better pay but they gained a measure of job security in industry without having to sever their rural links.

The general level of wages in the cotton industry appears to have been 'remarkably stable', except for the plague years of 1896–8, when thousands of people fled from the city in panic, and until the 1920s, when wages and industrial relations were permanently affected by new economic and institutional pressures.[26] Morris and Mehta agree that wages were stable but they differ sharply in their assessment of the availability of labour. Morris, who claims that there was never a shortage of labour, has much the best of the argument; indeed, it is difficult to see how a labour shortage could possibly have continued in the face of the plentiful supply of *badlis*.[27] But if a shortage of labour did not push wages up, why did not an abundance pull them down? Here too it seems that the jobbers have not been given due credit for the way in which they provided institutional support for wage levels, albeit informally, for several decades before the advent of trade unions.

The plague epidemic was an important episode in the history of the mills because it was the only occasion in the early years when anything like a free labour market was operating. The plague began in Bombay in the autumn of 1896 and the exodus of frightened citizens reached its climax in the first quarter of 1897. Among the fugitives were many Gujarati *banias* from the mill area. Their departure disrupted the interlocking supplies of grain and credit, forcing the millhands to take short-term loans from Marwaris in order to buy food.[28] The workers then put pressure on the mills to relax the usual system of monthly wage payments; as the Inspector of Factories reported, 'Their first demand . . . was not higher wages, but daily wages; and daily wages they speedily got.'[29] After this the shortage of labour helped wages to rise and jobbers began bidding for workers in the streets.[30] This situation did not last long. From April onwards the refugees returned to work and between June and October the mills were able to move back to their normal method of payment by combining ordinary monthly wages with special bonuses to overcome the continuing shortage of credit. The strikes which occurred in these months seem to have been concerned with bonuses rather than basic rates of pay.[31] While it is probably true that the millhands could not, in any case, have defended their inflated wages because of the restoration of an adequate labour supply, it also seems to be the case that they did not see the situation in those terms, being less concerned with levels of wages than with the way that frequency of payment was related to patterns of expenditure.

It seems, therefore, that for most of the industry's history the relationship between wage levels and labour supply was less close than has generally been supposed, because it was a relationship established through jobbers instead of directly between management and men. It was the jobbers' brokerage in the labour market that helped to keep the general level of wages stable while perpetuating the differences between mills. Complaints about labour shortages should be seen in this context. Morris has grasped the essential point about the labour supply when he concludes that 'the millowners were really complaining about mill-hand instability and truculence and not about shortages'.[32] At the same time it is necessary to recognize that 'instability and truculence' were only those aspects of labour organization that were most visible to the millowners. Beneath the turbulent surface of the labour force lay a discipline, commitment and stability appropriate to the ties of patronage around which the whole system was organized.

The Position of the Substitute Workers

Recognition of the jobber's powers can also help to solve some of the problems raised by the substitutes. The need for an organized supply of *badlis* arose out of the custom, followed by most workers, of returning periodically to their native villages. Some absenteeism was also inevitable in an unhealthy industrial city where men worked long hours and were given few holidays.

Dr D. Mazumdar has recently argued that the *badli* system was a useful way of screening potential millhands so that permanent jobs could be given to those with the most skill and 'the best potentiality for a stable commitment to industrial work'.[33] The trouble with this hypothesis is that both criteria were irrelevant to the labour force as it was then constituted. Only a tiny fraction of jobs required real skill and it was pointless to look for a 'stable commitment to industrial work' when the actual selection of recruits still rested with the jobber, who chose men that would be committed to his leadership.

Some mills tried unsuccessfully to dispense with *badlis* by keeping spare hands on the permanent staff. Unfortunately these hands were as irregular as their fellows, disappearing after pay day or migrating to their villages during the monsoon or the marriage season, just when their services were most required. There may also have been some difficulty in deploying spare hands around the departments without the prior approval of the jobbers concerned.

At first sight it might appear that the *badlis* were a threat to the jobs and pay of the permanent hands. As a body of men who were underemployed, yet already partly trained as millhands, they might have served as strike-breakers; as men who could subsist on a low and irregular income, they might have encouraged the millowners to dismiss their permanent hands and recruit new ones at a lower wage. Any millowner who considered such action had to face the problem of supplanting his jobbers and recruiting and organizing his workforce across the social and cultural gulf that separated management from men, the situation that had made jobbers necessary in the first place. *Badlis* had neither the organization nor the inclination to go along with an attack on the existing system of recruitment; they had already attached themselves to jobbers and many of the permanent hands were their relatives or friends. Large scale replacement of labour was not likely to succeed until the millowners could find a body of workers who saw themselves as underprivileged and possessed an organization which management could exploit for recruiting purposes. The first such opportunity came in 1929, when a general strike coincided with the political awakening of the untouchables.[34] Developments of this kind, together with the advent of trade unionism and the retrenchment of the inter-war years, probably did more to undermine the jobbers' influence than the decasualization schemes promoted by the government.

Mazumdar has tried to explain the differential between regular and *badli* wages by distinguishing between the supply price of the two kinds of labour. According to him the supply price of permanent hands was higher because they were permanent residents in the city, living with their wives and children, whereas *badlis* were temporary migrants to the city who came alone and could therefore afford to take jobs at a lower wage. Permanent hands were also more committed and became more skilled at their work, so that employers were willing to pay a higher price for their labour. Mazumdar's most detailed evidence comes, apparently, from a survey of working-class budgets, made in 1921, which collected 2,473 family budgets compared with 603 single men's budgets.[35] In fact, the investigators intended to bias this survey towards the budgets of families and its data cannot be taken as representative of the ratio between family men and single men among the millhands.[36] Furthermore, the results of the survey contradict Mazumdar's hypothesis. While average family incomes tended to be slightly higher than the single man's, as might be expected when some families had more than one earner, the difference was certainly not great enough to confirm a difference in the supply price. Indeed, the average monthly income of single men (who, according to Mazumdar, were likely to be casual workers with a low price on their labour) was virtually the same as the average monthly income of two-loom, full-time weavers in the textile mills.[37]

There is a considerable amount of evidence to suggest that a large proportion of the Bombay millhands had some rural links, whatever their residential arrangements in the city.[38] Two tables in the 1921 census put the number of Bombay-born among the regular millhands as low as 4,000 at a time when the average daily complement of the mills was 146,300.[39] Surveys based on samples point to a similar conclusion.[40] Morris, who has examined this evidence with great care, concludes that the Bombay-born proportion is far too small and favours 18.87 per cent as a more realistic estimate for 1921.[41] Even this proportion seems unlikely to be large enough to fit Mazumdar's hypothesis of a settled labour force providing all the permanent hands.

It would also be a mistake to assume that single migrants could always afford to take lower pay than men with families. It is a well-established fact that many single migrants regard themselves as urban extensions of a joint family which continues to be centred in the village and which expects its city members to send back money as a contribution to the common income. The working-class budget survey showed that, on average, 26.2 per cent of earnings were remitted to the villages.[42] Recent studies have shown that industrial earnings are essential to villages where agriculture is inadequate or where families are competing for status and influence. Urban migrants will therefore feel a heavy obligation to continue sending support.[43] In any case, as Ames has shown in another context, the property-owning dimension of a family may differ from its household dimension;[44] in the former, all members of the joint family may have common rights and obligations, wherever they live, whereas in the latter, the membership may fluctuate from month to month as brothers come and go in search of work and wives circulate between city and village according to the season.

Mazumdar's hypothesis is therefore based upon false assumptions about the nature of the working-class family. Factual evidence from the textile labour force is also weighted against it. The real explanation of the *badlis*' ambiguous position can be found in the influence of the jobber, for it was his control of recruiting that prevented an oversupply of labour from threatening the pay and security of the permanent hands. 'Stable commitment to industrial work' meant in practice a commitment to the jobber system, a commitment that was made as willingly by the *badlis* as by the regular workers because it eased their transition to an urban environment.

Caste and Kinship as Channels of Recruitment

Another attractive feature of the jobber system may have been the familiar quality of its intra-group relationships. The exact nature of these relationships is the most difficult problem raised by recruitment through intermediaries. Was the jobber's gang a new voluntary association arising out of industrial organization? Or was it a more or less faithful reproduction of traditional relationships, in particular, of caste?

Morris has rightly pointed out the inadequacies of the data on caste groupings among the millhands: categories of *varna* and caste are intermingled with classifications of a completely different nature, like language, region or religion, while *jati*, the most significant unit in the caste system, does not appear in any of the statistical evidence.[45] But while the caste categories are too vague, so are the industrial categories with which they are often equated. Any visitor to a cotton mill will quickly see how the machinery forces men into groups: squads of doffer boys move along the spindle frames, or groups of men attend to the various functions of a sizing machine, to name two of the most obvious examples. The effective units of industrial organization are not the mills, or even the mill departments, but the functional groups within the departments. Any correspondence between caste and industrial organization will therefore have to be between *jati* and functional group.

There is no direct historical evidence of such a correspondence; indeed, as Morris has shown, there is not even any firm evidence of a link between broad caste categories and whole departments. On the other hand, in view of the absence of information, it is surely too dogmatic to conclude, as Morris does, that caste 'is virtually irrelevant to the recruitment, utilization, and behaviour of the labour force in industry'.[46] The truth is that we do not know, one way or the other.

At the same time the circumstantial evidence suggests that ties of *jati* or kinship may well have been alive in the industrial environment. In the first place there is the volume of impressionistic comment about caste as a determinant of factory occupation, at least some of the comment coming from people who would have been unlikely to confuse *jati* with other groupings. More important is the fact that the jobber, the agent who organized the transition from village society to the factory floor, operated at a level which could have linked the *jati* with the functional group inside the mill; migrant villagers who came into the jobber's gang through *jati* or kinship connections were employed in the functional group which was the jobber's limited area of responsibility in the mill. As long as the jobber arranged recruitment and the employer refrained from disturbing the layout of his mill by rationalization or technical change, the social traditions of the workers could be transferred to the mill and accommodated to its technology. The absence of caste tensions, which Morris takes to be a sign of the absence of caste consciousness, may in fact be a sign of the ease with which caste had become a part of factory organization.

Census tables and special surveys reveal some clustering of castes in different departments.[47] Vague though these clusters may be, they do reflect a tendency on the part of the workers to associate with people of similar background. This being so, one might reasonably expect the same tendency to lead to clusters of subcastes, particularly if the subdivision of departments into functional groups reduced the number of other workers with whom it was necessary to associate. The mixing of castes in the department as a whole proves nothing; it is the mixing of castes within the functional group that has to be proved if caste is to be discounted.

There is also some evidence that traditional criteria might have influenced the choice of job and produced echoes of the traditional hierarchy of occupations; untouchables, for example, tended to enter menial jobs like sweeping.[48] More detailed similarities are unlikely to have appeared since factory jobs carried no ritual stigma. It is possible that some castes did not see factory work as a break with their traditions because they had a background of mobility or skill which was appropriate to industrial work. Moreover, the internal relationships of amorphous caste-clusters, like the Marathas and the Mahars (both of whom were prominent in the textile labour force), could well have facilitated occupational adjustment and harmonious working relationships in the mills.[49] The crucial point was not the nature of the work done but the nature of the tie between the *jati* and the jobber responsible for that aspect of production. Although in theory 'most groups seem willing to take all jobs and all groups seem willing to take most jobs',[50] in practice most *jatis* and kinship clusters became associated with particular jobs through the patronage of the jobbers and their choice of occupations became limited accordingly.

Modern analogies are few, partly, it seems, because sociologists exaggerate the contrast between industry and village labour. Although Gould is correct in saying that the 'nature of industrial technology works in strong opposition to the premises underlying ascription-oriented occupational stratification', the process by which this opposition becomes manifest may be gradual and prolonged.[51] The extreme division of labour which occurred in the mills (as it does in the factory system generally) was a rather hospitable environment for traditions of stratification and it remained hospitable for so long because employers did not recruit according to achieved characteristics. It is therefore possible that the social traditions of the millhands were no more affected by their industrial work—conceivably even less affected by it—than the traditions of non-factory occupational groups, like building workers or rickshawallas, who were hardly touched by industrial technology. Gould has pointed out that Lucknow rickshawallas detach 'work from its caste contexts without necessarily altering the extent to which other features of caste continue to operate'; in fact, they tend to cling to corporate groupings of kin and caste because they are 'the most important real and potential source[s] of support and preferential treatment wherever they go'.[52] Bellwinkel has found that, for Delhi building workers, 'kinship and caste norms have changed their context but not their content', acting as models for all other interpersonal relationships within the industrial system.[53] The evidence from Bombay suggests that this could also have been true of the millhands for the first six or seven decades of their history.

Conclusion

Recruitment through intermediaries made it possible for the labour force to organize itself; workers could then arrange their life in the factory to conform more closely to the patterns of life outside. The Bombay jobber played an important part in this process. He assisted the workers' transition to industrial employment by accommodating traditional relationships to factory organization and by providing various forms of patronage to newcomers to city life. It may well be the case that intermediaries such as the Bombay jobbers are helpful to the early stages of industrialization, even though their behaviour seems to be at odds with the rationality and technical values of modern industry. Moreover, if the social effects of industrial development were less sudden than has usually been supposed, the jobber appears a less anachronistic figure, a leader appropriate to that stage in the evolution of an industrial society.

A number of other modifications follow from a softening of the contrast between industrial organization and past traditions. This article has already pointed to the dangers of seeing employer–worker relations solely in terms of cash and economic self-interest; it is clear that these alone cannot explain the history of wages rates and labour supply in the Bombay mills. It is also necessary to be cautious in using some of the terminology of modern industrial relations. The millhands may have appeared to the management to be unstable, uncommitted and unresponsive, but none of these characteristics was true of the relationship which was most important to the millhands themselves: the relationship with their jobbers. For example, commitment to industry, in a situation where so many functions were delegated to intermediaries, was seen by workers as a commitment to the norms of the jobber system. To confuse this with indiscipline is to adopt the subjective view of management; it is also to ignore the fact that effective leadership can be exercised informally. Finally, the jobbers' leadership made possible a form of bargaining between management and men even though many of the prerequisites of a modern system of industrial relations did not exist. For the first sixty years of the cotton industry's existence, the jobbers seem to have been reasonably successful in reconciling the preferences of the workers with the adequate performance of the industry. This was certainly the view of the millowners, who shrank from taking direct control of their workforce because of the problems this would have posed in housing and welfare as well as recruitment and deployment.

It was not until rationalization overtook the textile industry in 1927–34 that the Bombay millhands were faced with the logical consequences of industrial employment. Thereafter labour organization had to be determined less by their social traditions and more by the economic interests of management and the technical requirements of production. Whether, and how far, this drew the Bombay millhands closer to the western model of an industrial labour force, or whether the new traditions of jobber organization continued to be felt, shaping the composition and structure of the labour force as pre-industrial relationships had influenced the period before 1927, is still an open question.

NOTES

1 S. D. Mehta, *The Indian Cotton Textile Industry: An Economic Analysis* (Bombay, 1953), p. 67.

2 Interviews with mill staff past and present; A. R. Burnett-Hurst, *Labour and Housing in Bombay* (London, 1925), *passim*; Royal Commission on Labour in India, *Evidence*, 8:1 (London, 1931), 11–12; for a description of gang organization in cotton presses see Bombay Factory Commission, *Report* (Bombay, 1875), pp. 112–13.

3 Royal Commission on Labour in India, *Evidence*, 1:1 (London, 1930), 185.

4 Burnett-Hurst, op. cit., pp. 46–7.

5 N. M. Joshi, 'Welfare Work in Bombay Cotton Mills', *Journal of Indian Industries and Labour*, 1:1 (February 1921), 21; Indian Tariff Board, *Report of the Indian Tariff Board (Cotton Textile Industry Enquiry) 1927*, 3 (Calcutta, 1927), p. 570 [this report is hereafter referred to as *ITB*]. For a good description of a jobber's wide-ranging powers as they appeared to an

ordinary millhand see the Defence Statement of G. R. Kasle in the Meerut Communist Conspiracy Case, pp. 1000–1.

6 *Bombay Chronicle*, 29 December 1925, p. 7; R. C. James, 'The Casual Labor Problem in Indian Manufacturing', *Quarterly Journal of Economics*, 74:1 (February 1960), 108; interview with S. H. Jhabvala on 1 June 1967.

7 Royal Commission on Labour in India, *Evidence*, 1:1 (London, 1930), 10.

8 From 1935 attempts were made to formalize this system, share substitute work more equally and limit the jobbers' power over the *badlis*. See M. D. Morris, *The Emergence of an Industrial Labor Force in India: A Study of the Bombay Cotton Mills, 1854–1947* (Berkeley and Los Angeles, 1965), pp. 138ff.

9 Ibid., p. 142.

10 Labour Office, Government of Bombay, 'Deductions from Wages or Payments in Respect of Fines' (typescript evidence, n.p., n.d.), 3, p. 71.

11 Morris, op. cit., p. 145.

12 For an extended discussion of the relationship between jobbers and trade unions see my doctoral dissertation, 'Labour Organisation in the Bombay Cotton Mills, 1918–1929' (University of Sussex, 1970).

13 Morris, op. cit., p. 135.

14 J. H. Kelman, *Labour in India* (London, 1923), p. 106.

15 There were less than a dozen strikes against bribery by jobbers during the 1920s, the first decade for which records are available (*Labour Gazette*, *passim*). Morris has suggested (op. cit., p. 135) that *dasturi* was a form of surcharge on wages which the millowners were prepared to allow to the jobbers in order to save the greater trouble and expense of employing labour officers to conduct recruiting. This arrangement shifted the risks of recruitment on to the jobbers, whose *dasturi* would have fluctuated according to the supply of labour and the availability of jobs. Unfortunately there is no proof of this; what little evidence exists on the size of *dasturi* suggests, on the contrary, that payments were fixed by custom and changed very little over the years in spite of wage rises and the variable demand for labour.

16 Morris, op. cit., p. 129.

17 When labour officers became responsible for hiring *badlis* under the decasualization schemes, they usually took jobbers to the mill gates to help them pick recruits and they normally approved the jobbers' selection (interviews with mill staff; Labour Office, *General Wage Census, Part 1, Third Report* (Bombay, 1937), p. 16). This contradicts Morris, who argues (op. cit., p. 131) that the jobbers owed their position, not to socio-linguistic differences between employers and workers, but to the fact that they were a cheaper form of middle management than specially-appointed labour officers. In practice, however, the socio-linguistic differences were real enough and difficult to overcome without the jobbers' help.

18 *ITB*, 2, p. 350.

19 Jobbers, or their equivalent, seem to have been much more common in the early stages of Indian industrialization than Morris (op. cit., p. 131) will allow. See Royal Commission on Labour in India, *Evidence*, *passim*. Two recent studies have shown how social differences have persisted in other industrial centres. It has been reported from Jamshedpur that caste ties still affect labour recruitment to some extent even though the management tried

to eliminate them (M. M. Ames, 'Class, caste and kinship in an industrial city of India', *Asia*, 15 (Summer 1969), 58–71). A study in Bengal has found that 'Cliques in the form of pseudo-kinship groups have developed within the factory in which the boss is the pseudo-elder brother.' This boss distributes patronage much as the Bombay jobber used to do (G. Chattopadhyay and A. K. Sen, 'Growth of a Disciplined Labour Force: A Case Study of Social Impediments', *Economic and Political Weekly*, 4:28–30 (July 1969), 1211. The recruitment practices of Bombay were not, therefore, exceptional because of the unusually wide area from which the workers were drawn.

20 R. D. Lambert, 'Urban Society and the Village', in *India's Urban Future*, ed. R. Turner (Berkeley and Los Angeles, 1962) and *Workers, Factories, and Social Change in India* (Princeton, 1963), pp. 76–9; K. Patel, *Rural Labour in Industrial Bombay* (Bombay, 1963), pp. 28–9; W. L. Rowe, 'Caste, Kinship and Association in Urban India', in *Urban Anthropology*, ed. A. Southall (London, 1972), pp. 228–9.

21 Morris, op. cit., p. 157. For examples of differences between neighbouring mills under the same management see Bombay Strike Enquiry Committee, *Proceedings* (Bombay, 1928–9), *passim.*

22 *ITB*, 3, p. 570.

23 Morris, op. cit., p. 165, fn.42.

24 Indian Industrial Commission, 1916–17, *Memorandum of Evidence on 'Industrial Employees' submitted by Mr A. E. Mirams* (Bombay, 1917), p. 58.

25 *Labour Gazette*, 9:5 (January 1930), 458–61.

26 Mehta, op. cit., pp. 27–30.

27 Morris, op. cit., pp. 39–62.

28 *Times of India Overland Weekly*, 10 October 1896, p. 7, 9 January 1897, p. 30, and 30 January 1897, p. 102; Chief Inspector of Factories, *Annual Factory Report of the Presidency of Bombay 1897* (Bombay, 1898), p. 8.

29 *Annual Factory Report 1897*, p. 8.

30 Ibid. Even then it is not certain that a free labour market was operating. It was alleged that much of the increase in wages went to the jobbers (*Times of India Overland Weekly*, 1 May 1897, p. 407; *Annual Factory Report 1898*, p. 6), who may have led their workers from mill to mill in search of the highest wages (*Times of India Overland Weekly*, 23 January 1897, p. 78). The jobbers would have been released from their usual ties to the departmental heads if the latter had joined the exodus from the city (ibid., 9 January 1897, p. 30 and 16 January 1897, p. 57).

31 *Annual Factory Report 1897*, p. 9.

32 Morris, op. cit., p. 59.

33 D. Mazumdar, 'Labour Supply in Early Industrialization: the Case of the Bombay Textile Industry', *Economic History Review*, 2nd series, 24:3 (August 1973), 492.

34 See my dissertation, 'Labour Organisation in the Bombay Cotton Mills, 1918–1929', chapter IX. Gail Omvedt, 'Non-Brahmans and Communists in Bombay', *Economic and Political Weekly*, 8 (1973), 749–59 and 800–5, sees the non-Brahman movement among the Bombay millhands as a radical, anti-capitalist force and does not refer to the use of untouchables as strike-breakers in 1929.

35 G. F. Shirras, *Report on an Enquiry into Working Class Budgets in Bombay* (Bombay, 1923); Mazumdar, loc. cit., p. 489.

36 Labour Office, Government of Bombay, *Report on an Enquiry into Working Class Family Budgets in Bombay City* (Bombay, 1935), p. 1.

37 Shirras, op. cit., p. 10.

38 There are innumerable references to the rural origins of the regular millhands in, for example, the Indian Factory Labour Commission, 2, *Evidence* (London, 1909) and the Royal Commission on Labour in India, *Evidence*, 1:1 (London, 1930). This view has recently been challenged by Baniprasanna Misra, 'Factory Labour during the Early Years of Industrialization: An Appraisal in the Light of the Indian Factory Commission, 1890', *Indian Economic and Social History Review*, 12:3 (1975), 210–14. While Misra is certainly right to attack the myth of the millhand-agriculturist, it does appear that millhands with very tenuous village links still saw the countryside as a place of retirement in old age or refuge in emergencies such as strikes. It is also possible that the workforce became less urbanized between 1890 and 1920 as the mills expanded and had more jobs to offer to rural migrants.

39 *Census of India 1921*, 9: 2, Tables XI and XII, Bombay City.

40 *Labour Gazette*, 9:5 (January 1930), 457–61; Bombay Millowners' Association, *Confidential Summary of Workmen's Service Records* (Bombay, 1941).

41 Morris, op. cit., p. 65 and Appendix IV.

42 Shirras, op. cit., p. 35.

43 W. L. Rowe, op. cit., pp. 225–8; M. B. Padki, 'Outmigration from a Konkan Village to Bombay', *Artha Vijnana*, 6:1 (March 1964), 27–36.

44 M. M. Ames, loc. cit.

45 M. D. Morris, 'Caste and the Evolution of the Industrial Workforce in India', *Proceedings of the American Philosphical Society*, 104:2 (April 1960), 128.

46 Ibid., 132.

47 *Census of India 1921*, 9: 2, City Table XI; R. G. Gokhale, *The Bombay Cotton Mill Worker* (Bombay, 1957), p. 116; for a discussion of these sources see Morris, *Emergence of an Industrial Labor Force*, Appendix V.

48 Niehoff and Lambert have both found a tendency for castes at the extremes of the traditional hierarchy to occupy similar relative positions in the factories; A. Niehoff, *Factory Workers in India* (Milwaukee, 1959), pp. 53–7; and R. D. Lambert, *Workers, Factories, and Social Change in India*, p. 158.

49 H. Orenstein, 'Caste and the Concept "Maratha" in Maharashtra', *Eastern Anthropologist*, 16:1 (January–July 1963), 1–9. This raises the possibility of regional variations in the evolution of an industrial workforce with regional caste structure as one of the variables.

50 M. D. Morris, 'The Effects of Industrialisation on "Race" Relations in India', in *Industrialisation and Race Relations: A Symposium*, ed. G. Hunter (London, 1965), p. 153.

51 H. A. Gould, 'Some Preliminary Observations Concerning the Anthropology of Industrialization', in *Peasants in Cities*, ed. W. Mangin (Boston, 1970), p. 138.

52 H. A. Gould, 'Lucknow Rickshawallas: The Social Organisation of an

Occupational Category', *International Journal of Comparative Sociology*, 6:1 (March 1965), 30 and 32.

53 M. Bellwinkel, 'Rajasthani Contract Labour in Delhi: A Case Study of the Relationship between Company, Middleman and Worker', *Sociological Bulletin*, 22:1 (March 1973), 96.

Part IV

TOWNS

12

Changing Form and Function in the Ceremonial and the Colonial Port City in India: An Historical Analysis of Madurai and Madras

SUSAN J. LEWANDOWSKI
Amherst College, Amherst, Mass.

> The city has usually been first of all a 'place'—a clearly defined space visibly possessed and controlled by human beings and often sacred to their gods, a statement of man imposed upon the chaotic and threatening vastness of nature. It has represented the desire of man to master his own world, creating an environment reflecting his powers of reason, his desire for convenience and order, and his aesthetic predilection for beauty and meaningfulness in his surroundings.[1]

The model of urban building most familiar to us in the West is one which relies on certain conceptions of the use of space dictated by modern technology and advanced modes of productivity. We have created cities in the twentieth century that correspond to our notions of progress, industrial development, social welfare and aesthetic beauty that differ intrinsically from cities in other parts of the world, built at different points in history and embodying different notions of the use of space. This paper will concern itself with the origin, development and changing form and function of two types of cities found throughout Asia, the ceremonial and the colonial port city. Urban geographers have long used these models in defining urban development outside the Euro-American context, but historians have yet to employ such models in their examination of cities, particularly in India.[2] In this analysis, the ceremonial model will be used as a point of departure to further our knowledge of the nature of the colonial port city in India. For this reason, secondary sources have been relied on to a greater extent in the discussion of the ceremonial city, and more emphasis has been placed on historical change within the colonial port city.

By choosing two cities within the same geographical and linguistic region of South India, Madras and Madurai, it is hoped that some of the cultural variables will be limited, and the different world views that have created these cities will be brought into focus. What this analysis will attempt to do is to examine these cities at different periods in their historical development in the hope that the premises underlying their growth will become clear. Therefore, we will focus on Madurai during the Śaṅgam period (between the first and fifth centuries A.D.) and again during the Nāyaka period in the sixteenth and seventeenth centuries. Since the coming of the British to India, the form and functions of Madurai have changed, and it no longer clearly illustrates the world view of those who created it. Madurai is one of the few cities in South India that can be subjected to this type of investigation for it is possible to find historical data on the city, and its early form is still in evidence today. Although many cities in India have been destroyed and rebuilt in the course of their history, Madurai's form was preserved by its architects. Then we will turn to Madras City and examine its development from the seventeenth through the nineteenth centuries. Twentieth-century industrial Madras is a topic for another paper.

The purpose of this paper is four-fold. First of all, it will try to show that the unitary urban form of pre-British Madurai was a direct reflection of the Hindu world view which stressed the interrelationship of the sacred and the secular, and the hierarchical position of different groups within the society; that Madras, on the other hand, developed a tripartite urban form which was predicated on a western ideology that allowed for horizontal linkages within the society. In this way it will be possible to test the hypothesis that the British were, in part, responsible for the way in which the spatial form of Madras developed. But the paper will also ask to what extent the use of models is a productive exercise for the historian; what can a comparison of two cities at different points in time tell us about urban development in India; and what can be learnt about the histories of Madras and Madurai from such an examination.

The Ceremonial City of Madurai

India is a country with one of the earliest traditions of town planning. Sanskrit texts, such as the *Arthaśāstra* of Kautilya (ascribed to the fourth century B.C.) and the *Mānasāra Śilpaśāstra*, written between the fifth and sixth centuries A.D., speculated on abstract principles of urban design that were essentially idealized versions of what a city should look like. Since the *Mānasāra* was translated into the languages of South India, and its precepts were followed in the construction of cities, we will use it to reveal the ideal urban form. It must be stressed here that there was no one ancient Indian urban form, but that cities differed on the basis of their origins and functions. For the purposes of this paper, the ceremonial city will be defined as one which combines both the characteristics of a sacred centre with that of a political capital. The term ceremonial is not used in the literature describing ancient cities in India, and the form it most closely resembles is that of a *rājadhāni* city, a seat of royal power and administration.[3]

Although literature can be a misleading source for the historian in that it often presents an idealized version of reality, it is capable of eliciting not only 'images' of cities, but also their underlying structural features.[4] It is the structure of the city we will look for in the images presented to us of Madurai in the Tamil epic, *Śilappadikāram*, reputedly written during the Śaṅgam Age sometime around the fifth century A.D. when it is first possible to piece together references to the city.

The epic begins with 'The Blessings' that capture the imagery of the royal umbrella, beneath which all else was contained.

> Blessed be the Moon!
> Blessed be the Moon that wraps the Earth
>   in misty veils of cooling light,
>   and looms, a royal parasol
>   festooned with pollen-laden flowers,
>   protecting us.[5]

Madurai has been characterized by a number of writers as a city of the moral order.[6] In the images of the city presented in the epic, the secular is subordinated to the sacred. The Pandyan king wears the broad chain of rule given to him by the gods.[7] In the later writings of the medieval period, such as the *Madurai Sthala-purāṇa*, the local chronicle that records the early activities of the Pandyan kings, dating from about the twelfth century, the sacred origins of the city are stressed. According to one myth a merchant discovered a lingam in a *kadamba* forest and informed the ruler of the Pandyan kingdom of this. The king dreamt that a city should be built in this place, and subsequently had a city constructed around a temple, and named it Madura or sweetness, after the Lord Śiva had sprinkled the city with nectar from his hair. Another myth that recounts the creation of the Pandyan kingdom cites the first rulers as children of the god Śiva and the patron goddess of Madurai, Mīnākshi.[8]

The source of the king's power was *dharma*, religious and moral law, symbolized by the imagery of the umbrella. The sacrifices that legitimized the position of the ruler were, in fact, performed by the priest who was the representative of the deity. The French sociologist, Louis Dumont, has argued that spiritual and temporal authority are absolutely distinguished in India, and if we agree with him that 'hierarchy integrates the society in relation to its ultimate values', then in India religion holds a higher rank than power—and kingly cities or *rājadhāni* cities must be, by extension, sacred cities.[9] As we shall see in the following analysis of Madurai, it was not until the medieval period that this ideology was clearly reflected in the physical form of the city.

Although it is almost impossible to date the founding of Madurai, Kautilya's *Arthaśāstra* refers to trade between Madurai and the Mauryan Empire of North India. We know from the Aśokan inscriptions of the third century B.C. that the great rival kingdoms of the Pandyas, Cheras and Cholas were already in existence in the South. It has been speculated that with the rise of the Chera and Chola kingdoms, the Pandyas, who had previously been oriented primarily towards maritime trade, shifted their administrative headquarters inland to better protect their territory.[10] The Vaigai Valley could easily be defended from attack, a factor that has contributed to the long history of the city, but it was also the physical centre of the Pandyan kingdom. The valley was bounded by a large plain which stretched to the sea on the east and south; on the west were the Western Ghat mountains, beyond which was the kingdom of the Cheras. The Cholas were to the north, but the valley was protected from them by a range of low hills, outcroppings of the Western Ghats that were surrounded by forests. The Śaṅgam Age was one in which the three ruling powers of the South attempted to expand their power base, and vied with one another for control over smaller independent chieftaincies.

Although Madurai was a political capital, and a base from which the Pandyan ruler extended his military control over a wider area, the city also had an economic dimension, for it was an inland market centre. One might argue that the economic function of Madurai was to sustain the city as the centre of an empire—that *artha*, or material gain, was subordinated under the overarching umbrella of *dharma*. The Pandyan king was primarily interested in expanding his holdings, and he needed funds to achieve his ends. This being so, both the cultivator and the merchant were in an interdependent relationship with the king.

Madurai was built on the banks of the Vaigai River, described in *Śilappadikāram* as a 'Most cherished possession of the Pandya kingdom'.[11] This reference reflects not only the fact that the river provided a natural defence barrier to the city on the north, but it was used for ritual bathing, drinking, sanitation and irrigation. The river watered the fertile land surrounding Madurai which supplied paddy, sugar cane, millet, garlic, plantains, areca nuts, coconuts and mangoes necessary for sustaining the city.[12] It also provided a means of transportation and communication with a wider area than the immediate countryside. The epic gives us descriptions of inland and overseas trade that centred around the city. Tribute such as silk, sandalwood, incense, perfumes, and camphor was brought by convoys of ships down the Vaigai River from Tondiamandalam.[13] Greek and Roman writers and geographers of the first and second centuries A.D. attest to the well-developed overseas trade networks that linked southern India with the Greco-Roman world. The fact that Roman coins were found in large numbers in the Vaigai River bed has led many scholars to believe that a colony of Roman merchants may have lived there at one time.[14] With regard to inland trade, *Śilappadikāram* mentions three highways that existed connecting Madurai with Kodumbalur, possibly Cranganore in Kerala. It is known that goods were brought from the Pandyan kingdom over, or through the passes of, the Western Ghats to Chera desam.[15] It is also believed that trade was carried on over the rugged roads linking north and south India. We know that Madurai was famous for its production of fine cloth, and its markets contained foreign cloth, silk and wool. From the literary sources one receives an impression of markets filled with luxury goods such as ivory, and pearls which the city exported, emeralds, rubies, diamonds and gold.[16] Although the revenue structure of Madurai remains obscure, both the petty traders and larger merchants, as well as the peasants tilling the hinterland, appear to have provided the economic support for the city. The political and economic functions of Madurai were, in effect, undifferentiated at a time when an expanding empire demanded an expanding economy.

When we turn from a discussion of the functions of Madurai to its urban form it becomes clear that Madurai shared many of the characterstics of the *durga-sanniveśa* tradition relating to the layout of forts.[17] Presumably the royal city incorporated elements from the earlier tradition of fort building, for common to both were the use of high walls and gates necessary for defending the city. There was often a moat or ditch beyond the walls that not only contributed to the protection of the city, but also provided water. Moats were an intrinsic part of the expansion of walled cities, for they were a source of earth used for building new walls, levelling the ground and raising the urban site.[18] *Śilappadikāram* describes the solid wall that surrounded the city, its gates and moat, and 'ramparts, covered with thick overgrowth', which would remain a feature of the landscape until the advent of the British.[19]

In the idealized urban plan, the four gates facing the cardinal points on the compass, determined the four main streets that led to the centre of the city, for the favourite design was that of a square or rectangle bisected in the middle. The grid pattern familiar to us in the West was most often employed in the layout of streets that ran directly from east to west and from north to south.[20] As Julian Smith has pointed out in his study of the architecture of Madurai, sacred geometry determined the layout of the city, the village and the dwelling place.[21] A ritual diagram or *vāstu-maṇḍala* (*vāstu*- meaning abode and *maṇḍala*, circle) was used to define the space on which construction would take place. Although the *maṇḍala* was in theory a circle, in actuality it formed a square for the drawing of the *maṇḍala* was determined by the cardinal directions.[22] After laying out the axes of the diagram, the perimeter was located, and lines were drawn linking the corners of the *maṇḍala*. The completion of the sacred diagram involved its division into *padas* or plots where the different deities resided.

An understanding of this geometry is useful in analysing Madurai. The wall which surrounded the city during the Śaṅgam period and defined its outer limits was theoretically also the boundary of the *maṇḍala*. However, it should be pointed out that it is historically difficult to document the use of *maṇḍalas* by urban architects during this period.[23] *Śilapaddikāram* mentions the initial journey that the hero and heroine of the epic take around the walls of Madurai before entering the eastern gate (one of the four city gates) indicative of a ritual circumambulation of the city.[24] That Madurai was divided into quarters occupied by different caste groups is clear from the epic which mentions four caste groups, Brahmins, warriors, merchants and craftsmen, protected by four gods.[25] Yet, on the basis of descriptions given in this epic and *Maduraikānchi* (dated from the second to the fourth century), it is impossible to give an accurate spatial analysis of the city. For example, it is not clear whether the centre of Madurai was occupied by a royal palace or a temple. Today the Tamil word *koyil* is translated as temple, but during the Śaṅgam period it apparently referred to a royal palace.[26] There is mention made of four streets surrounding the palace where Brahmins, princes, ministers, rich merchants and royal household servants resided, suggesting the palace as a central focus.[27] Although there are four major temples cited in the Madurai of *Śilappadikāram*, none of these is given a central place in the descriptions, nor does the worship of Śiva and Vishnu referred to in *Maduraikānchi* appear to have been more important than that of the 'dreaded' Dravidian deities, Muruga, Tirumal and Kotravai.[28] In spite of the fact that the goddess of Madurai appears at the end of *Śilapaddikāram* to placate the heroine of the epic, there is no mention of her shrine, and if a shrine to Śiva or Mīnākshi did occupy a central place, which seems rather unlikely during the Śaṅgam period, it did not dominate the urban landscape.

However, the Tamil puranas and other sources dating from the twelfth century reflect the growing prominence of the Brahmin community, and Aryan religious traditions in South India and their impact on the spatial evolution of Madurai. It is from this period that one can document the emergence of the Śiva temple in the centre of the city. Although the temple complex was increasing in importance from the twelfth to the thirteenth centuries, the Pandyan kings were struggling to maintain their power base. In the early fourteenth century, Muslim armies destroyed part of the Śiva temple and its adjacent residential areas, and occupied the city and its hinterland until 1372 when they were forced out of the area by an agent of the Vijayanagar rajas. Although the Pandyas were allowed to remain in power, under the authority of a viceroy or Nāyaka of Vijayanagar, by the middle of the sixteenth century the Nāyakas had themselves established a semi-independent dynasty. The temple city of Madurai visible to us today is a by-product of the Nāyaka period.

In the centuries that preceded Nāyaka rule, much of Madurai had been destroyed and rebuilt. In order to protect the city from further destruction, the earliest Nāyaka ruler, Viswanātha, who came to power in 1559, dismantled the Pandyan ramparts and built an elaborate double-walled fortress in their place.[29] He was responsible for clearing the jungle that had grown up around the city, and constructing two dams across the upper Vaigai River that facilitated the irrigation of the land around the capital, and turned the valley once again into a fertile rice producing belt.[30] Madurai could now resume its position as capital of a kingdom comprising the modern districts of Madura, Trichinopoly, Tinnevelly and the southern parts of Travancore.

As Nāyaka warriors from the Telugu-speaking region to the north of Madurai who were representatives of the Vijayanagar Empire now replaced the Tamil Pandyas as rulers, they insured their power base in the Tamil heartland by sponsoring the building of temple cities and pilgrimage centres; and as the Tamil texts tell us, Viswanātha 'received the sceptre in the presence of the goddess Minatchi'.[31] Burton Stein stresses that these warriors were 'most often men of low ritual origin whose participation in temple-oriented Hinduism reflected their pretensions to higher rank commensurate with their political power'.[32] Local merchants also contributed to the construction of temples, and their status rose in South Indian cities as their wealth buttressed the power of the new warrior rulers.

One might argue that the Telugus were essentially a colonial ruling group in the Tamil country; however, they were working within the same Hindu cosmological framework as that of the Tamils, and with accepted notions of hierarchy; one reinforced one's political position by building temples. The replacing of one Hindu power group by another did not alter significantly the form or functions of the city. With the rebuilding of Madurai, it became a visual expression of the strength and expandability of the Nāyaka kingdom, and a reflection of its relationship to the sacred and divine.

The Nāyaka ruler, Viswanātha, not only improved the fortifications of Madurai, but allegedly had his civil architect redesign the city in strict accordance with the principles laid down in the Śilpa-śāstras.[33] It is for this reason that Madurai expresses the sense of unitary planning which is not visible in ceremonial cities such as Benares. Madurai was laid out in the shape of a square with a series of concentric streets (squares within squares) culminating in the great temple of Mīnākshi. These squares continue to retain their traditional names, Adhi, Chitrai, Avani-moola, and Masi Streets (north, south, east and west). The names of these streets correspond to the Tamil months in which the most important temple deities process along the streets surrounding Mīnākshi Temple.[34] It was along these streets that quarters were laid out for the different castes and professional groups. The streets around the king's palace (now located southeast of the temple) contained the houses of the royal ministers and merchants, whereas the Brahmin community resided in *agraharams* or residential enclaves of their own near the temple. It is alleged that Viswanātha was able to gain the support of the Brahmins by repairing and building new temples and *agraharams* in the city.[35] The layout of the wards corresponded to the occupational requirements of their inhabitants, and were diversified in their appearance. But the pattern remained for the wealthiest inhabitants to reside near the urban centre, a common pattern in pre-industrial cities.[36]

In the *Mānasāra Śilpaśāstra* there are elaborate prescriptions for the expansion and reconstruction of ancient cities. Where a temple city is to be rebuilt, it is important to begin with the central shrine and to fashion the city around it.[37] In Viswanātha's design, the temple remained the focus of centrality as it had been throughout the medieval period. By the early thirteenth century, prior to the temple's partial destruction by Muslim invaders, it was apparently surrounded by an outer wall with fourteen towers, indicating that the notion of architectural monumentality witnessed under the Nāyaks was not new to Madurai.[38] It has been argued that the type of architecture employed by the Nāyaks of Madurai was a continuation of the style used by the Pandyas, involving the addition of a series of extensions onto the original structure but always with the overall plan of the city in mind.[39] The design of the Mīnākshi Sundareśvara temple has been attributed to Viswanātha Nāyaka who began construction of the outermost walls surrounding the original shrines of the god and goddess, the oldest part of the temple. However, further additions were made by princes, nobles and wealthy merchants who competed with one another to complete the structure without changing his original design.

The temple as well as the city faced east—for the direction of the rising sun holds the greatest cosmological significance for the Hindus. In accordance with orthodox principles of urban planning in India, the city's axes were aligned with the four quarters of the compass, and four gateways gave access to the city. One might argue, in effect, that the city, and the temple at its centre, were microcosms of the Hindu universe, for they both followed similar plans. The temple of Madurai had gate-towers (*gopurams*) facing the car street; and at times of procession the presiding deity would be drawn past these gates as it circled the temple, symbolic of the universe. The axis of Madurai was essentially a vertical one, for one of the *gopurams* which allowed access to the temple was 150 feet high.[40] These *gopurams* were visible for miles outside the city, thus attracting pilgrims to the deity and place of worship. If one were to look at the temple from above, one would see a square within a square; the cardinal points on the compass defined by these *gopurams*, with the central temple shrine marked by a *sikara*. What is important here is that the outer *gopurams* were the last ones to be built, symbolizing an infinitely expandable temple universe.[41]

Secular architecture was also an important element in the new plan of Madurai, but subordinate to that of the sacred. It was under Tirumala Nāyaka, who ruled from 1623–59 and who severed his ties with Vijayanagar and created an independent kingdom centring on Madurai, that secular architecture reached its zenith. It is speculated that the whole front half of the fort, located in the southeastern sector of the city, consisted of mansions, pavilions, elephant stables and barracks.[42] Tirumala is given credit for constructing the great palace of Madurai on a large plot of land that included a series of detached buildings and an arena for sports. The palace was an elaborate structure, supported by stone pillars and decorated with carved *chunam*, a fine stucco made of limestone. The architect who designed the palace may have come from Bisnagur where Mughal styles were popular.[43] The palace is the best example of monumental secular architecture undertaken during the reign of the Nāyaks.

The spatial relationship between the temple and the palace, between sacred and secular architecture is an important theme in the history of Madurai. Although the Nāyaks allegedly made a careful attempt to follow urban planning principles laid down in the *śāstras*, the location of the palace in the southeast does not accord with the texts, for the northwest and southeast were considered inauspicious.[44] As to why the palace was moved south, one might speculate that there was more room for monumental building in the southern sector of the city. It also appears that the Vaigai River may have shifted its course. Maps of contemporary Madurai show the southeast boundary of the city to be further from the temple (at the theoretical centre) than the northeast boundary. One might argue that because of the directional flow of the river, there was more land available for the stabling of elephants, and the housing of armies in the eastern and southern sectors, and this accounted for the substantial remains of secular architecture in this area. It would appear that the Nāyaka rulers, if they did use the *śāstras* in planning the city, were much less concerned about the cosmological significance of the location of their palaces and administrative buildings than they were about maintaining the temple in the centre of the sacred *maṇḍala*.

The city of Madurai was a product of a particular Hindu world view that stressed both the sacred and secular aspects of the political capital of an empire. It was created and developed by Hindu rulers and the wealthier stratum of urban society which saw the city as a symbolic expression of the empire. Like the deity who circled the temple (his universe) on processional occasions, the king theoretically circled his capital city at the time of his coronation, accepting the obligation to protect the kingdom over which he ruled.[45] At a time when Nāyaka rule was extending itself in South India, Madurai was remodelled on a monumental scale. But the form chosen was a unitary one expressive of the complementary relationship of king and deity in Hindu society—with the first position given to the latter, as signified in the divine palace, the Great Mīnākshi Temple. As one moved away from the symbolic centre, one moved down the Hindu hierarchy of caste, with the wealthiest and ritually purest stratum in closest proximity to the temple and palace, and the poorest on the urban fringes. The city was a visual reflection of the world view of those who occupied it and whose values were mirrored in its functions and residential patterns. It was also a reflection of the infinite expandability of such a universe.

With the coming of the British, Madurai ceased to be a *rājadhāni* city, a ceremonial city which was both the seat of royal power, and of a Hindu moral order, for the umbrella of *dharma* had collapsed. Although the British located their administrative offices in the Nāyaka Palace, and thus symbolically replaced their Telugu predecessors without changing the urban form, the longer they remained in Madurai, the more it came to look like the colonial city of Madras.

In the nineteenth century the old fortifications of Madurai were torn down, and the urban wall was made into Veli Street, a broad avenue circumscribing the city. (See map of Madurai.) Although at first new settlements were formed on the outskirts of the old city, with the building of the railroad in the 1870s and a bridge which spanned the Vaigai in 1889, the form of Madurai began to change.[46]

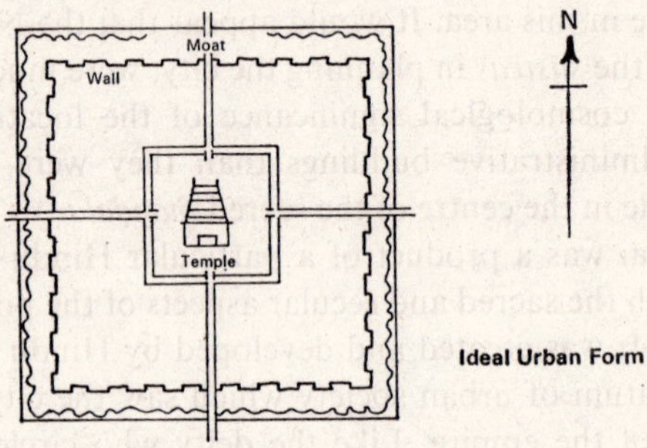

Madurai City (1937)

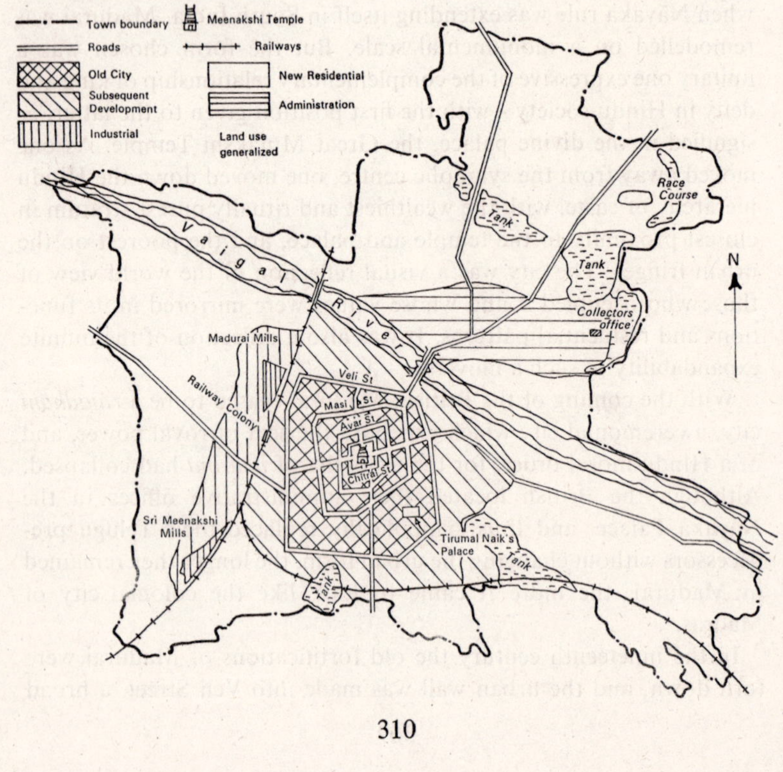

Now development took place north of the river and along the railway line to the west. Whereas previously Europeans lived to the east of the old city, now bungalows for European residents, clubs and a race course were constructed on the northern bank of the river.[47] It was here as well that government offices were located for the district of Madurai. On the western limits of the town, the major industrial development began to take place. Textile factories grew up in this sector, and a colony of railway workers has existed here since the nineteenth century. By the early twentieth century, the southern portion of the city, bounded by several large tanks which prevented expansion in this direction, provided an impoverished residential zone for handicraft weavers.[48]

Today, Madurai still remains a pilgrimage centre, as it had been prior to the British, and as Julian Smith has argued, the yearly cycle of festival processions that move along the car streets surrounding the temple, the divine palace where the king-deity resides, have maintained the morphology of the city intact since the Nāyaka period.[49] Yet, in the course of the nineteenth and twentieth centuries, Madurai became the district headquarters of a larger colonial political complex and an industrial town. The city was now predicated on different notions of the relationship between political and economic power than had existed under its Hindu rulers. One could suggest that Madurai no longer retained its unitary form, and instead became a collection of urban nuclei functionally related to one another, the old city centre representing only a sector of the city. The next section of this paper will illustrate how a city created, in part, by a European world view, emerged with a different urban form in India, and one which bears certain similarities to what we see in contemporary Madurai.

The Colonial Port City of Madras

In contrast to the Hindu world view expressed in the ceremonial city of India is that of the colonial city founded by Europeans. Over time, its form and functions became a direct reflection of its foreign origins, and as such it represented the microcosm of the larger colonial empire of which it was a product. The world view of those who created the colonial city was purely secular in orientation. The city did not stand alone as the centre of its own universe, but was linked to a series of other satellite cities, and ultimately subordinate to the foreign capital on which it depended for its existence.

Although there are no treatises that define the colonial city in India *per se*, social science literature has long used the colonial model as a means of examining cities founded or developed by European powers. We shall review here some of the basic characteristics ascribed to the colonial scene before turning to Madras. G. Balandier in an article which draws on a number of different disciplines points out several traits of what he calls the 'colonial situation'. First of all it involves the economic and political domination of a foreign minority from one ethnic (or racial) and cultural set of origins over an indigenous majority from a different background. Secondly, 'this domination' links 'radically different civilizations into some form of relationship'. Thirdly, it places an industrialized society in contact with a pre-industrial society, and fourthly, the tension between the two societies results primarily from the 'subservient role to which the colonial people are subjected as "instruments" of the colonial power'.[50] All of these characteristics are clearly evident in the form of the colonial port city of Asia. It is important to make a distinction between different stages in the development of the colonial port city, for as we shall see in the case of Madras, the city initially had a form similar to that of the ceremonial city, but as the British gained greater control over India there was an unleashing of Western notions of power which were in direct conflict with those embedded within the Hindu tradition, and became manifest in the urban form.

Before the coming of the British, Madrasapatam was an insignificant town on the Coromandel Coast, almost 350 miles northeast of the ceremonial city of Madurai. But in the course of its history, it was to become the capital for the whole of South India, and Madurai was to be reduced to a regional satellite—the administrative headquarters of one of the many districts of Madras Presidency. Although Madras was first and foremost a port city, over time it assumed the multi-functional roles of a political, social and cultural centre, and its dominance was felt over a wide territory. It is the particular nature of colonial dominance that will concern us in the following analysis of the development of Madras from its founding in the seventeenth century through the late nineteenth century.

Madrasapatam was already a cloth-producing centre when the East India Company came in search of cotton goods that could be traded in Bantam, Java, for cloves, spices and nutmeg that brought such a good price in England.[51] In 1639, after several abortive attempts to establish factories on the Coromandel Coast, the Company chose a site south of the town of Madrasapatam. It was on the sea, and was protected on the south by the Triplicane River (River Cooum), and on the west by the River North. This was a rich rice growing country, laced with lagoons and rivers that were capable of supporting an expanding population. But the site was considered to be waste land by the Tamilians who referred to it by the name '*Narimedu*' or jackal mound.[52]

Dr S. Krishnaswami Aiyangar who has studied the early evolution of Madras argues that the prosperity of the settlement was linked to its economic success. He asserts that cotton cloth was 20 to 30 per cent cheaper at this site than in Armagon in the Telugu-speaking region to the north of Madras where the Company had established an earlier factory; and that ships could come closer to the shore to pick up and deliver goods. Goods were also free from an import–export duty, although a customs duty was paid to the local ruler of the area for items bought or sold within his domain.[53] Permission was also granted to the British to build a fort, and to mint coins. Within a few decades Madras became an important emporium of trade. Goods were carried to Madras from China and the Malay Archipelago where they were sorted and repacked before being shipped to Europe.[54] This led to an increase in the number of English ships, seamen and traders involved in transferring foodgrains, fruits, vegetables, oils, oil seeds and livestock from Madras to the ports scattered around the Bay of Bengal and the Malabar Coast. In 1653 Madras was made a Presidency and five years later all English settlements on the Coromandel Coast and in Bengal were subordinated to it. Although commerce and trade continued to thrive during the late seventeenth and early eighteenth centuries, rivalry between France and England over control of the Coromandel Coast interfered with the commercial expansion of Madras, and ultimately relegated her to a secondary position in relation to the growing port cities of Calcutta and Bombay.

In order to enhance the commercial growth of Madras, it was necessary to fortify the site. By 1640 walls had been constructed to enclose the factory and Fort St George came into existence. Offices, warehouses and stores were soon built on the site.[55] The meagre British garrison was supplemented by Eurasian and native troops, and by the end of the year an estimated 300 to 400 families of weavers had migrated to the settlement.[56] Until the early nineteenth century, the fort and factory continued to remain the nucleus of military, commercial and government activities in Madras, and to dominate both the physical and functional development of the presidency capital.

The ethnic and cultural heterogeneity of the city was expressed at the outset by the different residential enclaves that began to be formed. Like settlement patterns in the city of Madurai, those of Madras appear to have initially followed a hierarchical pattern. The wealthiest and most prestigious residents of the city resided in closest proximity to the inner fort, containing the factory house. White Town developed on the north side of the Fort to house the European, Eurasian and Native Christian population of the settlement. Black Town, the extension of Madrasapatam, was the residential quarter for the city's indigenous inhabitants. This segregation of residential patterns was to characterize the city's subsequent evolution.

Expansion to the north of the fort was demarcated first by the European residential plots in White Town and those of the Portuguese traders who moved from the weaving village of San Thome further to the south. They were attracted to the new settlement by offers of better commercial facilities, a thirty year exemption from taxation, and the protection of the fort. The Portuguese were useful to the British for they had been on the Coromandel Coast for more than 100 years and knew the local languages. By the late seventeenth century there was also a community of Armenian traders who had migrated from North India.[57]

The houses of the Europeans, Portuguese and Native Christians of White Town were bounded by those of Black Town, occupied by the Telugu Komati, Balija and Beri Chetty trading castes employed as East India Company merchants and agents of private traders in the city. They functioned as *dubashes* (from *do basha*—speaker of two languages) or go-betweens, advancing money to the weavers of calico, chintz and muslin (who resided further to the north), and delivering the finished goods to the port for shipment to Bantam, Surat and the Persian Gulf. Telugu merchants also sold wine and other goods imported from England to the European and Black Town community.[58] Before reaching the hands of the merchants, cloth woven in the city was dyed on the northern limits of the settlement. To the east of the dyers, in a concentric arc, was the area where the Hindu and Muslim food processors, such as the fishermen, butchers, milk suppliers and oil-mongers resided, and where boatmen, potters, barbers and manual labourers were increasingly attracted to the growing settlement.

White Town was initially planned by the British. Its streets formed a uniform grid pattern, and had both British and Indian names.[59] Houses here were built of brick and were several stories high with thick walls to insure coolness in the summer heat, but unlike the later garden house designs adopted in Madras, the early White Town house had no garden or extensive courtyard, and was located very close to the street. As White Town expanded, more families were encouraged to move into Black Town, and by 1710 its western sector was occupied by the Portuguese, Native Christian and Armenian communities.[60]

The streets of Black Town were also laid out on a grid in the form of a square, a little more than a mile and half in circumference.[61] In the early eighteenth century, the town was surrounded with a brick wall seventeen feet thick on which bastions had been constructed for defence. Black Town was bounded by a river on the west, and the sea on the east. A canal built to join the river with the sea formed a natural moat on the north. The streets of Black Town were described as being wide, and a few were planted with trees, but the majority of houses were made of clay, rather than brick, and thatched, like those in the South Indian village. To the north of Black Town were gardens stretching for half a mile, planted by the British with mangoes, coconuts, orange trees, guavas, and other fruit trees for urban consumption and export.

It is clear from the preceding description that the nucleus of Madras was planned by the British, and that its form was designed to meet its principal function of trade and commerce. The early plan of Madras exhibits both economic dominance of the colonists over the colonial city with the fort providing the visible centre, and cultural heterogeneity with residential patterns segregated by ethnic origin. Colonial and indigenous quarters reflected distinctly different urban images, although this was much less pronounced in the early eighteenth century than it was 100 years later. Settlement of different caste groups was encouraged by the British under the direction of their *dubashes* and castes were given streets on which to reside in Black Town. During the Governorship of Elihu Yale (1687–92), for instance, fifty weavers were brought into the city and settled on Weavers' Street (now Nyniappa Naick Street).[62] As long as those who lived in Black Town contributed to the economic prosperity of the settlement, the British did little to interfere with their life-styles, and during the seventeenth and eighteenth centuries considerable power over Black Town inhabitants lay in the hands of Telugu and Tamil mercantile families who had connections with the East India Company. The British did, however, restrict the number of Muslim settlers in the town by placing a limit on the amount of land Muslims could occupy. This was a period when the Sultan of Golconda and the Nawab of the Carnatic, the latter being the hereditary Muslim ruler of the area on which the British settlement bordered, were still powerful forces in South India.

With the expansion of Madras in the eighteenth century, new villages were founded and those already in existence were incorporated into the urban nexus.[63] The British influenced the founding of a series of villages that functioned as economic satellites in relation to Fort St George. As a result of the shortage of cloth in South India in the early part of the century, the Company established colonies of weavers on the outskirts of Black Town to regulate its production. One such colony was Chintadripet to the west where settlement was controlled by a Hindu East India Company merchant, and spinners and weavers were brought from Salem shortly after the village was set up in 1734 to stimulate calico printing. The village contained two important Śiva and Vishnu temples, and had its own bazaar. Within a period of four years, 230 families were allegedly residing in the village.[64] Washermanpet was a similar satellite complex designed for the washers and dyers of cloth.

Aside from these planned settlements, there were a series of loosely linked self-contained villages incorporated into the city which remained for a while only marginally dependent on the commercial centre. They were an economic asset to the Company which leased them from the local ruler at a minimal charge for privileges of rent collection. Villages such as Mylapore and Triplicane, both eighth century temple complexes, were initially pilgrimage centres with large populations of Brahmans. They had their own functions, service castes, bazaars and temples. But under the British, the character of these villages slowly began to change as they were brought into closer relationship with the Fort and Black Town. Triplicane is perhaps the best example of this for it continued to remain an important Vaishnava religious centre. In the 1750s the Nawab of Arcot, a Muslim ruler, was given land on which to build a palace on the outskirts of the village. The Nawab sought the protection of the British at a time when the French were seeking control of the eastern coast of India. By granting him land within the city, the British were able to politically encapsulate the powerful ruler of a large territory of South India. The resettlement of the Nawab in the following decades led to the growth of a substantial Muslim community in the

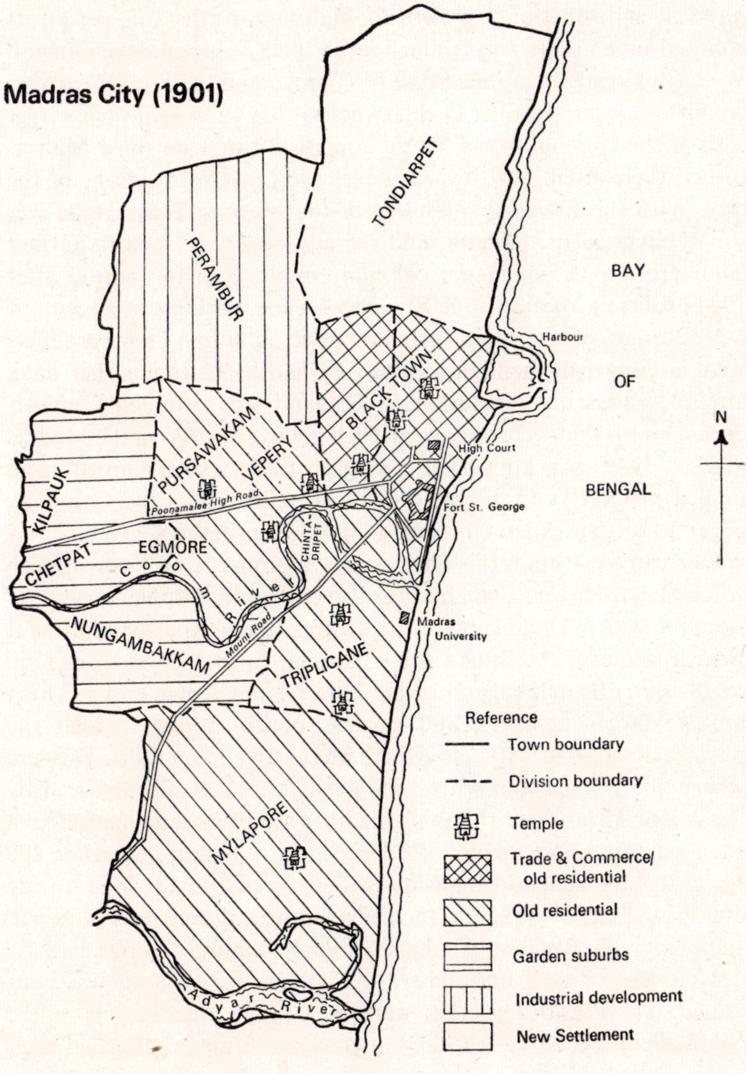

vicinity of Triplicane, initially comprising migrants from Arcot, the Nawab's former capital. Muslim service castes, merchants, weavers and artisans were subsequently attracted to Triplicane, and this led to the rapid development of bazaars and markets in the village. Triplicane soon became a subsidiary market centre, and satellite of Black Town and the Fort.

The mid-eighteenth century can be viewed as a turning point in the physical and functional growth of Madras for after this period its colonial inhabitants play a much larger role in urban development. We have already mentioned that the French and the English were in conflict with one another at this time, as they each vied for a larger slice of the colonial world. In the process, those who ruled Madras turned their attentions towards developing the fortifications of the city. With the French harassment of the Madras Coast, trade was slowly diverted to Calcutta, and the city never regained its former commercial position in the colonial empire.[65] In the period after 1744 profits in Madras trade began to decline, partially as a result of a great influx of silver that increased prices. But handloom products were no longer of the high quality they had been at an earlier date, and the industrial revolution in England was producing power-driven looms that were to have an even greater impact on the Madras market. Given slacking profits, English traders began investing in landed property and dabbling in local politics, and the Company began to further expand its territorial holdings in the South.

One can look upon this change as symptomatic of a new British colonial world view, emanating out of the metropole capital of London, which would culminate a century later in the assumption of British rule over the Indian sub-continent. In the period from 1750 to 1850, the British began moving out of Black Town and the Fort area in larger numbers, and garden suburbs began to alter the physical form of the city. Now there was clearly a separation between where one worked and where one lived. This was accompanied by the decentralization of shopping facilities as a European market area emerged, the construction of administrative buildings outside the Fort, and the general expansion of the colonial sector over a wide area of the city. Unlike the smaller administrative centres of North India such as Benares, Allahabad and Lucknow, Madras had no cantonment or civil lines where the colonial population was contained. The Presidency cities were, in essence, microcosms of the colonial empire, and as the empire grew and firmly established itself as a political entity, the colonists began to control more of the cities, and to leave an impact on their physical structures. One can argue that as power shifted out of the centre of the city, building became more decentralized. As such, the cities themselves became an expression of the colonial world view.

After 1770 when the city of Madras was made secure against the incursions of the French, north beach (between the Fort and the watering place for ships) owned by the Company but occupied by native merchants, was reclaimed by the Government; and new warehouses were constructed and rented out to merchants. This further extended British colonial control over mercantile activities in the city, particularly those of the native merchants.[66] In 1798, the Government came to a major decision to decentralize commercial activities by moving the port, located since its origin in front of the Fort, to the north outside of the town where the Master Attendant's Office and the Customs House had already been located.[67] This meant the colonial domination of the entire shoreline from the Fort northwards to the outer limits of the city. In the course of the nineteenth century this was to become the area where the major insurance, import–export firms and banking companies constructed their offices.

During this period, the Government slowly began moving outside the Fort as well. As Britain began to assume greater control over the Indian subcontinent, it expressed itself in monumental building.

In 1833, the British Government revoked the East India Company trading privileges and delegated to it full administrative responsibility over its colony. In 1857, the Crown itself assumed control over India. From the 1860s onwards administrative buildings began to appear outside the Fort in larger numbers, but their construction followed no central plan. The High Court buildings, comprising the Small Causes Court and the City Civil Court, were built in the area just to the north of the Fort, whereas Madras University was spread along the beach on open land a considerable distance to the south of the Fort. Although there is no one government complex in Madras, the apparent random location of buildings did have the impact of creating a sense of colonial monumentality, for wherever one turned within a few mile radius of the Fort, there was a symbol of colonial power.

European architects were responsible for the design of civic buildings in Madras, and by the era of Victoria were generally officers of the Royal Engineers or members of the Department of Public Works. Although many of the buildings constructed during the first half of the nineteenth century show influences of 'popularized Renaissance style' with classical façades and pillared porticos, during the second half of the century, Madras architecture was in the hands of several designers who preferred to incorporate indigenous forms, and who popularized the Hindu–Saracenic style with cupola-crowned minarets, arches and arabesque ornamentation.[68]

As the government functions of Madras increased in the course of the nineteenth century, and were reflected in the changing form of the city, so too the number of native employees needed to staff government offices and the burgeoning bureaucracy also increased. In the process, Triplicane, the temple village of Mylapore, as well as the villages of Puraswalkam and Vepery, inhabited by the Eurasian community, were brought into closer satellite relationship with the Black Town area which was now the city's central business district. These served as residential suburbs for indigenous white collar employees of the British who commuted daily to the urban centre.

From the mid-eighteenth century Europeans began moving out of the Fort and Black Town into the newly developing garden suburbs where their commercial and administrative dominance was now expressed in terms of their residential domination over a larger part of the city that had previously been under cultivation. Not only were they claiming a substantial portion of the urban landscape, but they were segregating themselves in the process. What clearly emerges from this point onwards are two distinct settlement patterns, the colonial and the indigenous.

After 1750 Black Town became increasingly inhabited by traders and weavers, and Europeans who could afford to build their own houses from the wealth acquired by the Company or government service began investing in property in the outlying portions of Madras where it was far less expensive to live than in the crowded urban centre.[69] River sites were among the most popular in Madras for they provided open vistas, and were often thought to afford protection from the spread of disease, particularly those located on high ground, conducive to suitable drainage. The banks of the Adyar and the Cooum (Triplicane) Rivers were two of the earliest areas sought for the construction of such homes. Another condition which affected the choice of a site was that of its defensibility; and the Choultry Plain, located further inland, was a second popular site because it was protected by four outposts.[70] This was a vast undeveloped area which was intersected by two important roads, one of which, Mount Road, had for centuries connected the Fort with the Portuguese settlement of San Thome. The other, a military road, Poonamallee High Road, led from the Fort west to the village of Poonamallee and crossed Mount Road. The area between these two roads was favoured for settlement, and by 1780 there were an estimated 500 to 600 garden houses stretching over six to seven miles of the Choultry Plain.[71]

The European sectors of Madras were characterized by low population densities, for each family constructed its own house surrounded by a large compound often consisting of several acres of land.[72] The most common house-type was the colonial bungalow, consisting of one or two stories divided into a verandah, dining rooms and bedrooms, each with attached baths.[73] These bungalows set in their compounds essentially functioned as oases of cultural space. They were located off wide, tree-lined streets built over time to serve the needs of the colonists, and the entire area of settlement was usually landscaped with an occasional park or cultivated public garden, in keeping with urban designs familiar in the West.

The increasing segregation of the colonists from the indigenous inhabitants of the city went hand in hand with growing permanence among colonial settlers in India. Until the mid-eighteenth century Englishmen viewed India as a place to earn their fortunes, before retiring in Britain. In the course of the following century the political hold of the mother country over the colony increased, and those who lived in Madras began to invest their savings in urban land with the notion of remaining in the city. The development and maintenance of colonial areas, however, placed a great drain on the resources of the city, and diverted municipal funds from the more crowded sectors where basic needs of water supply, health and sanitation were being neglected.[74] This led to a growing inequality in the civic amenities of different sectors of the city.

Indigenous settlement patterns were formulated on the basis of a very different set of principles. As in the city of Madurai, prestige was related to proximity to the centre, and the wealthiest merchants and *dubashes* in the employ of the East India Company chose to construct their houses in Black Town. They also patronized the building of temples and other Hindu institutions in the city, which led to the development of a series of small ceremonial complexes in Madras.[75] It is my hypothesis that in the eighteenth century, the *dubash* class used a South Indian model of kingship in their exercise of power in these centres, for they were responsible for arbitrating caste conflicts and protecting the Hindu sacred order in the city during this period.[76] In the course of the nineteenth century this pattern changed as the indigenous élite began to emulate the colonial pattern of settlement, and to participate in colonial institutions founded in the city. For the majority of the city's inhabitants, however, the notion of living in isolated homesteads was culturally alien, and they preferred to reside in the vicinity of a temple. What one finds, then, is areas of high population density, particularly towards the centre of Madras.[77] The most typical house-type of the wealthy was the courtyard house, built on a square or rectangular plan with rooms running around an inner courtyard. By the nineteenth century, the wide streets of Black Town originally designed by the British were reduced to narrow thoroughfares as Indians modified their environment to fit their own needs, and built additions onto the front of houses to accommodate more people.

Black Town and other indigenous areas of settlement were divided into neighbourhoods where groups belonging to the same caste or occupation resided. Over time, as migrants entered the city, the initial composition of neighbourhoods underwent change, and some became significantly mixed. Caste neighbourhoods remained more intact in the outlying villages of Madras. Nineteenth century Mylapore, for example, had clearly demarcated streets inhabited by particular castes who constructed and supported their own temples and choultries.[78] Pradip Sinha argues that the development of the heart of Calcutta shows the juxtapositioning of huts with substantial masonry houses, indicating that artisan and service castes were attracted to employment in large houses and settlement took place in the vicinity.[79] The centre of eighteenth and nineteenth century Black Town contained a large *paracheri* where members of the untouchable caste resided, who may have served similar functions as sweepers for the houses on which they bordered.

What this analysis of Madras has revealed is a tripartite urban form that evolves in the period after 1750. Prior to this date the city resembles in form that of the ceremonial city of Madurai, although the factory rather than the temple is the organizing principle. After this date, however, there is a slow process of diffusion and decentralization that affects both the colonial and indigenous populations and the institutions they found, for the British and their élite Indian employees begin to live and work in different locales. This new form is characterized by: (1) British residential sectors with forms and functions that reflect English cultural and spatial concerns; (2) native residential areas organized on the basis of their cultural orientations, with not one but several small ceremonial foci, reflecting the desires of the *dubash* class to attain king-like status; (3) a commercial and administrative nexus, now more loosely defined spatially than at an earlier period, but marked by its colonial monuments, and providing an area of interaction for the English and Indian residents of the city. This configuration then reflects a new form in urban India, and one which is intrinsically Western, characterized by the separation of work and residence—related in part to the growth of an industrial mentality, and an ideology of individualism becoming prevalent in the European world.

Summary and Conclusion

This paper set out to examine the origins, development and changing form and functions of two cities in South India, employing social science models of the ceremonial and colonial port city as a way of highlighting their historical evolution. Two different periods were chosen in the history of each city in order to determine whether there was continuity or change in the urban form. In the process, the paper raised the questions to what extent Madurai and Madras conformed to these urban types, and of what use models are to the historian.

In the case of Madurai, we have seen a continuity in its urban form that spanned several centuries. Madurai was first and foremost a political, religious and cultural capital, hence its ceremonial designation. The relationship between the sacred and secular in Hindu society was reflected in the urban form of the city. Centrality underscored its basic design, for the centre was an auspicious place in the world view of the Hindus, and Madurai was a Hindu city. It was around the temple in the urban centre that the city developed as we know it today, and in the course of Madurai's history, the temple was to grow to monumental proportions—symbolic of notions of the ever-expandable Hindu universe.

It was the king and secular nobility who were responsible for the building of the temple of Mīnākshi, and for the existence of the city itself, for Madurai was for centuries the capital of the Pandyan Empire and later the Nāyaka dynasty. Although the sacred and secular functions of Madurai were separable on a theoretical level, and the first rank in Hindu society went to religion, rather than power (this being a reflection of the ultimate values that integrated the society), the king and priest who represented the deity were dependent on one another for legitimation and protection, respectively, and during the Nāyaka period, sacred and royal power were concentrated in one portion of the city. Subordinate to the kingly functions of Madurai were those of the merchants, who in part provided the capital to keep the city going, and the funds for further expansion. As the priest was dependent on the king, so too the merchant was in an interdependent relationship with those who governed the city. The economic, political and religious spheres were essentially undifferentiated in pre-British India. The use of space and the concentration of power in Madurai were essentially a reflection of the *varna* system, with wealth, social status and ritual purity corresponding to proximity to the temple and palace, and diminishing as one moved toward the urban periphery. The unitary urban form of Madurai was an expression of hierarchical relations within Hindu society which integrated it into a single entity and as such it can be seen as a microcosm of the Hindu world view.

In contrast to the ceremonial city of Madurai, the colonial port city of Madras was predicated on different notions of the relationship between religious, political and economic power. The site of Madras was chosen with an eye to commercial advantage rather than political or religious motivations. In the West, economic wealth and political power were differentiated and the former was protected by the legal system. The initial form of Madras resembles that of Madurai, with the factory and the fort replacing the temple and palace as an organizing principle. Those who had the highest economic status in the new city, the European and Indian merchants, resided closest to the factory, for economic power was of prime importance in early Madras.

Even in the initial decades of the settlement one can see three distinct areas within the town, the Inner Factory or Fort; White Town, the residential quarters for Europeans; and Black Town, the area where the indigenous inhabitants lived and worked. The Europeans, who were a minority in the city, encouraged the early development of indigenous areas of settlement by patronizing temples and festivals, for these guaranteed an economic return for the colonizers. By the mid-eighteenth century, however, as the notion of empire evolves outside of India, it has an impact on the city of Madras. Now there is a decentralization and diffusion of power as government activities move out of the Fort, and are expressed in terms of monumental architecture. Now villages on the outskirts of the city are drawn into the urban sphere, and develop a satellite relationship with the commercial and administrative nexus. One might argue that a new type of power based on Western ideology has released a new urban form. In the modern West, as economic power is differentiated from the political sphere, so too political power is differentiated from religion, thus allowing for the development of the secular nation. Although Madras grew into a political capital, it never became a city of the moral order. In pre-British India, this was the only possibility for a *rājadhāni* city, for, as we have seen in Madurai, the king could not exist without the deity represented by the priest.

Thus, the unitary form of the ceremonial city gave way in Madras to a tripartite urban form, characterized by the separation of residential and work space, particularly among the élite of the city, and reflected in the mature urban form of the city in the nineteenth century. The reason why the British generate a new form in Indian cities has to do with their notions of political and economic dominance based on a Western ideology that stresses the individual, no longer primarily holds membership in a corporate group, and, as Balandier has pointed out, this horizontally links intrinsically different civilizations into a relationship with one another. As we have seen in British Madurai, it is possible to argue that the unitary form gave way to a series of multinucleated urban enclaves.

What, then, is the benefit to the historian of employing models such as the ceremonial and colonial port city in understanding the evolution of two South Indian cities? In the first place it has enabled us to trace continuity and change over extended periods of time, and to identify the nature of change. Secondly, it has highlighted the differences in the urban development of two cities in India which represent two different urban types; one based on traditional notions of design motivated by a particular Hindu world view, and the other based on particular Western notions of economic and political dominance. Thus, the colonial city emerges into sharper focus when placed against an indigenous urban form, the ceremonial city, that has existed for centuries in India.

NOTES

An earlier version of this paper was presented at the Conference on Indian Economic and Social History sponsored by the Social Science Research Council at St. John's College, Cambridge, England in July 1975. I would particularly like to thank Arjun Appadurai, Dennis Hudson, Julian Smith and Burton Stein for their useful comments on this paper, and John Robertshaw for the maps of Madurai and Madras.

1 Norma Evenson, *Chandigarh* (Berkeley, 1966), p. 2.

2 For a discussion of the ceremonial city see Paul Wheatley, *Pivot of the Four Quarters* (Edinburgh, 1971) and 'The City as Symbol' (London, 1969); Nelson I. Wu, *Chinese and Indian Architecture* (New York, 1963); and of the colonial city, Ronald J. Horvath, 'In Search of a Theory of Urbanization: Notes on the Colonial City,' in *East Lakes Geographer*, 5 (1969), 69–82.

3 *Architecture of Mānasāra*, translated by Prasanna Kumar Acharya (London, 1933), vol. IV, p. 95 (Chapter X, paras. 44–7).

4 See A. K. Ramanujan, 'Toward an Anthology of City Images,' in *Urban India*, ed. Richard G. Fox (Durham, 1970), p. 224.

5 Prince Ilanko Atikal, *Shilappadikaram* [The Ankle Bracelet] (New York, 1965), translated by Alain Danielou, p. 3.

6 See particularly A. K. Ramanujan, 'Toward an Anthology of City Images', pp. 235–40.

7 *Shilappadikaram*, pp. 89–90.

8 For the text of this and other stories see J. H. Nelson, *The Madura Country: A Manual* (Madras, 1868), Part III, pp. 3ff and *Oriental Historical Manuscripts in the Tamil Language*, translated by William Taylor (Madras, 1835), vol. I, p. 13.

9 See Louis Dumont, *Homo Hierarchichus* (London, 1972), p. 111, and *Religion/Politics and History* (Paris, 1970), p. 67.

10 *Madura: A Tourist's Guide* (Madras, 1913), p. 2.

11 *Shilappadikaram*, p. 90.

12 Ibid., pp. 72, 92.

13 Ibid., pp. 91, 96.

14 *Imperial Gazetteer of India*, vol. XVI (Oxford, 1908), p. 391.

15 *Oriental Historical Manuscripts*, vol. I, p. xiii, and K. K. Pillay, *A Social History of the Tamils*, pt. I (Madras, 1969), p. 239.

16 *Shilappadikaram*, pp. 97–8.

17 Julian Smith, 'Madurai, India: The Architecture of a City' (unpublished M.A. dissertation, M.I.T., February 1976), p. 12.

18 Amita Ray, *Villages, Towns and Secular Buildings in Ancient India* (Calcutta, 1964), pp. 71–2.

19 *Shilappadikaram*, p. 92. Inscriptions also refer to moat, flagstaff, rampart and parapet as parts of the fort. T. V. Mahalingam, *South Indian Polity* (Madras, 1967), p. 83.

20 This plan is mentioned not only in the *Mānasāra* but also in the *Agni Purāṇa* and the *Śukranītisara*. Ray, *Villages, Towns and Secular Buildings*, p. 53.

The ancient Tamil settlement of Uttaramerur has an overall plan that fits well with certain prescriptions of the *Śilpaśastras*. François Gros and R. Nagaswamy, *Uttaramērūr* (Pondicherry, 1970), pp. 90–5.

21 Julian Smith, 'Madurai, India', Chapter III, which gives a detailed description of this process.

22 Ibid., p. 22.

23 Ibid., p. 37.

24 *Shilappadikaram*, p. 91.

25 *Shilappadikaram*, pp. 98, 133–5.

26 George Hart, *The Poems of Ancient Tamil Nadu* (Berkeley, 1975), p. 13.

27 C. P. Venkatarama Ayyar, *Town Planning in Ancient Dekkan* (Madras, *c.* 1916), p. 42. Although his sources include Śaṅgam literature, they also rely heavily on Tamil works written after the twelfth century.

28 *Maduraikanchi*, in *Pattupattu: Ten Tamil Idylls*, translated by J. V. Chelliah, (Tinnevelly, 1962), pp. 227, 257.

29 *Oriental Historical Manuscripts*, vol. II, p. 15.

30 *Madura*, p. 26.

31 *Oriental Historical Manuscripts*, vol. II, p. 15.

32 Burton Stein, 'Integration of the Agrarian System of South India', in Robert Eric Frykenberg, ed., *Land Control and Social Structure in Indian History* (Madison, 1969), pp. 194–5.

33 J. P. L. Shenoy, *Madura, The Temple City* (Madura, 1937), p. 6.

34 Julian Smith, 'Madurai, India', p. 70.

35 J. H. Nelson, *The Madura Country*, p. 93.

36 Gideon Sjoberg, *The Pre-Industrial City* (New York, 1960), p. 323.

37 Binode Behari Dutt, *Town Planning in Ancient India* (Calcutta, 1925), p. 326.

38 J. H. Nelson, *The Madura Country*, p. 81.

39 K. A. Nilkanta Sastri, *A History of South India*, p. 485.

40 *Imperial Gazetteer of India*, vol. XVI, p. 405.

41 Nelson Wu, *Chinese and Indian Architecture*, p. 27.

42 *Madura*, p. 123.

43 *Oriental Historical Manuscripts*, vol. I, p. vii.

44 Venkatarama Ayyar, *Town Planning*, p. 44.

45 This is a reference to the symbolic circling of the capital by the king mentioned in the *Agni Purāṇa* and the *Mānasāra* which comes from the Hindu rite Pradakshina, or delimitation of sacred space. Paul Wheatley cites examples of this rite in several Southeast Asian cities. See *Pivot of the Four Quarters*, p. 466. Dennis Hudson suggests that Tirumala Nāyaka not only had two large cars constructed to pull the deities Śiva and Mīnākshi around the city of Madurai during the yearly festival celebrating their marriage, but also incorporated into the festival the coronation of Mīnākshi as queen of the city. 'Siva, Minakshi and Vishnu: Reflections on a Popular Myth in Madurai' (unpublished paper, 1975), p. 5.

46 K. V. Sundaram and C. S. Chandrasekhara, 'Urban Morphology and Internal Structure of Indian Towns—Some Case Studies,' in *National Geographical Journal of India*, 14 (March 1968), 56.

47 *Madura*, p. 13 and *Imperial Gazetteer*, vol. XVI, p. 404.

48 *Madura*, p. 12.

49 See Julian Smith, 'Madurai, India', Chapters VI and VII for a very interesting discussion of the different festivals in the city, their historical development and their relationship to the urban morphology.

50 G. Balandier, 'The Colonial Situation: A Theoretical Approach,' in Immanuel Wallerstein, ed., *Social Change: The Colonial Situation* (New York, 1966), pp. 54–5. For a discussion of the Asian Port City see Rhoads Murphey, 'Urbanization in Asia,' in *The City in Newly Developing Countries*, ed. Gerald Breese (Englewood Cliffs, 1972), pp. 58–75.

51 John Bruce, *Annals of Honourable East India Company* (London, 1810), pp. 359, 378.

52 Dr S. Krishnaswami Aiyangar, 'The Character and Significance of the Foundation of Madras,' in *Madras Tercentenary Commemoration Volume* (London, 1939), pp. 39–40, and *Manual of Administration of Madras Presidency*, vol. III (Madras, 1885), p. 446.

53 Mrs Frank Penny, *Fort St. George, Madras* (London, 1900), p. 4 and *Census of India, 1961*: Madras, vol. IX, Part X-(I), p. 4.

54 David Leighton, *Vicissitudes of Fort St. George* (Madras, 1902), p. 6.

55 This description is taken from one of the official records of Madras Presidency, 'Account of the Present Localities of Madras as Existing in the Middle of the Seventeenth Century', reprinted in the *Manual of Administration*, vol. I, p. 163.

56 Henry Davison Love, *Vestiges of Old Madras* (London, 1913), vol. I, p. 35.

57 *Manual of Administration*, vol. I, p. 163 and C. W. Ransom, 'The Growth of the Population of Madras', in *The Madras Tercentenary Commemoration Volume*, p. 320.

In 1688 the Directors of the East India Company granted the Armenians a contract enabling them to travel on Company ships and to establish settlements where they could build their own churches. C. S. Srinivasachari, *History of the City of Madras* (Madras, 1939), pp. 106–7.

58 Ibid., p. 52.

59 Some of the streets were named Middle, Charles York and Choultry Streets. *Manual of Administration*, vol. I, p. 163.

60 Although there is much discrepancy in population figures for early Madras, one fairly reliable estimate places the population at about 50,000 in 1688, the year in which Madras was made a Corporation by Royal Charter of the East India Company. *Census of the Town of Madras, 1871* (Madras, 1873), p. 26.

61 The following description is taken from the account of Thomas Salmon of the city in 1707. See H. V. Lanchester, *Town Planning in Madras* (Madras, 1916), pp. 87–8. Maps of early Madras, such as 'Prospect of Fort St. George and Plan of the City of Madras' (1710) surveyed by order of Governor Thomas Pitt, clearly attest to the physical layout of the city. This map is located in the British Museum, London.

62 Glyn Barlow, *The Story of Madras* (Madras, 1921), p. 23.

63 During the first 100 years, villages that existed on the periphery of the Fort were acquired on lease by the British. In 1708, for example, five villages were given in free grant to the Company, among the most important of which were Trivatore and Nungambakkam. *Census of Town of Madras*, 1871, p. 34.

64 C. S. Srinivasachari, 'Stages in the Growth of the City of Madras', in *Journal of Madras Geographical Association*, 2:3 (October 1927); and *Manual of Administration*, vol. III, p. 446.

65 In fact, the Regulating Act of 1773 limiting the political role of Madras was an acknowledgement by the British that Calcutta and Bombay had more commercial and industrial potential.

66 In 1772, of the 33 merchants who rented warehouses, only 9 were English. The merchants protested against the sale of land for they feared it would be re-rented at prohibitive rates. Love, *Vestiges of Old Madras*, vol. III, p. 163.

67 Jacques Dupuis, *Madras et le Nord du Coromandel* (Paris, 1960), p. 404.

68 For a description see Percy Brown, *Indian Architecture*, Third Edition (Bombay, 1942), vol. 2, p. 135.

69 In 1775, of the 356 lots of 2,400 sq. ft. each that were available in Black Town 253 were given to one family whose land was taken over by the Company after the attack of French in 1746. Love, *Vestiges of Old Madras*, vol. III, p. 53.

70 Richard Ellefsen, 'The Evolution of Areal Patterns in Madras City' (unpublished mimeographed paper), p. 6. There were four important forts in Egmore, San Thome, Nungambakkam and Puraswalkam which attracted a colonial population.

71 J. Dupuis, *Madras et le Nord du Coromandel*, p. 405. For a more detailed description of this development see *Census of Town of Madras, 1871*, p. 53.

72 *The Book of Grants of Ground* for 1774 mentions an unusual grant of 25 acres of land on Choultry Plain to a civil servant and Member of Council (Henry Brooke) for a period of ninety-nine years on condition that he build a brick house on it. Love, *Vestiges of Old Madras*, vol. III, p. 56.

73 For an excellent discussion of the bungalow see A. D. King, 'The colonial-bungalow compound complex', *Journal of Architectural Research*, 312 (May 1974).

74 Susan J. Lewandowski, 'Urban Growth and Municipal Development in the Colonial City of Madras, 1860–1900', *Journal of Asian Studies*, 34:2 (February 1975).

75 V. R. Ramachandra Dikshitar, 'Around the City Pagodas', *Madras Tercentenary Commemoration Volume*, pp. 359ff.

76 Susan J. Lewandowski, 'Merchants, Temples and Power in the Colonial Port City of Madras', presented at the Comparative Conference on The Colonial Port City in Asia, Santa Cruz, California, June 1976. In this paper I have focused on the Hindu sector of Madras.

77 For figures on the late nineteenth century, see Lewandowski, 'Urban Growth,' p. 350.

78 S. Kalyanasundaram, *A Short History of Mylapore* (Madras, 1913), p. 23, and *Manual of Administration*, vol. III, p. 447.

79 Pradip Sinha, 'The City as a Physical Entity—Calcutta, 1750–1850,' in *Bengal Past and Present*, 89:2, No. 168 (July-December 1970).

13

Urbanization and the Introduction of Modern Town Planning Ideas in India, 1900–1925[1]

H. E. MELLER
University of Nottingham

In the late nineteenth century, Britain had become the most highly urbanized nation of the world, though North-West Europe as a whole was undergoing, in this period, a process of rapid urbanization. The population growth of Europe which had fed the cities, spilled over into the great migratory flows which took European man to the underdeveloped regions of the world. Wherever the European migrants were dominant, as for example in the U.S.A. and Australia, there was a tendency for cities to develop, and where industrialization was rapid, it was matched by rapid urban growth.[2] The response to this fact amongst western nations was slow in developing. Nevertheless it was sufficient, by the end of the century, to generate a new interest in the social problems inherent in rapid urbanization. In the period 1890–1914, fresh ideas on how to control modern urbanization were put forward, and a more professional response to urban problems encouraged by the passing of town planning legislation. This proved to be the crucial, formative period of the modern town planning movement.

By contrast, in those areas of the world, in Africa, Asia, and the Far East, which had been seized by the great powers in the scramble for Empire, the rate of urbanization, though significant for commercial and capital cities, was overall very much lower. In India the impact of the British had led to urban decline for cities not commercially strategic to the British. The problems inherent in large scale urbanization, with industrialization, hardly impinged on the consciousness of either rulers or ruled. The lower level of population growth and economic development had pushed the matter into the background. Town planning in colonial countries in the late 1880s and 1890s was largely a matter of asserting the Imperial presence by the construction of impressive buildings for colonial rulers and their officers.[3]

Yet in the space of the next half century, the centre of most rapid population growth was to shift dramatically from West to East, to contribute an ever increasing flow of migrants to the cities; and economic development along modern technological lines was to advance greatly.[4] In India, in the period 1890–1925, there were certain people who had foreseen such a possibility occurring, and had recognized that they had a unique chance of trying to prevent some of the worst social side-effects of massive urbanization as experienced in the West. They were few in number: one or two Governors of states in which the great Presidency cities were situated; enlightened Indian princes concerned with the future of their own capital cities; some members of the nationalist Congress party who saw a chance of using the relative political autonomy of municipalities as a stepping-stone to political independence.

The modern town-planning movement in the West gave them encouragement to pursue fresh ways of responding to the growth of Indian cities. Pioneers of the movement in Britain were invited to India to work in this field, one of the earliest being Patrick Geddes.[5] For a brief while, a concerted attempt was made to introduce the concepts of town planning to India. The purpose of this paper is to discuss the context in which this attempt was made, and the extent of its influence.

The Urban Context

Contemporary understanding of the economic, social and administrative problems of cities in India is not easy to ascertain, with the present lack of historical data and monographs on individual cities. Perception of the need for control over changes in the urban environment, both in the West and in the East, was often attendant on the incidence of disease and the deterioration of standards of public health. Compounded with this were the problems of trying to improve the city's structure, particularly in the provision of roads, to meet the growing requirements of business and commerce. Solving such problems demanded administrative and political expertise of a new kind, directly concerned with the economic and social needs of the local urban community.

The situation for Indian cities was certainly not helped by colonial status. The administration of most cities was closely controlled by the Indian Civil Service and there was less necessity, politically, to consider the needs of different groups of citizens. Furthermore, any technical expertise called upon to help in solving urban problems was uniformly Western-orientated. The sanitary and civil engineers had a field day with little questioning of their priorities. Their priorities obviously suited the British; cut mortality figures by clearing slums, if possible by driving large straight roads through them (in a manner copied directly from European cities); fill up all tanks to eliminate the habitat of the mosquito; and make sure that the 'civil lines' were supplied with running water, a sewage system and street cleaners, paid for by a tax on the entire municipality, but mainly benefiting the British residents.

When ideas of comprehensive, full-scale planning were introduced in India, they were dominated by the latest level of Western technological advance and the pragmatic considerations of the ruling race. New Delhi and Jamshedpur both date from 1911 and both provide classic instances of the Westernization of urban form in India. The former designed appropriately by a British architect, the latter by a Pittsburg engineer, they mark India's baptism of fire in the modern town planning movement. They succeeded initially in maintaining their Westernized urban form because their functions, as the administrative centre of the British Raj, and as an industrial city based on Western technology, were as alien as their plans.[6] But these importations provided few guidelines for dealing with the problems of established Indian cities. Even the great Presidency cities, Bombay, Calcutta and Madras, which had grown large during the period of British rule, did not conform to the Western experience of urbanization, to which Western solutions of urban problems could be readily applied.[7]

However, by the turn of the century, there was mounting pressure to find at least some solution to India's urban problems. The activities of the engineers had not solved the problem of disease. The need for economic development in India was being taken more seriously,[8] and industries were naturally located in the cities. Further, the trend towards encouraging local self-government had placed cities in a new light as possible centres for 'modernizing' Indian society;[9] whilst the nationalist movement was not unappreciative of the crucial importance of cities as centres of communication and propaganda. Above all, the pace of Indian urbanization began to accelerate, almost imperceptibly at first, but gathering momentum in the twentieth century as the population began to grow faster than before, and greater numbers found their way to the cities. The trend of the future was becoming increasingly clear and was enough to encourage some new responses to urban problems.

Population Growth and Urbanization

Numerically, the ratio of urban to rural population was very small in the period 1881–1941. It was a mere 10 per cent. As for the pace of urbanization, India was only able to match that of the United States in the period 1790–1850 when the techniques of the Industrial Revolution in transport and manufacture had hardly been developed.[10] Yet the figures for the first four decades of the twentieth century show that the cities were absorbing a larger share of the population increase; and the sheer scale of the Indian population as a whole meant that the proportion of the population living in cities, numerically, was as much as three-quarters of the entire British population in 1901. See table below.[11]

	Pop. in millions	Per cent variation per decade	Urban pop. (in millions)	Per cent variation per decade	Per cent urban of total pop.	Per cent relative growth of urban pop.
1901	236.3	—	25.7	—	10.91	—
1911	252.1	+ 5.73	26.6	+ 2.4	10.57	− 3.12
1921	257.4	− 0.31	28.6	+ 7.3	11.38	+ 7.66
1931	279.0	+11.01	33.8	+18.4	12.13	+ 6.59
1941	318.7	+14.22	44.3	+31.1	13.91	+14.67

A. F. Weber, working at the end of the nineteenth century, highlighted three major features of the Indian experience of urbanization which could be statistically determined with differing degrees of accuracy.[12] The first was that some Indian cities had grown very large in the pre-industrial era when modern technology was unknown. According to estimates made in 1823, Madras had a population of 817,000; Benares 580,000; Delhi 400,000; Calcutta 900,000; and Surat 450,000. Thus the size of large cities at the beginning of the twentieth century was not unprecedented, though large cities were as likely to contract as to grow with shifts in their administrative, political or religious importance. A second significant point was that the statistics for growth in the decade 1881–91 showed a large increase in the case of industrial cities. Weber cites the examples of a 43.4 per cent increase of Hubli, 43.01 per cent of Karachi, and 41.26 per cent of Ajmer. Rapid growth was thus now closely allied to economic development. Finally, the largest towns were gaining an increasing proportion of the total urban population. Weber, from his vantage point of 1899, was cautious about generalizing on this latter tendency. He pointed out that the growth rates of individual large cities fluctuated according to the importance of the industrial, religious or administrative functions of the city, and to the ravages of epidemics and diseases. But, in this respect at least, time was to show that Indian urbanization was following a similar trend to that in Britain. The following diagram illustrates this.[13]

GROWTH OF CITIES, 1891-1941. BY SIZE IN 1891

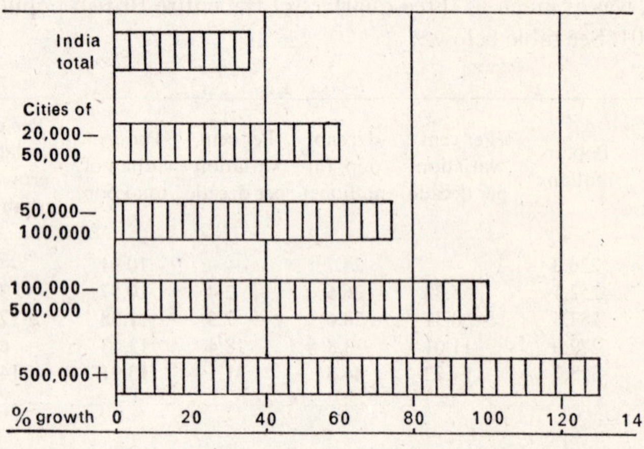

Large towns of 100,000 inhabitants or more thus gained a predominance in this period which became ever more firmly entrenched. Weber was prepared to describe a city of this size as a 'great' city which had a vital economic, social and cultural role to play, not only for those within its boundaries, but for those in the rural hinterland as well. G. S. Ghurye seized on this idea when he suggested that one of the most significant trends in Indian urbanization was the development in the period 1881–1941 of such large cities in practically every major region of the country.[15] In 1881, there were only eighteen great cities. By 1921 there were thirty-five, and by 1941 there were forty-seven. The distribution of these cities was not very even with some territories, such as Bombay State and Uttar Pradesh, far outdistancing the rest. But if large cities are a vital factor in the modernizing process, then the period 1891–1931 was the transitional stage.

The Political and Administrative Response to Urbanization

In Britain, when the majority of the population became urbanized, and the largest proportion in the late nineteenth century was to be found in great cities of over 100,000, the initial political response of the government had been to reform local administration.[16] As a result of these changes, two elements were developed in the government of cities, apart from better municipal administration, which were to lead directly to a greater responsiveness to the quality of the urban environment. These were the encouragement which local autonomy gave to leading citizens to involve themselves in local government, using their own wealth to supplement municipal resources, because they felt directly responsible for the city they governed. The other was the need to democratize local government elections because better municipal administration cost money, and the primary source of income for municipal councils was still the rates. These elements were further reinforced by the fact that some councillors inevitably found themselves representing the poorer wards of the city, and to those of them with a social conscience, this involved a new and more vigorous concern over the social and physical environment of the poor.[17]

One of the leading organizations promoting town planning in Britain was the National Housing Reform Council, founded in 1900, which was supported by a small group of people with experience in local government.[18] After many years of trying to improve the environment of the poor in cities, by providing open spaces and cultural and recreational facilities, it had been recognized that the basic problem was housing, and any future improvement had to start with the housing of the poor. The ambition of the National Housing Reform Council, beyond promoting town planning ideals, was to encourage local authorities to purchase land on the outskirts of cities and to supervise its development. If this was done economically, it could facilitate the movement of the respectable poor with a steady wage, to the outskirts, and their present homes would thus become available for those at the core of the housing problem, the inhabitants of the slums. It was an idea based on the possibility of rising real incomes for the poor, orderly and controlled administration, and the efficacy of private initiative. It was a major influence on the drafting of Britain's first piece of town planning legislation, the Housing, Town Planning Act 1909.

Conditions in Indian cities could not have been more different. It is true that the extension of services in municipalities, particularly sanitation, education and medical care since the late 1870s, made greater demands on local taxation, and gradually the British, under Mayo and Ripon, had extended the principle of local self-government to all municipalities under British rule. But apart from a few exceptions, such as the great Presidency cities, this was a dead letter in political terms since the chairman, the municipal commissioner, was usually a British official.[19] The kind of response which could be expected from such an official was a concern for the efficient administration of a minimum of municipal services. Concern over the social and physical condition of the poor or even the introduction of new civic improvements was totally outside the sphere of duty.

However, some Indian nationalists did begin to see, in local self-government, a chance to exercise some power in spite of the British. In the period 1909–25, local self-government in the municipalities was taken more seriously and it became the exception rather than the norm to have a British official as chairman.[20] In these circumstances, several prominent Indian national leaders, such as Surendra Nath Banerjea, Pherozeshah Mehta, Lala Lajpat Rai, G. K. Gokhale, Vallabhbhai Patel, C. R. Das, Subhash Chandra Bose and Jawaharlal Nehru, became associated with municipal work.[21]

But both political ambitions and hopes for improving the urban environment remained unfulfilled. Freedom of action was severely curtailed by the framework of municipal administration and the lack of resources. As Jawaharlal Nehru put it: 'The whole steel-frame of municipal administration as erected by Government, prevented radical growth or innovation. The financial policy was such that the municipality was always dependent on the Government. Most radical schemes of taxation or social development were not permissible under the existing municipal laws. Even such schemes as were legally permissible had to be sanctioned by Government, and only the optimists, with a long stretch of years before them, could confidently ask for, and await this sanction.'[22] Nehru resigned before his three year term of office was completed. There was no opportunity for him to expand the range and impact of municipal work, as the governing classes in British municipalities had been able to do half a century before.

The Emergence of the Improvement Trusts

Poverty, lack of resources, little modern economic development; these were the major problems of the municipalities. Meanwhile the population of the large cities just grew, not on such a scale as was subsequently reached in the post-Independence period, but significantly enough. First, the central areas of these cities reached levels of density quite beyond the highest ever found in the West. Secondly, suburban development, even for the affluent, was hampered by a lack of efficient and rapid transport, such as suburban railways, and by the lack of an infrastructure of services, water, sewage, etc., which was not extended to outlying areas. The outer rings of the Presidency cities became dominated by the shanty towns of the poorest rural immigrants. As the situation deteriorated, particularly as the incidence of disease mounted, the British established a new administrative body, a city Improvement Trust, whose job was to try and bring some order out of this chaos.

Improvement Trusts remained for most of the early decades of the twentieth century the sole bodies totally concerned with the development of the city. But by and large they were not planning bodies in any comprehensive sense, as understood by the supporters of the modern town planning movement in the West. The main function of the Improvement Trusts (though there were some variations in different cities) was to purchase land outside the built-up areas, and to supervise its orderly development. The profits made on the resale of plots of land to the builders and developers provided the income of the Trust. In a sense, the Trusts were fulfilling the objectives outlined by the National Housing Reform Council in Britain, though without the social purpose or concern for the quality of the housing of the poor which, alone, could have lifted such development schemes into the realm of town planning.

Yet the Improvement Trusts were born out of a growing anxiety about the social conditions of Indian cities. In Bombay, for instance, the rate of growth was exceptional. In 1838 the city had a population of 236,000. By 1872 this number had multiplied to 644,000. By 1891 it was 821,764, and by 1921, 1,175,914. Yet expansion of the city's area was confined by its geographical location. The result of population growth thus led to overcrowding and a proliferation of slums. Between 1896 and 1910 plague was endemic in the city, each fresh visitation carrying away many victims, weakened by the periodic famines endured by the city's poor.[23] The Bombay Improvement Trust was established in 1898.

This proved to be one of the earliest, as Calcutta did not get its Improvement Trust until 1912, even though in many respects conditions in Calcutta were worse than Bombay. Calcutta's slums, for instance, were more extensive. They were divided into great 'blocks' of building, ranging over 20 to 270 acres (but most commonly about 100 acres) consisting of streetless dense building. The total area covered in this way in the city in 1912 was 2,200 acres covering an area of three square miles.[24] Conditions like this were not commonly found in Indian cities, for all their overcrowding, apart from Bombay; though they were found in Cairo, Constantinople, and Chinese cities such as Pekin, Canton and Mukden. Calcutta, however, had the misfortune of possessing a far higher percentage of slums than any other city.

The objective of the Calcutta Improvement Trust on its inception in 1912 was to direct city improvement in the central areas. Unfortunately its powers were not matched to its objective. Improvements in central areas were extremely expensive, they tended to conflict with the interests of institutions, groups and influential citizens, who benefited from the absence of regulations; and all plans had to be submitted to the municipality, which made the final decision on any plan since it also controlled the financing of such schemes. Even more unfortunately, the Calcutta Improvement Trust was not able to supplement its income by controlling land development on the outskirts of the city. The Act under which it had to operate was largely based on the 1890 English Housing Act which was directed towards the problems of working class housing and slum clearance. The 1890 Act had identified the key social problem of the growing cities, but it provided no solution beyond recommending local authorities to deal with it as they saw fit.

However, as an indication of the new administrative response to the social problems of cities, it is worth pausing over the report on Calcutta's problems made by the first chairman of the Calcutta Improvement Trust, E. P. Richards. His report 'On the Condition, Improvement and Town Planning of the city of Calcutta and contiguous areas' was published privately in England in 1914, when he was recuperating there after a complete breakdown in his health. In it, he displayed the three most common responses to the huge problems of the Presidency cities. First, he was an engineer by training and his practical outlook encouraged him to concentrate on a root and branch approach to public health problems, armed with the preconceptions of Western bye-law and sanitary legislation. The answer to congestion and slums was wholesale demolition and the construction of wide new thoroughfares.

Secondly, he attempted to gain a correct estimate and correct scale of Calcutta's needs by comparing the city with other cities, especially those in the West. Since Calcutta was basically a commercial city, the examples he chose were London, Paris, Berlin, Rome, Venice, Hamburg, Dresden, Budapest and Chicago. The result was depressing in the extreme as Calcutta was poorer and more squalid than any of these. For ways of improving Calcutta, Richards turned to the town planning acts and manuals being produced at this time in the West, quoting extensively all the expensive methods of reform which even in the West were not gaining universal support. Finally he displayed an engineer's impatience of working alongside the slow process of fostering 'civic spirit'. In his view, the magnitude of Calcutta's problems was so great that only complete authoritarian rule and a massive injection of resources would make any difference.[25] It was a classic statement of the Western response to Indian urbanization.

The facts concerning public health in Indian cities seemed to justify his pessimism. At the All India Sanitary Conference of 1911, the appalling fact had been revealed that conditions were actually deteriorating rapidly. A paper by Dr Kailas Chundar Bose on the spread of tuberculosis in Calcutta showed a four-fold increase in the incidence of the disease between 1880 and 1911.[26] As for that most sensitive indicator of public health conditions, the infant mortality rates, these were quite shocking in Calcutta. The figures for the worst slum areas showed a death rate of more than 1 in 2. (See table on p. 340.)

The average for the whole city in 1911 was 362.1 per thousand; in Bombay it was 379.8, Bangalore 267.83, London 91, Birmingham 111, and Liverpool 125. It is not surprising, thus, to find the unfortunate officials of the Improvement Trusts turning to Western public health legislation as drowning men clutch at straws. Plague and high death

JORASANKO AND BURRABAZAR: INFANT MORTALITY FIGURES

	1907	1908	1909	1910	1911
Births	725	725	810	663	756
Deaths	432	450	462	448	436
Balance living	293	275	348	215	320
Death rate per 1,000	595	621	580	675	577

rates had always been features of Indian cities. But in the twentieth century, the old Indian custom of the whole town deserting the plague-ridden site and re-building afresh on an adjacent site, was not possible. Modern Indian cities had to contend with two unprecedented factors, the permanence of the modern urban infrastructure and of the transport systems, particularly the railways; and a continuing rapid growth rate, in some important cases accompanied by industrialization. There was a need for new ideas for controlling these public health hazards.

The Introduction of Modern Town Planning Concepts

Whilst the Improvement Trusts in Bombay and Calcutta battled on against impossible odds, an attempt was made to introduce more comprehensive legislation to facilitate urban control. Enthusiasm for town-planning, though, was somewhat lukewarm. A report produced by the Bombay Development Committee in 1914 rather smugly outlined the numerous incidences of government concern over city development dating back to 1877, though a dissenting minute from Sir Ibrahim Rahimtoola pointed out that to date, all effort had been directed to the making of roads and the improvement of communications.[27] Yet what else to do, how to do it, and how to pay for it, were not questions to which there were any easy answers. The I.C.S. administrators found little to help them in the British Housing and Town Planning Act of 1909. The Hon. Mr E. G. Turner, I.C.S., described the Act as 'the least cast-iron piece of legislation imaginable', and he recommended those seeking practical advice on how to set about improvement schemes to consult the 1910 Finance Act, The Kingsway Improvement Scheme Act, and the German Laws of 1893, 1911 and 1913.[28]

This lack of enthusiasm from the administrators was understandable, as the 1909 Act was hardly a manifesto for city development. Its significance lay not so much in its specific clauses but in the fact that it was a symptom of changing attitudes to urban improvement.[29] One of the major practical obstacles inhibiting more detailed and effective town planning legislation was the lack of professional expertise available for the drafting and carrying out of town plans. The profession of town planner, even in the West, was very much in its embryo stage.

In India, the situation was much worse as regards the necessary expertise for modern town planning. Bombay bravely took the lead by passing the first Town Planning Act in India in 1915. The Bombay act was an amalgam of English and German legislation in an attempt to find legislation more appropriate to Indian conditions. Yet the major problem was not so much the form of the legislation, as the lack of knowledge of town planning and its advantages. Bombay did have a consulting Surveyor to the Government, A. E. Mirams, who took up the cause of town planning in the state with considerable enthusiasm and energy.[30] He concentrated his efforts on the small towns and villages and travelled ceaselessly from Sind in the north, to Belgaum in the south, giving lectures on the Town Planning Act, and the advantages of planning for future development. However, his efforts were isolated and the propaganda work that he carried out, for all his personal enthusiasm, rather amateurish. His lectures were illustrated by slides which he had sent from England from the Garden Cities and Town Planning Association.[31]

However, a more practical approach was in some ways out of the question. Mirams found that not only did the municipal authorities have no knowledge of town-planning principles; they did not have at hand the tools or trained personnel even to begin.[32] There were very few detailed ordnance survey maps of towns, no trained valuers, and often only the Government Surveyor to service large numbers of municipalities. Further, the small towns and large villages themselves were not subject to the same kinds of pressure for change and development that were found in the West. Industrial expansion was concentrated in a very few places and, in the absence of economic factors, reformers had to rely on legislation, coupled with persuasion, to encourage a favourable response to their ideas. Quite often the only hope for improvement, if all the practical obstacles of ignorance and indifference were to be overcome, lay in developing new moral attitudes amongst municipalities and their inhabitants, to the environment in which they lived. It was a task of such magnitude that only the most enthusiastic and optimistic supporters of the modern town planning movement would have been tempted to respond to it. In 1914, as Europe plunged into war, perhaps only one man could have taken up the challenge so wholeheartedly. This was the ever enthusiastic town planning propagandist, Patrick Geddes.

The Contribution of Patrick Geddes

The introduction of modern town-planning ideas really came to India with Geddes. He was invited to India by Lord Pentland, Governor of Madras, to bring the Cities and Town Planning Exhibition and to continue his educational and propaganda work in India. Pentland was also able to persuade his old friends, Lords Willingdon and Carmichael, respectively Governors of Bombay and Bengal at that time, to interest themselves in Geddes' work.[33] Geddes was thus able to gain engagements for taking his Exhibition to the major Presidency towns. The original exhibition, however, was lost on its way to India, through enemy action. Geddes himself arrived safely on another ship, and friends and supporters of town planning in Britain and Europe sent him fresh material to recreate the Exhibition so that he could meet these engagements.[34] Taking the second exhibition round in different cities remained one of his major activities over the next ten years, a propaganda effort which he supplemented by running summer schools on city and community development in the hill station of Darjeeling.

In 1914, Geddes was sixty years old. But in the next ten years, which mark the period of his close association with India, he was able, for the first time in his life, to supplement extensively his educational and propaganda work with well paid commissions for town planning reports. These reports (and in ten years he was able to undertake forty or so different commissions) represent the first major contribution to the development of modern town planning in India on a fairly wide scale. Geddes was indefatigable in his constant travelling, constant enthusiasm for towns and cities, large and small, and his willingness to offer practical advice on all occasions. He did more than any other individual to promote town planning ideas.

Yet much of the ephemeral nature of India's initiation into the problems of modern urbanization was due to Geddes' particular approach to planning, his enormous enthusiasm and his lack of concern for the mundane, administrative problems of creating and training the necessary expertise to maintain a momentum for the professionalization of planning. Perhaps the basis for such a development was not there in a country under colonial status. Geddes did persuade Lord Pentland to influence the state government of Madras to appoint the first official town planner in India, and suggested the name of H. V. Lanchester, architect, and editor of *The Builder*. Lanchester was appointed in 1915, but the conditions experienced earlier by Mirams in Bombay state were all too prevalent elsewhere. There was a total lack of professional expertise for planners to draw upon. A small class was set up in Madras, under the direction of Lanchester, to train recruits in the range of skills necessary for the pursuit of efficient town planning.

However, these activities were so small-scale and isolated, they could never have been built up as a thriving nucleus for a newly professional approach to planning. Geddes himself was not particularly interested in such a possibility. He had always maintained that the sociological implications of town planning were so important that a training in the social sciences was fundamentally more important for the would-be planner. In 1919, he was offered, and accepted, the first chair of Sociology at Bombay University, which he got renamed as the chair of Civics and Sociology. Since the early days of British sociology (Geddes was a founder member of the British Sociological Society in 1903) he had always tried to direct the study of the subject towards a very definite practical purpose. He believed that sociologists should be men of action who took a direct part in the great evolutionary struggle between society and its environment, to ensure that progressive tendencies were encouraged and retrogressive tendencies repressed. For him, the sociologist was a man who could identify the former, and plan for their future development.[35]

This positivist approach was reinforced by a further legacy of Geddes' evolutionism. He saw the struggle between environment and society as continuous and never-ending. As a town planner, therefore, he saw no point in providing municipal councils with Master Plans or 'ultimate' solutions. He believed in an ameliorist approach, involving officials, administrators and people equally, all being responsible on a macro or micro scale for the overall quality of the environment.[36] The Geddesian town planner was thus not a professional who knew the most efficient ways of laying out roads, organizing sewage systems, and the like. For him, the town planner was the propagandist, the inspirational genius who would raise the consciousness of the whole community, to the life and death evolutionary struggle in which all were inexorably involved. Geddes' ideas on modern town planning were thus hardly representative of even the modern town planning movement in the West. Geddes considered the objectives of the National Housing Reform Committee, the Garden Cities Association and other pioneering bodies, were all useful as means of promoting interest and concern, but they were never wide enough to encompass the breadth of his cosmic vision.

Only in India, largely cut off by the European holocaust from normal ties with Europe, was Geddes able to flourish. The profound social and political changes which had been taking place in India in the late nineteenth and early twentieth centuries, and which were now speeded up by the first world war, created an atmosphere in which the enthusiasm of Geddes could meet with some response. On a practical level, his ameliorist approach had the very great advantage over other planning schemes, put forward by the British public health officers and sanitarians, of being relatively cheap. Princely rulers of native states were particularly responsive to this. The Maharaja of Indore, for instance, had spent crores of rupees on an alternative water supply for Indore which was designed to flush water through the sewers and cut the incidence and intensity of the plague. But all the elaborate schemes to find and harness extra water singularly failed in their objective. The Maharaja was thus more than willing to commission Geddes, with his reputation for efficiency and cheapness, to prepare a report on how to deal with Indore's economic and social problems and its future development.

What he got for his money may have surprised him, for Geddes put his heart and soul into his Indore Report.[37] He came to the city and stayed for ten months, in great contrast to his usual practice of paying flying visits of a week or two at a time. He had paid assistants to collect and arrange all relevant data for him. After months of intensive work, he produced a report in two volumes in which detailed attention was given to problems of housing and water supply.[38] But the main thrust of his arguments was directed towards the future position of Indore in the evolution of modern India. The second volume was largely taken up with a daring suggestion that a great new University of Central India should be set up in Indore. Students at this centre of higher education should be exposed to those kinds of study, his concept of civics and sociology being high on the list, in which book study would be supplemented by social action. Such students would then, in the future, spearhead attempts to nurture the civic spirit and civic cooperation in Indore and other cities, and by such enlightened and corporate action the future trends of urbanization would be made beneficial for the coming generations.

Geddes' approach to practical planning commissions was thus highly original and totally different from that of most of the town planning propagandists operating in the West. However, in the context of Indian cities, his approach had one outstanding advantage. He was prepared to operate in the economic and social circumstances in which he found himself; and he was not prepared to adopt without question any of the Western responses to controlling the problems of cities. He was totally scathing about the expensive and unrealistic activities of the British engineers and sanitarians with their belief in wide, open thoroughfares, wholesale destruction of slum areas, flushed sewers, etc;[39] whilst Improvement Trusts rarely had the powers to make a comprehensive impact on the total environment of the city. Geddes produced his plans and reports on an individual basis, as a 'guru' of city-development, but he did try to operate according to his own two cardinal rules. First, the prime objective of the planner should be to understand the nature and historical evolution of the society whose environment was to be planned; secondly, the planner had to make sure that the planning objectives were realistic, appropriate and satisfying on economic and social, aesthetic and spiritual levels.[40] This was quite the opposite of the normal treatment meted out to cities in colonial countries by their rulers, and marks Geddes' most significant contribution.

The Modern Town Planning Movement in Pre-Independence India

The impact of the introduction of modern town planning ideas in India was, however, very limited in spite of Geddes' personal effort. Given the unfavourable political and administrative circumstances for encouraging town planning, it was perhaps unfortunate (though possibly realistic) that Geddes put so much emphasis on long term objectives. As far as immediately pressing problems were concerned, Geddes was prepared to deal with them, but only on the basis that common sense and thrift could be applied to practical details, once the vision of the ultimate objective, a higher civilization, had been understood. For hard pressed municipalities, only the message of common sense, and particularly thrift, was likely to get through. A higher civilization was a Utopian dream when too many political and economic obstacles lay in the path of orderly urban development and control.

In India, Geddes was viewed with suspicion by the British, who did not like their administrative apparatus upset by an apparent crank. His contact with the nationalists, to judge by his brief correspondence with Mahatma Gandhi,[41] was more sympathetic, since he was working for social change. But the divergence between their ultimate objectives made any positive cooperation impossible. In a very few places, the roots of the modern town planning movement did find congenial soil and flourished. In Madras, training and survey work was carried out even after the departure of Lanchester, and some Improvement Trusts in capital cities of native states, the most important that of Hyderabad, did exercise a strong influence on the development of the city. A small trickle of Western planners found their way to India in the footsteps of Geddes and Lanchester, a notable example being Linton Bogle, a graduate of the first British university department of civic design at Liverpool.

Bogle wrote a treatise on *Town Planning in India* in 1929 after his experience as Chief Engineer of the Lucknow Improvement Trust. In it he wrote a credo for town planning in India which was obviously, though anonymously, influenced by Geddes, which he set out as follows.[42]

What town planning means:

1. DEFINITE PLAN of orderly development for the Town into which each improvement will fit as it is wanted.	NOT the immediate execution of the whole plan.
2. CARE AND PRESERVATION of human life and energy, particularly child life.	NOT indifference to congestion and insanitation.
3. PROVISION of good building sites.	NOT leaving narrow and awkward shaped plots.
4. ENCOURAGEMENT OF TRADE and increased facilities for business.	NOT interruption of trade.
5. PRESERVATION OF HISTORICAL BUILDINGS and buildings of religious veneration with all their traditions.	NOT destruction of old landmarks.
6. THE DEVELOPMENT of an INDIAN CITY worthy of civic pride.	NOT an imitation of European cities but the utilization of what is best in them.

7. HEALTH, PLEASANT SURROUNDINGS AND RECREATION for all inhabitants.	NOT merely expensive roads and parks available only for the rich.
8. CONTROL over the FUTURE GROWTH of the town with adequate provision for future requirements.	NOT haphazard laying out of buildings and roads with resultant COSTLY improvement schemes.
9. ECONOMY.	NOT WASTE.

It was symptomatic of the context in which town planners, East and West, worked in the interwar period that Bogle should present an ideal response, with emphasis on improving the quality of the urban environment, rather than a head-on attack on the political and administrative obstacles which inhibited any practical expression of the ideal. Lucknow, with the sensible advice of Mr. Bogle at hand, as a very small municipality, was able to effect many improvements at small cost.[43] But the great industrial city of the United Provinces, Kanpur, grew rapidly with relatively little consideration being given to the quality of the environment that was being produced, particularly the environment of the poor. Kanpur suffered all the same social evils that accompanied industrialization, with unplanned urbanization, in the West.[44]

Thus, in many ways, the introduction of the modern town planning movement in India was a still birth, since the context for its growth and nourishment was missing. Town planning legislation and activity even in Britain in the interwar period were modest, since the powers of planners were heavily curtailed for fear of impinging on the property rights and freedom of individuals. In India, where authoritarian rule could have overcome these problems, concern over the quality of the urban environment took very low priority over the other pressing needs of the government at the time. The only exceptions were those cities where leading Indian citizens, or rulers, themselves took an interest in their cities. The dedicated work of some of the wealthy Bombay families, particularly the Parsees, provided their city with parks and hospitals, statues and civic buildings considered appropriate for any great city, East or West, in the late nineteenth and early twentieth centuries. In Hyderabad, where the powers of the Improvement Trust were extended and supported wholeheartedly by the Nizam, three-fifths of the city was rebuilt between 1880–1930, and an active policy was pursued for rehousing the poor in sanitary accommodation.[45]

But none of this latter effort was enough to create the necessary conditions for working out an Indian response to modern urbanization. The question of a suitable urban form for modern development was rarely asked and hardly answered. Western models like Jamshedpur and New Delhi were maintained only by rigid adherence to a Master Plan, which could be amended at later stages, but which always had clear objectives with alien political and economic overtones. This technique was of strictly limited value and could not be applied at all to most of the major Indian cities, of 100,000 inhabitants or more, destined to grow larger and more congested, ever more rapidly. Indian cities were not to be spared, any more than Western cities had been, the task of facing the social consequences of unplanned urbanization and industrialization, which had been accumulating in the West over the previous century.

NOTES

1 An earlier version of this paper was read at the S.S.R.C. Conference on 'India' at Cambridge, July 1975. My research work on Geddes has been supported by a grant from the Social Science Research Council.

2 A. F. Weber, *The Growth of Cities in the Nineteenth Century* (1899, Reprinted, New York, 1965), pp. 155–8.

3 For an exploration of the elements which combine to make the colonial city see R. J. Horvath, 'In Search of a Theory of Urbanisation: Notes on the Colonial City', *East Lakes Geographer*, 5 (1969), 69–82.

4 Though the relationship between population growth, industrialization and urbanization was to be markedly different from the earlier European experience. A. Bose, *Urbanisation in India* (Bombay, 1970), p. 63. See also B. F. Hoselitz, 'Generative and Parasitic Cities', *Economic Development and Cultural Change*, 3 (1954), 278–94.

5 The most easily available published material of Geddes' work in India is J. Tyrwhitt, ed., *Patrick Geddes in India* (London, 1947) which contains extracts from the Indian Reports. In the course of my research, I have collected thirty Reports in their entirety and will be depositing copies shortly in the National Library of Scotland at Edinburgh.

6 A. K. Dutt, 'Critique of Town Plans of Jamshedpur', *National Geographical Journal of India*, 5:4 (1959), 205–11.

7 N. V. Sovani, *Urbanisation and Urban India* (London, 1966), provides an analysis of the concept of 'over-urbanization' in relation to India, pp. 1–13.

8 An example of this was the *Indian Industrial Commission 1916–18* (Calcutta, 1918).

9 See M. N. Srinivas, *Social Change in Modern India* (Berkeley and Los Angeles, 1967), pp. 50–6.

10 K. Davis, *The Population of India and Pakistan* (Princeton, 1951), p. 128.

11 M. S. Thacker, *India's Urban Problem* (Mysore, 1965), p. 49.
12 Op. cit., pp. 123–8.
13 Taken from Davis, op. cit., p. 130.
14 Ibid., pp. 132–3.
15 G. S. Ghurye, 'Cities of India', *Sociological Bulletin*, 2 (1953), 47–51.
16 A study of the social impact of local government reform is E. P. Hennock's *Fit and Proper Persons: ideal and reality in nineteenth century urban government* (London, 1973).
17 This concern was nurtured by the radical clergy in large cities; see, for example, A. Briggs, 'Birmingham: The Making of a Civic Gospel', in *Victorian Cities* (London, 1963), pp. 185–244.
18 W. Ashworth, *The Genesis of Modern British Town Planning* (London, 1954), pp. 178–9.
19 H. Tinker, *The Foundations of Local Self-Government in India, Pakistan and Burma* (London, 1954), p. 333.
20 H. T. S. Forrest, *The Indian Municipality and some practical limits on its everyday work* (Second Edition, Calcutta, 1925).
21 A. Bose, 'Administration of Urban Areas', *Survey of Research in Social Sciences* (Major Group III, I.C.S.S.R.) (Delhi, unpublished paper, 1970), p. 12.
22 J. Nehru, *An Autobiography* (1936, Reprinted, London, 1958), p. 142.
23 E. G. K. Hewat, *Christ and Western India: A Study of the Growth of the Indian Church in Bombay City from 1813* (Bombay, 1950), p. 313.
24 E. P. Richards, *Report on the Request of the Improvement Trust on the Condition, Improvement and Town Planning of the city of Calcutta and contiguous areas* (published privately, 1914), Section IV.
25 Ibid., p. 167.
26 Ibid., p. 246.
27 *Bombay Development Committee Report* (Government Records, Bombay, 1914).
28 E. G. Turner, I.C.S., *Notes on the Operation of the Housing and Town Planning Etc. Act 1909 and Allied Matters* (Government Records, Bombay, 1914).
29 Ashworth, op. cit., p. 167.
30 Mirams was appointed a member of the select committee to consider Bombay Town Planning Bill 1914–15. In the interwar period, he went to Africa to become Town Planning Adviser to the Government of Uganda.
31 As reported in *Garden Cities and Town Planning*, 1914, pp. 196–8.
32 A. E. Mirams, *Town Planning in Bombay under the Town Planning Act 1915* (Lecture to Town Planning Institute, London, 1919).
33 Lady Pentland, *The Rt. Hon. John Sinclair, Lord Pentland G.C.S.I. A Memoir* (London, 1928), p. 214.
34 H. V. Lanchester, editor of *The Builder*, collected and dispatched the items.
35 The earliest articles in which Geddes expressed these views are entitled 'Civics: as Applied Sociology', in *Sociological Papers* (London, 1904 and 1905), Parts I and II.
36 See P. Geddes, *Cities in Evolution* (London, 1915), especially Chapters 14 and 17.
37 He sunk himself in his work after the double tragedy of the death of his

eldest son, killed in action in France in May 1917, and the death of his wife in Calcutta in June 1917.

38 P. Geddes, *Town Planning towards City Development: A Report to the Durbar of Indore*, Parts I and II (Indore, 1918).

39 See, for example, P. Geddes, *Town Planning in Balrampur: A Report to the Hon'ble the Maharaja Bahadur* (Lucknow, 1917), p. 56.

40 *Cities in Evolution*, Chapter 13.

41 In the Geddes Collection, National Library of Scotland, MS 10515.

42 J. M. Linton Bogle, *Town Planning in India* (London, 1929), p. 6.

43 Geddes and Lanchester had both worked previously in Lucknow. Geddes' first report to the Municipal Council was published in 1916.

44 U. Singh, 'Origin and Growth of Kanpur', *National Geographical Journal of India*, 5:1 (March 1959), 1–11. Geddes did produce a plan for Cawnpore, but it has now been lost.

45 B. S. Townroe, 'Town Planning: An Indian example' (Hyderabad), *Asiatic Review*, 30:104 (October 1934).

INDEX